Chiroptical Spectroscopy: Fundamentals and Applications

Chiroptical Spectroscopy: Fundamentals and Applications

Editor

Mikolaj Tosto

scitus academics

Chiroptical Spectroscopy: Fundamentals and Applications
Edited by **Mikolaj Tosto**

ISBN: 978-1-68117-690-1
Library of Congress Control Number: 2016958853

www.scitusacademics.com

Notice

Printed in United States of America on Acid Free Paper

Preface

Chiroptical spectroscopy is one of the most developing areas of chiral analysis which role has been enhanced in recent years. There have been great advances in the fields of laboratory and astronomical spectroscopy. These have been equally matched by large-scale computations using state-of-the-art theoretical methods. The accurate atomic opacities that are available today play a great role in the field of biomedical research using nanotechnology. Spectroscopic techniques have been applied in virtually all technical fields of science and technology. Radio-frequency spectroscopy of nuclei in a magnetic field has been employed in a medical technique called magnetic resonance imaging (MRI) to visualize the internal soft tissue of the body with unprecedented resolution. This title provides an overview of the applicability range of chiroptical methods as a principle tool for chirality investigation, and typical applications of chiral coordination chemistry, such as circular dichroism (CD) spectroscopy is a spectroscopic technique where the CD of molecules is measured over a range of wavelengths. CD spectroscopy is used extensively to study chiral molecules of all types and sizes, but it is in the study of large biological molecules where it finds its most important applications. A primary use is in analysing the secondary structure or conformation of macromolecules, particularly proteins as secondary structure is sensitive to its environment, temperature or pH, circular dichroism can be used to observe how secondary structure changes with environmental conditions or on interaction with other molecules. Structural, kinetic and thermodynamic information about macromolecules can be derived from circular dichroism spectroscopy. Because of this sensitivity, the most accurate physical measurements have been frequency measurements.

This book, Chiroptical Spectroscopy: Fundamentals and Applications, provides an introduction to the important methods of chiroptical spectroscopy in general, and circular dichroism in particular, which are increasingly important in all areas of chemistry, biochemistry, and structural biology. The book is to be intended a valuable tool for advanced graduate students along with researchers in academia and industry.

Table of Contents

Chapter 1

The Use of a Combination of RDC and Chiroptical Spectroscopy for Determination of the Absolute Configuration of Fusariumin A from the Fungus *Fusarium* sp.

Liang-Yan Liu[1] . Han Sun[2,3] . Christian Griesinger[2] . Ji-Kai Liu[4]

[1]*College of Agronomy and Biotechnology, Yunnan Agricultural University, Kunming 650201, China*

[2]*Department of NMR-based Structural Biology, Max-Planck-Institute of Biophysical Chemistry, Am Fassberg 11, 37077 Go¨ttingen, Germany*

[3]*Leibniz-Institut fu¨r Molekulare Pharmakologie, 13125 Berlin, Germany*

[4] *School of Pharmaceutical Sciences, South-Central University for Nationalities, Wuhan 430074, China*

ABSTRACT

A new alkylpyrrole derivative, fusariumin A (**1**), was isolated from the culture broth of the fungus *Fusarium* sp. The absolute configuration of fuasiumin A has been established as (2′*R*,3′*R*) using a combination of RDC (residual dipolar coupling)-based NMR and DFT-supported chiroptical spectroscopy. It is worth to note that in this study without the aid of the RDC analysis, an unambiguous determination of configuration and conformation was not feasible due to the excessive conformational possibilities of this open-chain compound.

Keywords: NMRResidual dipolar couplingRelative configuration Absolute configuration Chiroptics

Fusarium is a large genus of filamentous fungi which widely distributed in soil and associated with plants. Most species are harmless saprobes, and are relatively abundant members of the soil microbial community. Some species infest rice, maize, oats, barley, and wheat as pathogens and produce mycotoxins in cereal crops that can affect human and animal health if they enter the food chain [1]. The main toxins produced by these *Fusarium* species are fumonisins and trichothecenes. When contaminated food and feed are ingested, toxins initiate a wide range of acute and chronic symptoms, including cardiovascular lesions, hypotension, anemia and lymphoid necrosis [2, 3]. Chemically, *Fusarium* species are productive fungi which produce secondary metabolites with diverse structures. According to the structure types, compounds reported from *Fusarium* sp. can be divided into trichothecens, fumonisins, zearalenones, enniatins, butenolides, equisetins, and fusarins, respectively [4–7]. Some of these compounds exhibit notable biological activities. For instance, chlorofusin, a cyclic peptide isolated from the broth of *Fusarium* sp., showed significant antagonistic activity to the p53/MDM2 [8]. In this study, a new alkylpyrrole derivative was isolated from the culture broth of the fungus *Fusarium sp.*, and named it as fusariumin A (**1**, Fig. 1). The gross structure of **1** was established by extensive spectroscopic analysis, including MS, 1D and 2D NMR spectroscopy. Since the two stereocenters are located in a flexible alky chain, their relative configurations are difficult to be determined due to insufficient experimental data of scalar couplings and NOEs. Following the recent success in the determination of relative and absolute configuration of flexible and complex organic molecules by using a combination of residual dipolar coupling (RDC)-based NMR spectroscopy [9–15] and chiroptics [16–19], the complete stereochemistry and preferred conformation of fusariumin A has been determined. Our study here demonstrates again the power of RDC analysis in combination with chiroptics for the configurational and conformational analysis of challenging organic molecular systems.

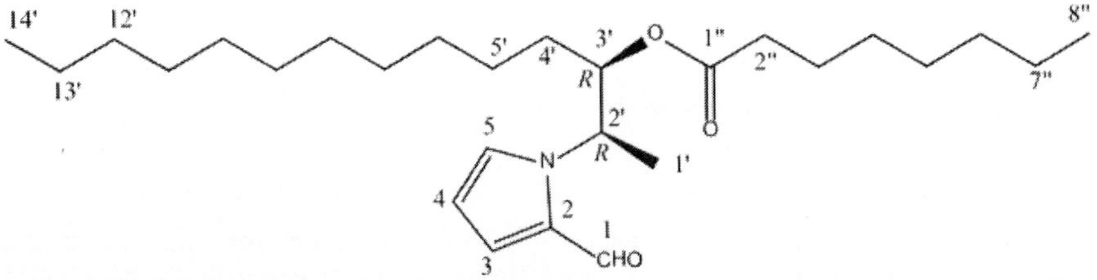

Fig. 1: The structure of fusariumin A (**1**)

Fusariumin A was isolated as colorless oil with the molecular formula of $C_{27}H_{47}NO_3$ which was deduced from the M^+ ion at *m/z* 433.3556, corresponding to 5 degrees of unsaturation. One aldehyde proton at δ_H 9.53 (1H, s), and three aromatic protons at δ_H 6.92 (1H, dd, $J = 4.3$, 1.7 Hz), 6.22 (1H, dd, $J = 4.3$, 2.9 Hz) and 7.08 (1H, dd, $J = 2.9$, 1.7 Hz) in the down-field region of ^1H NMR spectrum ($CDCl_3$, Table S1, Electronic supplementary material), together with the carbons at δ_C 179.9 (d), 131.5 (s), 125.6 (d), 110.0 (d) and 127.7 (d) ($CDCl_3$, Table S1) were empirically deduced to be a 1*H*-pyrrole-2-carbaldehyde moiety which was confirmed by the cross-peaks from H-5 to C-2, from H-1 to C-2 and C-3 in the HMBC experiment. In addition to the 1*H*-pyrrole-2-carbaldehyde moiety, the left 22 carbons involving one ester carbonyl, two methines, sixteen methylenes and three methyls required a linear structure to fulfil the degrees of unsaturation. The connection of C-1′/C-2′/C-3′/C-4′ was established from the correlations from H-1′ to C-2′ and C-3′, and from H-2′ to C-4′ in the HMBC spectrum (Fig. S2, Electronic supplementary material). C-2′ was deduced to be lined with the 1*H*-pyrrole-2-carbaldehyde moiety by the *N* atom from its chemical shift at δ_C 54.2 (d) and the HMBC correlation from H-2′ to C-2 and C-5. Similarly, the ester carbonyl group was determined at C-3′ by the chemical shift at δ_C 75.4 (d) and the HMBC correlation from H-3′ to C-1″. Up to now, the core structure of compound **1** was determined and the remaining two methyls and sixteen methylenes required two side chains extending from C-3′ and C-1″, respectively. In order to determine the length of each chain, high-resolution ESI-MS/MS technique was employed. When the $[M + H]^+$ was selected for MS/MS analysis, the characteristic fragmentation ion at *m/z* 290.2483 with the chemical composition $C_{19}H_{31}NO$ was detected, which could be explained by the elimination of a $C_8H_{16}O_2$ part, namely an octanoic acid (Fig. S3, Electronic supplementary material). Therefore, the acyl at C-3′ was determined as an octanoyl group, and the left side chain extending from C-3′ was deduced with fourteen carbons (Table 1).

Fusaiumin A (Fig. 1) is a molecule that contains a large number of potentially rotatable bonds, leading to a complex conformational space that is difficult to sample. In this study, in order to simplify the conformational problem, only the conformations stemming from the rotation of the bonds C4′-C3′, C3′-C2′, and C2′-N, which are close to the two unknown stereocenters, were considered. This approach is further justified, since the long poly-methylene chains predominantly have antiperiplanar conformation, the NMR parameters except for RDCs are local and we have shown on at least two examples, i.e., sagittamide A [11] and fibrosterolsulfate A [14], that the single-tensor assumption is valid even if large parts of the molecule are not characterized in detail. Because of a small proton-proton coupling between H4′a and H3′ (around 3 Hz) and a large coupling between H4′b and H3′ (around 9 Hz), as shown in Table 2; Fig. S4 (Electronic supplementary material), only two out of three conformers of the C5′-C4′-C3′-O dihedral are possible main conformations. Since from the *J*-coupling analysis no conclusive results can be obtained regarding the major conformation of the C4′-C3′-C2′-N dihedral, all three conformations (C4′/N: +*gauche*,-*gauche*, *anti*) needed to be considered. Besides, two conformations for the H2′-C2′-N-C5 dihedral (H2′/C5: *trans*, *cis*) were found from DFT calculations. Taken together, 12 (= 2 × 3 × 2) conformations were generated and DFT optimized for the two possible relative configurations (2′*R*,3′*R*) and (2′*R*,3′*S*), respectively (Fig. S5; Table S2). For all these 12 conformations of each configuration, the alkyl chain from C4′ to C14′ and from C2″ to C8″ was assumed to adopt an *anti* conformation, which is the energetically most preferable conformer [20].

After the attempt to determine the relative configuration of the two neighboring stereocenters C2′ and C3′ using $^{2,3}J$-couplings (Table 2) exclusively had failed, we decided to use residual dipolar couplings to probe the conformation and relative configuration of fusariumin A. Because only limited amount of sample (about 1 mg) was available, a slim PH-gel was prepared for a 1.7 mm NMR tube to acquire the RDC data [21]. 10 $^{1}D_{CH}$ (Table S3, Electronic supplementary material) were extracted from the spectra and they were used to calculate the alignment tensor for each possible conformation using the SVD method

Table 1. ^{1}H and ^{13}C NMR spectroscopic data of fusariumin A (**1**) in DMSO at 700 MHz

No.	^{1}H NMR	^{13}C NMR
1	9.50, s	180.2, d
2		131.7, s
3	7.04, dd, 4.3, 1.7	126.0, d
4	6.24, dd, 4.3, 2.9	110.3, d
5	7.45, dd, 2.9, 1.7	129.6, d
1′	1.44, d, 7.2	15.1, q
2′	5.37, m	54.4, d
3′	5.03, m	75.1, d
4′a	1.43, m	30.6, t
4′b	1.34, m	
5′a	1.22, m	25.2, m
5′b	1.16, m	
1″		172.6, s
2″	2.24, m	33.9, t
3″	1.46, m	24.9, t

Table 2. Long-range proton-proton and proton-carbon coupling constants of fusariumin A (**1**), *n* no signals in the HSQMBC and HMBC spectra

Atoms	$^{3}J_{HH}$ [Hz]	Atoms	$^{2,3}J_{CH}$ [Hz]
H3′-H4′a	3.3	H2′-C3′	−1.4
H3′-H4′b	9.4	H3′-C2′	−2.6
		H3′-C1′	3.0
		H3′-C5′	2.8
		H4′b-C2′	n
		H5′a-C3′	1.7
		H5′b-C3′	n
		H2′-C4′	n

[22]. In the RDC analysis, it was necessary to assign the two pairs of prochiral protons of C4′ and C5′, which has been achieved as follows: H5′a was defined as the proton that is closest to H3′ based on the strong NOE peak (Fig. S6); H4′b was defined as the proton which is *anti* to H3′ based on the large scalar couplings (Table 2; Fig. S4). The quality of the fit (*Q* factor) between the experimental RDCs and the back-calculated ones was used to identify the correct configuration and conformation [23]. The results summarized in Fig. 2 clearly show that the two lowest *Q* factors were obtained for conformations 9 and 11 of (2′*R*,3′*R*) or (2′*S*,3′*S*) with *Q* factors of 0.20 and 0.09, whereas the *Q* factors of all other possible conformers of (2′*R*,3′*S*) or (2′*S*,3′*R*) are significantly higher (Figs. S7, S8, Electronic supplementary material). Furthermore, as shown in Table S3 and Figure S8 (Electronic supplementary material), no significant violation of the experimental data is observed for any RDC of the best fitting conformer 11 of the relative configuration (2′*R*,3′*R*) or its enantiomer.

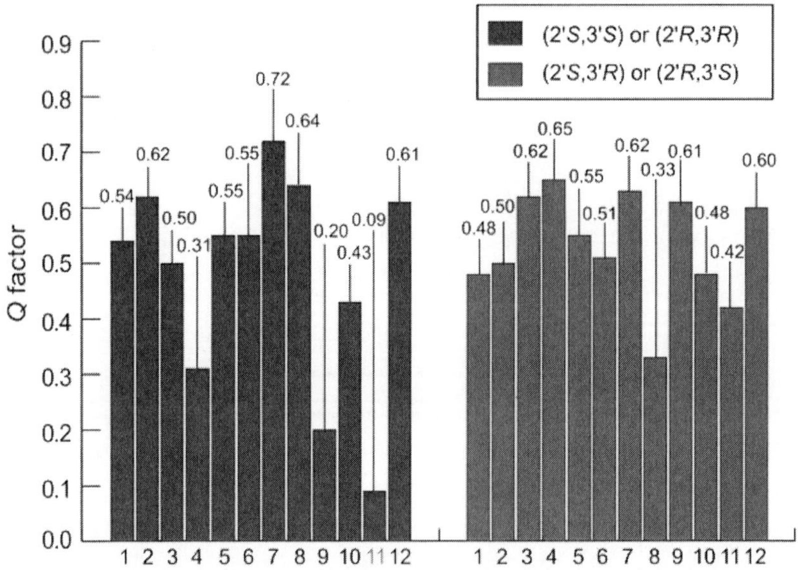

Figure 2. Comparison of the *Q* factors of the RDC fitting for the two possible relative configurations (2′*R*,3′*Rblack*) and (2′*R*,3′*Sgrey*) or their enantiomers. For each configuration 12 different conformers were considered in the RDC fitting. The conformer 11 of the configuration (2′*R*,3′*R*) or (2′*S*,3′*S*), which exhibits the significantly lowest *Q* factor, is highlighted in bold

Conformations 9 and 11 that exhibit the lowest *Q* factor of the RDC fitting (Fig. 2) mainly differ in the dihedral H3′-C3′-C2′-H2′. According to pervious studies [24, 25], for dihedral angles O-CA-CB-H, where CB bears one oxygen or nitrogen, the observed ^{2}J values range from -6 to 0 Hz. In addition, the *anti* conformation between proton and heteroatom leads to a small value of the two bonds C/H coupling constant ($^{2}J_{CH}$), whereas a large negative coupling constant is associated with a *gauche* conformation. Due to the fact that small negative coupling constants for both H2′/C3′ and H3′/C2′, and a small positive coupling for H3′/C1′ (Table 2) were observed, the *anti* relationship between H3′ and N, as well as between H2′ and O was determined as the main conformation. This is the case for conformer 11, but not for conformer 9, as shown with the aid of the Newman projections in Fig. 3. Additionally, NOE peaks that are relevant in the configurational and conformational analysis have been integrated (Table S4, Electronic supplementary material). The relationship between NOE integrals and the distance to the power of minus six is in a good agreement for the following proton pairs: H3′ and H5′a, H1′ and H5, H3 and H1, H4′b and H3, H4′a and H3, H2′and H1, which further supports conformer 11 as the major conformer. However, a relatively smaller NOE integral of H5′b and H2′, together with a relatively larger NOE integral of H5′a and H2′, were observed compared to the predicted ones. The reason for this could be a conformational averaging around the dihedral C4′-C5′, which nevertheless does not change the conclusion that conformer 11 was determined as the main conformation, because only dihedrals of C3′-C4′, C2′-C3′ and C2′-N define the conformation for the configurational analysis of C2′ and C3′.

The energy and free energy of each possible conformer of the relative configuration (2′*R*,3′*R*) or (2′*S*,3′*S*) was calculated by DFT using the B3LYP/6-31G(d) basis set that has been employed in the structure optimizations as well. Comparison of the computational energy of individual conformers (Table S5, Supporting Information) identifies the conformer 2 (**Δ**E = 0, **Δ**G = 0) and NMR-determined conformer 11 (**Δ**E = 0.5 kcal mol^{-1}, **Δ**G = 1.1 kcal mol^{-1}) as the lowest energy conformations. However, due to bad agreement with the RDC data

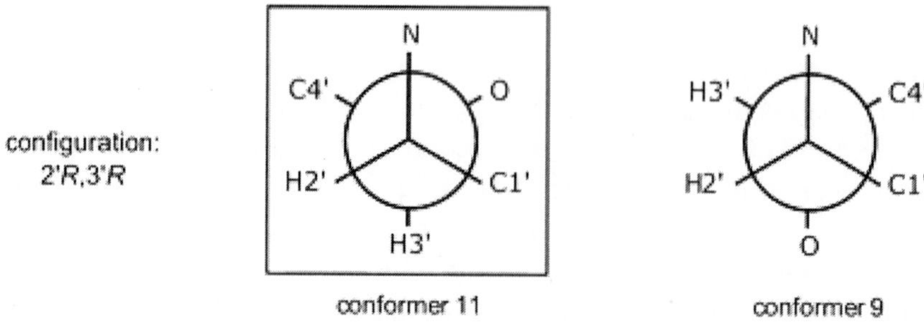

^3J(H2'-H3')	very small	very weak cross peak in COSY
^2J(H2'-C3')	-1.4 Hz	extracted from [^{1}H-^{13}C]-HECADE
^2J(H3'-C2')	-2.6 Hz	extracted from [^{1}H-^{13}C]-HECADE
^2J(H3'-C1')	3.0 Hz	extracted from [^{1}H-^{13}C]-HECADE

Figure 3. Newman projections of the conformers 9 and 11 for dihedral C2′-C3′. All conformers have a configuration of (2′*R*,3′*R*)

(*Q* = 0.62) as well as NOE violations, as the expected NOE between H2′ and H5 cannot be observed in the spectrum, the energetically most preferential conformation (conformer 2, see Table S2; Fig. S5) can be excluded to be the major conformation. Although many studies show that the NMR data are corroborated by DFT-based energy calculations [26, 27], on our example the DFT computation with the B3LYP functional do not accurately predict the relative energies [28].

In short, the relative configuration of fusariumin A was established as (2′*R*,3′*R*) or (2′*S*,3′*S*) by the RDC analysis exclusively. Furthermore, the preferential population of a single local conformation around the dihedrals of C3′-C4′, C2′-C3′ and C2′-N (conformer 11) was determined by the excellent fit of the RDC data, and was further corroborated by the *J*-coupling and NOE analysis. The long alkyl side chains were not analysed further, since they are assumed to be predominantly all-*trans* and were shown to have little influence on the RDC enhanced NMR analysis presented here [11, 14].

To determine the absolute configuration, ECD spectra of both enantiomeric forms (2′*R*,3′*R*) and (2′*S*,3′*S*) of NMR-determined conformation 11 have been calculated with time-dependent density functional theory (TD-DFT). The ECD spectrum calculated for (2′*R*,3′*R*) shown in Fig. 4 reproduced both the signs and the shape of the measured one. The agreement between the recorded spectrum and the calculated one is excellent, when the calculated spectrum of (2′*R*,3′*R*) is red-shifted by 25 nm. This procedure is in general allowed, because it has been shown in many previous studies that using the TD-DFT calculation with the B3LYP functionals the excitation energy can be predicted either too high or too low, depending on which system class is taken into account [29]. Based on the ECD data, the absolute configuration of fusariumin A was assigned as (2′*R*,3′*R*).

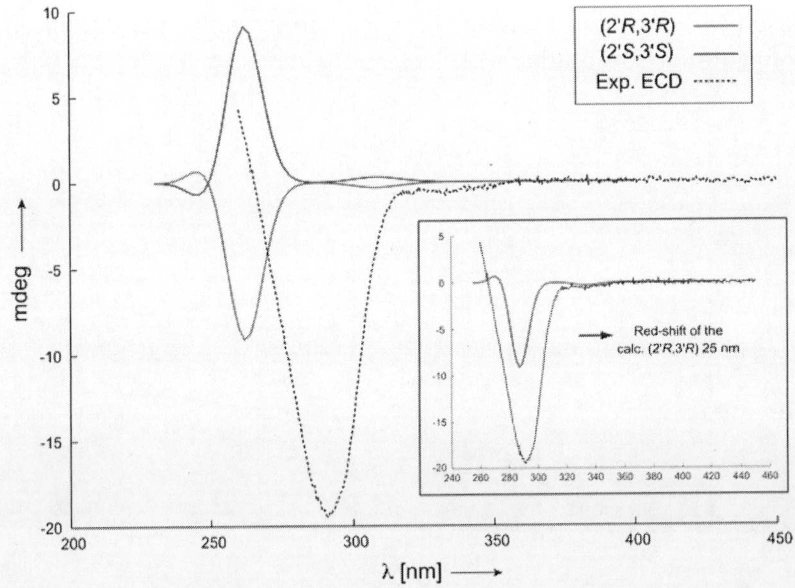

Figure 4. Comparison of experimentally measured ECD spectrum of fusariumin A in DMSO (*dashed line*) to the calculated ones using the RDC determined conformer 11 for both enantiomers (2′*R*,3′*R*) and (2′*S*,3′*S*). A 25 nm shift to higher wavelength of the calculated ECD spectrum of (2′*R*,3′*R*) results in a good fit to the experimental spectrum

Furthermore we measured ORD values at five different wavelengths (365, 436, 546, 578, 589 nm) in DMSO for fusariumin A, and calculated them for the conformer 11 with DFT. Figure 5 shows that the calculated ORD curve of (2′*R*,3′*R*) has a excellent agreement with the experimental one, which further supports the assignment of the absolute configuration from the ECD data. Interestingly, conformer 2 which was found by DFT to have the lowest energy shows an opposite sign of ECD and ORD as the ones of conformer 11 (Figs. S9, S10, Electronic supplementary material). Thus, without the NMR spectroscopic investigation which ruled out conformer 2 to be present in the solution ensemble, the wrong absolute configuration would have been determined. This result agrees with a previous finding [17] and further supports that the accurate determination of the conformation by RCD-based NMR analysis is essential for the correct assignment of absolute configuration for fusariumin A.

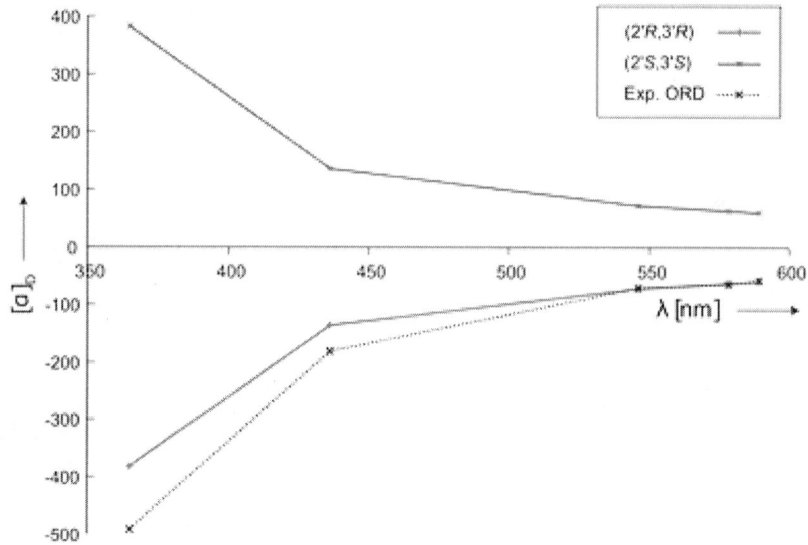

Figure 5. Comparison of experimentally measured ORD spectrum of fusariumin A in DMSO (*dashed line*) to the calculated ones using the RDC determined conformer 11 for both enantiomers (2′*R*,3′*R*) and (2′*S*,3′*S*)

In conclusion, the absolute configuration of fusariumin A has been established as (2′*R*,3′*R*) using a combination of NMR and DFT-supported chiroptical spectroscopy. It is worth to note that in this study without the aid of the RDC analysis, an unambiguous determination of configuration and conformation was not feasible due to the excessive conformational possibilities of this open-chain compound. Using the SVD fitting of the $^{1}D_{CH}$ data on the individual possible conformers, not only the relative configuration was successfully established, but also the selection of the correct conformations has been remarkably simplified, which is the basis for the DFT calculation of the chiroptical properties. A NOE and *J*-coupling analysis was subsequently utilized to validate the RDC-determined conformation and configuration. To our surprise, prevalence of one conformer around the dihedral of C3′-C4′, C2′-C3′ and C2′-N has been determined in solution. Of course, there will be the normal conformational flexibility in the long alkyl chains with predominance of the all-*trans* conformation. According to the previous study [30], it is interesting to note that preferences with high weight for a specific conformation have been already observed for numerous open-chain polyketides, especially when the alkyl chains contain certain functional groups. For example, the methyl groups in the alkyl chains do not affect the flexibility of the backbone, nevertheless they reduce the number of low energy local conformers. Our study here shows that fusariumin A is another case, in which nature has chosen an acyclic backbone with a high preference to populate a preferred local conformation.

1 EXPERIMENTAL SECTION

1.1 General Experimental Procedures

Optical rotations were measured on a Horiba SEPA-300 polarimeter (Horiba, Tokyo, Japan). Optical rotations for the determination of absolute configuration were measured at 22–25 °C using a 2 mL cuvette at 589, 578, 546, 436 and 365 nm with a Perkin Elmer model 241 polarimeter (Waltham, Massachusetts, USA). IR spectra were obtained on a Bruker Tensor 27 FT-IR spectrometer (Bruker, Ettlingen, Germany) using KBr pellets. CD spectra were recorded at room temperature using a Jasco-J-810 CD spectrometer (Tokyo, Japan). Standard 1D and 2D NMR spectra of fusariumin A in $CDCl_3$ were acquired on Bruker DRX-500 and

AM-400 instruments at room temperature with TMS as internal standard (Bruker, Rheinstetten, Germany).Standard 2D NMR spectra with DMSO solvents, together with [^{1}H,^{13}C]-CLIP-HSQC [31], [^{1}H,^{13}C]-HECADE [32], [^{1}H,^{13}C]-HSQMBC [33] and NOESY [34] spectra, which were used for determination of relative configuration, were recorded on Bruker 700 MHz with 1.7 mm PA-TXI room temperature probe head (Bruker, Rheinstetten, Germany). Chemical shifts (δ) were expressed in ppm with reference to the solvent signals. Mass spectra (MS) were recorded on an API QSTAR time-of-flight spectrometer (MDS Sciex, Ontario, Canada) or a VG Autospec-3000 spectrometer (VG, Manchester, England). Silica gel (200–300 mesh, Qingdao Marine Chemical Inc., Qingdao, China), Sephadex LH-20 (Amersham Biosciences, Sweden), and RP-18 gel (40–75 μm, Fuji Silysia Chemical Ltd. Japan) were used for column chromatography (CC). Preparative HPLC (Prep-HPLC) was performed on an Agilent 1200 liquid chromatography system equipped with a ZorbaxSB-C_{18} column (9.4 mm × 150 mm). Pre-coated silica gel GF254 plates (Qingdao Marine Chemical Inc., Qingdao, China) were used for TLC. Fractions were monitored by TLC, and spots were visualized by heating silica gel plates sprayed with 10% H_2SO_4 in ethanol.

1.2 Fungal Material

The fungus *Fusarium* sp. was collected in Botanic Garden of Kunming Institute of Botany, Chinese Academy of Sciences and identified by Prof. Zhu-Liang Yang (Kunming Institute of Botany, Chinese Academy of Sciences). A voucher specimen has been deposited in the School of Pharmaceutical Sciences, South-Central University for Nationalities. The culture medium consists of potato (peeled, 200 g), glucose (20 g), aneurine hydrochloride (10 mg), KH_2PO_4 (3 g), and $MgSO_4$ (1.5 g) in deionized water (1 L). The pH was adjusted to 6.5 before autoclaving, and the fermentation was carried out in a shaker (150 rpm) at 25 °C for 25 days.

1.3 Extraction and Isolation

The culture broth (18 L) was extracted with EtOAc for three times, and the organic layer was concentrated under reduced pressure to give a crude extract (8.0 g), which was subjected to silica gel column chromatography (CC) using a petroleum ether–acetone gradient (1:0 → 0:1) to afford fractions A–F. The fraction A was chromatographed first on a silica gel column eluted with petroleum ether–acetone (50:1, v/v), and then on a Sephadex LH-20 column eluted with $CHCl_3$-MeOH (1:1) to afford two fractions A1 and A2. The fraction A1 was purified by Preparative HPLC (CH_3CN/H_2O, 60:40 → 100:0) to give fusariumin A (3.0 mg).

Fusariumin A (1). colorless oil; $[\alpha]_D^{21} = -108.6$ (*c* 0.19, $CHCl_3$); IR (KBr) ν_{max} 2926, 2855, 1741, 1668, 1467, 1164, 776 cm^{-1}; ^1H NMR (500 MHz, $CDCl_3$) δ: 9.53 (1H, s, C*H*O), 7.08 (1H, dd, *J* = 2.9, 1.7 Hz, H-23), 6.92 (1H, dd, *J* = 4.3, 1.7 Hz, H-25), 6.22 (1H, dd, *J* = 4.3, 2.9 Hz, H-24), 5.55 (1H, m, H-21), 5.11 (1H, m, H-12), 2.23 (2H, m, H-14), 1.56 (4H, m, H-11 and H-15), 1.46 (3H, d, *J* = 7.1 Hz, H-22), 1.23 (26H, H-2 ~ H-10 and H-16 ~ H-19), 0.88 (6H, m, H-1 and H-20); ^{13}C NMR (125 MHz, $CDCl_3$) δ: 179.9 (d, *C*HO), 172.9 (s, C-13), 131.5 (s, C-26), 127.7 (d, C-23), 125.6 (d, C-25), 110.0 (d, C-24), 75.4 (d, C-12), 54.2 (d, C-21), 34.2 (t, C-14), 31.9 ~ 22.6 (C-2 ~ C-11 and C-15 ~ C-19), 14.7 (q, C-22), 14.1 (q, C-1 and C-20); ESIMS (positive): *m/z* 456 $[M + Na]^+$, 890 $[2 M + Na + H]^+$, 434 $[M + H]^+$, 290; HREIMS: *m/z* 433.3564 (calcd. for $C_{27}H_{47}NO_3$, 433.3556); 290.2473 (calcd. for $C_{19}H_{32}NO$, 290.2483).

1.4 Preparation of the PH-gel for 1.7 mm NMR Tube

2-(Acrylamido)-2-methyl- propanesulfonic acid (1 M), *N,N*-dimethylacrylamide (1 M), *N,N*-methylenebisacryl- amide (0.03 M), and ammonium persulfate (8 mM) were dissolved in purified water followed by devolatilization, in vacuo, for 15 min. The stock solution was inserted into a gel cylinder (material: PEEK) with an inner diameter of 2 mm and polymerized for 8–9 min at 70 °C. The gels were washed twice with aqueous HCl (0.02 M), three times with purified water (each time for 1–2 h) and finally dried under ambient conditions (air + room temperature) for at least 1 day.

1.5 Molecular Mechanics and DFT Calculations

The initial structure of each possible conformation was built with Discovery Studio 2.5 (Accelrys) and all trial structures were first minimized based on molecular mechanics calculations (CFF force field) [35] and followed by DFT optimizations at B3LYP/6-31G (d) levels. DFT optimizations were performed by using Gaussian09 [36] by using the IEFPCM solvent continuum model with DMSO as the solvent.

1.6 RDC Fitting

The fitting procedure of the experimental RDC data was performed by using the MSpin program (Mestrelab Research) [37].10 experimental ${}^{1}D_{CH}$ couplings and the coordinate files obtained from DFT optimizations were given as the input data. Five independent members of the alignment tensor were determined by using the singular value decomposition (SVD) method. The goodness of fit between experimental and back-calculated RDCs was expressed in terms of the Cornilescu quality factor *Q* [23].

1.7 ECD Computations

Time-dependent DFT (TD-DFT) with the basis set B3LYP/6-31G(d) was used to calculate the spin-allowed excitation energies, rotatory and oscillator strengths of the lowest 50 excited states. The calculations were performed with Gaussian09 [36] by using the IEFPCM solvent continuum model with DMSO as the solvent.

1.8 ORD Computations

The optical rotation dispersion calculations were performed at the four wavelengths 365, 436, 546, 578 and 589 nm by using the optimized structures as input coordinates. The calculations were carried out with the basis set B3LYP/6-31G(d) by using the IEFPCM solvent continuum model as implemented in Gaussian09[36] with DMSO as the solvent.

ACKNOWLEDGMENTS

Support by the National Natural Science Foundation of China (U1132607) to J. K. L. and the DFG (Forschergruppe FOR 934) to C. G. as well as the Chinese/German foundation (GZ1104) to H.S. and C.G. is acknowledged.

CONFLICT OF INTEREST

The authors declare no competing financial interest.

REFERENCES

1. C.M. Placinat, J.P.F. D'Mello, A.M.C. Macdonald, Anim. Feed Sci. Technol. **78**, 21–37 (1999)

2. Q.H. Wu, V. Dohnal, K. Kuča, Z.H. Yuan, Curr. Drug Metab. **14**, 641–660 (2013)

3. 3.S.P. McCormick, A.M. Stanley, N.A. Stover, N.J. Alexander, Toxins **3**, 802–814 (2011)

4. 4.A.E. Desjardins, R.H. Proctor, Int. J. Food Microbiol. **119**, 47–50 (2007)

5. 5.C.M. Maragos, M. Busman, R.D. Plattner, Food Addit. Contam. **25**, 105–114 (2008)

6. 6.K. Kleigrewe, F. Aydin, K. Hogrefe, P. Piecuch, K. Bergander, E.U. Würthwein, H.U. Humpf, J. Agric. Food Chem. **60**, 5497–5505 (2012)

7. 7.C. Dall'Asta, C. Falavigna, G. Galaverna, P. Battilani, J. Agric. Food Chem. **60**, 3800–3808 (2012)

8. 8.S.J. Duncan, S.G. Dudley, H. Williams, C. McNicholas, R. Purewal, M. Hajek, M. Gerlitz, S. Martin, S.K. Wrigley, M. Moore, J. Am. Chem. Soc. **123**, 554–560 (2001)

9. 9.C. Aroulanda, V. Boucard, F. Guibe, J. Courtieu, D. Merlet, Chem. Eur. J. **9**, 4536–4539 (2003)

10. 10.C.M. Thiele, A. Marx, R. Berger, J. Fischer, M. Biel, A. Giannis, Angew. Chem. Int. Ed. **45**, 4455–4460 (2006)

11. 11.A. Schuetz, J. Junker, A. Leonov, O.F. Lange, T.F. Molinski, C. Griesinger, J. Am. Chem. Soc. **129**, 15114–15115 (2007)

12. 12.M.E. Garcia, S. Pagola, A. Navarro-Vázquez, D.D. Phillips, C. Gayathri, H. Krakauer, P.W. Stephens, V.E. Nicotra, R.R. Gil, Angew. Chem. Int. Ed. **45**, 4455–4460 (2009)

13. 13.G. Kummerlöwe, B. Luy, TrAC Trend. Anal. Chem. **28**, 483–493 (2009)

14. 14.H. Sun, U.M. Reinscheid, E.L. Whitson, E.J. d'Auvergne, C.M. Ireland, J. Am. Chem. Soc. **133**, 14629–14636 (2011)

15. 15.V. Schmids, M. Fredersdorf, T. Lübken, A. Porzel, N. Arnold, L. Wessjohann, C.M. Thiele, J. Nat. Prod. **76**, 839–844 (2013)

16. 16.U.M. Reinscheid, M. Koeck, C. Cychon, V. Schmidts, C.M. Thiele, C. Griesinger, Eur. J. Org. Chem. **2010**, 6900–6903 (2010)

17. 17.H. Sun, E.J. d'Auvergne, U.M. Reinscheid, L.C. Dias, C.K. Andrade, R.O. Rocha, C. Griesinger, Chem. Eur. J. **17**, 1811–1817 (2011)

18. 18.M. Schmidt, H. Sun, P. Rogne, G.K. Scriba, C. Griesinger, L.T. Kuhn, U.M. Reinscheid, J. Am. Chem. Soc. **134**, 3080–3083 (2012)

19. 19.P. Trigo-Mouriño, R. Sifuentes, A. Navarro-Vázquez, C. Gayathri, H. Maruenda, R.R. Gil, Nat. Prod. Commun. **7**, 735–738 (2012)

20. 20.D. Nasipuri, *Stereochemistry of organic compounds: principles and applications*, 4th revised ed. edn. (New Academic Science, London, 2012)

21. 21.H.M. Ge, H. Sun, N. Jiang, Y.H. Qin, H. Dou, T. Yan, Y.Y. Hou, C. Griesinger, R.X. Tan, Chem. Eur. J. **18**, 5213–5221 (2012)

22. 22.J.A. Losonczi, M. Andrec, M.W. Fischer, J.H. Prestegard, J. Magn. Reson. **138**, 334–342 (1999)

23. 23.G. Cornilescu, J. Marquardt, M. Ottiger, A. Bax, J. Am. Chem. Soc. **120**, 6836–6837 (1998)

24. 24.N. Cyr, G.K. Hamer, A.S. Perlin, Can. J. Chem. **56**, 297–301 (1978)

25. 25.R. Riccio, G. Bifulco, P. Cimino, C. Bassarello, L. Gomez-Paloma, Pure Appl. Chem. **75**, 295–308 (2003)

26. 26.V.M. Sánchez-Pedregal, R. Santamaría-Fernández, A. Navarro-Vázquez, Org. Lett. **11**, 1471–1474 (2009)

27. 27.C. Pérez-Balado, H. Sun, C. Griesinger, A.R. de Lera, A. Navarro-Vázquez, Chem. Eur. J. **17**, 11983–11986 (2011)

28. 28.M.D. Wodrich, C. Corminboeuf, P.R. Schreiner, A.A. Fokin, P. von RaguéSchleyer, Org. Lett. **9**, 1851–1854 (2007)

29. 29.C. Diedrich, S. Grimme, J. Phys. Chem. A **107**, 2524–2539 (2003)

30. 30.R. Hoffmann, Angew. Chem. Int. Ed. **39**, 2054–2070 (2000)

31. 31.A. Enthart, J.C. Freudenberger, J. Furrer, H. Kessler, B. Luy, J. Magn. Reson. **192**, 314–322 (2008)

32. 32.W. Kozminski, D. Nanz, J. Magn. Reson. **124**, 383–392 (1997)

33. 33.R.T. Williamson, B.L. Márquez, W.H. Gerwick, K.E. Kövér, Magn. Reson. Chem. **38**, 265–273 (2000)

34. 34.M.J. Thrippleton, J. Keeler, Angew. Chem. Int. Ed. **42**, 3938–3941 (2003)

35. 35.S. Lifson, A. Warshel, J. Chem. Phys. **49**, 5116–5129 (1968)

36. 36.M.J. Frisch, G.W. Trucks, H.B. Schlegel, J.V. Ortiz, J. Cioslowski, D.J. Fox, *Gaussian 09 revision A.1* (Gaussian Inc., Wallingford, 2009)

37. Navarro-Vázquez, Magn. Reson. Chem. **50**(S1), S73–S79 (2012)

Chapter 2

Determination of the Absolute Configurations of Chiral Drugs Using Chiroptical Spectroscopy

Prasad L. Polavarapu

Department of Chemistry, Vanderbilt University, Nashville, TN 37235, USA

ABSTRACT

Chiroptical spectroscopy has emerged as a promising tool for the determination of absolute configurations and predominant conformations of chiral molecules in academic laboratories. This promise has led to the adaption of chiroptical spectroscopic methods as valuable tools in chiral drug discovery research programs of the pharmaceutical industry. Most major pharmaceutical companies have invested in in-house chiroptical spectroscopy applications and reported successful outcomes. In the context of continuously increasing applications of chiroptical spectroscopy for chiral molecular structure determination, a review of recent developments and applications for chiral drugs is presented in this manuscript.

Keywords: chiral; spectroscopy; drugs; electronic circular dichroism; optical rotation; vibrational circular dichroism; vibrational Raman optical activity; absolute configuration; conformation

1. INTRODUCTION

Life on planet Earth owes its existence to chirality or handedness. Chiral molecules are those that possess handedness, i.e., in simple terms, they are either left handed or right handed. Only one type of handedness is preferred by the biological molecules that control the life machinery. L-amino acids and D-sugars, are the chiral constituents of proteins and nucleic acids that make up biological systems. As a consequence of the preferential dominance of chirality, drugs that are developed for the treatment of human diseases or upkeep of human health, have to possess the correct handedness. Determination of the handedness of chiral molecules, also referred to as the determination of absolute configuration (AC), has become an important research area. Chiroptical Spectroscopy [1,2] is becoming an invaluable tool for this purpose.

Historically the AC determination was accomplished using X-ray crystallography, nuclear magnetic resonance (NMR) or stereoselective synthetic schemes. These three methods require, respectively, good quality crystals, diastereomeric complexes and labor-intensive chemical synthetic procedures. These disadvantages are avoided in chiroptical spectroscopic applications, where investigations on native samples in solution phase (or vapor phase in favorable situations) can be directly undertaken.

Optical rotation (OR) in the visible spectral region is one chiroptical property that elicited interest in the early days [3]. When normalized with concentration (in $g{\cdot}cc^{-1}$) and pathlength (in dm), the resulting quantity is referred to as Specific rotation (SR), or specific optical rotation (SOR) as it is called in the recent literature. SOR is normally considered to be a molecular property that is independent of concentration, although exceptions are known [4]. In the older literature, attempts were made to correlate SOR with AC, mostly via empirical models, but they did not survive the test of time. Circular dichroism (CD) associated with electronic transitions, referred to as electronic CD (ECD), is another chiroptical property that was popularized among synthetic organic chemists by Nakanishi, Harada, Berova, and their coworkers, via the use of an exciton chirality model [5,6]. The scope of this approach is limited to molecules that possess two interacting electronic chromophores that absorb light in the visible spectral regions. A large array of chiral molecules, that do not contain electronic chromophores absorbing visible light, cannot be studied using this method. This limitation was overcome by the development of two new methods that measure optical activity associated with vibrational transitions, which do not depend on the absence or presence of electronic chromophores. One method utilizes the CD associated vibrational transitions, referred to as vibrational CD (VCD) [7] and the other utilizes the differential vibrational Raman scattering referred to as vibrational Raman optical activity (VROA) [8,9]. These two vibrational transition-based methods are applicable for all chiral molecules. The four methods, namely, SOR, ECD, VCD and VROA, are collectively categorized as chiroptical spectroscopic methods. The advances in chiroptical spectroscopic instrumentation and the availability of commercial instruments allowed many new researchers to undertake these measurements.

The experimental data obtained with any or all four of the chiroptical methods mentioned in the previous paragraph, however, cannot by themselves directly reveal the ACs of chiral molecules. These experimental data must be analyzed with theoretical predictions of corresponding chiroptical properties to infer the ACs.

The theoretical methods used for predicting chiroptical properties can range from approximate models to semi empirical methods and to modern quantum chemical (QC) methods. The predictions resulting from approximate models and semi empirical methods are not reliable enough for determining the ACs. Due to the revolutionary developments that took place in QC theories [10,11,12], theoretical predictions resulting from the QC calculations are providing high enough confidence to reliably analyze the experimental data. The availability of software to undertake the QC calculations, and of fast computer processors to expedite the calculations has made the applications of chiroptical spectroscopic methods routine in recent years.

The current practice of determining the ACs of chiral molecules involves experimental measurement of chiroptical properties for the chemical substance of interest and undertaking QC calculations for possible structures of the molecules making up that substance. These two steps are followed by comparative analysis of the experimental and predicted chiroptical spectra.

2. CHIROPTICAL SPECTROSCOPIC TOOLS

In three of the following sub-sections, the instrumentation needed for experimental measurements and software used for QC predictions and spectral comparison analysis are summarized, to facilitate the introduction to newcomers. The fourth subsection illustrates a detailed procedure for AC determination.

2.1. Instrumentation

The instrumentation for optical rotation measurements for liquid samples is well established and commercial instruments are available (from Jasco Inc., Easton, MD, USA and Rudolph Research Analytical Inc., Hackettstown, NJ, USA). These instruments, which cost under $20,000, provide a measurement accuracy of 2 mdeg which is sufficient for most typical cases. Commercial laser polarimeters (from PDR Chiral Inc., Lake Park, FL, USA), which cost about $40,000, provide a measurement accuracy of 20 μdeg, and are mostly used with chromatography applications. Optical rotation measurements for gas phase samples can be undertaken using specialized instruments that use cavity ring down methods [13,14,15]. However, these instruments are quite expensive and are currently limited to academic laboratories. The instrumentation for ECD measurements for liquid samples is well established and commercial instruments are available (from Jasco Inc., Olis Inc., Bogart, GA, USA; Applied Photophyscis Inc., Leatherhead, Surrey, UK). These instruments cost ~$150,000. The instrumentation for VCD measurements for liquid samples is well established and commercial instruments (from Jasco Inc., Bruker Inc., Billerica MA, USA; BioTools Inc., Jupiter, FL, USA) cost under ~$200,000. The instrumentation for VROA measurements for liquid samples is also well established and currently there is only one commercial instrument (from BioTools Inc.), which costs ~$275,000.

2.2. QC Software

QC calculations of chiroptical properties can be undertaken on a variety of computer platforms, ranging from desktop computers to supercomputing clusters, using commercially available as well as freeware software. Freeware packages include DALTON [16], Psi4 [17] and NWChem [18], while popular commercial software packages include Gaussian [19] and ADF [20].

2.3. Spectral Comaprison Software

Spectral comparison involves comparing the digital experimental spectra with corresponding predicted spectra using spectral overlap integral methods [21,22]. A general purpose freeware program, CDSpecTech, has been developed in the author's laboratory, to analyze the ECD, VCD and/or VROA spectra, corresponding absorption/Raman spectra and also their ratio spectra [23]. SpecDis, a program restricted to the analysis of ECD and corresponding absorption spectra, is also a freeware program [24]. CompareVOA (from BioTools Inc.) is a commercial program for analyzing the VCD and corresponding absorption spectra [25].

2.4. A Step-by-Step Guide for AC Determination

Centratherin (see Figure 1), a natural product with anti-inflammatory and anti-microbial properties, will be used in this article as an example to lead the reader through different steps involved in the AC determination [26].

The experimental chiroptical spectral data are obtained for the sample of interest dissolved in an appropriate solvent. If the solvent used does not participate in solute-solvent intermolecular hydrogen bonds, then corresponding QC calculations can be handled, relatively easily, with implicit solvation models. If intermolecular hydrogen bonding between solvent and solute is involved, then corresponding QC calculations need to incorporate explicit solvent molecules to effectively incorporate solvent effects into the calculations. The use of solvents that do not participate in intermolecular hydrogen bonding are to be favored, unless the goal is to unravel the intermolecular hydrogen bonding itself. Nevertheless, experimental measurements in different solvents at different concentrations are useful to assess the influence of solvents and concentrations.

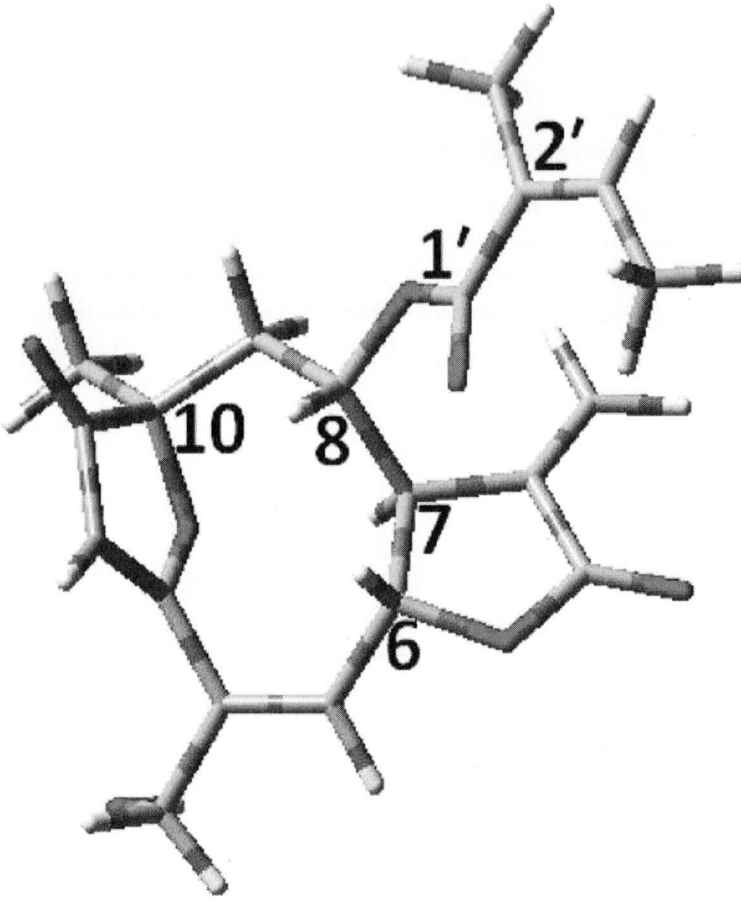

Figure 1. The (6R,7R,8S,10R,2'Z) structure of centratherin [26].

The experimental ECD and VCD spectra and corresponding absorption spectra for centratherin measured in acetonitrile solvent [26] are shown in Figure 2 and Figure 3, respectively. The experimental ROA spectra could not be measured for centratherin due to fluorescence issues and lack of the availability of enough sample. The experimentally measured SOR for centratherin [26] at 589 nm is −12 deg·cc·g^{-1}·dm^{-1}. Since the sample used for experimental measurements has negative SOR at 589 nm, this sample will be labeled as $(-)_{589}$-centratherin.

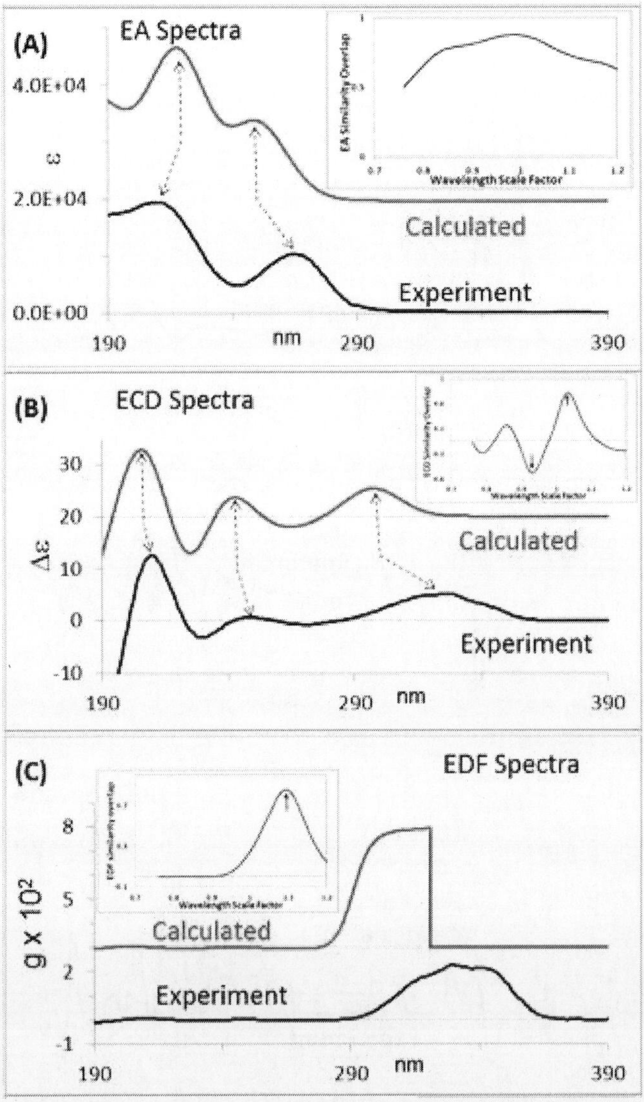

Figure 2. (**A**) Experimental and predicted electronic absorption spectra. Inset shows the similarity overlap plot as a function of wavelength scale factor; (**B**) experimental and predicted ECD spectra. Inset shows the similarity overlap plot as a function of wavelength scale factor; (**C**) experimental and predicted EDF spectra. Inset shows the similarity overlap plot as a function of wavelength scale factor. The experimental spectra are for $(-)_{589}$-centratherin and predicted spectra are for (6R,7R,8S,10R,2′Z) structure. Data taken from Reference [26].

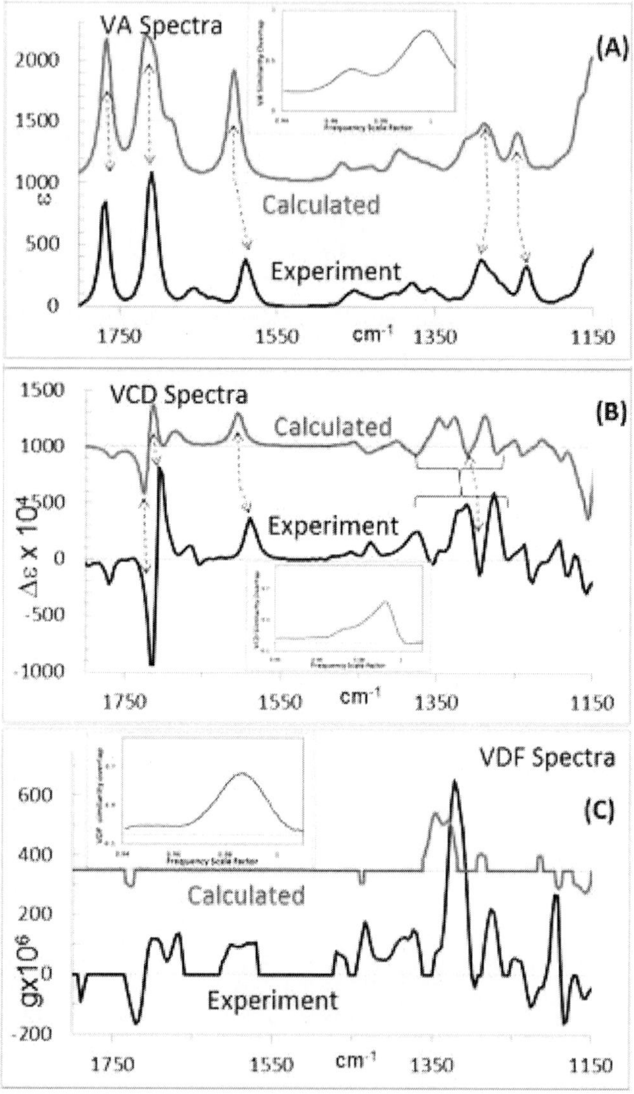

Figure 3. (**A**) Experimental and predicted vibrational absorption spectra. Inset shows the similarity overlap plot as a function of wavenumber scale factor; (**B**) experimental and predicted VCD spectra. Inset shows the similarity overlap plot as a function of wavenumber scale factor; (**C**) experimental and predicted VDF spectra. Inset shows the similarity overlap plot as a function of wavenumber scale factor. The experimental spectra are for $(-)_{589}$-centratherin and predicted spectra are for (6R,7R,8S,10R,2'Z) structure. Data taken from Reference [26].

Once a reliable set of experimental data has been gathered, QC calculations of chiroptical properties are initiated. The basic requirement for theoretical predictions of chiroptical properties is that the correct chemical structure of the compound of interest is known. Here chemical structure is meant to represent the chemical composition (atomic constituents) and the atomic connectivities (which atom is connected to which). Given that information, the three dimensional arrangement of atoms in a chiral molecule is the question that will be addressed by chiroptical spectroscopy. The three dimensional arrangement of atoms in a chiral molecule is defined by the ACs at individual chiral centers and dihedral conformations. Quite often, the relative ACs of the chiral centers may have been determined in the literature. If relative ACs are known with definite certainty, then theoretical predictions can be undertaken for that one diasteromer and conformational analysis conducted to predict the chiroptical properties. For situations where there is no prior information on the ACs of individual chiral centers, one would need to consider all possible diastereomers (and dihedral conformations associated with each diastereomer) and predict the chiroptical properties for all those possibilities. For a compound possessing "n" sources of chirality there will be 2^n diasteromers. Here, a source represents many of the types of chirality (for example, central chirality, axial chirality, etc.). One needs to consider 2^{n-1} diastereomers for theoretical predictions, because one-half of the 2^n diastereomeric structures are mirror images of the other half and their chiroptical properties would be opposite of the other half. For compounds possessing multiple sources of chirality, this situation can turn into a computational nightmare. More often than not, ACs for some of the chiral centers may have already been determined by other means (such as NOEs from NMR spectra), which will permit fixing the ACs at certain centers in the molecule, thereby reducing the computational demand.

The relative AC of centratherin (see Figure 1) is known from the literature as (6R,7R,8S,10R,2'Z), and therefore this disatereomer was used for the theoretical calculations [26].

The first step in the process for theoretical predictions is to build a molecular model. This involves pre-defining the chirality at individual chiral centers (and axial chirality, if one is involved) of the molecule of interest. There are several molecular visualization programs that can be used to build the molecular models. A popular freeware program is Avogadro [27]. Then a conformational search is carried out for the starting structure. A variety of commercial conformational search programs (Spartan [28], Conflex [29], Hyperchem [30], Macromodel [31]) are available for this purpose. It is important to make sure that all of the conformations found belong to the same diastereomer. If some conformers are found to have altered ACs then they need to be appropriately modified before further processing. The conformations determined with conformational search programs, within 20 kcal/mol of energy, need to be further refined using QC programs via geometry optimization options. A good compromise for the QC level of theory to be used here is B3LYP functional and 6-31G* basis set. The energies of optimized geometries at this level are compared and the lowest energy conformers within a certain energy range are retained for further geometry optimization at a higher level of theory. It is important to verify that the optimized conformers are at the minimum of potential energy, by performing vibrational frequency calculations and ensuring that there are no imaginary vibrational frequencies.

For the (6R,7R,8S,10R,2'Z) structure, sixteen lowest energy conformations, within 3 kcal/mol range at B3LYP/6-31G* level were reoptimized at B3LYP/aug-cc-pVDZ level of theory [26].

Then, chiroptical properties are calculated for all of these selected conformers with one particular AC. For the OR phenomenon, the predicted chiroptical property is the SOR at specific wavelengths. The chiroptical properties predicted for the CD phenomenon are the rotational strengths for each of the transitions. For the corresponding absorption phenomenon, the predicted properties are dipole strengths for each of the transitions. For the ROA phenomena, the properties predicted include normal coordinate derivatives of three different polarizability tensors (namely, electric dipole-electric dipole (EDED), electric dipole-magnetic dipole (EDMD) and electric dipole-electric quadrupole (EDEQ)) for each of the vibrational transitions. The anisotropies of these tensors are combined in an appropriate form to derive the activity associated with the ROA phenomena [9,32,33]. The anisotropy of EDED polarizability derivative tensor determines the activity associated with Raman spectra.

Rotational strengths in the case of CD phenomenon, and activities in the case of ROA phenomenon, are merely the signed numbers that represent integrated band intensities in the CD or ROA spectra. Dipole strengths in the case of absorption associated with CD, or Raman activities in the case of Raman associated with ROA, are positive numbers that represent integrated absorption band intensities in absorption or Raman spectra. They all can only be compared with corresponding integrated band intensities in the experimentally measured spectra. The task of integrating the band areas in the experimentally measured spectra is laborious, and may not provide easy comparison to the predicted quantities when multiple transitions overlap. Therefore, the opposite procedure is used by converting the predicted integrated band intensities into simulated predicted spectra, which can be compared with experimentally observed spectra. Simulation of theoretical spectra involves the assumptions of a band profile (Gaussian, Lorentzian, etc.) and a bandwidth for each of the transitions. For convenience, all transitions are assumed to have the same band profile and one chosen bandwidth. All these simulations can be conveniently undertaken using the spectral comparison software [23]. Since SOR is a cumulative effect from all electronic transitions, there is no simulation involved for theoretical SOR predictions.

For the (6R,7R,8S,10R,2′Z) structure, sixteen lowest optimized energy conformations were used for ECD and ORD calculations at CAM-B3LYP/aug-cc-pVDZ level and for VCD at B3LYP/aug-cc-pVDZ level of theory.

The calculated chiroptical properties for individual conformers (all with the same predefined AC) are to be weighted with their percent populations, referred to as Boltzmann populations or weights. These Boltzmann weights can be determined from the electronic energies or Gibbs energies obtained in the QC calculations. The Boltzmann weighted predicted ECD and VCD spectra for (6R,7R,8S,10R,2′Z) diastereomer are shown in Figure 2B and Figure 3B, while the corresponding absorption spectra are shown in Figure 2A and Figure 3A. The predicted population weighted SOR, for (6R,7R,8S,10R,2′Z) structure, is −44 deg·cc·g^{-1}·dm^{-1} at 589 nm.

Visual analysis of chiroptical spectra: At the simplest level of spectral comparison analysis, the experimental and predicted chiroptical spectra are visually compared to assess the agreement between them. To facilitate the visual comparison, lines are drawn correlating the bands observed in the experimental spectra with those in the calculated spectra. In the case of ORD, SOR values measured at discrete wavelengths are compared to those obtained in the calculations (keeping in mind that the calculated wavelengths may have been shifted from the experimental wavelengths). From Figure 2 and Figure 3, it can be seen that the experimental data for the enantiomer with negative SOR at 589 nm matches that predicted for (6R,7R,8S,10R,2'Z) diastereomer. Therefore, the AC of centratherin can be assigned [26] as $(-)_{589}$-(6R,7R,8S,10R,2'Z).

Table 1. Chiral molecules with pharmaceutical applications investigated for their absolute configurations.

Molecule	Methods Used	Practical Use	References
(1S,2S,3R)-1-acetoxymethyl-2,3,4,4-tetra-methylcyclopentane	VCD	pheromone	[34]
Aeroplysinin-1	VCD, ROA	treatment of antiangiogenic disease	[35]
(S)-alaptide	ECD, ORD	veterinary ointment	[90]
(S)-alternarlactam	VCD	fungal cytotoxin	[36]
(S)-AM3189	VCD, OR	diabetes treatment	[37]
(1S,4S)-amino-aza-benzimidazolone	VCD	positive allosteric modulators	[38]
(P)-9-amino-2-cyclopropyl-5-(2-fluoro-6-methoxyphenyl)-2,3-dihydro-pyrrolo[3,4-b]quinolin-1-one	VCD	atropisomers of GABA modulator	[39]
(S,R,R)-Aprepitant	VCD	neurokinin 1 (NK1) receptor antagonist.	[40]
(1R,5S)-1-azabicyclo[3.1.0]hexane	VCD	principle structural fragment of antitumor antibiotics azinomycins A and B	[41]
(S)-AZD624	VCD	NK3 antagonist	[42]
(S)-AZD6765	VCD	NMDA antagonist	[42]
(R,S) and (S,S)-Bedaquiline Analogs	ECD	Antituberculosis Agents	[43]
(S)-benzodiazepine	VCD	Active component of vasopressin receptor antagonist	[44]
(S) and (R)-2-(3,5-bis(trifluoromethyl)phenyl)-N-(4-(2-methylpyridin-4-yl)phenyl)propanamide	VCD, OR	γ-Secretase modulators	[45]
(2S,5R,6S)-2-Benzyl-5,6-bis(4-bromophenyl)-4-methylmorpholin-3-one	VCD, OR	MDM2 inhibitor	[46]
(R)-8-(4-bromophenyl)-8-ethoxy-8H-[1,4]thiazino[3,4-c][1,2,4]oxadiazol-3-one	ECD, ORD, VCD	Calcium Channel antagonist	[47,48]
(S) and (R)-(4-bromophenyl)(imino)(trifluoromethyl)-λ^6-sulfanone	VCD	synthesis of Glucokinase regulatory protein disruptor	[49]
(S) and (R)-(6-bromopyridin-3-yl)(methyl)(trifluoromethyl)-λ^4-sulfanol	VCD	synthesis of Glucokinase regulatory protein disruptor	[49]
(1R,6S,9R)-Buagafuran	ECD	antianxiety	[50]
(6R,7S)-chromenotriazolopyrimidine	VCD	MDM2-p53 inhibitor	[51]
(2R,3R) and (2S,3S)-2-chlorophenylglycidol	VCD, OR, ECD	functionality that can yield intermediates for the synthesis of chiral drugs	[52]
(2R,3R) and (2S,3S)-3-chlorophenylglycidol	VCD, OR, ECD	functionality that can yield intermediates for the synthesis of chiral drugs	[52]
(2R,3R) and (2S,3S)-4-chlorophenylglycidol	VCD,OR,ECD	functionality that can yield intermediates for the synthesis of chiral drugs	[52]
(S)-1-[(4-chlorophenyl)sulfonyl]-2-(2-thienyl)pyrrolidine	VCD	Calcium Channel antagonist	[53]
(S)-2-(2-chloro-4-pyridinyl)-1,1,1-trifluoro-2-propanol	VCD,OR	synthesis of Glucokinase regulatory protein disruptor	[54]
(1S,2S)-Cipralisant (GT-2331)	VCD	H_3 antagonist	[55]
(S)-3-cyanomethyl-3-hydroxyindole	VCD, ECD	antifungal agent	[56]
(S)-desflurane	VCD, OR	anesthetic	
(R)-dichlorprop	VCD	herbicide	[57–59]
(S)-dioxybrassinin	VCD, ECD	antifungal agent	[56]
(S)-Efavirenz	VCD	antiretroviral	[40]
(S)-enflurane	VCD, OR	anesthetic	[61]
(1S,2R)-ephedrine	VCD, ROA	antiinflammatory	[62,63]
(S,S)-Ethyl 6'-hydroxy-2',3'-dihydrospiro[cyclopropane-1,1'-indene]-2-carboxylate	VCD, OR	Head group in Potent GPR40 Full Agonists	[64]
(S)-etodolac	VCD	antiinflammatory	[65]
(1S,2R,3S)-Ezetimibe	VCD	to treat high cholesterol	[40]
(R,R)-Filorexant	VCD	Orexin Receptor Antagonist	[40]
(S)-Flecainide	VCD	antiarrhythmic	[60]
(2R,3R) and (2S,3S)-2-fluorophenylglycidol	VCD,OR,ECD	functionality that can yield intermediates for the synthesis of chiral drugs	[52]
(2R,3R) and (2S,3S)-3-fluorophenylglycidol	VCD, OR, ECD	functionality that can yield intermediates for the synthesis of chiral drugs	[52]
(2R,3R) and (2S,3S)-4-fluorophenylglycidol	VCD, OR, ECD	functionality that can yield intermediates for the synthesis of chiral drugs	[52]
(2R,3R) and (2S,3S)-4-(4-fluorophenyl)-3-hydroxymethyl-1-methylpiperidine	VCD	precursor to paroxetine and femoxetine	[52]
(1R,5S)-Frontalin	VCD	pheromone	[66]

Most of the reported chiroptical spectral analyses for chiral drugs were accomplished via visual spectral analyses. A table summarizing the chiral drugs whose ACs were investigated [34,35,36,37,38,39,40,41,42,43,44,45,46,47,48,49,50,51,52,53,54,55,56,57,58,59,60,61,62,63,64,65,66,67,68,69,70,71,72,73,74,75,76,77,78,79,80,81,82,83,84,85,86,87,88,89,90] using chiroptical spectroscopic methods are summarized in Table 1. Occasional reviews have also highlighted some of these chiral drugs [42,65,91,92]. There are several natural products with promising medicinal values where ACs were investigated using chiroptical spectroscopy, but it will be unwieldy to review all of them here.

2.5. Spectral Overlap Analysis

Visual spectral analysis does not provide any quantitative measure of agreement between experimental and predicted spectra and may introduce inadvertent user bias. To provide a quantitative measure of agreement, and eliminate the unintended bias, the digital experimental and predicted spectral data are used to calculate the normalized overlap integral between them. If the normalized overlap integral for signed chiroptical spectral data is 1, then the experimental data of the enantiomer used for experimental measurements are reproduced exactly by the AC used for calculations. On the other hand, if the normalized overlap integral for signed chiroptical spectral data is −1, then, the experimental data of the enantiomer used for experimental measurements would be reproduced exactly by the AC, which is opposite to that used for calculations. The normalized overlap integrals for the absorption and Raman spectra, which are between 0 and 1, do not reflect the AC. Nevertheless, it is important to verify that the predicted absorption or Raman spectrum also reproduces the corresponding experimental spectrum (vide infra). Similarity overlap plots for absorption and CD spectra are shown as insets in Figure 2A,B and Figure 3A,B. The ECD spectral overlap analysis (see inset in Figure 2B) yields a ECD spectral overlap of 0.78 for $(-)_{589}$-(6R,7R,8S,10R,2′Z) at a wavelength scale factor of 1.03 and also a overlap of −0.5 at a wavelength scale factor of 0.93. The later value indicates the level of agreement for the opposite enantiomer. This information could not have been obtained from the visual spectral analysis. Even though the overlap for $(-)_{589}$-(6R,7R,8S,10R,2′Z) is higher and that for the opposite enantiomer is lower, one should not be overconfident in assigning the AC from ECD spectral overlap alone (vide infra). The VCD spectral overlap analysis (see inset in Figure 3B) yields a overlap of 0.53 at a frequency scale factor of 0.99 for $(-)_{589}$-(6R,7R,8S,10R,2′Z) and none with opposite signs. Thus any possible assignment of opposite AC is ruled out from the VCD spectral analysis. Comparison of ORD data also supports $(-)_{589}$-(6R,7R,8S,10R,2'Z) assignment [26]. Thus, different chiroptical spectra provide complimentary information that that should be made use of. The spectral overlap analyses discussed in this paragraph have been reported for only a limited number of chiral drugs summarized in Table 1.

Advanced Spectral analysis: When chiroptical spectra are analyzed, a concomitant analysis for accompanying absorption and Raman spectra should also be provided. This is because some of the fundamental quantities involved are common to both of them. However, undertaking separate analyses for them represents an incomplete enquiry. A complete analysis includes comparison of ratio spectra, i.e., ratio of CD to absorption spectra and ratio of ROA to Raman spectra. The former is called dimensionless dissymmetry factor (DF), while the latter is called dimensionless circular intensity difference (CID). The ratio of ECD spectrum to corresponding absorption spectrum is called electronic dissymmetry factor (EDF) spectrum and the ratio of VCD spectrum to corresponding absorption spectrum is called vibrational dissymmetry factor (VDF) spectrum. The EDF and VDF spectra for centratherin are shown in Figure 2C and Figure 3C. The EDF spectral overlap analysis (see inset to Figure 2C) for $(-)_{589}$-(6R,7R,8S,10R,2'Z) yields a value of 0.85 and no negative values. Note that, in the previous paragraph, we stated that ECD spectra indicated a possibility for the opposite AC assignment, but EDF spectra now rule out that possibility. This example clearly shows the usefulness of EDF spectra. The VCD spectral overlap analysis (see inset to Figure 3C) for $(-)_{589}$-(6R,7R,8S,10R,2'Z) yields a value of 0.62 and no negative values. The overlap values for EDF and VDF are greater than the corresponding values for ECD and VCD. Thus the advanced spectral analysis also suggests the AC of centratherin as $(-)_{589}$-(6R,7R,8S,10R,2'Z).

The DF spectral analysis provides more insight than CD spectra alone. Furthermore, as literature studies indicate [69,93], the spectral overlap analysis for DF can be particularly useful when a distinction needs to be made out of several possible diastereomers. In addition, unexpected new information may ensue [94] from DF spectral analyses.

Since DF spectral analyses is a new concept, these analyses have not been yet been generally adopted. However, future investigations are recommended to incorporate the DF analyses, as there is more to gain and nothing to lose in such analyses.

Finally, it should be noted that for molecules with several chiral centers with unknown ACs, a unique solution results when only one diastereomeric structure provides the best match between experimental and predicted chiroptical property. But if multiple diastereomeric structures provide similar matches to the experiment, which is a common occurrence, then a given chiroptical property could not have provided the unique solution for AC. This later situation can be avoided if more than one chiroptical property is simultaneously analyzed for the compound of interest. This is because even if multiple diastereomers may possess the same chiroptical property in a given chiroptical method it is unlikely that they will have the same chiroptical property in another chiroptical method.

3. CONCLUSIONS

The pharmaceutical industry has widely adopted the chiroptical spectroscopic methods for establishing the ACs of chiral drugs that they are developing. There are some improvements that can be incorporated in to the methods that are being routinely used. The analysis of DF and CID spectra can improve the reliability of the AC assignments, help discriminate among multiple diastereomers and provide better insight. It is pragmatic, and generally important, to investigate more than one chiroptical property for determining the ACs of chiral molecules.

ACKNOWLEDGMENTS

Funding from NSF (CHE-1464874) is gratefully acknowledged. I would like to thank Fernando Martins, Cody Covington, and Mauro de Amorim for their participation in centratherin work [26]. I also thank Chris Welch and Leo Joyce of Merck, Oliver McConnell of Bristol-Myers Squibb and Michael Bartberger of Amgen for providing references to their published articles.

CONFLICTS OF INTEREST

The author declares no conflict of interest.

REFERENCES

1. Berova, N.; Polavarapu, P.L.; Nakanishi, K.; Woody, R.W. Comprehensive Chiroptical Spectroscopy: Instrumentation, Methodologies, and Theoretical Simulations; John Wiley & Sons: New York, NY, USA, 2012.

2. Berova, N.; Polavarapu, P.L.; Nakanishi, K.; Woody, R.W. Comprehensive Chiroptical Spectroscopy: Applications in Stereochemical Analysis of Synthetic Compounds, Natural Products, and Biomolecules; John Wiley & Sons: New York, NY, USA, 2012.

3. Eliel, E.L.; Wilen, S.H. Stereochemistry of Organic Compounds; John Wiley: New York, NY, USA, 1994.

4. Covington, C.L.; Polavarapu, P.L. Specific optical rotations and the Horeau effect. Chirality **2015**, 28, 181–185.

5. Harada, N.; Nakanishi, K. Circular Dichroic Spectroscopy: Exciton Coupling in Organic Stereochemistry; University Science Books: Sausalito, CA, USA, 1983; p. 460.

6. Berova, N.; Di Bari, L.; Pescitelli, G. Application of Electronic Circular Dichroism in Configurational and Conformational Analysis of Organic Compounds. Chem. Soc. Rev. **2007**, 36, 914–931.

7. Stephens, P.J.; Devlin, F.J.; Pan, J.-J. The determination of the absolute configurations of chiral molecules using vibrational circular dichroism (VCD) spectroscopy. Chirality **2008**, 20, 643–663.

8. Barron, L.D.; Zhu, F.; Hecht, L.; Tranter, G.E.; Isaacs, N.W. Raman optical activity: An incisive probe of molecular chirality and biomolecular structure. J. Mol. Struct. **2007**, 834–836, 7–16.

9. Nafie, L.A. Vibrational Optical Activity: Principles and Applications; John Wiley and Sons: New York, NY, USA, 2011.

10. Crawford, T.D.; Ruud, K. Coupled-Cluster Calculations of Vibrational Raman Optical Activity Spectra. ChemPhysChem **2011**, 12, 3442–3448.

11. Cheeseman, J.R.; Frisch, M.J.; Devlin, F.J.; Stephens, P.J. Ab initio Calculation of Atomic Axial Tensors and Vibrational Rotational Strengths Using Density Functional Theory. Chem. Phys. Lett. **1996**, 252, 211–220.

12. Autschbach, J. Computing chiroptical properties with first-principles theoretical methods: Background and illustrative examples. Chirality **2009**, 21, E116–E152.

13. Bougas, L.; Sofikitis, D.; Katsoprinakis, G.E.; Spiliotis, A.K.; Tzallas, P.; Loppinet, B.; Rakitzis, T.P. Chiral cavity ring down polarimetry: Chirality and magnetometry measurements using signal reversals. J. Chem. Phys. **2015**, 143.

14. Müller, T.; Wiberg, K.B.; Vaccaro, P.H. Cavity Ring-Down Polarimetry (CRDP): A New Scheme for Probing Circular Birefringence and Circular Dichroism in the Gas Phase. J. Phys. Chem. A **2000**, 104, 5959–5968.

15. Sofikitis, D.; Bougas, L.; Katsoprinakis, G.E.; Spiliotis, A.K.; Loppinet, B.; Rakitzis, T.P. Evanescent-wave and ambient chiral sensing by signal-reversing cavity ringdown polarimetry. Nature **2014**, 514, 76–79.

16. Dalton: A Molecular Electronic Structure Program. Available online: http://daltonprogram.org (accessed on 10 August 2016).

17. PSI4: A Open-Source Suite of Ab Initio Quantum Chemistry Programs. Available online: http://www.psicode.org/ (accessed on 10 August 2016).

18. Valiev, M.; Bylaska, E.J.; Govind, N.; Kowalski, K.; Straatsma, T.P.; van Dam, H.J.J.; Wang, D.; Nieplocha, J.; Apra, E.; Windus, T.L.; et al. NWChem: A comprehensive and scalable open-source solution for large scale molecular simulations. Comput. Phys. Commun. **2010**, 181, 1477–1489.

19. Gaussian09; Gaussian Inc.: Willingford, CT, USA, 2013.

20. ADF: Amsterdam Density Functional Molecular Modeling Suite; Software for Chemistry & Materials (SCM): Amsterdam, The Netherlands, 2014.

21. Shen, J.; Zhu, C.; Reiling, S.; Vaz, R. A novel computational method for comparing vibrational circular dichroism spectra. Spectrochim. Acta Part A **2010**, 76, 418–422.

22. Debie, E.; de Gussem, E.; Dukor, R.K.; Herrebout, W.; Nafie, L.A.; Bultinck, P. A Confidence Level Algorithm for the Determination of Absolute Configuration Using Vibrational Circular Dichroism or Raman Optical Activity. ChemPhysChem **2011**, 12, 1542–1549.

23. Covington, C.L.; Polavarapu, P.L. CDSpecTech: Computer Programs for Calculating Similarity Measures for Experimental and Calculated Dissymmetry Factors and Circular Intensity Differentials. Available online: https://sites.google.com/site/cdspectech1/ (accessed on 10 August 2016).

24. Bruhn, T.; Schaumlöffel, A.; Hemberger, Y.; Bringmann, G. SpecDis: Quantifying the Comparison of Calculated and Experimental Electronic Circular Dichroism Spectra. Chirality **2013**, 25, 243–249.

25. CompareVOA; BioTools Inc.: Jupiter, FL, USA, 2012.

26. Junior, F.M.S.; Covington, C.L.; de Albuquerque, A.C.F.; Lobo, J.F.R.; Borges, R.M.; de Amorim, M.B.; Polavarapu, P.L. Absolute Configuration of (−)-Centratherin, a Sesquiterpenoid Lactone, Defined by Means of Chiroptical Spectroscopy. J. Nat. Prod. **2015**, 78, 2617–2623.

27. Hanwell, M.D.; Curtis, D.E.; Lonie, D.C.; Vandermeersch, T.; Zurek, E.; Hutchison, G.R. Avogadro: An advanced semantic chemical editor, visualization, and analysis platform. J. Cheminform. **2012**, 4, 1–17.

28. Spartan: Wavefunction Inc. Available online: https://www.wavefun.com/products/spartan.html (accessed on 10 August 2016).

29. Conflex: High Performance Conformational Analysis. Available online: http://www.conflex.us/ (accessed on 24 May 2010).

30. HyperChem: Hypercube, Inc. Available online: http://www.hyper.com/ (accessed on 10 August 2016).

31. MacroModel 9.6; Schrodinger LLC: New York, NY, USA, 2008.

32. Barron, L.D. Molecular Light Scattering and Optical Activity, 2nd ed.; Cambridge University Press: Cambridge, UK, 2004.

33. Polavarapu, P.L. Vibrational Spectra: Principles and Applications With Emphasis on Optical Activity; Elsevier: Amsterdam, The Netherlands, 1998.

34. Figadere, B.; Devlin, F.J.; Millar, J.G.; Stephens, P.J. Determination of the absolute configuration of the sex pheromone of the obscure mealybug by vibrational circular dichroism analysis. Chem. Commun. **2008**, 1106, 1106–1108.

35. Nieto-Ortega, B.; Casado, J.; Blanch, E.W.; López Navarrete, J.T.; Quesada, A.R.; Ramírez, F.J. Raman Optical Activity Spectra and Conformational Elucidation of Chiral Drugs. The Case of the Antiangiogenic Aeroplysinin-1. J. Phys. Chem. A **2011**, 115, 2752–2755.

36. Jiang, N.; Tan, R.X.; Ma, J. Simulations of Solid-State Vibrational Circular Dichroism Spectroscopy of (S)-Alternarlactam by Using Fragmentation Quantum Chemical Calculations. J. Phys. Chem. B **2011**, 115, 2801–2813.

37. Ma, Z.; Lin, D.C.H.; Sharma, R.; Liu, J.; Zhu, L.; Li, A.-R.; Kohn, T.; Wang, Y.; Liu, J.; Bartberger, M.D.; et al. Discovery of the imidazole-derived GPR40 agonist AM-3189. Bioorg. Med. Chem. Lett. **2016**, 26, 15–20.

38. Pero, J.E.; Rossi, M.A.; Kelly, M.J.; Lehman, H.D.G.F.; Layton, M.E.; Garbaccio, R.M.; O'Brien, J.A.; Magliaro, B.C.; Uslaner, J.M.; Huszar, S.L.; et al. Optimization of Novel Aza-benzimidazolone mGluR2 PAMs with Respect to LLE and PK Properties and Mitigation of CYP TDI. ACS Med. Chem. Lett. **2016**, 7, 312–317.

39. Pivonka, D.E.; Wesolowski, S.S. Vibrational Circular Dichroism (VCD) Chiral Assignment of Atropisomers: Application to g-Aminobutyric Acid (GABA) Modulators Designed as Potential Anxiolytic Drugs. Appl. Spectrosc. **2013**, 67, 365–371.

40. Sherer, E.C.; Lee, C.H.; Shpungin, J.; Cuff, J.F.; Da, C.; Ball, R.; Bach, R.; Crespo, A.; Gong, X.; Welch, C.J. Systematic Approach to Conformational Sampling for Assigning Absolute Configuration Using Vibrational Circular Dichroism. J. Med. Chem. **2014**, 57, 477–494.

41. Rauk, A.; Yang, D.; Tsankov, D.; Wieser, H.; Koltypin, Y.; Gedanken, A.; Shustov, G.V. Chiroptical Properties of 1-Azabicyclo[3.1.0]hexane in the Vacuum-UV and IR Regions. J. Am. Chem. Soc. **1995**, 117, 4160–4166.

42. Wesolowski, S.S.; Pivonka, D.E. A rapid alternative to X-ray crystallography for chiral determination: Case studies of vibrational circular dichroism (VCD) to advance drug discovery projects. Bioorg. Med. Chem. Lett. **2013**, 23, 4019–4025.

43. Geng, Y.; Li, L.; Wu, C.; Chi, Y.; Li, Z.; Xu, W.; Sun, T. Design and Stereochemical Research (DFT, ECD and Crystal Structure) of Novel Bedaquiline Analogs as Potent Antituberculosis Agents. Molecules **2016**, 21.

44. Dyatkin, A.B.; Freedman, T.B.; Cao, X.; Dukor, R.K.; Maryanoff, B.E.; Maryanoff, C.A.; Matthews, J.M.; Shah, R.D.; Nafie, L.A. Determination of the absolute configuration of a key tricyclic component of a novel vasopressin receptor antagonist by use of vibrational circular dichroism. Chirality **2002**, 14, 215–219.

45. Chen, J.J.; Qian, W.; Biswas, K.; Yuan, C.; Amegadzie, A.; Liu, Q.; Nixey, T.; Zhu, J.; Ncube, M.; Rzasa, R.M.; et al. Discovery of 2-

methylpyridine-based biaryl amides as γ-secretase modulators for the treatment of Alzheimer's disease. Bioorg. Med. Chem. Lett. **2013**, 23, 6447–6454.

46. Gonzalez-Lopez de Turiso, F.; Sun, D.; Rew, Y.; Bartberger, M.D.; Beck, H.P.; Canon, J.; Chen, A.; Chow, D.; Correll, T.L.; Huang, X.; et al. Rational Design and Binding Mode Duality of MDM2–p53 Inhibitors. J. Med. Chem. **2013**, 56, 4053–4070.

47. Carosati, E.; Cruciani, G.; Chiarini, A.; Budriesi, R.; Ioan, P.; Spisani, R.; Spinelli, D.; Cosimelli, B.; Fusi, F.; Frosini, M.; et al. Calcium Channel Antagonists Discovered by a Multidisciplinary Approach. J. Med. Chem. **2006**, 49, 5206–5216.

48. Stephens, P.J.; Devlin, F.J.; Gasparrini, F.; Ciogli, A.; Spinelli, D.; Cosimelli, B. Determination of the Absolute Configuration of a Chiral Oxadiazol-3-one Calcium Channel Blocker, Resolved Using Chiral Chromatography, via Concerted Density Functional Theory Calculations of Its Vibrational Circular Dichroism, Electronic Circular Dichroism, and Optical Rotation. J. Org. Chem. **2007**, 72, 4707–4715.

49. Nishimura, N.; Norman, M.H.; Liu, L.; Yang, K.C.; Ashton, K.S.; Bartberger, M.D.; Chmait, S.; Chen, J.; Cupples, R.; Fotsch, C.; et al. Small Molecule Disruptors of the Glucokinase-Glucokinase Regulatory Protein Interaction: 3. Structure–Activity Relationships within the Aryl Carbinol Region of the N-Arylsulfonamido-N′-arylpiperazine Series. J. Med. Chem. **2014**, 57, 3094–3116.

50. Li, L.; Li, C.; Si, Y.-K.; Yin, D.-L. Absolute configuration of Buagafuran: An experimental and theoretical electronic circular dichroism study. Chin. Chem. Lett. **2013**, 24, 500–502.

51. Allen, J.G.; Bourbeau, M.P.; Wohlhieter, G.E.; Bartberger, M.D.; Michelsen, K.; Hungate, R.; Gadwood, R.C.; Gaston, R.D.; Evans, B.; Mann, L.W.; et al. Discovery and Optimization of Chromenotriazolopyrimidines as Potent Inhibitors of the Mouse Double Minute 2—Tumor Protein 53 Protein—Protein Interaction. J. Med. Chem. **2009**, 52, 7044–7053.

52. McConnell, O.; He, Y.; Nogle, L.; Sarkahian, A. Application of chiral technology in a pharmaceutical company. Enantiomeric separation and spectroscopic studies of key asymmetric intermediates using a combination of techniques. Phenylglycidols. Chirality **2007**, 19, 716–730.

53. Carosati, E.; Budriesi, R.; Ioan, P.; Cruciani, G.; Fusi, F.; Frosini, M.; Saponara, S.; Gasparrini, F.; Ciogli, A.; Villani, C.; et al. Stereoselective Behavior of the Functional Diltiazem Analogue 1-[(4-Chlorophenyl)sulfonyl]-2-(2-thienyl)pyrrolidine, a New L-Type Calcium Channel Blocker. J. Med. Chem. **2009**, 52, 6637–6648.

54. Pennington, L.D.; Bartberger, M.D.; Croghan, M.D.; Andrews, K.L.; Ashton, K.S.; Bourbeau, M.P.; Chen, J.; Chmait, S.; Cupples, R.; Fotsch, C.; et al. Discovery and Structure-Guided Optimization of Diarylmethanesulfonamide Disrupters of Glucokinase–Glucokinase Regulatory Protein (GK–GKRP) Binding: Strategic Use of a N → S ($n_N \rightarrow \sigma^*_{S-X}$) Interaction for Conformational Constraint. J. Med. Chem. **2015**, 58, 9663–9679.

55. Minick, D.J.; Copley, R.C.B.; Szewczyk, J.R.; Rutkowske, R.D.; Miller, L.A. An investigation of the absolute configuration of the potent histamine H_3 receptor antagonist GT-2331 using vibrational circular dichroism. Chirality **2007**, 19, 731–740.

56. Monde, K.; Taniguchi, T.; Miura, N.; Nishimura, S.-I.; Harada, N.; Dukor, R.K.; Nafie, L.A. Preparation of cruciferous phytoalexin related metabolites, (−)-dioxibrassinin and (−)-3-cyanomethyl-3-hydroxyoxindole, and determination of their absolute configurations by vibrational circular dichroism (VCD). Tetrahedron Lett. **2003**, 44, 6017–6020.

57. He, J.; Wang, F.; Polavarapu, P.L. Absolute configurations of chiral herbicides determined from vibrational circular dichroism. Chirality **2005**, 17, S1–S8.

58. He, J.; Polavarapu, P.L. Determination of the absolute configuration of chiral α-aryloxypropanoic acids using vibrational circular dichroism studies: 2-(2-chlorophenoxy)

propanoic acid and 2-(3-chlorophenoxy) propanoic acid. Spectrochim. Acta Part A **2005**, 61, 1327–1334.

59. He, J.; Polavarapu, P.L. Determination of Intermolecular Hydrogen Bonded Conformers of α-Aryloxypropanoic Acids Using Density Functional Theory Predictions of Vibrational Absorption and Vibrational Circular Dichroism Spectra. J. Chem. Theory Comput. **2005**, 1, 506–514.

60. Freedman, T.B.; Long, F.; Citra, M.; Nafie, L.A. Hydrogen-stretching vibrational circular dichroism spectroscopy: Absolute configuration and solution conformation of selected pharmaceutical molecules. Enantiomer **1999**, 4, 103–119.

61. Zhao, C.; Polavarapu, P.L.; Grosenick, H.; Schurig, V. Vibrational circular dichroism, absolute configuration and predominant conformations of volatile anesthetics: Enflurane. J. Mol. Struct. **2000**, 550–551, 105–115.

62. Freedman, T.B.; Ragunathan, N.; Alexander, S. Vibrational circular dichroism in ephedra molecules. Experimental measurement and ab initio calculation. Faraday Discuss. **1994**, 99, 131–149.

63. Yu, G.-S.; Che, D.; Freedman, T.B.; Nafie, L.A. Backscattering dual circular polarization raman optical activity in ephedrine molecules. Tetrahedron Asymmetry **1993**, 4, 511–516.

64. Wang, Y.; Liu, J.; Dransfield, P.J.; Zhu, L.; Wang, Z.; Du, X.; Jiao, X.; Su, Y.; Li, A.-R.; Brown, S.P.; et al. Discovery and Optimization of Potent GPR40 Full Agonists Containing Tricyclic Spirocycles. ACS Med. Chem. Lett. **2013**, 4, 551–555.

65. McConnell, O.; Bach, A.; Balibar, C.; Byrne, N.; Cai, Y.; Carter, G.; Chlenov, M.; Di, L.; Fan, K.; Goljer, I.; et al. Enantiomeric separation and determination of absolute stereochemistry of asymmetric molecules in drug discovery—Building chiral technology toolboxes. Chirality **2007**, 19, 658–682.

66. Ashvar, C.S.; Stephens, P.J.; Eggimann, T.; Wieser, H. Vibrational circular dichroism spectroscopy of chiral pheromones: Frontalin

(1,5-dimethyl-6,8-dioxabicyclo[3.2.1]octane). Tetrahedron Asymmetry **1998**, 9, 1107–1110.

67. Freedman, T.B.; Cao, X.; Oliveira, R.V.; Cass, Q.B.; Nafie, L.A. Determination of the absolute configuration and solution conformation of gossypol by vibrational circular dichroism. Chirality **2003**, 15, 196–200.

68. Regalado, E.L.; Sherer, E.C.; Green, M.D.; Hendersonl, D.W.; Thomas Williamson, R.; Joyce, L.A.; Welch, C.J. Chromatographic Separation and Assignment of Absolute Configuration of Hydroxywarfarin Isomers. Chirality **2014**, 26, 95–101.

69. Derewacz, D.K.; McNees, C.R.; Scalmani, G.; Covington, C.L.; Shanmugam, G.; Marnett, L.J.; Polavarapu, P.L.; Bachmann, B.O. Structure and Stereochemical Determination of Hypogeamicins from a Cave-Derived Actinomycete. J. Nat. Prod. **2014**, 77, 1759–1763.

70. Izumi, H.; Ogata, A.; Nafie, L.A.; Dukor, R.K. A Revised Conformational Code for the Exhaustive Analysis of Conformers with One-to-One Correspondence between Conformation and Code: Application to the VCD Analysis of (S)-Ibuprofen. J. Org. Chem. **2009**, 74, 1231–1236.

71. Santoro, E.; Mazzeo, G.; Petrovic, A.G.; Cimmino, A.; Koshoubu, J.; Evidente, A.; Berova, N.; Superchi, S. Absolute configurations of phytotoxins seiricardine A and inuloxin A obtained by chiroptical studies. Phytochemistry **2015**, 116, 359–366.

72. Polavarapu, P.L.; Cholli, A.L.; Vernice, G. Absolute configuration of isoflurane. J. Am. Chem. Soc. **1992**, 114, 10953–10955.

73. Polavarapu, P.L. Determination of Molecular Stereochemistry using Optical Rotatory Dispersion, Vibrational Circular Dichroism and Vibrational Raman Optical Activity. In Chiral Analysis; Busch, K.W., Busch, M.A., Eds.; Elsevier Science: Oxford, UK, 2011.

74. Dunmire, D.; Freedman, T.B.; Nafie, L.A.; Aeschlimann, C.; Gerber, J.G.; Gal, J. Determination of the absolute configuration and solution conformation of the antifungal agents

ketoconazole, itraconazole, and miconazole with vibrational circular dichroism. Chirality **2005**, 17, S101–S108.

75. Izumi, H.; Ogata, A.; Nafie, L.A.; Dukor, R.K. Structural determination of molecular stereochemistry using VCD spectroscopy and a conformational code: Absolute configuration and solution conformation of a chiral liquid pesticide, (R)-(+)-malathion. Chirality **2009**, 21, E172–E180.

76. Maryanoff, B.E.; McComsey, D.F.; Dukor, R.K.; Nafie, L.A.; Freedman, T.B.; Cao, X.; Day, V.W. Structural studies on McN-5652-X, a high-affinity ligand for the serotonin transporter in mammalian brain. Biorg. Med. Chem. **2003**, 11, 2463–2470.

77. Freedman, T.B.; Dukor, R.K.; van Hoof, P.J.C.M.; Kellenbach, E.R.; Nafie, L.A. Determination of the Absolute Configuration of (−)-Mirtazapine by Vibrational Circular Dichroism. Helv. Chim. Acta **2002**, 85, 1160–1165.

78. Horne, D.B.; Tamayo, N.A.; Bartberger, M.D.; Bo, Y.; Clarine, J.; Davis, C.D.; Gore, V.K.; Kaller, M.R.; Lehto, S.G.; Ma, V.V.; et al. Optimization of Potency and Pharmacokinetic Properties of Tetrahydroisoquinoline Transient Receptor Potential Melastatin 8 (TRPM8) Antagonists. J. Med. Chem. **2014**, 57, 2989–3004.

79. Thiel, O.R.; Achmatowicz, M.; Bernard, C.; Wheeler, P.; Savarin, C.; Correll, T.L.; Kasparian, A.; Allgeier, A.; Bartberger, M.D.; Tan, H.; et al. Development of a Practical Synthesis of a p38 MAP Kinase Inhibitor. Org. Process Res. Dev. **2009**, 13, 230–241.

80. Shen, J.; Yang, J.; Heyse, W.; Schweitzer, H.; Nagel, N.; Andert, D.; Zhu, C.; Morrison, V.; Nemeth, G.A.; Chen, T.-M.; et al. Enantiomeric characterization and structure elucidation of Otamixaban. J. Pharm. Anal. **2014**, 4, 197–204.

81. Mazzeo, G.; Santoro, E.; Andolfi, A.; Cimmino, A.; Troselj, P.; Petrovic, A.G.; Superchi, S.; Evidente, A.; Berova, N. Absolute Configurations of Fungal and Plant Metabolites by Chiroptical Methods. ORD, ECD, and VCD Studies on Phyllostin, Scytolide, and Oxysporone. J. Nat. Prod. **2013**, 76, 588–599.

82. Izumi, H.; Ogata, A.; Nafie, L.A.; Dukor, R.K. Vibrational Circular Dichroism Analysis Reveals a Conformational Change of the Baccatin III Ring of Paclitaxel: Visualization of Conformations Using a New Code for Structure—Activity Relationships. J. Org. Chem. **2008**, 73, 2367–2372.

83. Goljer, I.; Molinari, A.; He, Y.; Nogle, L.; Sun, W.; Campbell, B.; McConnell, O. Unexpected rearrangement of enantiomerically pure 3-aminoquinuclidine as a simple way of preparing diastereomeric octahydropyrrolo[2,3-c]pyridine derivatives. Chirality **2009**, 21, 681–691.

84. Sen, A.; Bouchet, A.; Lepère, V.; Le Barbu-Debus, K.; Scuderi, D.; Piuzzi, F.; Zehnacker-Rentien, A. Conformational Analysis of Quinine and Its Pseudo Enantiomer Quinidine: A Combined Jet-Cooled Spectroscopy and Vibrational Circular Dichroism Study. J. Phys. Chem. A **2012**, 116, 8334–8344.

85. Tamayo, N.A.; Bo, Y.; Gore, V.; Ma, V.; Nishimura, N.; Tang, P.; Deng, H.; Klionsky, L.; Lehto, S.G.; Wang, W.; et al. Fused Piperidines as a Novel Class of Potent and Orally Available Transient Receptor Potential Melastatin Type 8 (TRPM8) Antagonists. J. Med. Chem. **2012**, 55, 1593–1611.

86. Izumi, H.; Futamura, S.; Tokita, N.; Hamada, Y. Fliplike Motion in the Thalidomide Dimer: Conformational Analysis of (R)-Thalidomide Using Vibrational Circular Dichroism Spectroscopy. J. Org. Chem. **2006**, 72, 277–279.

87. Vanthuyne, N.; Roussel, C.; Naubron, J.-V.; Jagerovic, N.; Lázaro, P.M.; Alkorta, I.; Elguero, J. Determination of the absolute configuration of 1,3,5-triphenyl-4,5-dihydropyrazole enantiomers by a combination of VCD, ECD measurements, and theoretical calculations. Tetrahedron Asymmetry **2011**, 22, 1120–1124.

88. Wang, F.; Zhao, C.; Polavarapu, P.L. A study of the conformations of valinomycin in solution phase. Biopolymers **2004**, 75, 85–93.

89. Yamamoto, S.; Straka, M.; Watarai, H.; Bour, P. Formation and structure of the potassium complex of valinomycin in solution studied by Raman optical activity spectroscopy. Phys. Chem. Chem. Phys. **2010**, 12, 11021–11032.

90. Julíneka, O.; Setnicka, V.; Rezácová, A.; Dohnal, J.; Vosátka, V.; Urbanová, M. Product of alaptide synthesis: Determination of the absolute configuration. J. Pharm. Biomed. Anal. **2010**, 53, 958–961.

91. Nafie, L.A.; Dukor, R.K. Applications of Vibrational optical activity in the Pharmaceutical Industry. In Applications of Vibrational Spectroscopy in Pharmaceutical Research and Development; Pivonka, D.E., Chalmers, J.M., Griffiths, P.R., Eds.; John Wiley: New York, NY, USA, 2007; pp. 129–154.

92. Tsankov, D.; Polyanichko, A.; Wieser, H. Vibrational Circular Dichroism: Ensuring Quality of Pharmaceutical Products. In Pharmaceutical Sciences Enctclopedia: Drug Discovery, Development, and Manufacturing; Gad, S.C., Ed.; John Wiley and Sons: New York, NY, USA, 2011.

93. Junior, F.M.S.; Covington, C.L.; de Amorim, M.B.; Velozo, L.S.M.; Kaplan, M.A.C.; Polavarapu, P.L. Absolute Configuration of a Rare Sesquiterpene: (+)-3-Ishwarone. J. Nat. Prod. **2014**, 77, 1881–1886.

94. Covington, C.L.; Polavarapu, P.L. Solvation dependence observed in the electronic dissymmetry factor spectra: How much information are we missing by analyzing the circular dichroism spectra alone? Phys. Chem. Chem. Phys. **2016**, 18, 13912–13917.

Chapter 3

Homoconjugation *vs.* Exciton Coupling in Chiral α,β-Unsaturated Bicyclo[3.3.1]nonane Dinitrile and Carboxylic Acids

Gintautas Bagdžiūnas [1,2], Eugenijus Butkus [1] and Sigitas Stončius [1,*]

[1]*Department of Organic Chemistry, Vilnius University, Naugarduko 24, 03225 Vilnius, Lithuania*

[2]*Present address: Department of Polymer Chemistry and Technology, Kaunas University of Technology, Radvilėnų pl. 19, 50254 Kaunas, Lithuania*

ABSTRACT

The chiroptical properties of enantiomerically pure bicyclo[3.3.1]nona-2,6-diene-2,6-dicarbonitrile and related acids were studied by circular dichroism spectroscopy and theoretical computations. A consideration of the molecular structure of the synthesized difunctional compounds revealed that chromophores are predisposed to transannular through-space interaction due to a favourable conformation of the bicyclic skeleton and a rather small interchromophoric distance. Evidence for non-exciton-type coupling between the two acrylonitrile and acrylate moieties in **3** and **4**, respectively, was obtained by chiroptical spectroscopy and DFT calculations.

Keywords: circular dichroism; conformational analysis; TD-DFT calculations; transannular interactions; homoconjugation

1. INTRODUCTION

Cyclic α,β-unsaturated carboxylic acids are found in various chiral natural products such as the heteroyohimbine alkaloids [1] or shikimic and chorismic acids, which are involved in biosynthetic processes and used in enzyme action studies [2]. The latter acids are precursors for the synthesis of biologically active compounds [3,4] and are important biochemical intermediates [5]. Chiroptical methods and, in particular, circular dichroism (CD) spectroscopy are nowadays well-established techniques for the determination of the absolute stereochemistry of chiral compounds. A variety of methodologies, ranging from empirical rules to *ab initio* quantum mechanical methods, have been devised for the correlation of the chiroptical properties with the absolute configuration [6]. In particular, rapid development of high-level quantum mechanical methods led to the use of advanced calculations, not only for the absolute stereochemistry determination of model, relatively small compounds, but also for studies of conformational changes and chromophore interactions in large biochemically relevant structures, such as proteins [7]. Nevertheless, the question of setting the absolute configuration of polyfunctional molecules remains a nontrivial task and may become a complicated issue in cyclic α,β-unsaturated carboxy compounds [8] due to the complex character of the chromophore. In general, the application of electronic circular dichroism measurements led to the correlation of the sign and magnitude of the observed Cotton (CE) effect with the absolute configuration of chiral molecules containing various chromophores [9,10]. In particular, the related α,β-unsaturated ketone chromophore belongs to the group of chromophores that have been investigated both experimentally and theoretically over the last years [11]. A number of various sector and/or helicity rules have been proposed to correlate the sign of the CEs that is observed in the spectral region between 200 and 350 nm with the absolute configuration of α,β-enone molecules [12]. These rules are derived from the observation that the CD and UV spectra of enones are affected by substituents located in the proximity of this chromophore altering its electronic structure as well as spatial dimension [13].

Thus, suitable model structures with several chromophores are of considerable interest for studying chiroptical properties in more detail. Our attention turned to acrylonitrile and acrylate chromophores in the chiral bicyclo[3.3.1]nonane framework that has been shown to be a proper conformationally diverse molecular structure for stereochemical studies [14,15,16]. In addition, these chromophores have received little attention over last years.

In this work the synthesis of bicyclo[3.3.1]nonane α,β-unsaturated dinitrile and the corresponding acids was accomplished. The molecular conformation of unsaturated derivatives was investigated through a combination of molecular mechanics and DFT calculations. Enantiomerically pure compounds of this framework were employed as suitable models to study chiroptical properties, *i.e.*, the effects of electronic interactions in the generation of rotational strength in the electronic transitions and conceivable chromophore interaction by CD spectroscopy and TD-DFT computations.

2. RESULTS AND DISCUSSION

Difunctional α,β-unsaturated nitrile **3** and acid **4** (Scheme 1) were prepared using the typical synthetic methodology, which involves sequential dehydration of ketone cyanohydrins using phosphorus oxychloride/pyridine or thionyl chloride, followed by acidic or alkaline hydrolysis of the resulting conjugated nitrile. Quast *et al.* [17] used this method for the synthesis of bicyclo[3.3.1]nona-2,6-diene-2,6-dicarbonitrile and 2,6-dicyanobarbaralanes from the racemic bicyclo[3.3.1]nonane-2,6-dione **1**. Herein we report on the synthesis of enantiomerically pure dinitrile **3** from (+)-(*1S,5S*)-bicyclo[3.3.1]nonane-2,6-dione (**1**) (Scheme 1).

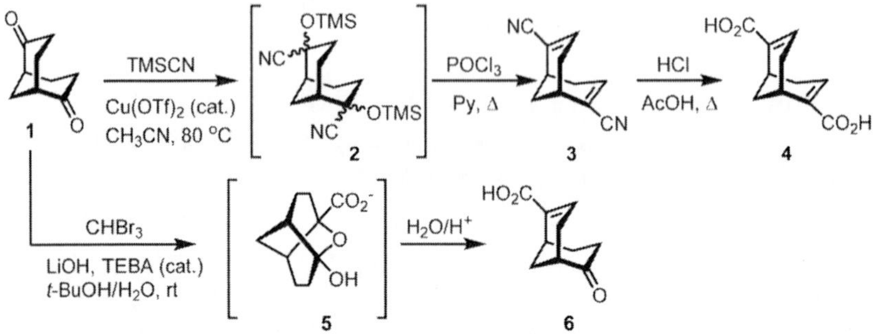

Scheme 1. Synthesis of unsaturated derivatives **3**, **4**, **6**.

We found that the $Cu(OTf)_2$ is an effective catalyst [18] for nucleophilic addition of TMSCN to diketone **1**. The cyanohydrin **2** was dehydrated using phosphorus oxychloride and pyridine and the so formed dinitrile **3** was hydrolyzed with concentrated HCl in acetic acid to yield corresponding α,β-unsaturated acid **4**. An attempt to synthesize diacid **4** via an addition of bromoform to ketone **1** under alkaline conditions [19] was also made. Interestingly, only unsaturated keto carboxylic acid **6** was isolated, whose structure was confirmed by its ^{13}C-NMR spectrum in which characteristic ketone and carboxyl group carbonyl signals were observed at 213.9 and 171.5 ppm, respectively. It is likely that the reaction takes place through tricyclic oxatwistane intermediate **5**, formation of which precludes the nucleophilic addition of the Br_3C^- nucleophile to the second carbonyl group to give difunctional derivative **4**. Subsequently, the oxatricyclic intermediate **5** was easily hydrolyzed under acidic conditions to afford **6** (Scheme 1). A compound similar to **5** was isolated and identified by Quast in the reaction of **1** with trimethyl(trifluoromethyl)silane [20].

Conformational analysis of dinitrile **3**, diacid **4** and monoacid **6** was performed with SPARTAN 10 using the Monte-Carlo method and MMFF94 force field. The minimum energy conformers found by molecular mechanics have been further optimized at the DFT/B3LYP/aug-cc-pVDZ level, followed by calculations of their harmonic vibrational frequencies to verify their stability and to calculate conformational free energies (Table 1).

Table 1. .Relative free energies, populations, symmetries, and torsion angles for low energy conformers of **4** and **6**.

Compound	Conformer [a]	ΔG, kcal/mol	Distribution,%	Angle (C=C-C=O), deg. (Symmetry)
	trans-trans	0.00	69.4	178.6 (C_2)
4	*cis-trans*	0.53	28.0	−0.3, 178.6 (C_1)
	cis-cis	1.93	2.6	−0.9 (C_2)
	trans-chair	0.00	77.7	179.5 (C_1)
6	*cis-chair*	0.78	20.4	−0.6 (C_1)
	trans-boat	2.26	1.6	−179.4 (C_1)
	cis-boat	3.14	0.3	0 (C_1)

[a] chair/boat denotes the conformation of the cyclohexanone ring.

Conformational flexibility of the unsaturated bicyclic framework is notably reduced and for difunctional compounds **3** and **4** the double half-chair conformation was found to be the most stable. In the case of **6**, a half-chair/chair conformation of the bicyclic framework was found to be the most stable and prevailed over other conformations (Table 1). However, for compounds **4** and**6** the carboxyl group could be either s-*cis* or s-*trans* with respect to the C=C–C=O bond, thus yielding three and four conformers of **4** and **6**, respectively. The conformational analysis of dinitrile **3** gave only one stable conformer. Chiroptical properties of chiral α,β-unsaturated nitrile**3** and carboxylic acids **4** and **6** were also investigated. The experimental CD and UV spectra are shown in Figure 1.

The positive CE around 290 nm in the CD spectrum of **6** is assigned to n→π* transition of the carbonyl group and the intensity is typical for this chromophore. The sign of this CE can be accurately predicted using the octant rule for the carbonyl chromophore. No CE's associated with the π→π* transitions of the α,β-unsaturated carboxylate moiety around 200–240 nm were observed in the experimental CD of **6**, suggesting negligible (canceling) external perturbation of virtually planar (non-skewed) chromophore (Table 1) by dissymetrically disposed substituents. By contrast, the interpretation of the experimental CD spectra of **3** and **4**, and the assignment of observed CE's to particular electronic transitions is

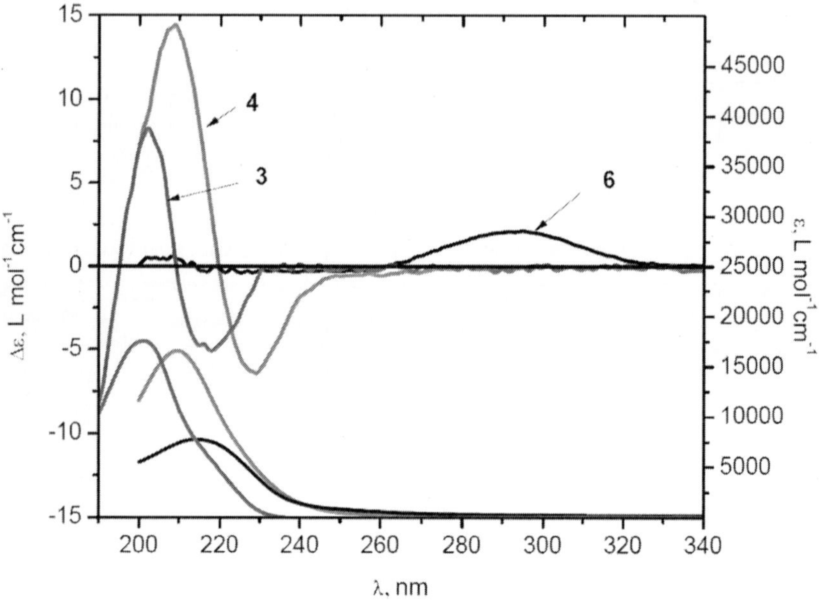

Figure 1. CD and UV spectra of dinitrile (+)-**3** (blue) in MeCN, diacid (+)-**4** (red) and ketoacid(+)-**6** (solid) in EtOH.

more complicated because the strong bisignate absorption band is not due to the exciton-type coupling [21]. The orientation of the two unsaturated chromofores in these dichromophoric molecules is close to parallel and the π→π* transition electric dipoles do not form a chiral array prerequisite for exciton coupling [22], as illustrated for the most stable *trans-trans* conformer of diacid **4** (Figure 2). In addition, the corresponding absorption band in the UV spectrum of **4** is blue-shifted in comparison with the monounsaturated congener **6**, as can be expected in the case of stacked chromophores with parallel orientation of the two relevant transition dipoles [23].

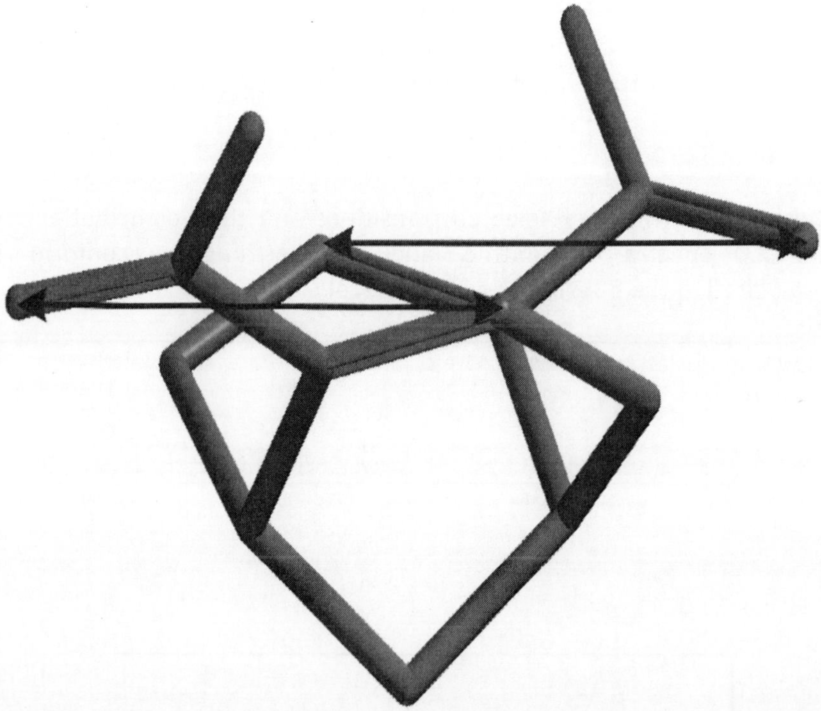

Figure 2. Orientation of the two long-axis polarized π→π* transition dipoles in **4**.

Nevertheless, the bisignate CE in the CD spectra apparently originates from the coupling between unsaturated fragments, e.g., in diacid **4**, because the signal around 200–240 nm is not observed in the case of monounsaturated derivative **6**. Linhard *et al.* assigned the CD spectra bands around 230 nm of related α-alkoxyacrylates to π→π* transition and related the sign of CE with the intrinsic chirality of the unsaturated moiety, reflected by the twist of carbonyl of carboxylate group in relation to C=C bond [24]. In the case of **3** and **4**, however, the sign of the observed CE's in the CD spectra (Figure 1) is not correlated with the twisting of the conjugated chromophores, which are essentially planar as suggested by DFT calculations (Table 1).

We calculated the CD spectra of dinitrile *(1S,5S)*-**3** and diacid *(1S,5S)*-**4** with the TD-DFT/B3LYP/aug-cc-pVDZ method and performed analysis of the molecular orbitals taking into account only intense rotatory strengths (Table 2). Thus, the negative CE band at 218 nm in

CD spectra of **3** is congruous with theoretical transition at 217 nm with −44.91 (in 10^{-40} cgs units) rotational strength (Figure 3).

Table 2. Properties of selected transitions and their contribution to the CD spectra of dinitrile **3** and diacid **4**(*trans-trans* conformer) calculated at the B3LYP/aug-cc-pVDZ level.

Comp.	λ, nm (Δε) [a]	Transition	λ, nm	f [b]	R_{vel} [c]	Contributions [d]
3	218 (−5.16)	3	217.5	0.0015	−44.91	45–47 (61%), 44–46 (34%)
	202 (8.46)	4	207.5	0.501	126.42	44–47 (48%), 45–46 (33%)
4	229 (−6.41)	5	226.2	0.0019	−50.62	54–57 (66%), 55–56 (29%),
	209 (14.4)	8	215.2	0.530	74.32	55–57 (45%), 54–56 (45%)

[a] experimental CD; [b] oscillator strength; [c] Rotatory strength in velocity form (10^{-40} cgs); [d] contributions more than 5% are selected.

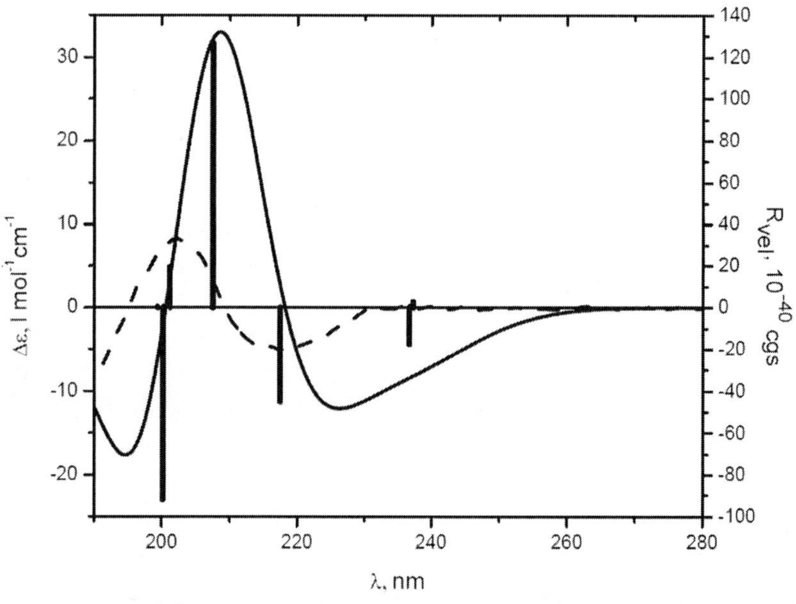

Figure 3. Comparison of the calculated (solid) and experimental (- -) CD spectra of dinitrile **3** at the B3LYP/aug-cc-pVDZ level (σ = 0.30 eV); bars represent the rotatory strength.

Accordingly, single-electron excitation at 226 nm with similar rotatory strength (-50.62×10^{-40}cgs) for prevailing *trans-trans* conformer of diacid **4** was predicted (Figure 4 and Table 2). The positive CE's in CD spectra of **3** and **4** at 202 and 209 nm could be attributed to the calculated excitations at 207 nm (126.42×10^{-40} cgs) and 215 nm (74.32×10^{-40} cgs), respectively. The predicted spectra for the minor *cis-trans* and *cis-cis* conformers of **4** were very similar to that of*trans-trans*-**4** regarding the pattern, absolute and relative intensity of the Cotton effects (Figure 4).

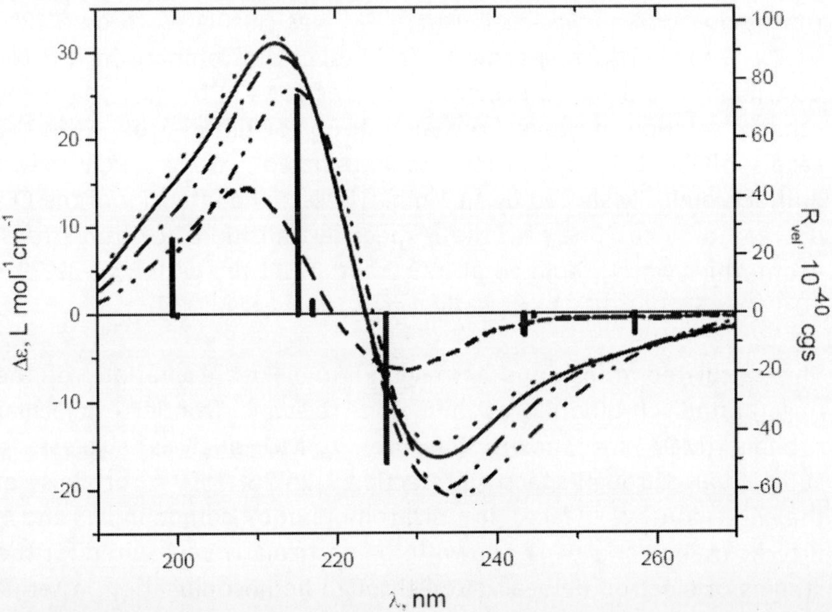

Figure 4. Comparison of experimental (- -) and theoretical spectra of diacid **4**, calculated at the B3LYP/aug-cc-pVDZ level (σ = 0.30 eV) for individual conformers (*trans-trans* (····),*cis-trans* (-·-), *cis-cis* (-···)), and Boltzmann-averaged (solid) CD spectrum; bars represent the rotatory strength for the most abundant *trans-trans* conformer.

To address the possible solvent effect on the conformational equilibrium and calculated chiroptical properties, dinitrile **3** and conformers of diacid **4** were reoptimized using the polarizable continuum model (PCM) in conjunction with B3LYP/aug-cc-pVDZ, followed by calculation of their harmonic vibrational frequencies and CD spectra at the same level of theory. Apart from a slight bathochromic shift (ca 2 nm) and notably (*ca.* 20%) increased CD intensity, the calculated CD spectra for dinitrile **3** in the gas phase and acetonitrile solution were virtually identical. In the case of **4**, the geometry of the respective conformers reoptimized using PCM were similar to those obtained in the gas phase, but the relative stability of *cis-trans-* and *cis-cis-*conformers, characterized by a substantial dipole moment, increased in ethanol solution. Population of *trans-trans-*, *cis-trans-* and *cis-cis-***4** using PCM was calculated to be 51.8%, 41.7% and 6.5%, respectively (cf. Table 1). Comparison of the Boltzmann-averaged CD spectra calculated for **4** in the gas phase and ethanol solution, however, revealed no major differences. As in the case of **3**, CD spectrum of **4** predicted using PCM was bathochromically shifted by ca 6 nm, whereas the intensity of the CEs decreased by ca 20%, e.g., the respective transitions for *trans-trans-***4**conformer were predicted at 229.0 and 221.1 nm with R_{vel} −39.79 × 10^{-40} and 57.17 × 10^{-40}, respectively (cf. Table 2).

The calculated transitions correspond to π→π* excitations of the unsaturated chromophores and the relevant frontier molecular orbitals (MO) are shown in Figure 5. MO analysis suggests a substantial through-space interaction [25,26] of π orbitals at the *endo* (concave) face in dichromophoric compounds **3** and **4**. Bicyclic frameworks were shown to be particularly well suited for the studies of electron delocalization through homoconjugation in terms of direct ("through-bond") and indirect ("through-space") interactions from localized sets of orbitals or chromophores. Such interaction of π–electron systems in norbornadienes [27], norbornenones [28], barrelenes [29], bicyclo[3.3.1]nona-dienones [30] and related frameworks [31] was evidenced by photoelectron, NMR and CD spectroscopy. In the case of **3** and **4**, two localized (isolated) chromophores are predisposed to transannular through-space interaction due to a favourable conformation of bicyclic skeleton and a rather small interchromophoric distance (ca. 3.2–3.3 Å, measured as C_2–C_6 and C_2–C_7 distance).

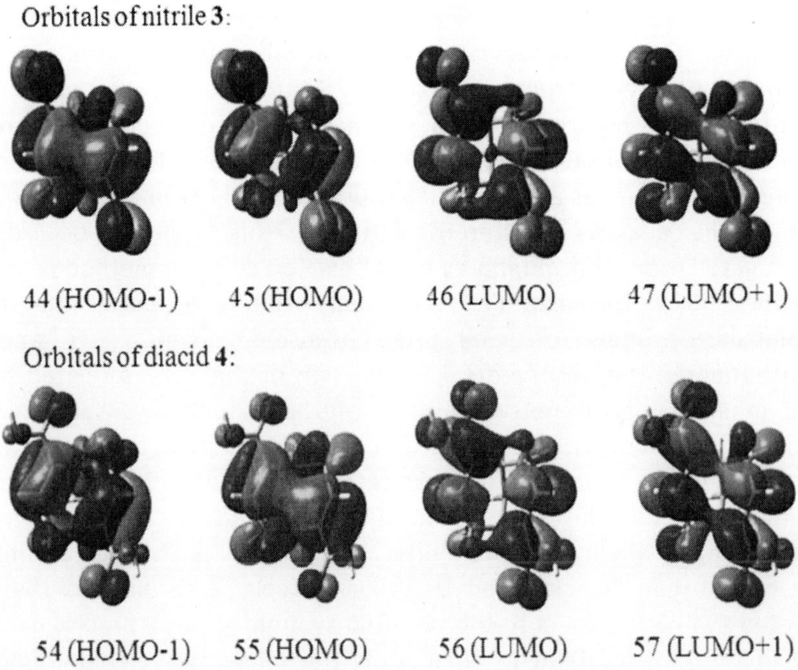

Figure 5. Molecular orbitals associated with the main transitions of dinitrile **3** and diacid **4**.

An in-phase (symmetric) linear combinations of the corresponding MO's results in π-extended (homoconjugated) molecular orbitals, *i.e.*, 44 (HOMO-1), 47 (LUMO+1) and 55 (HOMO), 57 (LUMO+1) for **3** and **4**, respectively. The negative CE in the calculated CD spectra of **3** and **4** at 218–229 nm originates from two single-electron transitions, involving excitations from "localized" to homoconjugated (MO(45)→(MO)47, MO(54)→MO(57)) and excitations from homoconjugated to "localized" (MO(44)→(MO)46, MO(55)→MO(56)) molecular orbitals (Table 2, Figure 5). The calculated positive rotational strength at 202 and 209 nm for **3** and **4**, respectively, are described as mixtures of excitations involving homoconjugated molecular orbitals, that is 44 (HOMO-1)→47 (LUMO+1) and 55 (HOMO)→57 (LUMO+1) (Table 2), and excitations form "localized" occupied MO to "localized" LUMO, *i.e.*, MO(45)→(MO)46 and MO(54)→MO(56) for **3** and **4**, respectively. HOMO and LUMO of **3** and **4** should be viewed as delocalized molecular orbitals, where a clear electronic communication between the π (and π*) orbitals of each unsaturated chromophore exists. That is to say the present system should be treated as a single conjugated electron system where the two unsaturated moieties are conjugated to each other, losing their nature as an independent unsaturated chromophore. As a result, the analysis of stereostructure of such fully delocalized conjugated monochromophores by the exciton chirality method is not justified [32]. The extended molecular orbitals resemble the π-molecular orbitals of conjugated transoid dienes [33] and, consequently, the observed/calculated sign of the CE's is related to the inherent dissymmetry (helicity) of the extended unsaturated monochromophore [34,35]. The latter is C_2-symmetric and acquires left-handed (M) helicity, roughly expressed as a C_2–C_1---C_5–C_6 dihedral angle (ca. −100 degrees), in *(1S,5S)*-**3** and *(1S,5S)*-**4**. In inherently dissymmetric (helical) C_2-symmetric chromophores the electronic excitations can be classified as A or B type, according to their orientation with respect to the two-fold symmetry axis. The bisignate CD in the case of **3**and **4**, negative at the longer wavelengths and positive at shorter wavelengths, is in accordance with a general helicity rule [36,37,38,39], which predicts a negative rotational strength for the transition of lowest energy, polarized perpendicular to the C_2 axis in a chromophore of M helicity; positive rotational strength is predicted for the higher energy transition, which is polarized parallel to the symmetry axis of the chromophore.

3. EXPERIMENTAL SECTION

3.1. General Information

Melting points were determined with a Gallenkamp melting apparatus in capillary tubes and are not corrected. IR spectra were recorded in KBr pellets on a Perkin–Elmer Spectrum BX spectrometer (Waltham, MA, USA). Proton (300 MHz) and carbon (75 MHz) nuclear magnetic resonance spectra were recorded on a Varian Inova 300 spectrometer and chemical shifts are reported in parts per million relative to solvent resonance signal as an internal standard. The CD and UV spectra were recorded with a JASCO J-815 spectrometer (Tokyo, Japan) at 20 °C in a 0.10 cm cell with scaning rate of 50 nm/min. The stock solutions were prepared by weighting compound into volumetric flask and diluting with UV-grade solvents. The CD spectra were measured in millidegrees and normalized into $\Delta\varepsilon_{max}$ [L mol^{-1} cm^{-1}]/λ[nm] units. Optical rotations were measured on a KRÜSS P3001RS automatic digital polarimeter (Hamburg, Germany) at 589 nm and $[\alpha]^{20}$ values are given in 10^{-1} deg cm^2 g^{-1}, and concentrations are given in units of g/100 cm^3. Elemental analyses were performed by the analytical laboratory of the Chemistry Faculty, Vilnius University. Thin-layer chromatography was carried out on Kieselgel 60 F254 (Merck, Darmstadt, Germany) plates coated with silica gel, and Kieselgel 60 silica gel (0.040–0.063 mm, Merck) was used for column chromatography. The synthesis of starting enantiomerically pure (+)-(*1S,5S*)-bicyclo[3.3.1]nonane-2,6-dione **1** was performed following the procedure described earlier [40].

3.2. Theoretical Calculations

Conformational search of diacid **4** and monoacid **6** was performed with SPARTAN'10 [41] using the Monte–Carlo method and MMFF94 force field. The minimum energy conformers found by molecular mechanics have been further optimized using Gaussian software [42] at DFT/B3LYP/aug-cc-pVDZ level, followed by calculations of their harmonic vibrational frequencies to verify their stability and to calculate conformational free energies; population percentages were calculated using ΔG and applying Boltzmann statistics at T = 293.15 K. The electronic circular dichroism CD calculations were performed using Gaussian software and employing TD-DFT approach with the B3LYP hybrid functional combined with the aug-cc-pVDZ basis set. Additionally, for compounds **3** and **4** the geometry of the conformers in acetonitrile (ε = 35.688) and ethanol (ε = 24.852) solution, respectively, was optimized using PCM model at B3LYP/aug-cc-pVDZ level; CD spectra were calculated at the same level of theory. The rotational strength calculations have been carried out both in velocity (R_{vel}) and length formalism (R_{len}); the results in the two formalisms were almost identical. Rotatory strengths are reported in the usual cgs units of 10^{-40} esu cm erg G^{-1}, where 1 esu cm erg G^{-1} corresponds to 3.336 × 10^{-15} C m J T^{-1}in SI units. The CD spectra of the individual conformers were simulated by overlapping Gaussian functions for each transition using SpecDis version 1.61 [43]. The half-width at 1/e of the peak maximum (σ) value of 0.30 eV and R_{vel} were used in this work. The calculated peak maxima were not wavelength corrected.

3.3. Preparation of Compounds 3–6

(+)-(*1S,5S*)-Bicyclo[3.3.1]nona-2,6-diene-2,6-dicarbonitrile (**3**). TMSCN (0.82 mL, 6.2 mmol) was added to a solution of **1** (234 mg, 1.54 mmol) and $Cu(OTf)_2$ (56 mg, 0.15 mmol) in abs. CH_3CN (5 mL) under an argon atmosphere. The reaction mixture was stirred at 80 °C temperature for 3 days in a closed vessel. The solvent was then evaporated, the residue was diluted with DCM and washed with dist. H_2O, brine and dried over Na_2SO_4. The solution was evaporated to dryness to yield crude **2** (480 mg, 89%) as an yellow oil, which was used without further purification. $POCl_3$(0.76 mL, 8.2 mmol) and pyridine (1.1 mL, 14 mmol) were added to **2** (480 mg, 1.4 mmol) under an argon atmosphere. The reaction mixture was refluxed for 4 h, then cooled to room temperature and quenched with ice. The resulting mixture was filtered through a pad of Celite, and the pad was washed with DCM. After separation of the layers, the aqueous phase was extracted with DCM (3 × 20 mL). The organic layers were combined, washed with 0.1 M HCl, sat. $NaHCO_3$ and dried over Na_2SO_4. The residue was purified by column chromatography (eluent ethyl acetate/petroleum ether, 1:3) to yield **3** (186 mg, 71%) as colorless crystals; mp 147–149 °C (racemate mp 189–190 °C [17]); $[\alpha]_D$ = +15.5 (*c* 0.71, $CHCl_3$); UV, λ_{max} (logε): 201 (4.24); IR (KBr) ν_{max}/cm^{-1} 2919, 2208, 1628, 1433; ^{1}H-NMR ($CDCl_3$, ppm) *δ* 6.62 (dd, *J* = 5.0, 2.5 Hz, 2H), 2.84–2.67 (m, 2H), 2.55–2.26 (m, 4H), 1.80 (t, *J* = 3.2 Hz, 2H); ^{13}C-NMR ($CDCl_3$, ppm) *δ* 142.6, 118.6, 116.2, 31.0, 29.0, 26.6; Anal. Calcd for $C_{11}H_{10}N_2$: C 77.62; H 5.92; N 16.46. Found: C 77.69; H 5.94; N 16.15.

(+)-(*1S,5S*)-Bicyclo[3.3.1]nona-2,6-diene-2,6-dicarboxylic acid (**4**). A solution of **3** (150 mg, 0.88 mmol) in a mixture of conc. HCl (4 mL) and acetic acid (3 mL) was refluxed for 6 h. The reaction mixture was then cooled to room temperature and kept in a refrigerator at −15 °C temperature for 2 days. The crystals were filtered and washed with Et_2O to give colorless solid, which was dried under vacuum; yield 140 mg (76%); (+)-**4** (and *rac*-**4)** mp > 220 °C (dec.); $[\alpha]_D$ = +28 (*c* 0.25, $CHCl_3$); UV, λ_{max} (logε): 209 (4.22); IR (KBr) ν_{max}/cm^{-1} 3074, 2931, 1677, 1636, 1417, 1254, 1243; ^{1}H-NMR (CD_3OD, ppm) *δ* 6.98 (dd, *J* =

5.0, 2.3 Hz, 2H), 2.97 (s, 2H), 2.54–2.43 (m, 2H), 2.24 (dd, *J* = 19.7, 5.0 Hz, 2H), 1.74 (t, *J* = 3.0 Hz, 2H); ^{13}C-NMR (CD_3OD, ppm) *δ* 170.1, 139.8, 134.8, 33.4, 29.2, 27.8; Anal. Calcd for $C_{11}H_{12}O_4$: C 63.45; H 5.81. Found: C 63.64; H 5.91.

(+)-(*1S,5S*)-6-Oxobicyclo[3.3.1]non-2-ene-2-carboxylic acid (**6**). Diketone **1** (170 mg, 1.12 mmol) and TEBA (51 mg, 0.22 mmol) in *t*-BuOH (5 mL) were added to a solution of $LiOH{\cdot}H_2O$ (1.88 g, 44.8 mmol) in H_2O (5 mL) and $CHBr_3$ (0.98 mL, 11 mmol). The reaction mixture was stirred at room temperature for 48 h under an argon atmosphere, then washed with toluene. The aqueous phase was acidified with 0.1 M HCl, stirred for 1 h and then extracted with DCM (3 × 10 mL). The organic phase was dried over Na_2SO_4 and evaporated. The residue was purified by column chromatography (eluent ethyl acetate / petroleum ether 1:2) to yield **6** (120 mg, 60%) as colorless crystals; mp 95–97 °C; $[\alpha]_D$= +166 (*c* 0.307, $CHCl_3$); UV, λ_{max} (logε): 214 (3.89); IR (KBr) ν_{max}/cm^{-1}2939, 1704, 1678, 1636, 1420, 1222; ^{1}H-NMR ($CDCl_3$, ppm) *δ* 10.4 (bs, 1H), 7.26 (dd, *J* = 4.2, 2.7 Hz, 1H), 3.02 (s, 1H), 2.74 (s, 1H), 2.62 (ddd, *J* = 21, 6.9, 2.7 Hz, 1H), 2.42–1.79 (m, 7H); ^{13}C-NMR ($CDCl_3$, ppm) *δ* 213.9, 171.5, 141.4, 132.5, 43.5, 35.8, 31.1, 30.8, 29.9, 27.6; Anal. Calcd for $C_{10}H_{12}O_3$: C 66.65; H 6.71. Found: C 66.46; H 6.54.

4. CONCLUSIONS

In conclusion, the synthesis of enantiomerically pure bicyclic dinitrile **3** and acids **4, 6** from (+)-(*1S,5S*)-bicyclo[3.3.1]nonane-2,6-dione (**1**) was accomplished and the chiroptical properties of the obtained α,β-unsaturated compounds were studied. The bisignate CE in the CD spectra of difunctional derivatives **3** and **4**, associated with the π→π* transitions apparently originates from the non-exciton-type coupling between the two unsaturated fragments. TD-DFT calculations suggest a substantial through-space interaction (homoconjugation) of π orbitals in **3** and **4**. As a result, the studied molecular structures should be treated as specific delocalized electron systems, where the two unsaturated moieties are conjugated to each other, losing their nature as an independent unsaturated chromophore. The analysis of stereostructure of such fully delocalized conjugated C_2-symmetric monochromophores, which acquire left-handed (M) helicity in *(1S,5S)*-**3**and *(1S,5S)*-**4**, by the exciton chirality method is therefore not justified. The sign of the CE's in the CD spectra of **3** and **4**, negative at the longer wavelengths and positive at shorter wavelengths, is decided by inherent dissymmetry (helicity) of the extended monochromophores and is in accordance with a general helicity rule.

ACKNOWLEDGMENTS

GB and SS acknowledge the support by the European Social Fund under the Global Grant measure (VP1-3.1-ŠMM-07-K-01-030). We are grateful to Dr. V. Šikšnys, Institute of Biotechnology, Vilnius University, for providing access to the CD spectrometer.

AUTHOR CONTRIBUTIONS

Authors contributed to the present work as described in the following: E.B. and S.S. suggested the idea of the work and analysed the data. S.S. and G.B. performed experimental work and calculations. All authors contributed to and approved the final manuscript.

CONFLICTS OF INTEREST

The authors declare no conflict of interest.

REFERENCES

1. Finch, N.; Taylor, W.I.; Emerson, T.R.; Klyne, W.; Swan, R.J. Optical rotatory dispersion curves of heteroyohimbine alkaloids. Tetrahedron 1966, 22, 1327–1333.

2. Campbell, M.M.; Sainsbury, M.; Searle, P.A. The biosynthesis and synthesis of shikimic acid, chorismic acid, and related compounds. Synthesis 1993, 179–193.

3. Pawlak, J.L.; Berchtold, G.A. Synthesis of disodium 3-[(1-carboxylatoethenyl)oxy]cyclohepta-1,6-diene-1-carboxylate: A seven-membered ring analog of chorismate. J. Org. Chem. 1988, 53, 4063–4069.

4. Zhang, Y.; Liu, A.; Ye, Z.G.; Lin, J.; Xu, L.Z.; Yang, S.L. New approach to the total synthesis of (−)-zeylenone from shikimic acid. Chem. Pharm. Bull. 2006, 54, 1459–1461.

5. Jiang, S.; Singh, G. Chemical synthesis of shikimic acid and its analogues. Tetrahedron 1998,54, 4697–4753.

6. Eliel, E.L.; Wilen, S.H. Stereochemistry of Organic Compounds; Wiley: New York, NY, USA, 1994; pp. 991–1118.

7. Karabencheva-Christova, T.G.; Carlsson, U.; Balali-Mood, K.; Black, G.W.; Christov, C.Z. Conformational Effects on the Circular Dichroism of Human Carbonic Anhydrase II: A Multilevel Computational Study. PLoS One 2013, 8, e56874.

8. Kurtán, T.; Jia, R.; Li, Y.; Pescitelli, G.; Guo, Y.W. Absolute configuration of highly flexible natural products by the solid-state ECD/TDDFT method: Ximaolides and sinulaparvalides.Eur. J. Org. Chem. 2012, 6722–6728.

9. Circular Dichroism: Principles and Applications, 2nd ed.; Berova, N., Nakanishi, K., Woody, R.W., Eds.; John Wiley and Sons: New York, NY, USA, 2000.

10. Berova, N.; di Bari, L.; Pescitelli, G. Application of electronic circular dichroism in configurational and conformational analysis of organic compounds. Chem. Soc. Rev. 2007,36, 914–931.

11. Orentas, E.; Bagdžiūnas, G.; Berg, U.; Žilinskas, A.; Butkus, E. Enantiospecific synthesis and chiroptical properties of bicyclic enones. Eur. J. Org. Chem. 2007, 25, 4251–4256.

12. Gawronski, J.K. Conformations, Chiroptical and Related Spectral Properties of Enones. InThe Chemistry of Enones; Patai, S., Rappoport, Z., Eds.; John Wiley and Sons: New York, NY, USA, 1989; pp. 55–105.

13. Frelek, J.; Szczepek, W.J.; Weiss, H.P.; Reiss, G.J.; Frank, W.; Brechtel, J.; Schultheis, B.; Kuball, H.G. Chiroptical properties of the cisoid enone chromophore. J. Am. Chem. Soc.1998, 120, 7010–7019.

14. Stephens, P.J.; McCann, D.M.; Butkus, E.; Stončius, S.; Cheeseman, J.R.; Frisch, M.J. Determination of absolute configuration using concerted ab initio DFT calculations of electronic circular dichroism and optical rotation: Bicyclo[3.3.1]nonane diones. J. Org. Chem. 2004, 69, 1948–1958.

15. Berg, U.; Butkus, E. An analysis of the circular dichroism spectra of bicyclo[3.3.1]nonane diones. J. Chem. Res.(S) 1994, 356–357.

16. Stončius, S.; Berg, U.; Butkus, E. Chiral bicyclic keto lactones: Determination of the absolute configuration by the study of chiroptical properties and chemical correlation. Tetrahedron Asymmetry 2004, 15, 2405–2413.

17. Quast, H.; Görlach, Y.; Stawitz, J.; Peters, E.-M.; Peters, K.; Schnering, H.G.V. Synthese und struktur von 2,6-dicyanbicyclo[3.3.1]nona-2,6-dienen und 2,6-dicyanbarbaralanen. Chem. Berichte 1984, 117, 2745–2760.

18. Saravanan, P.; Anand, R.V.; Singh, V.K. Cu(OTf)2 catalyzed trimethylsilyl cyanide addition to carbonyl compounds. Tetrahedron Lett. 1998, 39, 3823–3824.

19. Vitnik, V.D.; Ivanović, M.D.; Vitnik, Ž.J; Đorđević, J.B; Žižak, Ž.D; Juranić, I.O. One-step conversion of ketones to conjugated acids using bromoform. Synth.Commun. 2009, 39, 1457–1471.

20. Quast, H.; Becker, C.; Witzel, M.; Peters, E.-M.; Peters, K.; von Schnering, H.G. Syntheses and structures of 2,6-substituted barbaralanes. Liebigs Ann. Chem. 1996, 985–997.

21. Kasha, M.; Rawls, H.R.; El-Bayoumi, M.A. The exciton model in molecular spectroscopy.Pure Appl. Chem. 1965, 11, 371–392.

22. Person, R.V.; Monde, K.; Humpf, H.-U.; Berova, N.; Nakanishi, K. A new approach in exciton-coupled circular dichroism (ECCD)-insertion of an auxiliary stereogenic center.Chirality 1995, 7, 128–135.

23. Boiadjiev, S.E.; Lightner, D.A. Exciton chirality. (A) Origins of and (B) applications from strongly fluorescent dipyrrinone chromophores. Monatsch. Chem. 2005, 136, 489–508.

24. Vlahov, I.R.; Bazin, H.G.; Linhardt, R.J. Circular dichroism and absolute conformation of Δ4-uronate derivatives: A semi-empirical rule for inherent chiral α-alkoxy acrylates. Chem. Commun. 1998, 1819–1820.

25. Hoffmann, R. Interaction of orbitals through space and through bonds. Acc. Chem. Res.1971, 4, 1–9.

26. Hoffmann, R.; Heilbronner, E.; Gleiter, R. Interaction of nonconjugated double bonds. J. Am. Chem. Soc. 1970, 92, 706–707.

27. Lightner, D.A.; Gawronski, J.K.; Bouman, T.D. Electronic structure of symmetric homoconjugated dienes. Circular dichroism of (1S)-2-deuterio- and 2-methylnorbornadiene and (1S)-2-deuterio- and 2-

methylbicyclo[2.2.2]octadiene. J. Am. Chem. Soc. 1980, 102, 5749–5754.

28. Lightner, D.A.; Gawronski, J.K.; Hansen, A.E.; Bouman, T.D. Charge-transfer band of 7-norbornenone. Circular dichroism of (1R)-2-deuteriobicyclo[2.2.1]hept-2-en-7-one and (1R)-2-methylbicyclo[2.2.1]hept-2-en-7-one. J. Am. Chem. Soc. 1981, 103, 4291–4296.

29. Lightner, D.A.; Paquette, L.A.; Chayangkoon, P.; Lin, H.S.; Peterson, J.R. Synthesis and chiroptical properties of (1S)-[2,5-2H2]bicyclo[2.2.2]octa-2,5,7-triene (2,5-dideuteriobarrelene). J. Org. Chem. 1988, 53, 1969–1973.

30. Doerner, T.; Gleiter, R.; Robbins, T.A.; Chayangkoon, P.; Lightner, D.A. Homoconjugation and transannular orbital interactions detected by photoelectron and carbon-13 NMR spectroscopy. Bicyclo[3.3.1]nona-3,7-diene-2,6-dione and bicyclo[3.3.1]nonane-2,6-dione. J. Am. Chem. Soc. 1992, 114, 3235–3241.

31. Robbins, T.A.; Toan, V.V.; Givens, J.W., III; Lightner, D.A. Transannular orbital interaction between ketone and olefin chromophores detected by circular dichroism and carbon-13 NMR spectroscopy. Dimethanonaphthalenones and trimethanoanthracenones. J. Am. Chem. Soc. 1992, 114, 10799–10810.

32. Di Bari, L.; Guillarme, S.; Hermitage, S.; Jay, D.A.; Pescitelli, G.; Whiting, A. Absolute stereochemistry assignment of N-phosphorylimine-derived aza-Diels-Alder adducts with TDDFT CD calculations. Chirality 2005, 17, 323–331.

33. Salvadori, P.; Rosini, C.; di Bari, L. Conformation and Chiroptical Properties of Dienes and Polyenes. In The Chemistry of Dienes and Polyenes; Rappoport, Z., Ed.; John Wiley and Sons: New York, NY, USA, 1997; Volume 1, pp. 111–147.

34. Charney, E.; Ziffer, H.; Weiss, U. Optical activity of non-planar conjugated dienes-II transoid dienes. Tetrahedron 1965, 21, 3121–3126.

35. Rauk, A.; Peoples, H.A. The electronic structure and optical activity of conjugated dienes: 1,3-butadiene and α- and β-phellandrene. J. Comp. Chem. 1980, 1, 240–256.

36. Wagniere, G.; Hug, W. Polarization and the sign of the long-wavelength Cotton-effects in chromophores of symmetry C2. Tetrahedron Lett. 1970, 11, 4765–4768.

37. Hug, W.; Wagniere, G. The optical activity of chromophores of symmetry C2. Tetrahedron1972, 28, 1241–1248.

38. Buss, V.; Kolster, K. Electronic structure calculations on helicenes. Concerning the chirality of helically twisted aromatic systems. Chem. Phys. 1996, 203, 309–316.

39. Harada, N.; Uda, H.; Nozoe, T.; Okamoto, Y.; Wakabayashi, H.; Ishikawa, S. Absolute stereostructure of novel chiral troponoid spiro compounds as determined by theoretical calculation of CD spectra. J. Am. Chem. Soc. 1987, 109, 1661–1665.

40. Wallentin, C.J.; Orentas, E.; Butkus, E.; Warnmark, K. Baker's yeast for sweet dough enables large-scale synthesis of enantiomerically pure bicyclo[3.3.1]nonane-2,6-dione. Synthesis2009, 864–867.

41. SPARTAN'10 for Windows, Version 1.0.1.. Wavefunction, Inc. 1840 Von Karman Avenue, Suite 370, Irvine, CA, USA, 2010.

42. Frisch, M.J.; Trucks, G.W.; Schlegel, H.B.; Scuseria, G.E.; Robb, M.A.; Cheeseman, J.R.; Scalmani, G.; Barone, V.; Mennucci, B.; Petersson, G.A.; et al. Gaussian 09,

Revision A.02, Gaussian, Inc. Wallingford, CT, USA, 2009.

43. Bruhn, T.; Schaumlöffel, A.; Hemberger, Y.; Bringmann, G. SpecDis: Quantifying the comparison of calculated and experimental electronic circular dichroism spectra. Chirality2013, 25, 243–249.

Chapter 4

Synthesis and Properties of Poly(Isothianaphthene Methine)s with Chiral Alkyl Chain

Yu Innami [1], Hirotsugu Kawashima [1], Rafaël H. L. Kiebooms [2], Hideaki Aizawa [1], Kiyoto Matsuishi [1] and Hiromasa Goto [1,*]

[1]*Institute of Materials Science, Graduate School of Pure and Applied Sciences, University of Tsukuba, Tsukuba, Ibaraki 305-8573, Japan*

[2]*European Patent Office, Patentlaan 3-9, 2288 EE The Hague, The Netherlands*

Abstract

We synthesized poly(isothianaphthene methine)s with chiral alkyl chains in the substituent. Resultant polymers are soluble in THF and $CHCl_3$. Structure of the polymers was characterized with FT-IR, FT-Raman, and UV-Vis-NIR optical absorption spectroscopy. They showed low-bandgap both in solution and in a form of film. Optical activity of the polymers was confirmed with optical rotatory dispersion. Doping effects on the polymer were also examined with UV-Vis-NIR spectroscopy and ESR measurement.

Keywords: π-conjugated polymer; low-bandgap polymer; isothianaphthene; chiroptical activity

1. INTRODUCTION

In the search for new materials for plastic electronics, π-conjugated oligomers and polymers have received much recent interest. These materials are used in applications such as transistors [1,2,3], photovoltaic cells [4,5], molecular wires [6], electrochromic devices [7,8,9], and fluorescence sensors or imaging [10,11,12]. Chiral π-conjugated polymers show optical absorption and chiroptical activity in visible range [13]. Although natural materials such as cellulose and proteins show intense chiroptical activity in UV region (short wavelengths), they show no absorptions at the visible range. On the other hand, π-conjugated polymers have chromophore and show optical functionality in the visible region. The function of optical rotation in visible-near-infrared region can be useful as an optical isolator for optical fibers.

Furthermore, chiral π-conjugated polymers can show a helical structure. Helical structure is generally observed in natural polymers, such as DNA and starch. Synthesis of chiral π-conjugated polymers may lead to mimetic technology of natural polymers.

π-Conjugated polymers have been also studied as emission materials for application of 3D displays and backlights of liquid crystal displays [14]. Low-bandgap π-conjugated polymers have optical absorption at near-infrared region, and show good response to external stimulus [15,16,17]. A structure of poly(arylene methine)s is a candidate for low-bandgap polymers [18,19].

Isothianaphthene (benzo[*c*]thiophene) has attractive electric and optical properties [20,21,22,23]. Isothianaphthene is also well known as a monomer for low-bandgap polymers [24,25]. Polyisothianaphthene derivatives having functional groups such as long alkyl chains, liquid crystalline groups, and radicals were studied [26,27,28]. The isothianaphthene polymers could be materials for electrical and optical devices [29,30]. Combinations of polyisothianaphthene and poly(arylene methine) structures can afford improved characteristics. Additionally, introduction of chiral alkyl side chains for poly(arylene methine) can improve solubility, and provide a function of optical rotation at long wavelengths. Chiral π-stacking can be expected in the form of cast films. In this study, we report synthesis of poly(isothianaphthene methine)s with novel chiral alkyl chains and their optical, chiroptical, as well as doping effects.

2. EXPERIMENTAL SECTION

2.1. Technique

Chemicals were purchased from Tokyo Chemical Industry and Wako Pure Chemical Industries. 1,4-Dioxane was used after distillation and the other reagents were used as received. NMR spectra were obtained by using a JEOL JNM-ECS 400 spectrometer. The NMR were measured in chloroform-d ($CDCl_3$) and listed in ppm from TMS as the internal standard. Specific optical rotation of chiral compounds was measured in THF with a JASCO P-1010 polarimeter. Fourier transform infrared spectra (FT-IR) of the polymers were taken with a JASCO FTIR 300 spectrometer by the KBr method. Fourier transform Raman (FT-Raman) spectra were obtained by using a Nicolet NXR FT-Raman spectrometer with 1,064 nm excitation wavelength. Ultraviolet-visible-near-infrared (UV-Vis-NIR) absorption spectroscopy measurements were carried out at room temperature by using a JASCO V-630 UV-Vis optical absorption spectrometer and a SHIMADZU UV-3100PC spectrometer with a quartz cell. Optical rotation dispersion (ORD) measurements were performed using a JASCO J-720 spectrometer with an ORDE-307W ORD unit. Molecular weights of the polymers were determined by gel permeation chromatography (GPC) using a JASCO HPLC 870-UV detector with THF as the solvent, with the instrument calibrated with polystyrene standards. ESR measurement of the solid polymer sample packed into a 5 mm quartz tube was carried out with a JEOL JES TE-200 spectrometer.

2.2. Monomer Synthesis

Isothianaphthene monomer, 1,3-bis(*tert*-butyldimethylsilyl)isothianaphthene (abbreviated as ITN-2TBSi) was synthesized in three steps, according to the previously reported method by Okuda *et al.* [31]. Benzaldehyde monomers with chiral side chains were synthesized by the Mitsunobu reaction, as shown in Scheme 1. The monomer ((−)-mono and (+)-mono2) having chiral alkyl group can be obtained in one step.

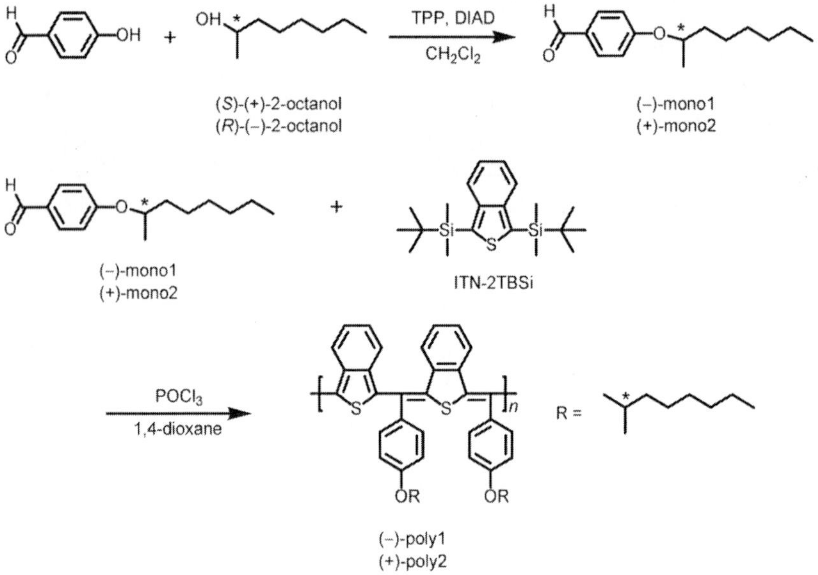

Scheme 1. Synthetic routes to poly(isothianaphthene methine)s with chiral side chains. DIAD = diisopropyl azodicarboxylate.

Reaction of a chiral alcohol with *p*-hydroxybenzaldehyde has been previously reported [32]. Triphenylphosphine (TPP) (2.79 g, 10.65 mmol) was added to a solution of *p*-hydroxybenzaldehyde (1.00 g, 8.18 mmol) and (*S*)-(+)-2-octanol (1.17 g, 9.02 mmol) in dichloromethane (16.00 mL). The mixture was cooled to 0 °C, then diisopropyl azodicarboxylate (DIAD) (40% in toluene, 5.17 mL, 9.82 mmol) was added dropwise. The reaction solution was stirred overnight at room temperature. The resultant mixture was subsequently extracted with dichloromethane, brine and water. The organic layer was dried over magnesium sulfate and filtered. The crude product was purified with column chromatography (silica gel, dichloromethane). Vacuum drying affords (−)-mono1 (Y = 50.7%). The (+)-mono2 was also obtained under the same conditions as synthesis of (−)-mono1 using (*R*)-(−)-2-octanol (Y = 48.7%).

(−)-Mono1: ^{1}H NMR (400 MHz, $CDCl_3$, δ from TMS): δ 9.85 (s, 1H), 7.80 (d, 2H, J = 8.8 Hz), 6.96 (d, 2H, J = 8.8 Hz), 4.47 (q, 1H, J = 6.0 Hz), 1.77–1.28 (m, 15H), 0.88 (t, 3H, J = 6.4 Hz). ^{13}C NMR (100 MHz, $CDCl_3$): δ 190.5, 163.4, 131.9, 129.4, 115.5, 74.2, 36.2, 31.7, 29.1, 25.3, 22.5, 19.5, 14.0. $[\alpha]^{20}_D$ = −1.39 deg·cm^2·g^{-1} (THF).

(+)-Mono2: ^{1}H NMR (400 MHz, $CDCl_3$, δ from TMS): δ 9.86 (s, 1H), 7.81 (d, 2H, J = 8.8 Hz), 6.96 (d, 2H, J = 8.4 Hz), 4.48 (q, 1H, J = 5.6 Hz), 1.76–1.28 (m, 15H), 0.88 (t, 3H, J = 6.8 Hz). ^{13}C NMR (100 MHz, $CDCl_3$): δ 190.7, 163.5, 132.0, 129.5, 115.5, 74.3, 36.3, 31.7, 29.2, 25.4, 22.6, 19.6, 14.1. $[\alpha]^{20}_D$ = +1.31 deg·cm^2·g^{-1} (THF).

2.3. Polymer Synthesis

Poly(isothianaphthene methine)s were synthesized with polycondensation between the ITN monomer (ITN-2TBSi) and the benzaldehyde monomer ((−)-mono1 or (+)-mono2) under oxidative conditions. ITN having no protection group at the β-position can be polymerized under oxidative conditions solely. Therefore, *tert*-butyldimethylsilyl groups were introduced onto β-position of the ITN monomer for preventing from polymerization of the ITN solely in the appropriate condition.

A solution of ITN monomer (0.11 g, 0.30 mmol) and (−)-mono1 or (+)-mono2 (0.07 g, 0.30 mmol) in 1,4-dioxane (2.40 mL) was refluxed at 85 °C in the presence of phosphoryl chloride (0.60 mL) for 24 h. Then, the solution was poured into 100 mL of methanol and the precipitate was collected to obtain a dark indigotic blue solid followed by vacuum drying ((−)-poly1; Y = 23.8%, (+)-poly2; Y = 30.5%). The polymers were subsequently neutralized with an excess amount of triethylamine. The polymer (as prepared) was treated with excess amount of triethylamine for obtaining neutral (dedoping) state of the polymer followed by vacuum drying to remove residual triethylamine in the polymer.

The polymerization results are summarized in Table 1. The (−)-poly1 and (+)-poly2 were obtained in the yield of 23.8% and 30.5%, respectively. The yields is comparable to synthetic yield of poly(isothianaphthene methine) having hexyloxy side chains [33]. The number-average molecular weights (M_n) of both (−)-poly1 and (+)-poly2 were estimated to be 2650, the weight-average molecular weights (M_w) were 3030 and 3130, respectively, evaluated by GPC against a polystyrene standard. These molecular weights were slightly higher than that of poly(isothianaphthene methine)s bearing di-*tert*-butylphenol substituents [28].

Table 1. Polymerization and optical absorption spectra results.\

Polymer	M_n [a]	M_w [a]	M_w/M_n	λ_{max}(solution) (nm)	λ_{max}(film) (nm)	E_g [b] (eV)
(−)-poly1	2650	3030	1.1	602	614	1.26
(+)-poly2	2650	3130	1.2	601	612	1.26

[a] Polystyrene standard, THF as solvent; [b] Estimated from onsets of optical absorption spectra in solution.

3. RESULT AND DISCUSSION

3.1. FT-IR and FT-Raman Spectroscopy

The FT-IR absorption spectra of (−)-poly1 and (+)-poly2 are shown in Figure 1. Intense absorption bands corresponding to C–O–C as an ether stretching were observed at 1,245 cm^{-1} for (−)-poly1 and 1,244 cm^{-1} for (+)-poly2, respectively. The polymers show absorption bands at 1,602 cm^{-1} due to C=C vibrations of a quinonoid isothianaphthene unit [34].

Figure 2 shows FT-Raman spectra of (−)-poly1 and (+)-poly2. The Raman bands of (−)-poly1 were mainly observed at 1,465, 1,303, 991 and 449 cm^{-1}. According to the FT-Raman spectroscopic studies for poly(isothianaphthene methine)s in the previous study, these Raman bands were associated with vibrations of benzenoid and quinonoid isothianaphthene units [28,34]. (+)-Poly2 also shows Raman bands at 1,460, 1,303, 989 and 447 cm^{-1}. The results of FT-IR and FT-Raman spectroscopy indicated that (−)-poly1 and (+)-poly2 constructed poly(isothianaphthene methine) units.

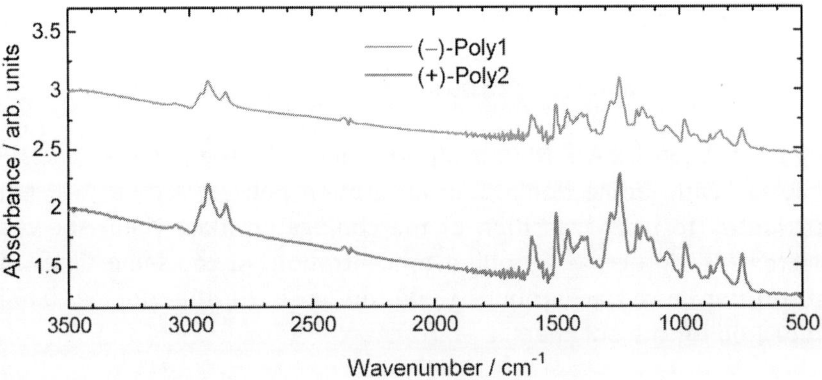

Figure 1. FT-IR spectra of (–)-poly1 and (+)-poly2.

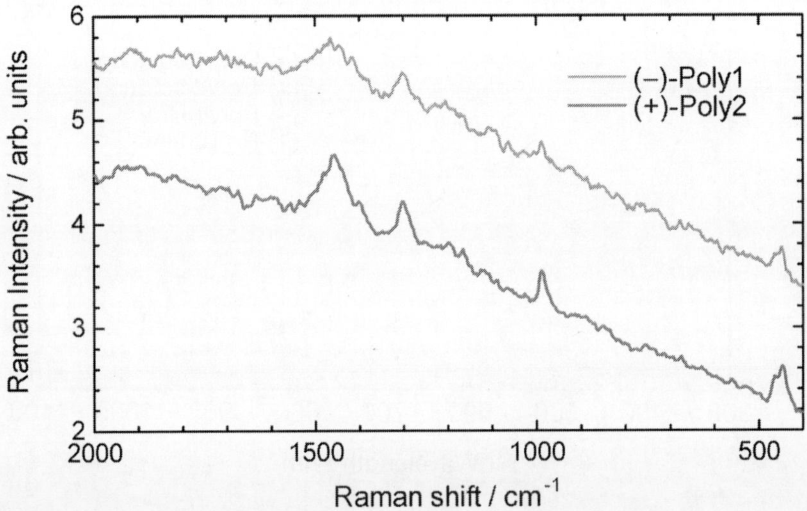

Figure 2. FT-Raman spectra of (–)-poly1 and (+)-poly2.

3.2. UV-Vis-NIR Absorption Spectroscopy

Figure 3 shows UV-vis-NIR absorption spectra of (–)-poly1 and (+)-poly2 in THF solution, and in the form of cast films. The polymers showed an absorption maximum (λ_{max}) at around 600 nm in solution state. In comparison with the polymers in solution state, λ_{max} of the polymer cast films on a quartz glass showed red shifts by 12 nm for (–)-poly1 and 11 nm for (+)-poly2. From the band-edge of the spectra of both polymers in THF solution, the bandgap (E_g) can be estimated to be 1.26 eV. λ_{max} and E_g of the polymers are listed in Table 1.

Figure 4 shows UV-Vis-NIR absorption spectra of the polymers in THF solution with iodine doping. An absorption peak at around 600 nm attributed to π-π* transition of the conjugated main chain showed decrease with increasing iodine concentration. At the same time, an absorption peak at around 1,000 nm due to the doping band appeared for the polymers.

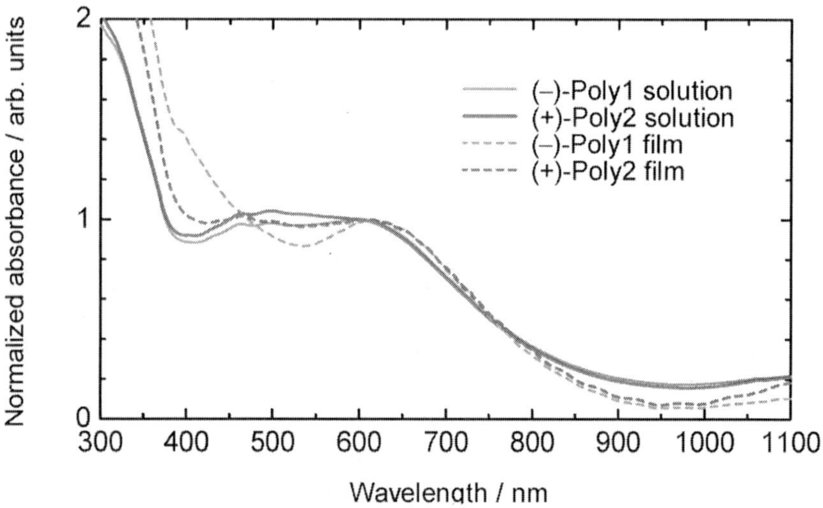

Figure 3. UV-Vis-NIR absorption spectra of (–)-poly1 and (+)-poly2 in solution (0.03 mM in THF) (solid line) and cast films (dashed line).

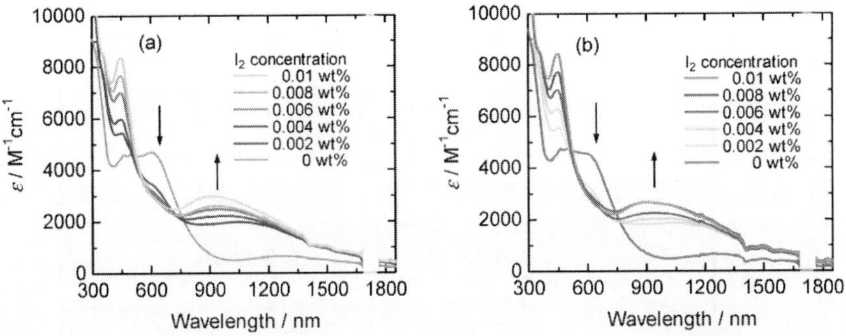

Figure 4. UV-Vis-NIR absorption spectra of (−)-poly1 (**a**) and (+)-poly2 (**b**) in THF solution with iodine doping.

3.3. ORD Spectroscopy

Figure 5 shows ORD spectra of (−)-poly1 and (+)-poly2. Optical rotations at visible range were observed in the ORD spectra of the polymers. (−)-Poly1 polymerized from (−)-mono1 showed a negative optical rotation around 560 nm, and (−)-mono1 also showed a negative optical rotation at 589 nm. (+)-Poly2 gave the same sign of optical rotation as the monomer. These results indicate that the optical rotations at around 560 nm of the polymers are derived from the chiral side chains, suggesting that the sign of optical rotation of the polymers depends on chirality of the side chains.

In the previous research, other types of poly(isothianaphthene methine)s with chiral side chains were reported [26]. However, in this case, poly(isothianaphthene methine)s with a chiral side chain showed no chiroptical activity in visible range. Moreover, poly(isothianaphthene methine)s bearing ferroelectric liquid crystalline groups with chiral center in the terminal displayed no chiroptical activity in the visible range. This is due to the fact that the asymmetric center of the polymers in the side chain has distance from the main chains. In the present study, the asymmetric centers of (−)-poly1 and (+)-poly2 are directly connected to ether oxygen in the substituent, resulting the polymers show chiroptical activity in the visible range.

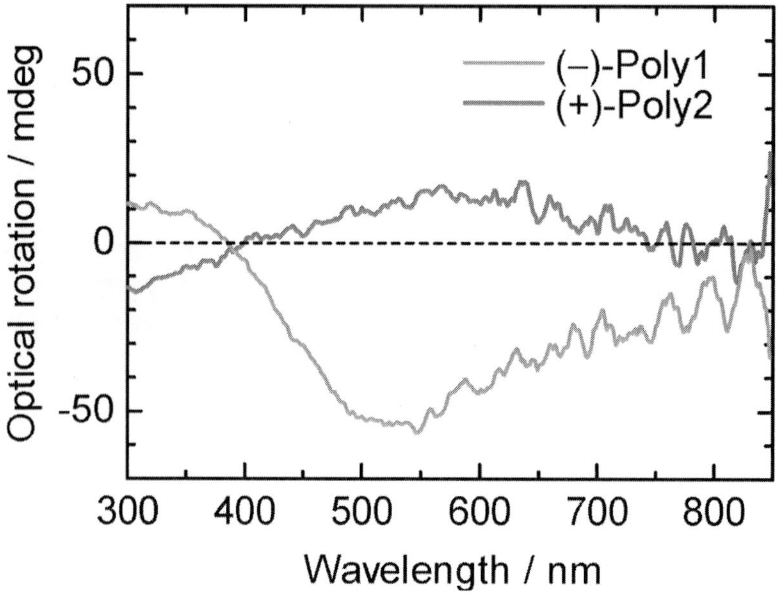

Figure 5. ORD spectra of (–)-poly1 and (+)-poly2 in cast films.

3.4. ESR Measurements

ESR measurements were carried out on a polymer bulk sample with vapor phase iodine doping. Figure 6 shows ESR spectra of (–)-poly1 with in-situ doping for 0–50 min. The ESR signal indicates that radical cations were generated along the polymer main chain. The generation of radical cations can enhance electrical conductivity of the polymer [25]. *g*-Value, intensity, and peak-width plots *vs.* the doping time of (–)-poly1 are shown in Figure 6b,c.

The signal intensity gradually increased with the doping time, indicating increase of spin concentration with doping time. However, *g*-value and peak width also increased with doping. Neugebauer *et al.* [34] reported occurrence of strong charge carrier localization with doping confirmed with IR spectroscopic and electrochemical analysis for PITN-methine. The increase of the peak width in the ESR measurements indicates that charge carriers (polarons (radical cations) and bipolarons (dications)) generated by the iodine doping may be localized.

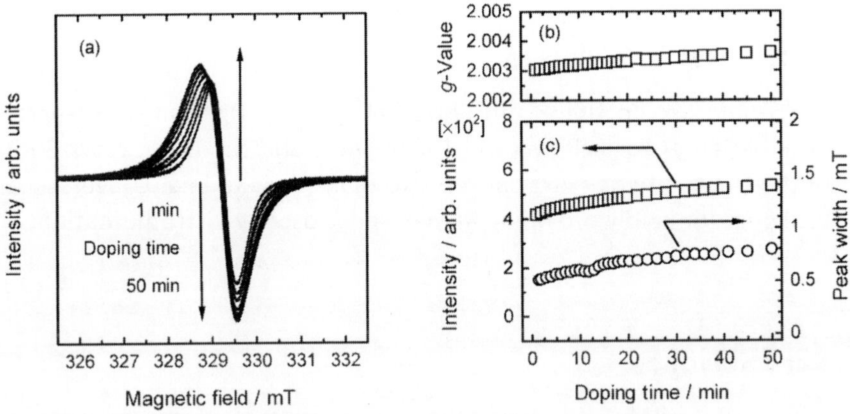

Figure 6. (**a**) ESR spectra of (–)-poly1 in bulk state with vapor phase iodine doping; (**b**) g-Value; (**c**) intensity, and peak width of (–)-poly1 with vapor phase iodine doping for 0–50 min.

4. CONCLUSIONS

Chiral π-conjugated polymers can be an important issue in the field of materials science from the view point of comparing basic science to bio-polymers. Industrial applications are expected for opto-electronic organic materials.

We synthesized low-bandgap polymers with chiral side chains under oxidative conditions. An introduction of alkyl side chains allows solubility of (–)-poly1 and (+)-poly2 in organic solvents such as THF or $CHCl_3$. Bandgap of the polymers is estimated to be 1.26 eV evaluated from optical absorption spectroscopy. Optical rotations of the polymers were identified in film state with ORD spectroscopy. Furthermore, the polymers showed complementary mirror-image optical rotations. This can be a first example of the synthesis of poly(isothianaphthene methine)s with chiral side chains showing chiroptical activity in the visible range. Doping and dedoping of an electron acceptor for the polymers may afford tuning of optical activity. The polymers may be applied for optical sensing devices by combining the function of optically active low-bandgap character with dopable properties.

ACKNOWLEDGMENTS

We would like to thank the Chemical Analysis Division of Research Facility Center for Science and Technology, and the Glass Work Shop of the University of Tsukuba. We also thank Seiji Kojima (University of Tsukuba) for kindly providing Raman spectroscopy instrumentation.

REFERENCES

1. Hu, W.; Nakashima, H.; Furukawa, K.; Kashimura, Y.; Ajito, K.; Liu, Y.; Zhu, D.; Torimitsu, K. A self-assembled nano optical switch and transistor based on a rigid conjugated polymer, thioacetyl-end-functionalized poly(*para*-phenylene ethynylene). *J. Am. Chem. Soc.* **2005**, *127*, 2804–2805.

2. Nelson, T.L.; Young, T.M.; Liu, J.; Mishra, S.P.; Belot, J.A.; Balliet, C.L.; Javier, A.E.; Kowalewski, T.; McCullough, R.D. Transistor paint: High mobilities in small bandgap polymer semiconductor based on the strong acceptor, diketopyrrolopyrrole and strong donor, dithienopyrrole. *Adv. Mater.* **2010**, *22*, 4617–4621.

3. Ortiz, R.P.; Yan, H.; Facchetti, A.; Marks, T.J. Azine- and azole-functionalized oligo and polythiophene semiconductors for organic thin-film transistors. *Materials* **2010**, *3*, 1533–1558.

4. Skompska, M. Hybrid conjugated polymer/semiconductor photovoltaic cells. *Synth. Met.* **2010**, *160*, 1–15.

5. Zhou, H.; Yang, L.; Stuart, A.C.; Price, S.C.; Liu, S.; You, W. Development of fluorinated benzothiadiazole as a structural unit for a polymer solar cell of 7% efficiency. *Angew. Chem. Int. Ed.* **2011**, *50*, 2995–2998.

6. Søndergaard, R.; Krebs, F.C. The challenge of synthesizing oligomers for molecular wires.*Polymers* **2011**, *3*, 545–557.

7. Liou, G.S.; Yen, H.J.; Chiang, M.C. Near-infrared electrochromic poly(aryl ether)s based on isolated electroactive tetraphenyl-*p*-phenylenediamine moieties. *J. Polym. Sci. Part A Polym. Chem.* **2009**, *47*, 5378–5385.

8. Baran, D.; Balan, A.; Celebi, S.; Esteban, B.M.; Neugebauer, H.; Sariciftci, N.S.; Toppare, L. Processable multipurpose conjugated polymer for electrochromic and photovoltaic applications. *Chem. Mater.* **2010**, *22*, 2978–2987.

9. Koldemir, U.; Graham, K.R.; Salazar, D.H.; McCarley, T.D.; Reynolds, J.R. Electron rich APFO polymer with dual electrochromism and electroluminescence. *J. Mater. Chem.* **2011**,*21*, 6480–6482.

10. Smith, R.C.; Tennyson, A.G.; Lim, M.H.; Lippard, S.J. Conjugated polymer-based fluorescence turn-on sensor for nitric oxide. *Org. Lett.* **2005**, *7*, 3573–3575.

11. Balamurugan, A.; Reddy, M.L.P.; Jayakannan, M. Carboxylic-functionalized water soluble π-conjugated polymer: Highly selective and efficient chemosensor for mercury(II) ions. *J. Polym. Sci. Part A* **2009**, *47*, 5144–5157.

12. Wang, G.; Pu, K.Y.; Zhang, X.; Li, K.; Wang, L.; Cai, L.; Ding, D.; Lai, Y.H.; Liu, B. Star-shaped glycosylated conjugated oligomer for two-photon fluorescence imaging of live cells. *Chem. Mater.* **2011**, *23*, 4428–4434.

13. Langeveld-Voss, B.M.W.; Janssen, R.A.J.; Meijer, E.W. On the origin of optical activity in polythiophenes. *J. Mol. Struct.* **2000**, *521*, 285–301.

14. Watanabe, K.; Sakamoto, T.; Taguchi, M.; Fujiki, M.; Nakano, T. A chiral π-stacked vinyl polymer emitting white circularly polarized light. *Chem. Commun.* **2011**, *47*, 10996–10998.

15. Ajayaghosh, A.; Eldo, J. A novel approach toward low optical band gap polysquaraines.*Org. Lett.* **2001**, *3*, 2595–2598.

16. Mühlbacher, D.; Scharber, M.; Morana, M.; Zhu, Z.; Waller, D.; Gaudiana, R.; Brabec, C. High photovoltaic performance of a low-bandgap polymer. *Adv. Mater.* **2006**, *18*, 2884–2889.

17. Soci, C.; Hwang, I.W.; Moses, D.; Zhu, Z.; Waller, D.; Gaudiana, R.; Brabec, C.J.; Heeger, A.J. Photoconductivity of a low-bandgap conjugated polymer. *Adv. Funct. Mater.* **2007**, *17*, 632–636.

18. Jenekhe, S.A. A class of narrow-band-gap semiconducting polymers. *Nature* **1986**, *322*, 345–347.

19. Chen, W.C.; Jenekhe, S.A. Small-bandgap conducting polymers based on conjugated poly(heteroary1ene methines). 1. Precursor poly(heteroary1ene methylenes).*Macromolecules* **1995**, *28*, 454–464.

20. Vangeneugden, D.; Kiebooms, R.; Adriaensens, P.; Vanderzande, D.; Gelan, J.; Desmet, J.; Huyberechts, G. "Formal" copolymers based on 1,3-dithienylisothianaphthene derivatives: Promising materials for electronic devices. *Acta Polym.* **1998**, *49*, 687–692.

21. Kisselev, R.; Thelakkat, M. Synthesis of novel 1,3-bis(5-diarylaminothiophen-2-yl)isothianaphthenes. *Chem. Commun.* **2002**, *14*, 1530–1531.

22. Mohanakrishnan, A.K.; Kumar, N.S.; Amaladass, P. Synthesis and characterization of 9,9-dialkylfluorene

capped benzo[*c*]thiophene/benzo[*c*]selenophene analogs as potential OLEDs. *Tetrahedron Lett.* **2008**, *49*, 4792–4795.

23. Salamonczyk, M.; Kovarova, A.; Svoboda, J.; Pociecha, D.; Gorecka, E. Switchable fluorescent liquid crystals. *Appl. Phys. Lett.* **2009**, *95*.

24. Kobayashi, M.; Colaneri, N.; Boysel, M.; Wudl, F.; Heeger, A.J. The electronic and electrochemical properties of poly(isothianaphthene). *J. Chem. Phys.* **1985**, *82*, 5717–5723.

25. Chandrasekhar, P.; Masulaitis, A.M.; Gumbs, R.W. Novel synthesis, spectroelectrochemical, electrochemical and chronovoltabsorptometric characterization of poly(isothianaphthene).*Synth. Met.* **1990**, *36*, 303–326.

26. Kiebooms, R.H.L.; Goto, H.; Akagi, K. Synthesis of a new class of low-band-gap polymers with liquid crystalline substituents. *Macromolecules* **2001**, *34*, 7989–7998.

27. Jung, Y.K.; Kim, H.; Park, J.H.; Lee, J.; Lee, S.K.; Lee, Y.S.; Shim, H.K. Alternating fluorene copolymers containing isothianaphthene derivatives: A study of their aggregation properties and small band gap. *J. Polym. Sci. Part A* **2008**, *46*, 3573–3590.

28. Innami, Y.; Kiebooms, R.H.L.; Koyano, T.; Ichinohe, M.; Ohkawa, S.; Kawabata, K.; Kawamatsu, M.; Matsuishi, K.; Goto, H. Synthesis of a low-bandgap polymer bearing side groups containing phenoxy radicals. *J. Mater. Sci.* **2011**, *46*, 6556–6562.

29. Kim, J.Y.; Qin, Y.; Stevens, D.M.; Kalihari, V.; Hillmyer, M.A.; Frisbie, C.D. High open-circuit voltage photovoltaic cells with a low bandgap copolymer of isothianaphthene, thiophene, and benzothiadiazole units. *J. Phys. Chem. C* **2009**, *113*, 21928–21936.

30. Yamamoto, T.; Usui, M.; Ootsuka, H.; Iijima, T.; Fukumoto, H.; Sakai, Y.; Aramaki, S.; Yamamoto, H.M.; Yagi, T.; Tajima, H.; *et al.* π-conjugated polymers consisting of isothianaphthene and dialkoxy-*p*-phenylene units: Synthesis, self-assembly, and chemical and physical properties. *Macromol. Chem. Phys.* **2010**, *211*, 2138–2147.

31. Okuda, Y.; Lakshmikantham, M.; Cava, M. A new route to 1,3-disubstituted benzo[*c*]thiophene. *J. Org. Chem.* **1991**, *56*, 6024–6026.

32. Wipf, P.; Graham, T.H. Photoactivated tungsten hexacarbonyl-catalyzed conversion of alkynols to glycals. *J. Org. Chem.* **2003**, *68*, 8798–8807.

33. Kiebooms, R.; Wudl, F. Synthesis and characterisation of poly(isothianaphthene methine).*Synth. Met.* **1999**, *101*, 40–43.

34. Neugebauer, H.; Kvarnström, C.; Brabec, C.; Sariciftci, N.S.; Kiebooms, R.; Wudl, F.; Luzzati, S. Infrared spectroelectrochemical investigations on the doping of soluble poly(isothianaphthene methine) (PIM). *J. Chem. Phys.* **1999**, *110*, 12108–12115.

Chapter 5

Probing Kinetic Mechanisms of Protein Function and Folding with Time-Resolved Natural and Magnetic Chiroptical Spectroscopies

David S. Kliger *, Eefei Chen and Robert A. Goldbeck

Department of Chemistry and Biochemistry, University of California, Santa Cruz, CA 95064, USA

ABSTRACT

Recent and ongoing developments in time-resolved spectroscopy have made it possible to monitor circular dichroism, magnetic circular dichroism, optical rotatory dispersion, and magnetic optical rotatory dispersion with nanosecond time resolution. These techniques have been applied to determine structural changes associated with the function of several proteins as well as to determine the nature of early events in protein folding. These studies have required new approaches in triggering protein reactions as well as the development of time-resolved techniques for polarization spectroscopies with sufficient time resolution and sensitivity to probe protein structural changes.

Keywords: circular dichroism; optical rotatory dispersion; magnetic circular dichroism; magnetic optical rotatory dispersion; heme proteins; cytochrome; phytochrome; polarization; quasi-null; ligand shuttle

1. INTRODUCTION

Circular dichroism (CD) spectroscopy has long been known as a valuable tool for determining the structural motifs of proteins. Like other structure-sensitive techniques, such as X-ray and NMR spectroscopies, in the past it had not been amenable to kinetic measurements and thus was useful only for determining static structural properties. In recent decades this changed, however, so that time-resolved CD measurements have become possible, thus opening up the capability of determining the time dependence of protein structural changes.

The first approach to time-resolved CD measurements involved the coupling of CD spectroscopy to stopped-flow kinetic techniques [1,2]. This approach used a standard technique for CD measurements in which the circular polarization of the light was alternated between left and right circular polarizations at frequencies on the order of 100 KHz. Stopped-flow techniques were capable of millisecond mixing times. The time course of CD signals was thus possible at single wavelengths with time resolution on the order of several milliseconds.

Efforts began in the mid 1980's to improve the time resolution of CD measurements in order to follow structural changes occurring in proteins on faster time scales. To do that, a different approach to CD measurements was developed [3]. While oscillating between two circular polarizations with higher frequency is possible, it would have meant using smaller aperture optics, thus reducing light intensities to levels that would make the signal to noise ratio of CD measurements poor. Instead, a pseudo-null approach to CD measurements was developed which made CD measurements possible on a nanosecond time scale, 6 orders of magnitude faster than previous capabilities.

In this article we will describe how this pseudo-null technique works, how modifications of the technique can be used for magnetic circular dichroism (MCD), optical rotatory dispersion (ORD), and magnetic optical rotatory dispersion (MORD) measurements, and how these techniques have been used for rapid measurements to determine early events in protein function and folding reactions.

2. QUASI-NULL POLARIZATION SPECTROSCOPY

Typical CD signals represent differences in the absorption of left and right circularly polarized light that are on the order of 10^{-3} to 10^{-5} of the unpolarized absorption. Phase-sensitive detection approaches were thus used to detect the small differences in large signals but, as mentioned above, this limited the time resolution of measurements. To increase the time resolution of CD measurements significantly a different approach was employed in which the differences in intensity due to CD represented a sizeable fraction of the background signal. This involved taking advantage of the fact that elliptically polarized light can be thought of as a vector addition of left and right circularly polarized light components of different amplitudes. When elliptically polarized light passes through a circularly dichroic sample, the relative amplitudes of the left and right circular components change. This results in a change in the eccentricity of the elliptically polarized light. By measuring this change in eccentricity one can determine the circular dichroism with high sensitivity. The experimental arrangement to accomplish such a measurement is shown in Figure 1.

As seen in Figure 1, the light that probes CD signals (typically from a high intensity, short duration xenon flashlamp) passes through a linear polarizer to produce linearly polarized light. This light then passes through a strained quartz plate with the strain axis oriented at +45° or −45° to produce left or right elliptically polarized light. Enough strain is placed on the quartz plate to produce a retardation on the order of 1 or 2 degrees, producing elliptically polarized light with major axis intensity on the order of 10^4 times the intensity of the

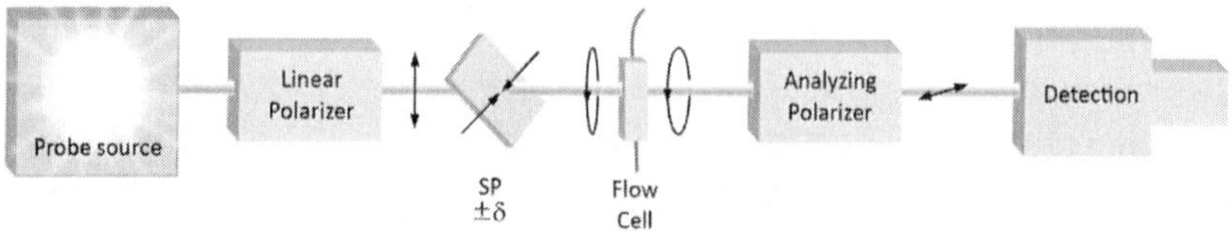

Figure 1. Apparatus for near-null ellipsometric time-resolved measurements of circular dichroism. Elliptically polarized light of high eccentricity is generated by sending initially unpolarized light through the first linear polarizer and then a strain plate (SP), which introduces a small phase retardance (δ). Right and left elliptically polarized light (REP and LEP) are obtained by rotating SP around its vertical axis by 180°. A circularly dichroic sample will change the eccentricity of elliptically polarized light because this light comprises components of LCP and RCP light with different amplitudes. After the sample, the LEP and REP probe light travel through a second, analyzing polarizer, and the minor axes (horizontally polarized light) of the two beams are detected by either an intensified photodiode array or intensified charge coupled device.

minor axis. When this light passes through a sample exhibiting CD the polarization ellipticity is changed. The degree to which the ellipticity changes is monitored by passing the probe light through a second linear polarizer oriented to pass light aligned along the minor axis of the ellipse. This measurement monitors the intensity along the minor elliptical axis, an intensity that is changed substantially by the CD of typical samples. The light emerging from the second polarizer is directed to a detection system, typically a gated multichannel detector capable of monitoring an entire spectrum with several nanoseconds time resolution. Making such measurements with both left and right elliptically polarized light then yields the sample circular dichroism according to:

$$\text{Signal} = (I_{\text{REP}} - I_{\text{LEP}})/(I_{\text{REP}} + I_{\text{LEP}}) = 2.3\ \Delta\varepsilon c l/\delta \quad (1)$$

where I_{REP} and I_{LEP} are the intensities reaching the detector from right and left elliptically polarized light, respectively, Δε is the circular dichroism, c is the sample concentration, l is the sample path length, and δ is the retardation (in radians) of the strain plate producing the elliptically polarized light. Because of the high intensity of the probe beam and the amplification factor, δ, gained by the use of elliptically polarized light, it is possible to achieve nanosecond time resolution with this technique. With a nanosecond pulsed laser pump source, it is possible to trigger protein reactions (as discussed below) and follow the change in CD as a function of time from nanoseconds to seconds.

Modification of this approach makes it possible to measure magnetic circular dichroism, as shown in Figure 2 [4]. Here, the same basic optical layout is used, but the sample is placed in a magnetic field whose field lines through the sample are parallel to the probe light propagation direction. This magnetic field induces a circular dichroism, which can have significant magnitude in aromatic moieties. Of course, the field also produces an optical rotation (Faraday rotation) which can be quite large as it is due to rotation from the sample cell and solvent as well as the molecules under study. Since the quasi-null technique relies on measuring the intensity of light from the minor elliptical polarization axis, a rotation of the elliptically polarized light would yield a signal at the detector that is generally much larger than the signal due to the direct MCD effect. To counter this, the light is passed through a reference cell with solvent that is matched to the sample cell and which is placed in a magnet of the same intensity but opposite field orientation as the sample magnet [5]. This rotates the polarization ellipse back to the original orientation so that the light directed to the detector reflects the true CD signal of the sample.

The CD signal measured in this way is composed of both the natural CD of the sample as well as the magnetically-induced CD. In other words, the measured signal is CD + H•MCD, where H is the magnitude of the magnetic field oriented parallel to the probe propagation direction. If one is interested in determining the pure MCD signal, it is necessary only to reverse the magnetic field direction (so the field is oriented antiparallel to the probe propagation direction), thus yielding a signal of CD − H•MCD. The sum of these two measurements yields 2 CD and the difference of the measurements yields 2H•MCD.

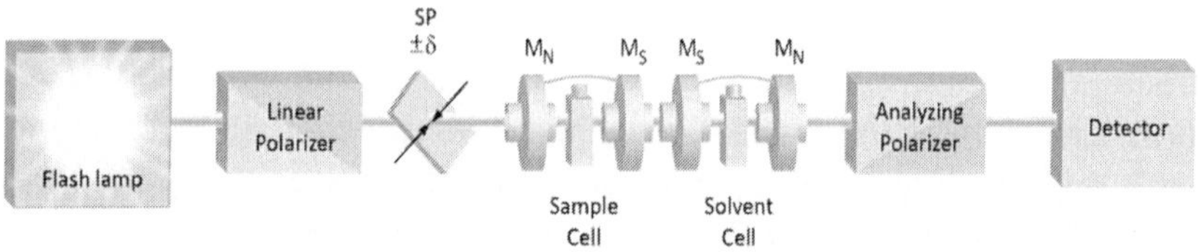

Figure 2. Apparatus for time-resolved measurements of magnetic circular dichroism. By addition of a magnet with the sample cell placed between the pole faces (M_N, M_S) and a compensator (solvent cell between pole faces of a second magnet), the TRCD approach can be extended to TRMCD measurements. The compensator counteracts the Faraday rotation of the probe beam polarization as it passes through the sample cell windows and the solvent in a magnetic field. It comprises a solvent blank in a cell matched with the sample cell and a magnetic field matched in magnitude but opposite in direction to that for the sample.

With a slight modification, indeed a simplification, of the approaches shown in Figures 1 and 2it is possible to measure ORD or MORD with high time resolution [6–8]. This involves removing the strain plate in the CD (MCD) apparatus and making measurements by rotating one of the polarizers by a small angle. This works in the following way. Starting with a sample between crossed polarizers, one of the polarizers is rotated by a small reference angle β (typically on the order of 1°). The light entering the second polarizer thus has its polarization altered by the rotation induced by the sample plus β. Rotating the first polarizer by −β results in the polarization entering the second polarizer changed by the rotation induced by the sample minus β.

$$\text{Signal}=[I(\beta)-I(-\beta)]/[I(\beta)+I(-\beta)]\approx-[\text{LD}+\text{ORD}]/\beta\approx-\text{ORD}/\beta \qquad (2)$$

Here LD is the sample linear dichroism, which will be negligibly small for a randomly oriented sample or for a photoselected sample that has been excited by a pump laser (propagating parallel to the probe beam propagation) whose polarization axis is parallel to the polarization axis of the fixed polarizer.

3. KINETICS OF PROTEIN STRUCTURAL CHANGES

3.1. Protein Function

3.1.1. Ligand Photolysis in Cytochrome c Oxidase

Since the development of the nanosecond time-resolved CD/ORD/MCD/MORD techniques described above they have been applied to the characterization of excited states of a number of inorganic metal complexes [9–12] as well as the study of tRNA [13] and a number of proteins. Proteins studied include heme proteins [7,14–24], phytochrome [25–29], PYP [30], Phot1-LOV2 [31], and rhodopsin [32]. As examples of the type of information obtainable from these time-resolved polarization spectroscopies, we will focus here on studies of bovine cytochrome *c*oxidase (cytox) and on phytochrome (phyt).

Cytox, the terminal enzyme in the respiratory chain of aerobic organisms, accepts electrons from cytochrome c. The reduced state of the protein binds molecular oxygen and reduces it to water. In this process, it creates a proton gradient across the mitochondrial membrane. This, in turn, drives the production of ATP within the mitochondria.

Bovine cytox is a complex, multi-subunit enzyme whose active site contains a heme *a*, with a nearby Cu_A and a heme a_3, with a nearby Cu_B. Heme *a* is a hexacoordinate heme A and it, with Cu_A, are involved in accepting electrons from cytochrome *c*. The electron is then transferred to the ligand binding site, heme a_3 and Cu_B. Heme a_3 is a pentacoordinate heme, with the fifth coordination site ligated to a histidine distal to the Cu_B and the sixth coordination site available to bind ligands such as O_2, CO, or NO.

In an effort to understand the mechanism of ligand reduction and proton transfer in cytox, early time-resolved studies used fast and ultrafast absorption spectroscopy, IR spectroscopy, and resonance Raman spectroscopy to study the reaction intermediates produced following photolysis of a CO ligand bound to heme a_3 [33]. The results of those studies suggested that the CO rapidly binds to Cu_B after it is photodissociated from heme a_3. The transfer of CO to Cu_Boccurs on a picosecond time scale and time-resolved IR measurements showed that the CO remains on Cu_B for a couple of microseconds. Time-resolved resonance Raman measurements showed that upon photolysis of CO, a Raman peak indicative of an iron-histidine bond disappears, suggesting that the iron is in a low-spin state or in a 5-coordinate species where the 5th ligand is a group other than an imidazole. A mechanism consistent with all these measurements was proposed as shown in Figure 3.

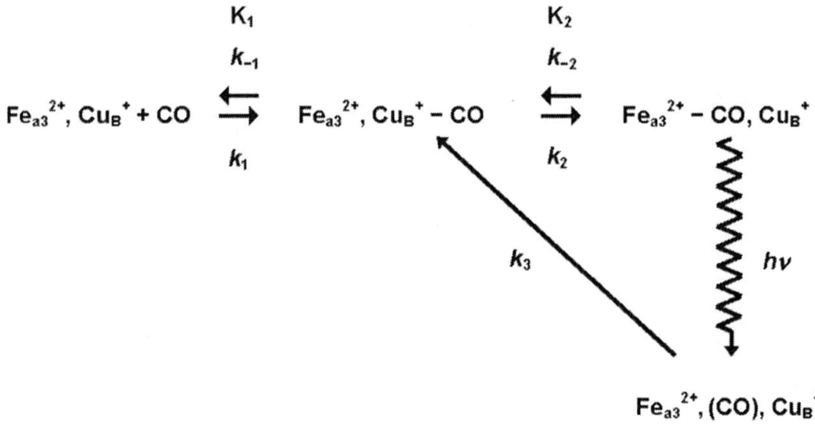

Figure 3. Mechanism of CO binding to cytochrome *c* oxidase deduced from time-resolved visible absorption, IR absorption, and Raman scattering experiments. Photolysis results in CO dissociating from heme a_3 and rapidly binding to nearby Cu_B. This mechanism would predict a high-spin state at the heme center for about a microsecond, at which point the high-field ligand CO would re-bind to heme a_3 and return the heme center to a diamagnetic ($S = 0$) state.

That mechanism suggested that heme a_3 should be high spin for a microsecond or so, until CO rebinds to it. To confirm this prediction time-resolved MCD measurements were made [16,19] because the MCD spectrum of fully reduced, unliganded cytox has a large contribution from high-spin heme a_3 and a much smaller contribution from a low-spin heme. Interestingly, the TRMCD signal showed that a high spin species is created within 10 ns of photolysis of CO from heme a_3 and the heme remains high spin for milliseconds, until CO rebinds to the heme. The apparent discrepancy between the Raman results and the MCD results was resolved with the proposal of a ligand shuttle model for cytox ligand binding, shown in Figure 4.

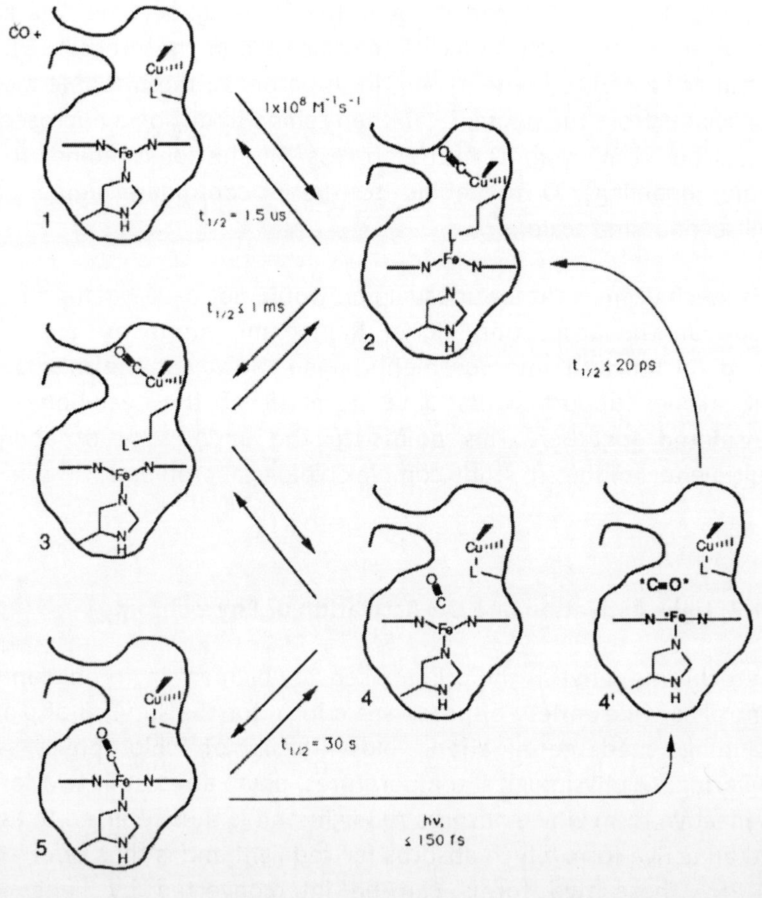

Figure 4. Cartoon of the Fe_{a3}-Cu_B bimetal site of cytochrome*c* oxidase showing the ligand shuttle mechanism for CO binding, as deduced by combining the results of TRMCD spectroscopy with the data of earlier TROA, TRIR, and TR^3studies (the latter data considered alone having first suggested the mechanism shown in Figure 3). The combined data suggested shuttling of a ligand L between the heme $a_3$iron atom and Cu_B, where L is a moiety endogenous to the protein. Species 1, 2, 3, 4, and 5 represent the thermal pathway. Species 4′ represents the photolytic generation of non-thermally equilibrated CO geminate to the heme a_3 and Cu_B (asterisks indicate excess excitation energy imparted to CO and the heme). See text for a discussion of this mechanism.

As Figure 4 shows, prior to photolysis, heme a_3 is ligated to a histidine residue and to CO and Cu_B is ligated to another ligand, designated L. Upon photolysis of CO from heme a_3 the CO group becomes ligated to Cu_B on a picosecond time scale, displacing L in the process. L then becomes ligated to heme a_3 and, in the process, the histidine moiety dissociates from the heme. L can then rebind to Cu_B on a microsecond time scale, displacing CO in the process. The histidine rebinds to the heme, enabling CO to rebind to the 5 coordinate heme on a millisecond time scale.

This mechanism is rather unusual and would not have been proposed based on the absorption, IR, or Raman measurements alone nor based on the MCD measurements alone. However, the mechanism has strong support when data from all of the techniques are considered together. This points to the importance of applying multiple techniques to study complex biological problems.

3.1.2. Light Activation and De-Activation of Phytochrome

Phytochrome (phyt) is the primary sensory pigment in green plants. It controls a wide variety of processes critical for the survival of plants, including seed germination, biosynthesis of chlorophylls, and flowering. At physiological temperatures, phyt can exist in two forms, an inactive form which absorbs red light and is thus referred to as Pr, and an active form which absorbs far-red light and is thus referred to as Pfr. These two forms can be interconverted by light, with absorption of red light by Pr producing Pfr and absorption of far-red light by Pfr producing Pr.

Time-resolved absorption experiments showed that the transformation from Pr to Pfr involves 5 intermediates with lifetimes in the microsecond and millisecond time scales [26]. The structural natures of these intermediates were probed by chromophore-band TRCD experiments discussed in [25]. The CD spectra of the later intermediates were similar to CD spectra obtained in studies where those intermediates were trapped at low temperatures. However, the earliest intermediate exhibited different CD spectra in the room temperature kinetic and low temperature trapping experiments. The difference in the CD spectra was interpreted as the result of structural strain in the low-temperature trapped intermediate, strain that relaxes within a microsecond at room temperature. This suggests that there is a structural change in the chromophore pocket at early times and, given that these differences are observable in CD spectra but not absorption spectra, that the early changes in the pocket involve motions of aromatic residues rather than charged groups.

To look at more global structural changes upon conversion of Pr to Pfr, TRCD measurements were carried out in the UV spectral region [29]. The results of this study showed that the major global structural change associated with the Pr to Pfr transition, an *N*-terminal α-helix folding, takes place in about 113 ms, significantly slower than the chromophore pocket structural changes observed at early times but faster than the last changes (slower than 266 ms) observed in absorption studies.

The photoreversion of Pfr to Pr was also studied by time-resolved absorption [27] and CD [28] studies. The absorption study showed that the reversion from Pfr to Pr reaction is simpler than the conversion reaction from Pr to Pfr in that it exhibits only 3 intermediates with lifetimes of 320 ns, 265 μs, and 5.5 ms in a sequential scheme. Interestingly, none of the intermediates involved in the Pfr to Pr reaction are the same as those observed in the Pr to Pfr reaction. As in the case of the Pr to Pfr reaction, TRCD measurements showed that the global unfolding process, involving a decrease in α-helix associated with the formation of the Pr form of the protein, does not occur in the last stage of the reaction, but is associated with the 265 μs process.

3.2. Protein Folding

3.2.1. Rapid Folding Triggers

In order to study reaction kinetics it is necessary not only to be able to make measurements on a time scale comparable to the speed of the reaction, but also to be able to trigger the reaction on such a time scale. Several approaches have been used to trigger protein folding reactions. Early approaches to this problem involved mixing techniques [1,2]. Proteins in denaturing solutions would be mixed with solvents to dilute denaturants such that folding could occur. Alternately, proteins could be mixed with denaturant solutions to induce unfolding. This typically allowed for millisecond time resolution, though recent microfluidics techniques have allowed for sub-millisecond mixing times [34–36]. For faster folding, a variety of photo-triggering techniques have been used.

In special cases, the photochemical properties of proteins can be used to trigger folding. This has been done with considerable success in the case of folding of cytochrome *c* (cytc) (see below). Two trigger methods have been used for this protein. The first takes advantage of the fact that, while the heme in cytc is six coordinate in its native state, with the iron ligated to a histidine and a methionine group of the protein backbone, addition of CO to a partially denaturing solution of cytc leads to a displacement of the methionine ligation by CO, resulting in further destabilization of the protein. Thus, one can add enough denaturant to a solution of CO and cytc to unfold the ligated protein but not enough to denature the native protein. By photodissociating the CO from the heme with a fast laser pulse the CO-unbound protein will be formed rapidly under conditions that facilitate formation of the folded state [37]. The advantage of this approach is that CO photolysis reverses through ligand rebinding so the measurements can be repeated many times on the same sample. The disadvantage is that this reversibility means that only short-lived folding intermediates can be studied since CO rebinding kinetically competes with the folding process. An alternative folding trigger for cytc takes advantage of the fact that oxidized cytc is less stable than reduced cytc. Thus, denaturant can be added to an oxidized sample to unfold the protein at a concentration in which the reduced protein remains folded [38]. If a photoreducing agent, such as NADH, is added to the sample, photolysis of the NADH results in an electron transfer to the cytc. This rapidly produces reduced cytc in an environment in which it will fold to the native state.

Another approach to trigger folding is to insert a group which sterically hinders folding until a phototrigger alters the group to relieve the steric constraint. This approach has been used to trigger peptide folding using an azobenzene group attached to the peptide such that isomerization of the azobenzene can facilitate folding or unfolding of the peptide [39].

Finally, various perturbation approaches can be used to facilitate folding or unfolding of proteins. For example, dyes which produce a pH jump upon photoexcitation can be used to trigger folding or unfolding for pH-sensitive folding processes. Also, temperature jumps can be produced by tuning a pulsed laser to about 1.5 μm, where water absorbs, to induce unfolding reactions under heat denaturing conditions or folding for cold denatured proteins. Temperature jumps can cause significant birefringence artifacts for TRCD measurements so for measurements on time scales faster than birefringence relaxation times, temperature jumps should be coupled to TRORD measurements since birefringence artifacts affect ellipsometric CD measurements to first order but affect ellipsometric ORD measurements to second order [40].

3.2.2. Monitoring Protein Folding Reactions

Perhaps the protein folding system most widely studied with ellipsometric polarization techniques is cytochrome *c*. TRCD, TRORD, and TRMCD have all been used to elucidate the early events in the folding mechanism of this protein. High time-resolution studies of cytc folding were first carried out using the CO photolysis approach to trigger folding and time-resolved absorption measurements to monitor folding [37]. TRCD experiments were later carried out to follow structural changes with more structure-sensitive far-UV CD measurements [41]. The first surprising result from this study was that absorption changes that were identified in the previous study as protein folding actually were due to changes in the ligation state of the heme. The second surprising result was that only about 7% of the native structure developed and that occurred within 500 ns of CO photolysis. Complete folding was prevented because of kinetic competition between the folding process and rebinding of the CO to the heme.

TRMCD studies of the cytc folding process revealed further interesting insights into the nature of folding. Folding had traditionally been described as a classical chemical reaction, with a reactant (unfolded protein) transforming into a product (folded protein) either directly or through some intermediate processes. An alternative model, the landscape view of folding, had been proposed [42] and supported by theoretical models. In this view, there are

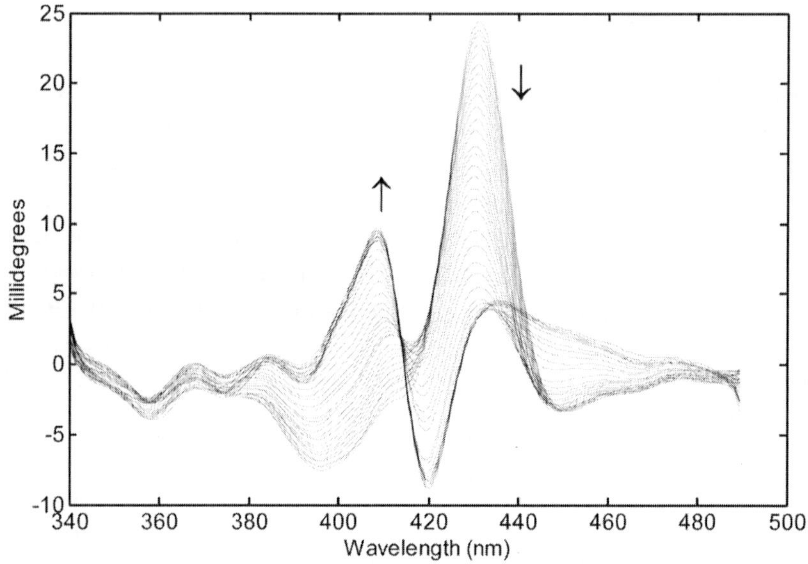

Figure 5. TRMCD spectra of cytochrome *c* measured at logarithmic time intervals from 330 ns to 25 ms after photolysis of the CO complex prepared under partially denaturing conditions. Arrows show direction of change with time. The spectra evolve through a complex mechanism, as revealed by the small blue shift over time of the ~430-nm MCD peak of the initial high-spin, 5-coordinate heme photolysis product. The mechanism proceeds first through unimolecular binding reactions between the heme iron atom and methionine or histidine residues, as the protein begins to fold, and finally through the bimolecular rebinding of CO, which stops refolding.

many unfolded protein states and each could, in principle, take different routes to the folded state. Thus, experimental observations monitored different folding routes with common observable features. The difference between these two views can be difficult to detect. If the rate of interconversion between different unfolded species (conformational diffusion) is fast relative to the rate of folding any observation will appear to monitor a classical reaction, *i.e.*, transformation from an average unfolded species to a folded species. On the other hand, if conformational diffusion times are comparable to folding times it would be possible to observe different folding pathways. TRMCD measurements of cytc folding, due to its rich spectral features (see Figure 5), were able to experimentally show, for the first time, that early events in the folding of cytc are better described by a landscape model than a classical model of folding [43]. Furthermore, by studying the folding in several cytc mutants the conformational diffusion time was determined to be about 3 μs [44], an order of magnitude faster than previous estimates for cytc based on absorption measurements [45]. Thus, folding processes occurring in microsecond times would best be described by a landscape view while millisecond or longer folding processes would adequately be described classically.

Beyond gaining understanding of the early events involved in cytc folding using the CO photolysis triggering approach, it is possible to monitor the whole folding process, from the earliest times to the formation of the native structure by using a photoreduction technique. This approach was first used in far UV-TRCD measurements [46]. Further evidence for the importance of the landscape view was demonstrated with this approach and an ultrafast folding process was observed which actually increased in amplitude with higher denaturant concentrations [47,48]. Interestingly, late folding processes leading to the native structure slowed down as expected as denaturant concentrations increased while early processes actually speeded up. This was shown to be related to a transient ligation to a non-native histidine group [49] associated with early formation of a molten globule folding intermediate [50].

4. CONCLUSIONS

From the examples cited above one can see that the ability to make CD, ORD, MCD, and MORD measurements on fast time scales is a valuable tool for biophysics. Two types of information of great value to understanding protein function are the structures of the proteins and the kinetics of protein reactions. The time-resolved polarization spectroscopies described here contribute to both of these areas and thus can provide important contributions to our mechanistic understanding of protein function. Furthermore, as our study of mechanistic features of cytox showed, different spectral techniques provide insights into different aspects of protein changes, so the ability to carry out protein studies with multiple spectroscopic probes is important for establishing mechanisms with confidence. The ability to link structural and kinetic information through these types of measurements has resulted in significant advances in our toolkit of biophysical methods for understanding proteins.

ACKNOWLEDGMENTS

This work was supported in part by grants EY00983 and EB02056 from the National Institutes of Health.

REFERENCES

1. Anson, M.; Bayley, P.M. Measurement of circular dichroism at millisecond time resolution: Stopped-flow circular dichroism system. J. Phys. E Sci. Instrum 1974, 7.

2. Bayley, P.M.; Anson, M. Stopped-flow circular dichroism: New fast-kinetic system.Biopolymers 1974, 13, 401–405.

3. Lewis, J.W.; Tilton, R.F.; Einterz, C.M.; Milder, S.J.; Kuntz, I.D.; Kliger, D.S. New technique for measuring circular dichroism changes on a nanosecond time scale: Application to (carbonmonoxy) myoglobin and (carbonmonoxy)hemoglobin. J. Phys. Chem 1985, 89, 289–294.

4. Goldbeck, R.A.; Dawes, T.D.; Milder, S.J.; Lewis, J.W.; Kliger, D.S. Measurement of magnetic circular dichroism (MCD) on a nanosecond timescale. Chem. Phys. Lett 1989, 156, 545–549.

5. Goldbeck, R.A.; Kliger, D.S. Nanosecond time-resolved absorption and polarization dichroism spectroscopies. Methods Enzymol 1993, 226, 147–177.

6. Esquerra, R.M.; Goldbeck, R.A.; Kim-Shapiro, D.B.; Kliger, D.S. Fast time-resolved magnetic optical rotatory dispersion

measurements. 1. Mueller analysis of optical and photoselection-induced artifacts. J. Phys. Chem. A 1998, 102, 8740–8748.

7. Shapiro, D.B.; Goldbeck, R.A.; Che, D.; Esquerra, R.M.; Paquette, S.J.; Kliger, D.S. Nanosecond optical rotatory dispersion spectroscopy: Application to photolyzed hemoglobin-CO kinetics. Biophys. J 1995, 68, 326–334.

8. Esquerra, R.M.; Goldbeck, R.A.; Kim-Shapiro, D.B.; Kliger, D.S. Fast time-resolved magnetic optical rotatory dispersion measurements. 2. Confirmation of Mueller analysis and application to myoglobin ligand photolysis. J. Phys. Chem. A 1998, 102, 8749–8758.

9. Gold, J.S.; Milder, S.J.; Lewis, J.W.; Kliger, D.S. Transient circular dichroism of the luminescent state of Ru(bpy)32+. J. Am. Chem. Soc 1985, 107, 8285–8286.

10. Milder, S.J.; Gold, J.S.; Kliger, D.S. Assignments of ground- and excited-state spectra from time-resolved absorption and circular dichroism measurements of the 2E State of (Δ)-Cr(bpy)33+. Inorg. Chem 1990, 29, 2506–2511.

11. Milder, S.J.; Gold, J.S.; Kliger, D.S. Time-resolved circular dichroism of the lowest excited state of (Δ)-Ru(bpy)32+. Chem. Phys. Lett 1988, 144, 269–272.

12. Milder, S.J.; Gold, J.S.; Kliger, D.S. Circular dichroism of a subnanosecond state: (Δ)-Fe(bpy)32+. J. Am. Chem. Soc 1986, 108, 8295–8296.

13. Milder, S.J.; Weiss, P.S.; Kliger, D.S. Time-resolved absorption, circular dichroism, and emission of transfer-RNA: Evidence that the photo-cross-linking of 4-thiouridine in transfer-RNA occurs from the triplet state. Biochemistry 1989, 28, 2258–2264.

14. Einterz, C.M.; Lewis, J.W.; Milder, S.J.; Kliger, D.S. Birefringence effects in transient circular-dichroism measurements with applications to the photolysis of

carbonmonoxyhemoglobin and carbonmonoxymyoglobin. J. Phys. Chem 1985, 89, 3845–3853.

15. Milder, S.J.; Bjorling, S.C.; Kuntz, I.D.; Kliger, D.S. Time-resolved circular dichroism and absorption studies of the photolysis reaction of (carbonmonoxy)myoglobin. Biophys. J 1988,53, 659–664.

16. Woodruff, W.H.; Einarsdottir, O.; Dyer, R.B.; Bagley, K.A.; Palmer, G.; Atherton, S.J.; Goldbeck, R.A.; Dawes, T.D.; Kliger, D.S. Nature and functional implications of the cytochrome-a3 transients after photodissociation of CO-cytochrome oxidase. Proc. Natl. Acad. Sci. USA 1991, 88, 2588–2592.

17. Bjorling, S.C.; Goldbeck, R.A.; Paquette, S.J.; Milder, S.J.; Kliger, D.S. Allosteric intermediates in hemoglobin. 1. Nanosecond time-resolved circular dichroism spectroscopy. Biochemistry 1996, 35, 8619–8627.

18. Chen, E.F.; Kliger, D.S. Time-resolved near UV circular dichroism and absorption studies of carbonmonoxymyoglobin photolysis intermediates. Inorg. Chim. Acta 1996, 242, 149–158.

19. Goldbeck, R.A.; Dawes, T.D.; Einarsdottir, O.; Woodruff, W.H.; Kliger, D.S. Time-resolved magnetic circular dichroism spectroscopy of photolyzed carbonmonoxy cytochrome coxidase (cytochrome-aa3). Biophys. J 1991, 60, 125–134.

20. Goldbeck, R.A.; Einarsdottir, O.; Dawes, T.D.; Oconnor, D.B.; Surerus, K.K.; Fee, J.A.; Kliger, D.S. Magnetic circular dichroism study of cytochrome ba3 from Thermus thermophilus: Spectral contributions from cytochrome b and cytochrome a3 and nanosecond spectroscopy of CO photodissociation intermediates. Biochemistry 1992, 31, 9376–9387.

21. O'Connor, D.B.; Goldbeck, R.A.; Hazzard, J.H.; Kliger, D.S.; Cusanovich, M.A. Time-resolved absorption and magnetic

circular dichroism spectroscopy of cytochrome c3 fromDesulfovibrio. Biophys. J 1993, 65, 1718–1726.

22. Esquerra, R.M.; Goldbeck, R.A.; Kim-Shapiro, D.B.; Kliger, D.S. Spectroscopic evidence for nanosecond protein relaxation after photodissociation of myoglobin-CO. Biochemistry 1998,37, 17527–17536.

23. Goldbeck, R.A.; Esquerra, R.M.; Kliger, D.S. Hydrogen bonding to Trp β37 is the first step in a compound pathway for hemoglobin allostery. J. Am. Chem. Soc 2002, 124, 7646–7647.

24. Vitale, D.J.; Goldbeck, R.A.; Kim-Shapiro, D.B.; Esquerra, R.M.; Parkhurst, L.J.; Kliger, D.S. Near-ultraviolet magnetic circular dichroism spectroscopy of protein conformational states: Correlation of tryptophan band position and intensity with hemoglobin allostery.Biochemistry 2000, 39, 7145–7152.

25. Bjorling, S.C.; Zhang, C.F.; Farrens, D.L.; Song, P.S.; Kliger, D.S. Time-resolved circular dichroism of native oat phytochrome photointermediates. J. Am. Chem. Soc 1992, 114, 4581–4588.

26. Zhang, C.F.; Farrens, D.L.; Bjorling, S.C.; Song, P.S.; Kliger, D.S. Time-resolved absorption studies of native etiolated oat phytochrome. J. Am. Chem. Soc 1992, 114, 4569–4580.

27. Chen, E.F.; Lapko, V.N.; Lewis, J.W.; Song, P.S.; Kliger, D.S. Mechanism of native oat phytochrome photoreversion: A time-resolved absorption investigation. Biochemistry 1996,35, 843–850.

28. Chen, E.F.; Lapko, V.N.; Song, P.S.; Kliger, D.S. Dynamics of the N-terminal α-helix unfolding in the photoreversion reaction of phytochrome A. Biochemistry 1997, 36, 4903–4908.

29. Chen, E.F.; Parker, W.; Lewis, J.W.; Song, P.S.; Kliger, D.S. Time-resolved UV circular dichroism of phytochrome A:

Folding of the N-terminal region. J. Am. Chem. Soc 1993, 115, 9854–9855.

30. Chen, E.F.; Gensch, T.; Gross, A.B.; Hendriks, J.; Hellingwerf, K.J.; Kliger, D.S. Dynamics of protein and chromophore structural changes in the photocycle of photoactive yellow protein monitored by time-resolved optical rotatory dispersion. Biochemistry 2003, 42, 2062–2071.

31. Chen, E.F.; Swartz, T.E.; Bogomolni, R.A.; Kliger, D.S. A LOV story: The signaling state of the Phot1 LOV2 photocycle involves chromophore-triggered protein structure relaxation, as probed by far-UV time-resolved optical rotatory dispersion spectroscopy. Biochemistry2007, 46, 4619–4624.

32. Thomas, Y.G.; Szundi, I.; Lewis, J.W.; Kliger, D.S. Microsecond time-resolved circular dichroism of rhodopsin photointermediates. Biochemistry 2009, 48, 12283–12289.

33. Woodruff, W.H.; Dyer, R.B.; Einarsdóttir, Ó.; Peterson, K.A.; Stoutland, P.O.; Bagley, K.A.; Palmer, G.; Schoonover, J.R.; Kliger, D.S.; Goldbeck, R.A.; et al. Ultrafast and not-so fast dynamics of cytochrome oxidase: The ligand shuttle and its possible functional significance. P. Soc. Photo-Opt. Instrum. Eng 1991, 1432. [CrossRef]

34. Akiyama, S.; Takahashi, S.; Ishimori, K.; Morishima, I. Stepwise formation of α-helices during cytochrome c folding. Nat. Struct. Biol 2000, 7, 514–520.

35. Knight, J.B.; Vishwanath, A.; Brody, J.P.; Austin, R.H. Hydrodynamic focusing on a silicon chip: Mixing nanoliters in microseconds. Phys. Rev. Lett 1998, 80, 3863–3866.

36. Hertzog, D.E.; Michalet, X.; Jager, M.; Kong, X.X.; Santiago, J.G.; Weiss, S.; Bakajin, O. Femtomole mixer for microsecond kinetic studies of protein folding. Anal. Chem 2004, 76, 7169–7178.

37. Jones, C.M.; Henry, E.R.; Hu, Y.; Chan, C.K.; Luck, S.D.; Bhuyan, A.; Roder, H.; Hofrichter, J.; Eaton, W.A. Fast events in protein folding initiated by nanosecond laser photolysis. Proc. Natl. Acad. Sci. USA 1993, 90, 11860–11864.

38. Pascher, T.; Chesick, J.P.; Winkler, J.R.; Gray, H.B. Protein folding triggered by electron transfer. Science 1996, 271, 1558–1560.

39. Chen, E.F.; Kumita, J.R.; Woolley, G.A.; Kliger, D.S. The kinetics of helix unfolding of an azobenzene cross-linked peptide probed by nanosecond time-resolved optical rotatory dispersion. J. Am. Chem. Soc 2003, 125, 12443–12449.

40. Chen, E.F.; Wen, Y.X.; Lewis, J.W.; Goldbeck, R.A.; Kliger, D.S.; Strauss, C.E.M. Nanosecond laser temperature-jump optical rotatory dispersion: Application to early events in protein folding/ unfolding. Rev. Sci. Instrum 2005, 76, 083120:1–083120:7.

41. Chen, E.F.; Wood, M.J.; Fink, A.L.; Kliger, D.S. Time-resolved circular dichroism studies of protein folding intermediates of cytochrome c. Biochemistry 1998, 37, 5589–5598.

42. Bryngelson, J.D.; Wolynes, P.G. Spin glasses and the statistical mechanics of protein folding.Proc. Natl. Acad. Sci. USA 1987, 84, 7524–7528.

43. Goldbeck, R.A.; Thomas, Y.G.; Chen, E.F.; Esquerra, R.M.; Kliger, D.S. Multiple pathways on a protein folding energy landscape: Kinetic evidence. Proc. Natl. Acad. Sci. USA 1999, 96, 2782–2787.

44. Abel, C.J.; Goldbeck, R.A.; Latypov, R.F.; Roder, H.; Kliger, D.S. Conformational equilibration time of unfolded protein chains and the folding speed limit. Biochemistry2007, 46, 4090–4099.

45. Hagen, S.J.; Hofrichter, J.; Szabo, A.; Eaton, W.A. Diffusion-limited contact formation in unfolded cytochrome c:

Estimating the maximum rate of protein folding. Proc. Natl. Acad. Sci. USA 1996, 93, 11615–11617.

46. Chen, E.F.; Wittung-Stafshede, P.; Kliger, D.S. Far-UV time-resolved circular dichroism detection of electron-transfer-triggered cytochrome c folding. J. Am. Chem. Soc 1999, 121, 3811–3817.

47. Chen, E.F.; Goldbeck, R.A.; Kliger, D.S. Earliest events in protein folding: Submicrosecond secondary structure formation in reduced cytochrome c. J. Phys. Chem. A 2003, 107, 8149–8155.

48. Chen, E.F.; Goldbeck, R.A.; Kliger, D.S. The earliest events in protein folding: A structural requirement for ultrafast folding in cytochrome c. J. Am. Chem. Soc 2004, 126, 11175–11181.

49. Chen, E.; Abel, C.J.; Goldbeck, R.A.; Kliger, D.S. Non-native heme-histidine ligation promotes microsecond time scale secondary structure formation in reduced horse heart cytochrome c. Biochemistry 2007, 46, 12463–12472.

50. Chen, E.; van Vranken, V.; Kliger, D.S. The folding kinetics of the SDS-induced molten globule form of reduced cytochrome c. Biochemistry 2008, 47, 5450–5459.

Chapter 6

Scalable Fabrication of Quasi-Three-Dimensional Chiral Plasmonic Oligomers Based on Stepwise Colloid Sphere Lithography Technology

Shiwei Xie[1,2], Jinzhe Yang[4] , Xiao Xiao[1] , Yidong Hou[1,3*,] Jinglei Du[1,3], Lin Pang[1] , Xie Li[1] and Fuhua Gao[1,3*]

[1] *Department of Physics, Sichuan University, Chengdu 610064, China.*

[2] *College of Science, China Three Gorges University, Yichang 443002, China.*

[3] *Key Laboratory for High Energy Density Physics and Technology, Ministry of Education, Sichuan University, Chengdu 610064, China. 4 Department of Physics, Key laboratory of Micro- and Nano-Photonic Structures (Ministry of Education) and State Key Laboratory of Surface Physics, Fudan University, Shanghai 200433, China*

ABSTRACT

We report a simple and scalable method for the fabrication of spiral-type chiral plasmonic oligomers based on the stepwise colloid sphere lithography technology. Through carefully adjusting the azimuthal angle Φ of polystyrene (PS) sphere array monolayer and the deposition thickness k_n, the chiral plasmonic oligomers composed of four achiral particles can be successfully fabricated on a desired substrate. And their chiral sign, i.e., left-hand or right-hand, is dependent on the anticlockwise or clockwise deposition sequence of the achiral particles. The measured results show a large chiroptical resonance in the visible region, and this resonance can be easily adjusted by using different sizes of PS spheres. Our in-depth theoretical and experimental researches further reveal that the obtained chiral plasmonic oligomers are indeed a kind of quasi-three-dimensional chiral nanostructures, which own a three-dimensional geometrical morphology, but with nonreciprocity chiroptical effect. The ease and scalability (>1 cm^2) of the fabrication method make chiral plasmonic oligomers promising candidates for many applications, such as chiral biosensor and catalysis.

BACKGROUND

According to Lord Kelvin, any geometrical figure or group of points is defined as chiral if its mirror image cannot be made to coincide with itself [1]. Chirality is ubiquitous in nature and plays a crucial role in the living body. Almost all of the important biomolecules, such as proteins, amino acids, and DNA, own the same chirality, i.e., left-hand (LH) and right-hand (RH). And distinguishing the chirality of molecules becomes very significative for life. Although enantiomers (i.e., left-handed (LH) and right-handed (RH) substances) possess the same physical and chemical properties, they usually interact differently with left- and right-circularly polarized light (LCP and RCP). In fact, the cross coupling between the electric and magnetic dipoles in the chiral medium can break the degeneracy between the helicity eigenmodes of light (i.e., LCP and RCP), leading to an absorption difference (i.e., circular dichroism, CD) or a phase retardation difference (i.e., circular birefringence, CB) for the LCP and RCP. This measurable chiroptical effect paves a way to achieve the structural characterization and spectroscopy of chiral molecules and manipulate the polarization state of light. However, the magnetoelectric coupling in the natural chiral molecules, such as DNA, proteins, amino acids, and viruses, is very weak [2]. This limits the ability of practical applications for the polarization manipulation and high-sensitivity sensing.

Recently, chiral plasmonic structures (CPS) have been demonstrated to own giant chiroptical effect [3] and attracted many attentions. These CPS cannot only be used to enhance the chiroptical effect of chiral molecules and improve the detection sensitivity [4, 5] but also be used to achieve some amazing physical phenomena, such as negative refraction [6, 7], repulsive Casimir force [8], and spin Hall effect [9].

These remarkable properties make CPS a very popular metamaterial in many fields, such as biology, pharmacology, and nanophotonics. Typically, the currently developed CPS can be divided into two categories: one is the two-dimensional (2D) CPS. This type of CPS owns a plane-like geometrical morphology, and the twist sense of their structures is reverse when looked from the opposite side, such as a gammadion structure [10], L-shaped structure [11], and rose-shaped structure [12]. The chiroptical effect from these CPS is nonreciprocal, which is similar to the Faraday effect [13]. The other is the three-dimensional (3D) CPS. The twist sense of this type of CPS is the same when looked from the opposite side, such as Helix [14], twisted arcs [3, 15], Y-shaped [16], U-shaped [17], cross-shaped [18], and three-dimensional triple-helical nanowires [19, 20]. The chiroptical effect from these CPS is reciprocal, just like that from natural light active medium [21]. However, the fabrication of these 2D or 3D CPS usually relied on the electron beam lithography technique [22], direct laser writing technique [23], and so on. The process technology usually is time-consuming, expensive, and small area limited, which limited the related research and applications.

Molecule assembly techniques, such as DNA origami technique [24, 25], have been demonstrated to a kind of efficient and low-cost method for the fabrication of CPS. The chiroptical resonance from the CPS is randomly dispersed in solvent usually located in the visible region. Glancing angle deposition technique is another low-cost, material-independent, and parallel fabrication technique for the fabrication of CPS. With the help of various masks, such random nanohole array [26], square nanoparticle array [27], and aligned ZnO nanorods [28], various CPS with chiroptical resonance located in the near-infrared and visible region have been achieved. Particularly, our previous work also demonstrates that with the help of assembled polystyrene (PS) sphere array, a kind of shell-like chiral nanostructures can be achieved [29]. This kind of CPS can combine the magnetic or dielectric spheres to form chiral “Janus particles” [30] or “patchy particles” [31, 32] and will find potential applications in the colloid field. However, the cancellation effect originated from the PS array limited the related applications. In this paper, we propose a new method for the fabrication of CPS based on stepwise colloid sphere lithography technology, which is quasi-three-dimensional chiral plasmonic oligomers (CPO) composed of four achiral particles. Furthermore, we systematically analyze the optical properties of our fabricated CPO with the help of full-wave simulation and the measurement of CD spectra and optical activity. And the results reveal the reciprocal chiroptical effect of our fabricated CPO.

METHODS

This section describes the design principle and methods of the CPO fabricated. Colloid sphere lithography technology is a powerful method for the fabrication of nanostructures. And a great number of nanostructures have been obtained by this method, such as triangle particle array [33], binary array [34], and multiplex quasi-3D grids [35]. The basic principle of this technology is the use of a PS array as mask, and the morphology and size of the obtained nanostructures are dependent on the projection of gap between PS spheres with respect to material vapor beam [36]. In this work, we employ this technology to arrange four achiral nanoparticles with different sizes in a concentric circle, and in this case a kind of new CPS, i.e., CPO, can be formed on substrate, as shown in Fig. 1a, b. The left-handed chiral plasmonic oligomers (LHCPO) are related to the anticlockwise deposition sequence (Fig. 1a), while the right-handed chiral plasmonic oligomers (RHCPO) are related to the clockwise deposition sequence (Fig. 1b). In order to obtain CPO with high optical chirality and geometrical chirality, the size and position of the four achiral particles should be properly adjusted in the fabrication process.

Figure 2a is the material deposition schematic diagram, where ϑ is the deposition angle, which is defined as the material vapor beam with respect to the substrate normal, and Φ is the azimuth angle with respect to the PS array monolayer. In the formation of CPO, the size of the achiral particles and the diameter of the circle where the achiral particles are located are dependent on the deposition angle ϑ, and the position is dependent on the azimuth angle Φ. The deposition thickness k is another important parameter and defined as the deposition thickness on the plane perpendicular to the vapor beam. In general, the height of the achiral particles is dependent on the deposition thickness k. However, due to surface energy minimization

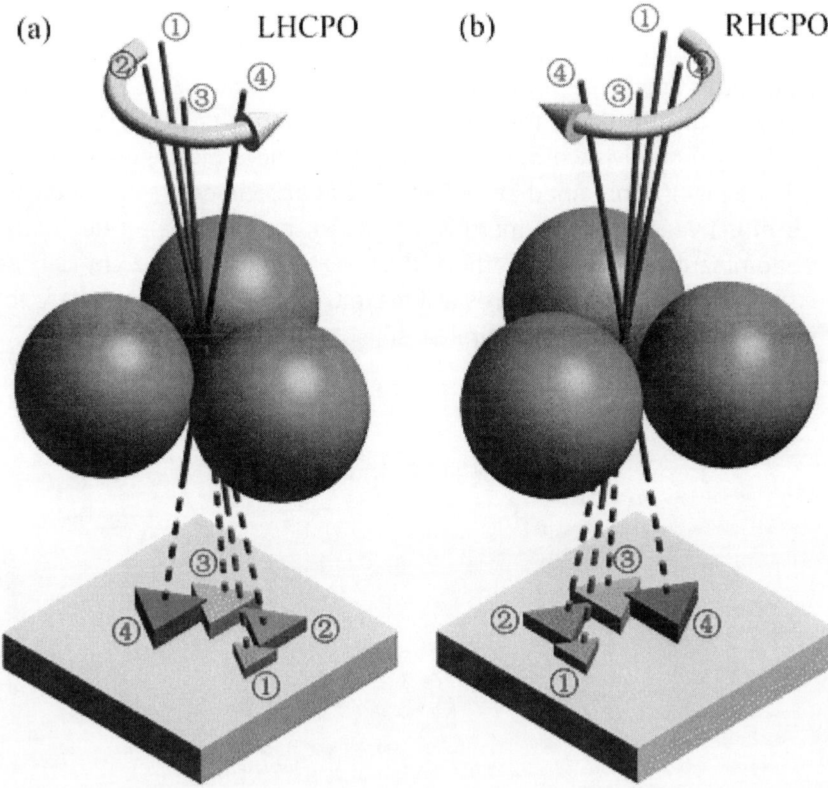

Figure 1. Design principle schematic of LHCPO (**a**) and RHCPO (**b**). The numbers ①, ②, ③, and ④ denote the *n*-th material deposition step and the formed achiral particles, and the *green curves with yellow arrow* denote the deposition sequence, where the anticlockwise deposition sequence refers to LHCPO and the clockwise deposition sequence refers to RHCPO

[27], the deposition thickness k will indirectly affect the size of achiral particles and result in great contraction of the achiral particles with small deposition thickness. In the fabrication of CPO, these influence factors should be considered. The inset scanning electron microscope (SEM) images shown in Fig. 2b are the obtained CPO with $\vartheta = 20°$, $k_{1,2,3,4} = 8$, 25, 40, and 55 nm, and $\Delta\Phi = \pm 60°$, where k_n is the deposition thickness in the n-th step material deposition process, $\Delta\Phi$ is the relative azimuth angle between the approaching two-step material deposition

processes, and the signs "+" and "–" refer to the anticlockwise deposition sequence (i.e., LHCPO) and the clockwise deposition sequence (i.e., RHCPO). The measured CD spectra show that the LHCPO and RHCPO nearly own opposite CD spectra and a maximum CD signal of ~180 mdeg is obtained at 637 nm. These experiment results indicate the effectiveness of the method proposed in this paper. Due to the predominant fabrication method, the CPO with area of >1 cm^2 can be easily obtained. These features will make CPO a promising candidate for many applications, such as chiral biosensor and catalysis.

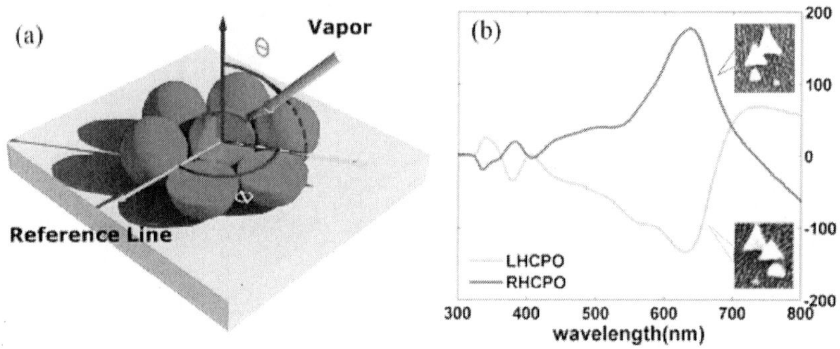

Figure 2. a Schematic diagram of material deposition on assembled PS array monolayer. Where ϑ is the deposition angle, which is defined as the material vapor beam with respect to the substrate normal, and Φ is the azimuth angle with respect to the PS array monolayer. **b** The measured CD spectra of LHCPO (*green*) and RHCPO (*aubergine*) with $\vartheta = 20°$, $k_{1,2,3,4} = 8$, 25, 40, and 55 nm, respectively, and $\Delta\Phi = \pm 60°$. The *insets* are the related CPO SEM images

The quasi-3D CPO are fabricated on a BK7 glass substrate through four-step Ag deposition on a monolayer of PS array. The detailed fabrication schematic diagram is shown in Fig. 3.

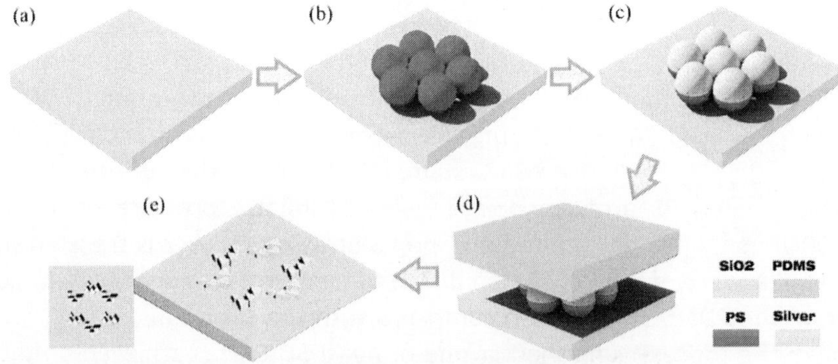

Figure 3. Schematic diagram of the preparation process. **a** BK7 glass substrate. **b** Self-assembly of polystyrene microspheres. **c**Glancing angle deposition of metal vapor. **d** Removal of unwanted portions with PDMS. **e** Resulting structure and its top view

Firstly, a BK7 glass is used as substrate. Before being used in the micro-sphere-assembled process, the BK7 glass substrate is immerged in a mixed solution of sulfuric acid/hydrogen peroxide (3:1) for more than 1 h at 80 °C. Then, the substrate is rinsed in deionized water for several times and immerged in another mixed solution of ultrapure water/ammonium hydroxide/30 % hydrogen peroxide (5:1:1) for 1 hour under ultrasonication, sequentially. Finally, the substrates were thoroughly rinsed with deionized water and stored under deionized water until required. Secondly, a monolayer of PS array with hexagonal symmetry is obtained on the BK7 glass substrate through the method reported in the literature, as shown in Fig. 3b. The PS spheres with a diameter of 750 nm and weight concentration of 10 % are purchased from Thermo Scientific Company and used without further treatment. Thirdly, the Ag deposition on the closely packed PS array monolayer is performed inside a vacuum thermal evaporation system, as shown in Fig. 3c. The base pressure, the deposition rate, and the temperature are 4×10^{-4} Pa, 1 nm/s, and 30 °C, respectively. For a single-step deposition, the deposition time needs to be precisely controlled (i.e., deposition thickness k), together with the angles ϑ and Φ, which can be easily adjusted by tilting and rotating the samples with the improved slide holder in the vacuum chamber, respectively. For stepwise depositions, the operational process is the repeat of the single deposition. All the deposition angle ϑ is set to 20°, $\Delta\Phi$ is set to ±60°for LHCPO (i.e., +60°)

and RHCPO (i.e., −60°), and the deposition thickness $k_{1,2,3,4}$ is set to 8, 25, 40 and 55 nm, respectively. Finally, a polydimethylsiloxane (PDMS) stamp is used to remove the silver-coated PS array monolayer. As shown in Fig. 3d, e, the PDMS stamp is placed on the surface of the silver-coated PS array monolayer with a uniform pressure of about 500 g/cm^2. After being lifted up, the PS array monolayer is transferred to the surface of the PDMS stamp, due to the larger Van der Waals force from the PDMS stamp when compared with the silica substrate. When all of the process is finished, a kind of quasi-3D CPO is achieved on the BK7 glass substrate.

RESULTS AND DISCUSSION

The SEM images are collected by the Hitachi S-4800 SEM. Figure 4a, b shows the SEM images of the obtained LHCPO and RHCPO, respectively. And the insets are the enlarged SEM images of single CPO. From these images, we can get that the CPO is well formed on the BK7 glass substrate. Obviously, the chiral sign (i.e., LH or RH) is dependent on the anticlockwise or clockwise deposition sequence. The Nikon Eclipse Ti-U atomic force microscopy (AFM) also has been used to verify the 3D geometric morphology of the quasi-3D CPO, and the obtained AFM images are shown in Fig. 4c, d, where the 3D geometric morphology is well presented. The deposition thickness in every material deposition step is also detected by AFM, and the results meet well with that designed thickness.

The finite difference time domain (FDTD) method is used to achieve the theoretical simulation and analysis of the obtained quasi-3D CPO. The geometric model of a single CPO used in simulation is four achiral particles with side length $L_{1,2,3,4} = 36, 96, 150$, and 175 nm and thickness $k_{1,2,3,4} = 8, 25, 40$, and 55 nm, respectively. These achiral particles are accurately arranged in a concentric circle like that shown in the obtained SEM images (i.e., Fig. 4a, b for LHCPO and RHCPO). Figure 5a shows the calculated CD spectra, where a maximum CD signal of about 320 mdeg is found at 680 nm. This obvious CD signal indicates that the CPO interact differently with LCP and RCP. Due to the small

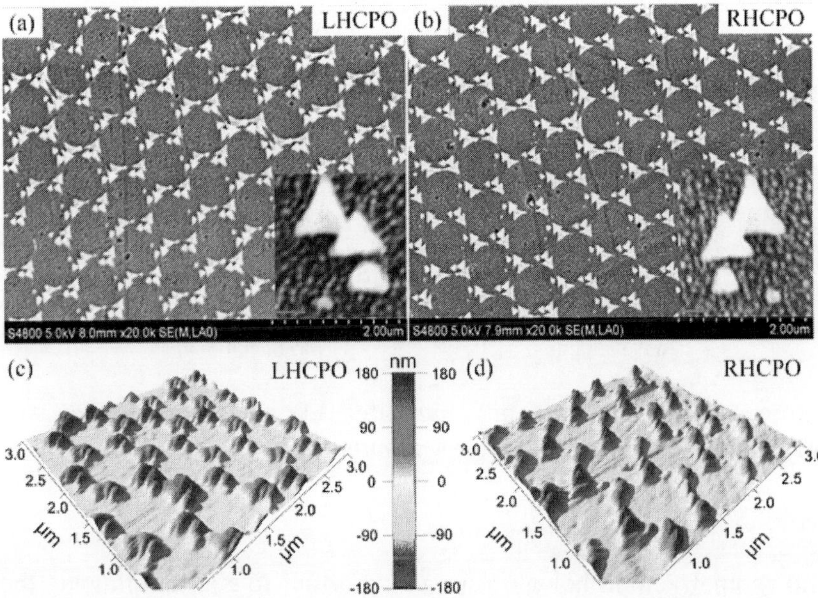

Figure 4. The measured SEM and AFM images of LHCPO and RHCPO with $\vartheta = 20°$, $k_{1,\ 2,\ 3,\ 4} = 8,\ 25,\ 40,$ and 55 nm, respectively, and $\Delta\Phi = \pm 60°$. **a**, **c** From LHCPO. **b**, **d** From RHCPO. The *insets* in **a** and **b** are the enlarged images of one CPO

duty ratio of CPO on the glass substrate, the transmittance coefficient for LCP and RCP is larger than 0.70 in the whole visible range. These calculated results meet well with the CD spectra measured from the Jasco J-810 circular dichroism spectroscopy system (as shown in Fig. 5b), where the maximum CD signal is ~180 mdeg at 640 nm. The differences between the simulated and measured results should be mainly attributed to the geometric morphology difference of CPO used in theoretical simulation and experiment process.

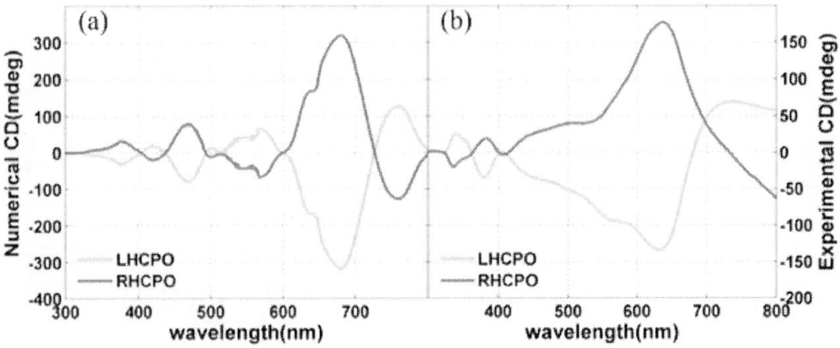

Figure 5. The simulated and measured CD spectra of LHCPO and RHCPO. **a** Calculated CD signal. **b** Measured CD

The geometric morphology plays an important role in determining the chiroptical effect. As discussed earlier, the chiroptical effect from 2D CPS usually is nonreciprocal, while the chiroptical effect from 3D CPS is reciprocal. This optical effect gives us a standard to determine the dimensionality of CPS. For the CPO obtained in this paper, it seems that they are a kind of 3D CPS from the point of view of geometric morphology. However, our in-depth theoretical and experimental researches reveal that the obtained CPO is indeed a kind of quasi-3D CPS, and their chiroptical effect is nonreciprocal, although they own a 3D geometrical morphology. Figure 6a, b shows the simulated CD spectra of LHCPO and RHCPO on the BK7 glass substrate when light incidents from the forward (blue curve) and backward (red curve) sides. The forward side is defined as the case that the BK7 glass substrate with the CPO side faces the light source, while the backward side is defined as the opposite case. These simulated results show that the CD signals from LHCPO and RHCPO own the same sign in the whole waveband from 300 nm to 800 nm, when light incidents from the forward and backward sides. These results meet well with the experiment, as shown in Fig. 6c, d. This 3D chiroptical effect indicates that the CPO together with BK7 glass substrate is a kind of 3D CPS.

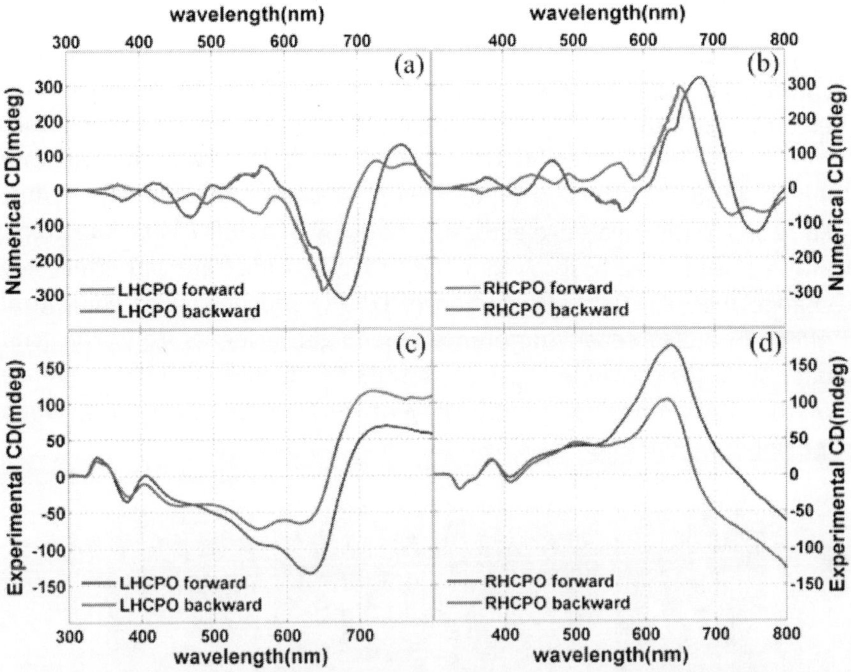

Figure 6. The simulated and experimental CD spectra. **a**, **b** Simulated CD spectra of LHCPO and RHCPO. **c**, **d** Measured CD spectra of LHCPO and RHCPO. The *blue* and *red curves* refer to the light incidence from the forward and backward sides of the samples

However, we note that the substrate also can affect the chiroptical effect from CPS. In fact, the excited surface plasmonic resonance in the air CPS and CPS substrate interfaces can destroy the mirror symmetry of 2D CPS and results in 3D chiroptical effect [37]. And this phenomenon happens again in this work. Figure 7e, f shows the simulated CD spectra of LHCPO and RHCPO without substrate when light incidents from the forward and backward sides. We can see that the CD signals almost own the opposite sign when light incidents from the opposite sides. This indicates that the chiroptical effect from CPO themselves is nonreciprocal, just like that from 2D CPS. And the 3D chiroptical effect shown in Fig. 6 should be attributed to the influence of the BK7 glass substrate, which adds another dimensionality for the quasi-3D CPO and results in reciprocal chiroptical effect. When comparing the simulated results in Fig. 6a, b with Fig. 7e, f, we find that the glass substrate also can suppress some plasmonic resonance modes and lead to a relatively smooth CD spectra shown in Fig. 6a, b. Figure 7a–d shows the surface electric distribution of LHCPO when LCP incidents from the backward side. Figure 7a, c is the electric distribution of LHCPO without substrate when incident lights are 650 and 705 nm, respectively. While Fig. 7b, d is the related electric distribution of LHCPO with substrate. These images clearly show that the BK7 glass substrate can effectively change the near-field distribution of LHCPO and finally the chiroptical effect. The CD intensity difference when light incidents from front and back sides (as shown in Fig. 7e, f) should be attributed to the influence of the 3D geometrical morphology of CPO, which is different when looking from the opposite sides.

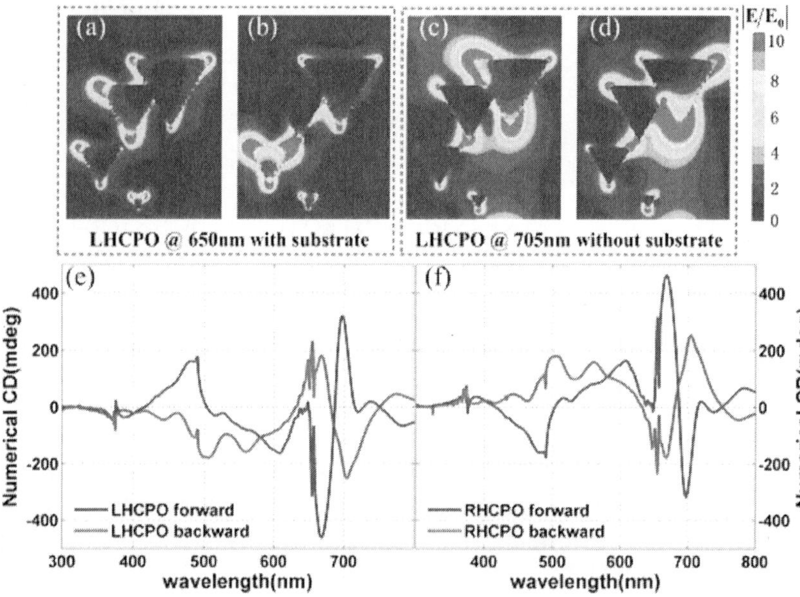

Figure 7. Images of the electric field distributions and simulated CD spectra of the CPO without substrate. **a–d** Electric field distribution at interface between CPO and BK7 glass substrate. **a, c** For LHCPO with substrate. **b, d** For LHCPO without substrate. The incident light is 650 nm for **a** and **b** and 705 nm for **c** and **d**. **e, f** Calculated CD spectra of LHCPO and RHCPO without substrate. The *blue* and *red curves* refer to the light incidence from the forward and backward sides

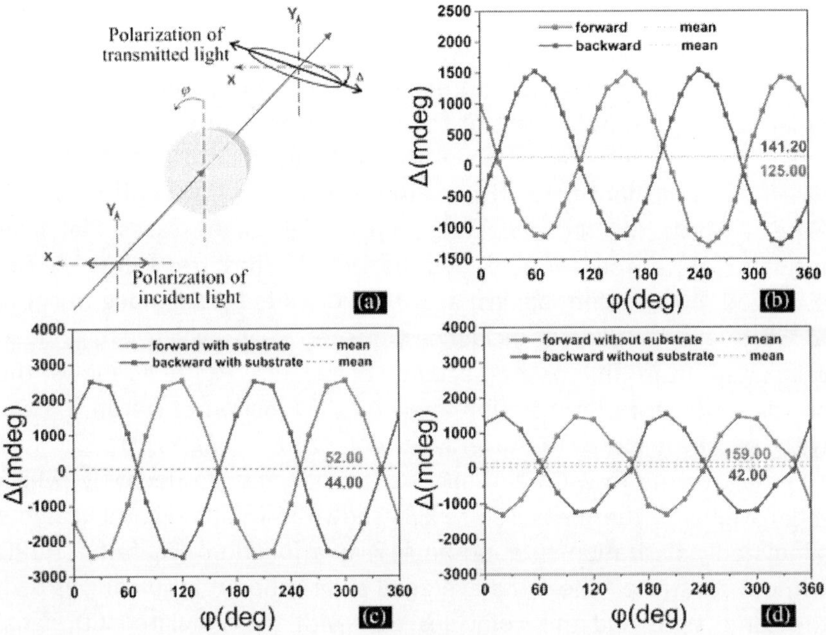

Figure 8. The experimental and simulated optical activity of LHCPO with wavelength of 632.8 nm. **a** Schematic illustration of the optical path used in the experiment. The angles φ and Δ refer to the incident polarization azimuthal angles of samples and polarization rotation angles, respectively. A He:Ne laser at 632.8 nm is used as a light source in the experiment, and the laser is replaced by a plane wave at 632.8 nm in simulations. **b** The measured polarization rotation angle Δ as a function of φ from LHCPO. **c**, **d** The simulated polarization rotation angle Δ as a function of φ from LHCPO with (**c**) and without substrate (**d**). The *blue* and *red colors* in **b**, **c**, and **d** refer to the light incidence from the backward and forward sides, while the *dashed lines* denote the averaged polarization rotation angles

The optical activity also has been investigated in this work. We note that the obtained CPO do not own a perfect in-plane rotational symmetry, and the polarization rotation of linear polarized light does not unambiguously determine the optical activity in the obtained CPO sample. Thus, the polarization analysis for linearly polarized incidence at a series of incident polarization azimuthal angles φ is performed to specify the linear birefringence and obtain the actual optical activity.

The measured diagram is shown in Fig. 8a, where a linear polarization light at 632.8 nm incidents normally to the sample surface, and the polarization rotation angle Δ of the transmitted light is defined as the longer axis of the polarization ellipse with respect to the polarization direction of incident light. The measured result for LHCPO is shown in Fig. 8b, where the red and blue curves refer to the cases that light incidents from the forward and backward sides, respectively. The averaged polarization angles are 125.00 and 141.20 mdeg for the forward and backward incidences, respectively, which are indeed originated from the optical activity of LHCPO. Figure 8c shows the simulated polarization rotation angle Δ as a function of φ from LHCPO with substrate, and the averaged polarization angles are 52 and 44 mdeg for the forward and backward incidences, respectively, which meet well with the measured results shown in Fig. 8b. Figure 8d is the simulated polarization rotation angle Δ as a function of φ from LHCPO without substrate, where the averaged polarization rotation angles own the same sign. And this coincides well with the simulated CD signal shown in Fig. 7e, f, indicating the effectiveness of our previous discussions.

CONCLUSIONS

In this paper, we have demonstrated that a kind of quasi-3D CPO can be easily achieved through the stepwise colloid sphere lithography technology. Through a four-step deposition process with proper fabrication parameters, the LHCPO and RHCPO are formed on a BK7 glass substrate with CD of ~180 mdeg and optical activity of ~140 mdeg. Due to the advantages of the fabrication method, the CPO with area of larger than 1 cm^2 can be easily achieved, and their chiroptical resonance also can be expediently tuned in the infrared and visible region through using proper micro-sphere array and deposition parameters, such as deposition time, angle, and thickness. The FDTD method also has been employed to investigate the chiroptical properties of CPO, and the simulated results meet well with that of the experiment. The in-depth theoretical and experimental researches reveal that the BK7 glass substrate plays an important role in the chiroptical effect of CPO. The substrate can restrain some plasmonic resonance modes and obviously break the mirror symmetry of CPO, leading to a 3D chiroptical effect in the experiment. The CPO with large area, tunable chiroptical spectra, and a low-cost fabrication method could find potential applications in many fields, such as stereochemical enantiomer sensors.

ACKNOWLEDGEMENTS

We would like to thank the National Natural Science Foundation of China, Grant No. 61377054.

COMPETING INTERESTS

The authors declare that they have no competing interests.

AUTHORS' CONTRIBUTIONS

SX produced the samples, carried out the test of CD spectra and optical activity, did digital simulations, and performed the statistical analysis. SX and YH drafted the manuscript. JY performed part of the simulations. FG and YH participated in the design of the study and made valuable proposals. XX, LP, and JD participated in the analysis and discussion. XL participated in the discussion for the revision. All authors read and approved the final manuscript.

REFERENCES

1. Thomson WH, Kelvin L (1904) Baltimore lectures on molecular dynamics and the wave theory of lightGoogle Scholar

2. Shieh J-Y, Kuo J-Y, Weng H-P, Yu HH (2013) Preparation and evaluation of the bioinspired PS/PDMS photochromic films by the self-assembly dip–drawing method. Langmuir 29(2):667–672

3. Cui Y, Kang L, Lan S, Rodrigues S, Cai W (2014) Giant chiral optical response from a twisted-arc metamaterial. Nano Lett 14(2):1021–1025

4. Hendry E, Carpy T, Johnston J, Popland M, Mikhaylovskiy R, Lapthorn A, Kelly S, Barron L, Gadegaard N, Kadodwala M (2010) Ultrasensitive detection and characterization of biomolecules using superchiral fields. Nat Nanotechnol 5(11):783–787

5. Tullius R, Karimullah AS, Rodier M, Fitzpatrick B, Gadegaard N, Barron LD, Rotello VM, Cooke G, Lapthorn A, Kadodwala M (2015) "Superchiral" spectroscopy: detection of protein higher order hierarchical structure with chiral plasmonic nanostructures. J Am Chem Soc 137(26):8380–8383

6. Pendry J (2004) A chiral route to negative refraction. Science 306(5700):1353–1355

7. Zhaofeng L, Mehmet M, Ekmel O (2013) Chiral metamaterials: from optical activity and negative refractive index to asymmetric transmission. J Opt 15(2):023001

8. Zhao R, Zhou J, Koschny T, Economou E, Soukoulis C (2009) Repulsive Casimir force in chiral metamaterials. Phys Rev Lett 103(10):103602

9. Wang H, Zhang X (2011) Unusual spin Hall effect of a light beam in chiral metamaterials. Phys Rev A 83(5):053820

10. Gao W, Tam WY (2011) Optical activities in complementary double layers of six-armed metallic gammadion structures. J Opt 13(1):015101

11. Helgert C, Pshenay-Severin E, Falkner M, Menzel C, Rockstuhl C, Kley E-B, Tuennermann A, Lederer F, Pertsch T (2011) Chiral metamaterial composed of three-dimensional plasmonic nanostructures. Nano Lett 11(10):4400–4404

12. Rogacheva AV, Fedotov VA, Schwanecke AS, Zheludev NI (2006) Giant gyrotropy due to electromagnetic-field coupling in a bilayered chiral structure. Phys Rev Lett 97(17):177401

13. Polevoy SY, Prosvirnin SL, Tarapov SI, Tuz VR (2013) Resonant features of planar Faraday metamaterial with high structural symmetry study of properties of a 4-fold array of planar chiral rosettes placed on a ferrite substrate. Eur Phys J Appl Phys 61(3):30501

14. Gansel JK, Thiel M, Rill MS, Decker M, Bade K, Saile V, von Freymann G, Linden S, Wegener M (2009) Gold helix photonic metamaterial as broadband circular polarizer. Science 325(5947):1513–1515

15. Ma X, Huang C, Pu M, Wang Y, Zhao Z, Wang C, Luo X (2012) Dual-band asymmetry chiral metamaterial based on planar spiral structure. Appl Phys Lett 101(16):161901

16. Xiaoliang M, Cheng H, Mingbo P, Wenbo P, Yangin W, Xiangang L (2013) Circular dichroism and optical rotation in twisted Y-shaped chiral metamaterial. Appl Phys Express 6(2):022001

17. Mutlu M, Ozbay E (2012) A transparent 90 degrees polarization rotator by combining chirality and electromagnetic wave tunneling. Appl Phys Lett 100(5):051909

18. Papakostas A, Potts A, Bagnall DM, Prosvirnin SL, Coles HJ, Zheludev NI (2003) Optical manifestations of planar chirality. Phys Rev Lett 90(10):107404

19. Esposito M, Tasco V, Cuscuna M, Todisco F, Benedetti A, Tarantini I, De Giorgi M, Sanvitto D, Passaseo A (2015) Nanoscale 3D chiral plasmonic helices with circular dichroism at visible frequencies. ACS Photonics 2(1):105–114

20. Esposito M, Tasco V, Todisco F, Cuscuna M, Benedetti A, Sanvitto D, Passaseo A (2015) Triple-helical nanowires by tomographic rotatory growth for chiral photonics. Nat Commun 6:6484

21. Fedotov V, Mladyonov P, Prosvirnin S, Rogacheva A, Chen Y, Zheludev N (2006) Asymmetric propagation of electromagnetic waves through a planar chiral structure. Phys Rev Lett 97(16):167401

22. Staude I, Decker M, Ventura MJ, Jagadish C, Neshev DN, Gu M, Kivshar YS (2013) Hybrid high-resolution three-dimensional nanofabrication for metamaterials and nanoplasmonics. Adv Mater 25(9):1260–1264

23. Radke A, Gissibl T, Klotzbuecher T, Braun PV, Giessen H (2011) Three-dimensional bichiral plasmonic crystals fabricated by direct laser writing and electroless silver plating. Adv Mater 23(27):3018–3021

24. Lan X, Chen Z, Dai G, Lu X, Ni W, Wang Q (2013) Bifacial DNA origami-directed discrete, three-dimensional, anisotropic plasmonic nanoarchitectures with tailored optical chirality. J Am Chem Soc 135(31):11441–11444

25. Shen X, Asenjo-Garcia A, Liu Q, Jiang Q, García de Abajo FJ, Liu N, Ding B (2013) Three-dimensional plasmonic chiral tetramers assembled by DNA origami. Nano Lett 13(5):2128–2133

26. Frank B, Yin X, Schäferling M, Zhao J, Hein SM, Braun PV, Giessen H (2013) Large-area 3D chiral plasmonic structures. ACS Nano 7(7):6321–6329

27. Mark AG, Gibbs JG, Lee TC, Fischer P (2013) Hybrid nanocolloids with programmed three-dimensional shape and material composition. Nat Mater 12(9):802–807

28. Yeom B, Zhang H, Zhang H, Park JI, Kim K, Govorov AO, Kotov NA (2013) Chiral plasmonic nanostructures on achiral nanopillars. Nano Lett 13(11):5277–5283

29. Hou Y, Li S, Su Y, Huang X, Liu Y, Huang L, Yu Y, Gao F, Zhang Z, Du J (2013) Design and fabrication of three-dimensional chiral nanostructures based on stepwise glancing angle deposition technology. Langmuir 29(3):867–872

30. Walther A, Mueller AHE (2013) Janus particles: synthesis, self-assembly, physical properties, and applications. Chem Rev 113(7):5194–5261

31. Pawar AB, Kretzschmar I (2010) Fabrication, assembly, and application of patchy particles. Macromol Rapid Commun 31(2):150–168

32. Larsen GK, He Y, Ingram W, Zhao Y (2013) Hidden chirality in superficially racemic patchy silver films. Nano Lett 13(12):6228–6232

33. Duyne CLHaRPV (2003) Dichroic optical properties of extended nanostructures fabricated using angle-resolved nanosphere lithography. Nano Lett 3(7):939–943

34. Zhang G, Wang D, Möhwald H (2007) Ordered binary arrays of Au nanoparticles derived from colloidal lithography. Nano Lett 7(1):127–132

35. Zhang G, Wang D, Möhwald H (2007) Fabrication of multiplex quasi-three-dimensional grids of one-dimensional nanostructures via stepwise colloidal lithography. Nano Lett 7(11):3410–3413

36. Su Y, Ye S, Hou Y, Shi S, Li S, Gao F, Du J (2014) Design and fabrication of diverse three-dimensional shell-like nanostructures. Microelectron Eng 115:6–12

37. Kuwata-Gonokami M, Saito N, Ino Y, Kauranen M, Jefimovs K, Vallius T, Turunen J, Svirko Y (2005) Giant optical activity in quasi-two-dimensional planar nanostructures. Phys Rev Lett 95(22):227401

Chapter 7

Synthesis and Properties of a Chiroptically Active Oligomer from 3,4-Ethylenedioxythiophene and (–)-Myrtenal

Hirotsugu Kawashima and Hiromasa Goto *

Institute of Materials Science, Graduate School of Pure and Applied Sciences, University of Tsukuba, Tsukuba, Ibaraki 305-8573, Japan

ABSTRACT

Oxidative polycondensation of 3,4-ethylenedioxythiophene and (–)-myrtenal was carried out with $POCl_3$. A π-conjugated system thus constructed consists of aromatic and quinoidal alternating structure linked via methine groups. We examined iodine doping effect for the resultant material with electron spin resonance spectroscopy. Circular dichroism spectra in chloroform solution showed blue-shift with increase of iodine concentration. This result indicates that the doping process can tune chiroptical activity of the chiral π-conjugated system.

Keywords: poly(3,4-ethylenedioxythiophene); chiroptically active materials; π-conjugated materials

1. INTRODUCTION

Many kinds of conjugated polymers have been widely studied for applications, such as transparent conductors, light-emitting diodes, thin film transistors, and photovoltaic devices [1,2,3,4,5,6,7,8,9]. Low-bandgap conjugated polymer is of interest because of its sensitivity in optical and electrical impulsions for external stimuli [10,11,12,13,14]. Poly(3,4-ethylenedioxythiophene) (PEDOT) and its derivatives are widely studied conjugated polymers due to their relatively low ionization potential, high electrical conductivity, and good stability [15,16,17,18,19,20]. A conjugated polymer which has benzenoid and quinonoid alternating structure in the main chain bridged via methine group (methine polymer) has been paid much attention because of the relatively small-bandgap [21,22,23,24,25,26,27]. Polycondensation between arylene unit and aldehyde group in the presence of sulfuric acid has been developed [28,29]. The polymerization is shown in Scheme 1. We synthesized a methine oligomer (abbreviated as ME1) from EDOT and (−)-myrtenal, a chiral compound (Scheme 2). Chiroptical activity and doping effect for the resultant thus prepared is examined based on consideration of high sensitivity derived from low-bandgap.

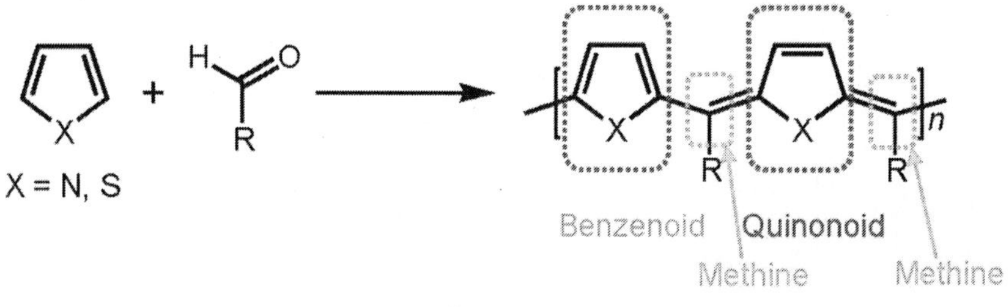

Scheme 1. Dehydrative polycondensation for methine type polymer.

2. EXPERIMENTAL SECTION

Polycondensation between aldehydes and thiophenes provides Novolac-type polymers [30]. In this reaction, the protonated aldehyde electrophile can sequentially react with active site (α,α'-position) of thiophene. Chen and Jenekhe proved following elimination of protons at methine linkages by sulfuric acid for producing full π-conjugated skeleton [29].

Polycondensation of pyrrole and 1-dodecanal was carried out for obtaining polypyrrole-methine type π-conjugated polymers [31]. The Rothemund type reaction for synthesis of porphyrine can be applied for polycondensation between EDOT and chiral aldehydes for construction of π-conjugated main chain [32,33]. In this case, bulky group in the substituents can prevent a formation of cyclic compounds.

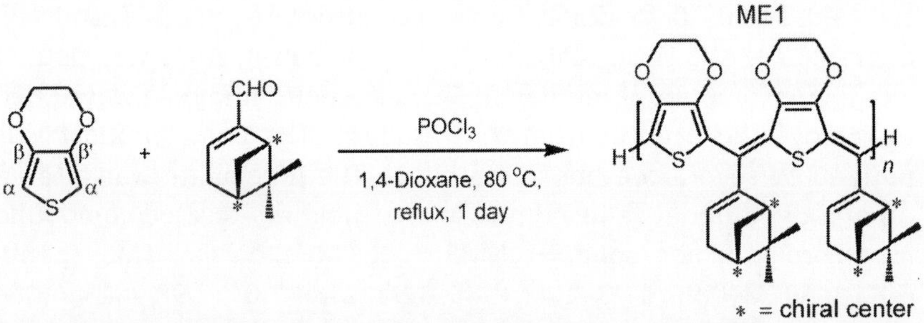

Scheme 2. Synthesis of methine bridged oligomer as a main product from 3,4-ethylenedioxythiophene (EDOT) and (–)-myrtenal.

Chemicals were purchased from Tokyo Kasei and Aldrich and used as received. ^{1}H NMR measurements of (–)-myrtenal and ME1 were performed in $CDCl_3$ with ECS 400 spectrometer (JEOL) at room temperature. Chemical shifts are reported in ppm downfield from $SiMe_4$, using the solvent's residual signal as an internal reference. Fourier transfer infrared (FTIR) absorption spectra of ME1 and (–)-myrtenal were obtained by FT/IR-300 spectrometer (Jasco), with the KBr method. Molecular weights of ME1 were determined by gel permeation chromatography (GPC) with MIXED-D HPLC column (Polymer Laboratories), PU-980 HPLC pump (Jasco) and MD-915 multiwavelength detector (Jasco), with THF used as the solvent, with the instruments calibrated by polystyrene standard. UV-visible absorption spectra were recorded on V-630 UV-vis optical absorption spectrometer (Jasco). Circular dichroism (CD) spectra were obtained with J-720 spectrometer (Jasco). Electron spin resonance (ESR) spectra were taken at room temperature using JES-TE200 ESR spectrometer (JEOL) during *in-situ* vapor phase doping process with iodine.

The target material was synthesized by dehydrative polycondensation between EDOT and (−)-myrtenal with $POCl_3$. The reaction was carried out in a Schlenk tube.

A solution of EDOT (0.50 g, 3.5 mmol), (−)-myrtenal (0.54 g, 3.6 mmol), and $POCl_3$ (0.061 g, 0.40 mmol) in 1,4-dioxane (5 mL) was refluxed at 80 °C for 25 h (molecular structure of EDOT and (−)-myrtenal are shown in Scheme 2). The reaction mixture was poured into a large amount of methanol. Then, aqueous ammonia was added to remove the catalyst from the resultant. The crude product was purified by several washes in methanol. The precipitate was filtered off and dried under reduced pressure to yield the desired compound as a brown color solid. ^{1}H NMR (400 MHz, δ from TMS (ppm), $CDCl_3$): δ0.73–0.96, 1.23–1.42, 1.85–1.97, 2.17–2.64, 2.98, 4.13, 6.06–6.39, 6.73. GPC measurement evaluated that the number average molecular weight (M_n) is 900, the weight average molecular weight (M_w) is 1600, polydispersity (M_w/M_n) is 1.72. This result indicates that the resultant is an oligomer with molecular weight dispersion (Figure 1). Employment of EDOT as an arylene unit can be expected to avoid side reaction at β and β′ positions in the oxidative polycondensation because these parts are protected by the ethylenedioxy group.

3. RESULTS AND DISCUSSION

IR absorption spectra of (−)-myrtenal and ME1 are examined, as shown in Figure 2. An absorption band of C–H stretching vibration of the aldehyde group of (−)-myrtenal is observed at around 1700 cm^{-1}. On the other hand, IR absorption spectrum of ME1 shows no signals at around 1700 cm^{-1}. The absence of the aldehyde signal in the IR absorption spectrum of ME1 indicates completion of the polycondensation reaction [34,35]. Characteristic absorption bands at 1089 cm^{-1} and 1360–1490 cm^{-1} of ME1 are attributable to C–O–C

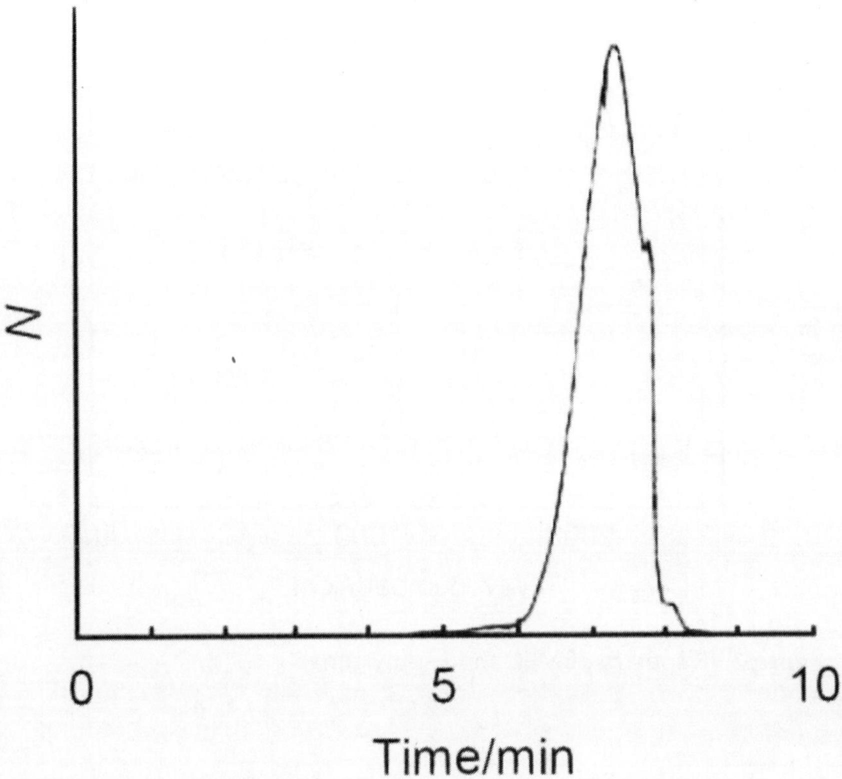

Figure 1. GPC curve of ME1.

asymmetric stretching vibration and C=C stretching vibration of EDOT, respectively. ^{1}H NMR measurements of ME1 and (–)-myrtenal were also performed for verification of completion of the reaction. NMR signals of ME1 were totally broadened. Typical signal at 9–10 ppm attributed to aldehyde group disappears after the reaction. This can be due to the fact that the polycondensation between the aldehyde group and arylene units was successfully carried out. The characteristic signals of EDOT (4.16 ppm, –O–CH_2–CH_2–O–) and (–)-myrtenal (0.7–2.9 ppm, each alkyl group) were observed in ME1 spectrum except aldehyde signal [36]. This result agrees with the IR measurements.

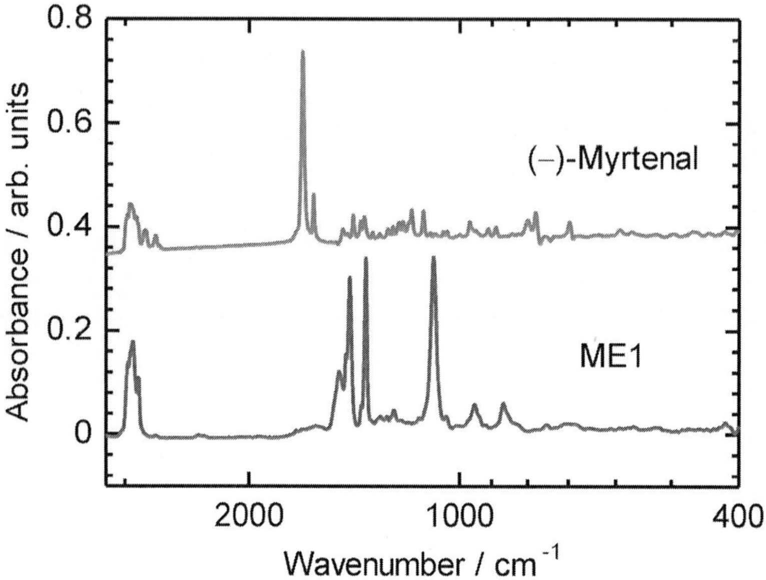

Figure 2. IR spectra of ME1 and (–)-myrtenal.

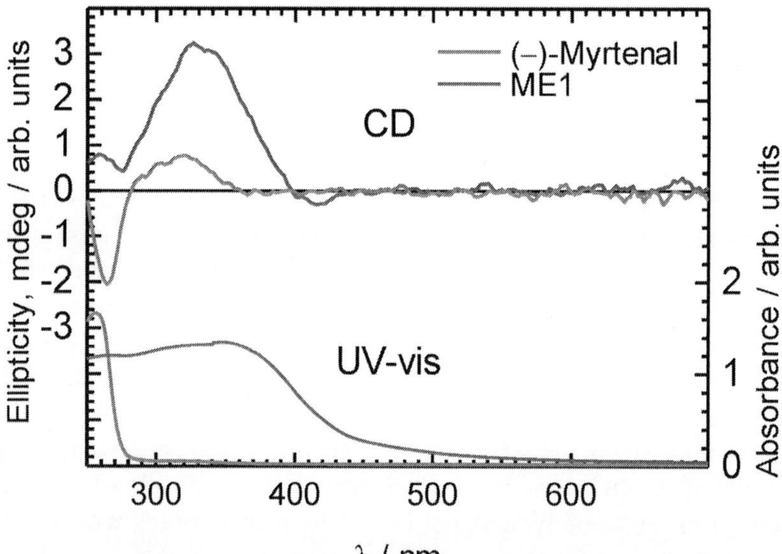

Figure 3. CD spectra of ME1 and (–)-myrtenal in $CHCl_3$ solution.

UV-vis absorption measurements of (−)-myrtenal and ME1 in $CHCl_3$ were examined (Figure 3). A broad absorption band of ME1 indicates that the π-conjugation length of the backbone is developed. An optical bandgap of ME1 calculated from the absorption spectrum is to be 2.8 eV. Therefore, ME1 is considered to be a semiconducting organic material. Although the previously reported methine type polymers exhibited extended π-conjugation and low-bandgap because of benzenoid and quinonoid alternating structure in the main chain, the bandgap value in the present study is relatively large [28,37]. This is mainly because of the low degree of the polycondensation. Besides, bulky (−)-myrtenal moieties in the side chain might decrease the coplanarity of the main chain.

CD absorption spectra of ME1 and (−)-myrtenal were obtained in $CHCl_3$ solution, as shown in Figure 3. Both spectra show clear CD curves. Broad CD signal of ME1 indicates that the backbone of ME1 individually shows chiroptical activity. After the polycondensation, chiroptical activity of the side chain remains and it induces chiroptical activity for the entire system. Such oxidative polycondensation can be simple and convenient method to introduce chiroptical activity for conjugated materials. We examined a doping effect of iodine (electron acceptor) for ME1 with UV-vis optical absorption, CD, and ESR. Figure 4 shows CD and UV-vis absorption spectra of ME1 in $CHCl_3$ with various iodine doping levels in solution. As for UV-vis spectra, clear changes in UV-vis absorption spectrum of ME1 were observed upon progress of the doping. New absorption peaks at 295 nm and 355 nm appeared with progress of the iodine doping. These two peaks indicate an occurrence of oxidation of ME1 by the doping. Furthermore, broad absorption band at 600–800 nm appeared gradually. This suggests generation of radical cations (charge species, polarons) for ME1 [38]. CD spectra of ME1 by the iodine doping show blue shift at short wavelengths and decrease of the intensities by the iodine doping. The blue shift implies that the short helical form induced by the chiral substituent is released by the doping. Color change of ME1 in solution with various iodine doping levels is shown in Figure 5. Original color of iodine in a solution is purple. However, addition of iodine leads changes in color for the material from orange to dark green. This result suggests that the iodine doping tunes the color and chiroptical activity of ME1. Commission Internationale de l'Eclairage (International Commission on Illumination, CIE) color space confirms the color in the solution, as shown in Figure 6.

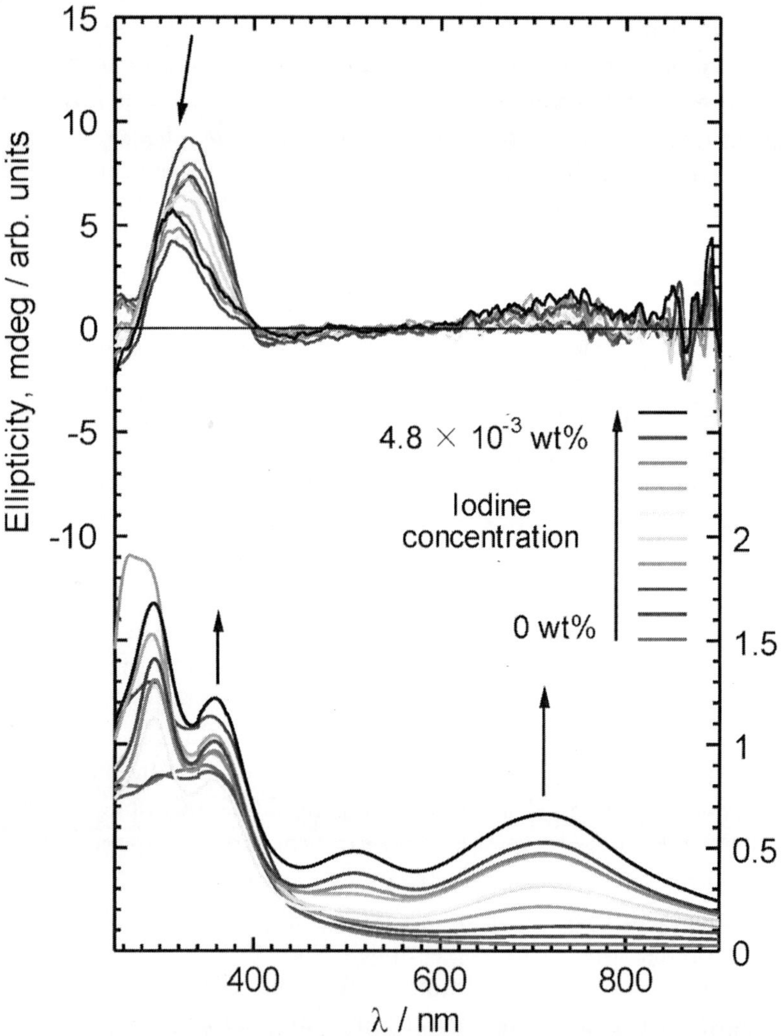

Figure 4. CD and UV-vis absorption spectra of ME1 in $CHCl_3$ with various iodine doping levels.

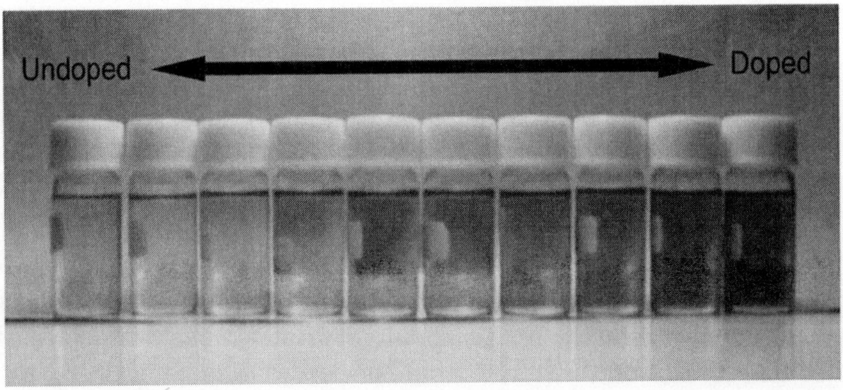

Figure 5. Color change of ME1 in $CHCl_3$ solution from orange to green with iodine doping.

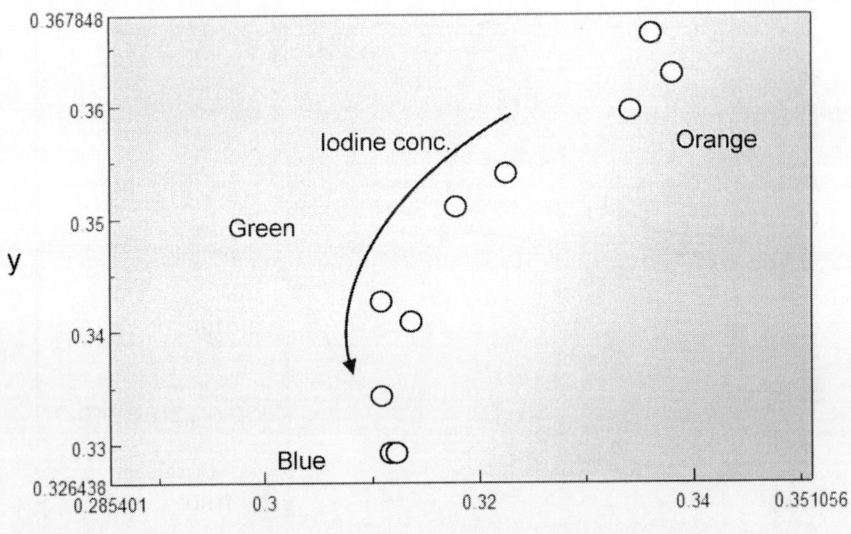

Figure 6. Change in CIE color space coordination diagram of ME1 with iodine doping.

In-situ ESR spectra of ME1 with vapor phase iodine doping were measured (Figure 7). As prepared oligomer shows weak ESR signal, indicating incomplete dedoping of $POCl_3$ with aqueous ammonia treatment, or doping with oxygen in the air. The spin concentration increased rapidly upon the doping. This indicates a generation of radical cations along the main chain. Figure 8 shows *g*-value, intensity, and peak width (ΔH_{pp}) plots *vs*. the doping time. The peak width and *g*-value are constant upon the doping. However, the intensity is increased by the doping, indicating that the doping is effectively carried out and charge species are generated along the main chain [39].

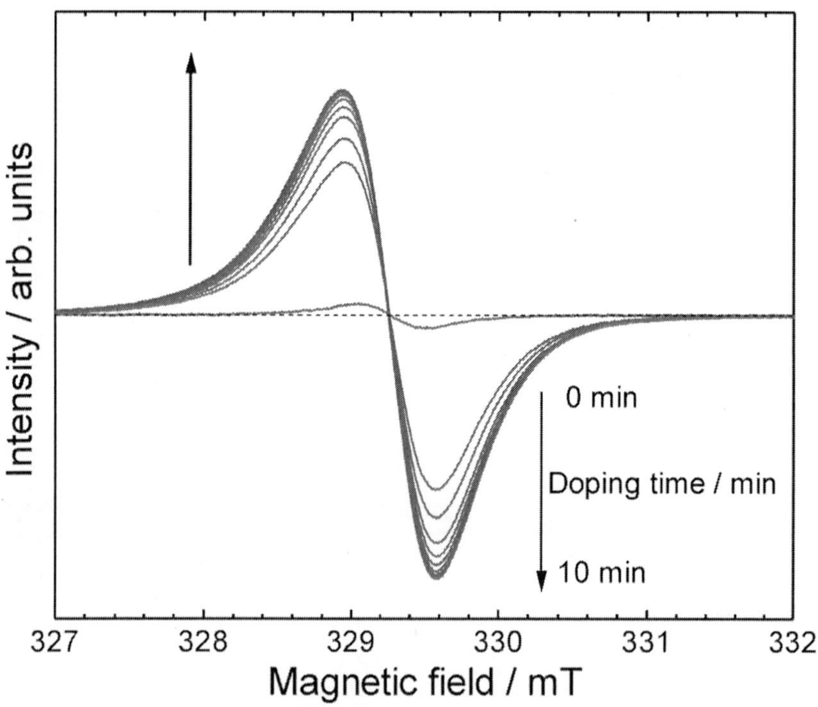

Figure 7. *In-situ* ESR spectra during vapor phase iodine doping.

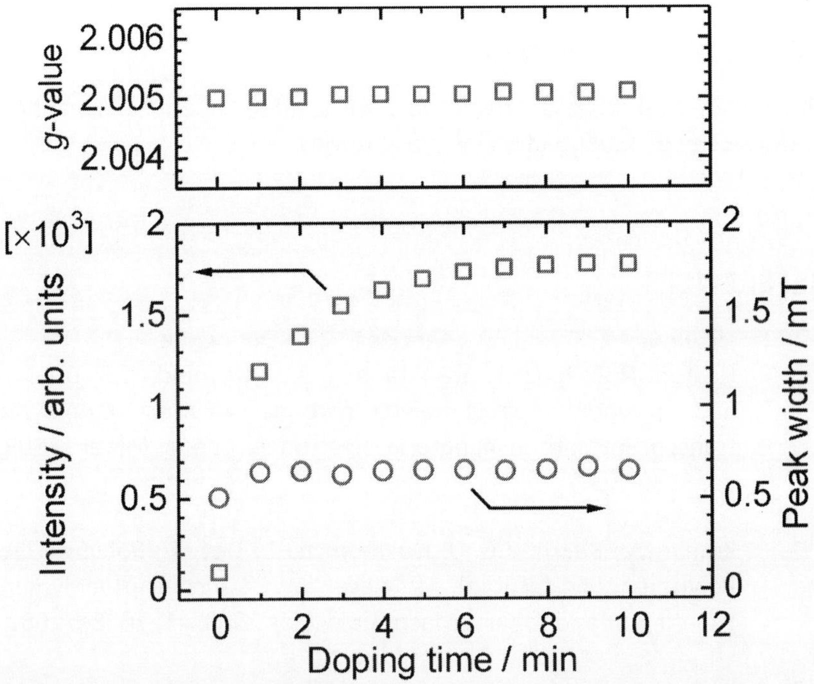

Figure 8. *g*-value, intensity, and peak width (ΔH_{pp}) of ME1 with vapor phase iodine doping for 0–10 min.

4. CONCLUSIONS

A new methine π-conjugated oligomer was synthesized from EDOT and (–)-myrtenal. This shows a broad absorption band and a CD signal in the long wavelengths. The chiral side chain induces helical conformation of the main chain to exhibit chiroptical activity. Iodine doping for the oligomer was examined, and the doped state was monitored with the UV-vis optical absorption, the CD, and the ESR spectroscopy. The UV-vis absorption and the ESR measurements confirm the formation of radical cations. CD spectra of the oligomer show blue shift of the CD signal during the doping. This suggests that the change in electronic structure upon doping tunes its chiroptical activity.

ACKNOWLEDGEMENTS

The author would like to thank Glass work shop of Central Workshop of University of Tsukuba for fine glass works.

REFERENCES

1. Nikolou, M.; Dyer, A.L.; Steckler, T.T.; Donoghue, E.P.; Wu, Z.; Heston, N.C.; Rinzler, A.G.; Tanner, D.B.; Reynolds, J.R. Dual n- and p-type dopable electrochromic devices employing transparent carbon nanotube electrodes. Chem. Mater. 2009, 21, 5539–5547.

2. Kumar, A.; Bokria, J.G.; Buyukmumcu, Z.; Dey, T.; Sotzing, G.A. Poly(thieno[3,4-b]furan), a new low band gap polymer: Experiment and theory. Macromolecules 2008, 41, 7098–7108.

3. Zerza, G.; Röthler, B.; Sariciftci, N.S.; Gómez, R.; Segura, J.L.; Martín, N. Photophysical properties and optoelectronic device applications of a novel naphthalene-vinylene type conjugated polymer. J. Phys. Chem. B 2001, 105, 4099–4104.

4. Pei, J.; Yu, W.-L.; Huang, W.; Heeger, A.J. A novel series of efficient thiophene-based light-emitting conjugated polymers and application in polymer light-emitting diodes. Macromolecules 2000, 33, 2462–2471.

5. Rathnayake, H.P.; Cirpan, A.; Lahti, P.M.; Karasz, F.E. Optimizing LED Properties of 2,7-Bis(phenylethenyl)fluorenes.Chem. Mater. 2006, 18, 560–566.

6. Crouch, D.J.; Skabara, P.J.; Lohr, J.E.; McDouall, J.J.W.; Heeney, M.; McCulloch, I.; Sparrowe, D.; Shkunov, M.; Coles, S.J.; Horton, P.N.; Hursthouse, M.B. Thiophene and selenophene copolymers incorporating fluorinated phenylene units in the main chain: Synthesis, characterization, and application in organic field-effect transistors. Chem. Mater.2005, 17, 6567–6578.

7. Tang, M.L.; Reichardt, A.D.; Wei, P.; Bao, Z. Correlating carrier type with frontier molecular orbital energy levels in organic thin film transistors of functionalized acene derivatives. J. Am. Chem. Soc. 2009, 131, 5264–5273.

8. Yang, M.; Peng, B.; Liu, B.; Zou, Y.; Zhou, K.; He, Y.; Pan, C.; Li, Y. Synthesis and photovoltaic properties of copolymers from Benzodithiophene and Thiazole. J. Phys. Chem. C 2010, 114, 17989–17994.

9. Kim, J.Y.; Qin, Y.; Stevens, D.M.; Kalihari, V.; Hillmyer, M.A.; Frisbie, C.D. High open-circuit voltage photovoltaic cells with a low bandgap copolymer of Isothianaphthene, Thiophene, and Benzothiadiazole units. J. Phys. Chem. C2009, 113, 21928–21936.

10. Zhen, F.Z.; Eshbaugh, A.A.; Schanze, K.S. Low-bandgap donor-acceptor conjugated polymer sensitizers for dye-sensitized solar cells. J. Am. Chem. Soc. 2011, 133, 3063–3069.

11. Hou, J.; Park, M.-H.; Zhang, S.; Yao, Y.; Chen, L.-M.; Li, J.-H.; Yang, Y. Bandgap and molecular energy level control of conjugated polymer photovoltaic materials based on Benzo[1,2-b:4,5-b′] dithiophene. Macromolecules 2008, 41, 6012–6018.

12. Huang, X.; Shi, Q.; Chen, W.-Q.; Zhu, C.; Zhou, W.; Zhao, Z.; Duan, X.-M.; Zhan, X. Low-bandgap conjugated donor-acceptor copolymers based on porphyrin with strong two-photon absorption. Macromolecules 2010, 43, 9620–9626.

13. Zou, Y.; Gendron, D.; Neagu-Plesu, R.; Leclerc, M. Synthesis and characterization of new low-bandgap diketopyrrolopyrrole-based copolymers. Macromolecules 2009, 42, 6361–6365.

14. Kiebooms, R.H.L.; Adriaensens, P.J.A.; Vanderzande, D.J.M.; Gelan, J.M.J.V. Grignard reactions on Ortho DicarboxylicArene derivatives. Synthesis of 1,3-Dithienylisothianaphthene compounds. J. Org. Chem. 1997, 62, 1473–1480.

15. Groenendaal, L.B.; Jonas, F.; Freitag, D.; Pielartzik, H.; Reynolds, J.R. Poly(3,4-ethylenedioxythiophene) and its derivatives: Past, present, and future. Adv. Mater. 2000, 12, 481–494.

16. Roncali, J.; Blanchard, P.; Frère, P. 3,4-Ethylenedioxythiophene (EDOT) as a versatile building block for advanced functional π-conjugated systems. J. Mater. Chem. 2005, 15, 1589–1610.

17. Segura, J.L.; Gómez, R.; Blanco, R.; Reinold, E.; Bäuerle, P. Synthesis and electronic properties of Anthraquinone-, Tetracyanoanthraquinodimethane-, and Perylenetetracarboxylic Diimide-functionalized Poly(3,4-ethylenedioxythiophenes). Chem. Mater. 2006, 18, 2834–2847.

18. Han, D.-H.; Kim, J.-W.; Park, S.-M. Electrochemistry of conductive polymers 38. Electrodeposited poly(3,4-ethylenedioxy-thiophene) studied by current sensing atomic force microscopy. J. Phys. Chem. B 2006, 110, 14874–14880.

19. Chahma, M.; Myles, D.J.T.; Hicks, R.G. Synthesis and electropolymerization behavior of bis (Oligothienyl) sulfides. Generation of heteroaromatic Poly(p-phenylene sulfide) analogs. Chem. Mater. 2005, 17, 2672–2678.

20. Pai, C.-L.; Liu, C.-L.; Chen, W.-C.; Jenekhe, S.A. Electronic structure and properties of alternating donor-acceptor conjugated copolymers: 3,4-Ethylenedioxythiophene (EDOT) copolymers and model compounds. Polymer 2006, 47, 699–708.

21. Jenekhe, S.A. Synthesis and characterization of carbon atom bridged heterocyclic polymers of specified conjugation length. 1. Novel polyterthiophenes. Macromolecules 1990, 23, 2848–2854.

22. Chen, W.-C.; Liu, C.-L.; Yen, C.-T.; Tsai, F.-C.; Tonzola, C.J.; Olson, N.; Jenekhe, S.A. Theoretical and experimental characterization of small band gap poly(3,4-ethylenedioxythiophene methine)s. Macromolecules 2004, 37, 5959–5964.

23. Chen, W.-C.; Jenekhe, S.A. New polyaniline derivatives: Poly(4,4'-diphenylamine methylenes) and Poly(4,4'-

diphenylimine methines). Macromolecules 1992, 25, 5919–5926.

24. Tsukamoto, N.; Ha, J.; Sato, H.; Strzelec, K. Chemical doping of Triphenylaminebenzaldehyde polymers. Int. J. Polym. Mater. 2004, 53, 799–807.

25. Toussaint, J.M.; Brédas, J.L. Theoretical analysis of the geometric and electronic structure of small-band-gap polythiophenes: Poly(5,5'-bithiophene methine) and its derivatives. Macromolecules 1993, 26, 5240–5248.

26. Stagnaro, P.; Pioli, F.; Panizza, M.; Gandini, A. Acid-catalyzed polycondensation of 2-acetoxymethyl-3,4-dimethylthiophene. Access to a novel poly(thienylenemethine) with alternating aromatic- and quinoid-like structures. Macromolecules 2009, 42, 2455–2461.

27. Kiebooms, R.; Wudl, F. Synthesis and characterisation of poly(isothianaphthenemethine). Synth. Met. 1999, 101, 40–43.

28. Chen, W.C.; Jenekhe, S.A. Small bandgap conducting polymers based on conjugated poly(heteroarylene methine). 1 Precursor poly(heteroarylene methylenes). Macromolecules 1995, 28, 454–464.

29. Chen, W.C.; Jenekhe, S.A. Small bandgap conducting polymers based on conjugated poly(heteroarylene methines). 2. Synthesis, structure, and properties. Macromolecules 1995, 28, 465–480.

30. Caesar, P.D.; Sachanen, A.N. Thiophene-formaldehyde condensation. Ind. Eng. Chem. 1948, 40, 922–928.

31. Aota, H.; Itai, Y.; Matsumoto, A.; Kamachi, M. Synthesis of π-conjugated polymer containing porphyrins. Chem. Lett.1994, 1994, 2043–2046.

32. Rothemund, P. Formation of porphyrines from pyrrole and aldehydes. J. Am. Chem. Soc. 1935, 57, 2010–2011.

33. Rothemund, P. A new porphyrin synthesis. The synthesis of porphin. J. Am. Chem. Soc. 1936, 58, 625–627.

34. Goto, H.; Akagi, K. Synthesis of a pyrrole-based methine bridge type liquid-crystalline conjugated polymer. J. Polym. Sci. A Polym. Chem. 2005, 43, 616–629.

35. Meng, L.-J.; Wu, H.-C.; Gao, C.; Yi, W.-H. Synthesis and characterization of a kind of poly(3-butylthiophene methine) with Azo side groups. J. Appl. Polym. Sci. 2005, 97, 1261–1265.

36. Multiplet signals at 6.0–6.5 ppm of ME1 were observed in the 1H NMR measurement. Although side reactions at the side chain might occur during the polycondensation process, the signals can be related with molecular weight dispersity.

37. Zaman, M.B.; Perepichka, D.F. A new simple synthesis of poly(thiophene-methine)s. Chem. Commun. 2005, 33, 4187–4189.

38. Neugebauer, H.; Kvarnström, C.; Brabec, C.; Sariciftci, N.S.; Kiebooms, R.; Wudl, F.; Luzzati, S. Infrared spectroelectrochemical investigations on the doping of soluble Polyisothianaphthene Methine (PIM). J. Chem. Phys.1999, 110, 12108–12115.

39. Patil, A.O.; Heeger, A.J.; Wudl, F. Optical properties of conducting polymers. Chem. Rev. 1988, 88, 183–200.

Chapter 8

Raman Optical Activity and Raman Spectra of Amphetamine Species—Quantum Chemical Model Calculations and Experiments

Rolf Willestofte Berg[1*], Irene Shim[1], Peter Cyril White[2], Salim Abdali[3]

[1]*Department of Chemistry, Technical University of Denmark, Lyngby, Denmark*

[2]*ReForensics, Lincoln, UK*

[3]*Biophysical Chemistry Group, Department of Chemistry, H.C. Ørsted Inst., University of Copenhagen, DK Copenhagen, Denmark*

ABSTRACT

Theoretical calculations and preliminary measurements of vibrational Raman optical activity (ROA) spectra of different species of amphetamine (amphetamine and amphetamine-H^+) are reported for the first time. The quantum chemical calculations were carried out as hybrid ab initio DFT-molecular orbital calculations by use of the Gaussian 03W program, based on complete geometry minimizations of the conformational energy of the S-(+)-amphetamine molecule, the S-(+)-amphetamine-H^+ion, and the R-(–)-amphetamine molecule. Following this, harmonic frequency calculations have been made, providing information about the cation vibrational bands, expected in salts of single anions (chlorides) as well as in salts of anions with internal bonds (sulfates, hydrogen phosphates, etc.). It shows that the kind of anion should be given better attention, as so far it has often not been the case, when the spectra are employed for identification purposes. The DFT calculations show that the most stable conformations are those allowing for close contact between the aromatic ring and the amine hydrogen atoms. The internal rotational barrier within the same amphetamine enantiomer has a considerable influence on the Raman and ROA spectra. As predicted the experimental ROA spectra were found to depend on the chirality. Two street samples, provided by the London Police, were also measured and compared to the calculated ROA spectra. The street samples were found to contain different enantiomers of the protonated amphetamine-H^+ sulfate. According to the present study the $AMPH^+$ ion in aqueous sulfate solution seems to adopt a conformation in which the phenyl and ammonium groups are in transpositions, similar to what has been found in the solid state.

Keywords: Amphetamine; Raman; ROA; DFT; Molecular Orbital; Drugs; Forensic

1. INTRODUCTION

Theoretical calculations and preliminary measurements of vibrational Raman optical activity (ROA) spectra of different species of amphetamine (amphetamine and amphetamine-H^+) are reported for the first time. Amphetamine (AMP) is a chiral compound, DL-amphetamine, with CAS no. [300-62-9] and a melting point of about 138°C - 146°C. The stereochemistry is such that the molecule can be found with two enantiomeric forms: a) the R-amphetamine (CAS reg. no. [156-34-3]), which also can be found named R-(-)-amphetamine, L-AMP or levo-AMP, and b) the S-amphetamine (CAS reg. no. [51- 64-9]), which also can be named S-(+)-amphetamine, D-AMP or dextro-AMP. The two enantiomeric forms differ from each other by the three-dimensional geometry around the asymmetric C* atom (C8), as expressed in the formula C_6H_5-CH_2-C*H(CH_3)NH_2. Consequently, difference in their biological functions can also be found, e.g. the S-(+)-isomer exhibits higher cardiovascular effect, but, greater pharmacologic potency than the corresponding R-(–)-isomer, perhaps up to 10 times [1-6]. This is why it is important that determination of AMP species should be carried out by methods that are capable of providing information on the enantiomeric purity and chirality. However, the amphetamine molecule has not, according to our knowledge, been chirally examined, except by electronic circular dichroism (CD), which showed that the AMP-CD signal was too weak to be conclusive [7]. Therefore, the following study can be considered as the first of its kind on the AMP molecules.

The interest in AMP is due to its effect on the nervous system, but mostly for its worldwide illegal abuse. It is one of the most common drugs for misuse found in the illegal market, and with various qualities due to the uncontrolled purity; a feature which unfortunately has been associated with mortal consequences. Identification of the provenience of a drug is of considerable interest from a forensic point of view and for legal matters. The purity and quality vary due to the illegality and lack of control of the market [8]. Medicaments on the market may in particular contain mixtures of S-(+)-isomer and R-(−)-isomeric forms—in varying amounts of one species with respect to the other—a matter that could influence the activity of the sample when used. Determination of the ratio of one enantiomer to the other, or the content of impurities in a sample has been a subject for different biophysical methods. However, we have earlier shown that confusions in determination of these molecules and in describing them were surprisingly more common than expected [9]. In that work, we showed that by using Raman and surface enhanced Raman spectroscopy (SERS) combined with quantum chemical DFT calculations, it was possible to demonstrate the differences between what people almost agreed on to be AMP and what really has been measured. The confusion among previously reported results occurred mainly in the differentiation between amphetamine itself and the protonated chloride or sulfate salts, formed because amphetamine is a weak base (pK_a is ~9.8) and thus has the ability to become protonated and occur as salts. The need for identifying this drug and its related species has been sought for long time, in that the available methods are either not very accurate, e.g. due to limited selectivity (as it is the case for colorimetric tools), or they are time consuming, costly and/or require high concentrations of the sample (like in the case of chromatographic, NMR and X-ray methods).

Our attempt here is to use Raman and Raman optical activity (ROA) measurements, combined with quantum chemical calculations in order to achieve a thorough vibrational optical activity determination. This determination method was used to compare the results on two street samples, which the London Police office has provided. According to our knowledge, calculated and measured ROA spectra of AMP or protonated AMP have never been reported. This fact could be explained by the lack of sensitive and reliable ROA instruments, becoming commercially available only recently [10-12]. The attempt here to fill the gap is therefore of importance, especially also with respect to impurities associated with chirality. In the following, two species will be subject of the ROA study: AMP and $AMPH^{+}$, which intentionally were chosen because, as mentioned above, they are found in most cases commonly referred to as AMP.

Today, Raman spectroscopy is a well-established tool for determination of structural changes of molecules regardless whether these molecules are found in gas, liquid or solid state, and it has been proven powerful for molecular studies, too. On the other hand, ROA, until a decade ago has suffered from the lack of commercial instrumentation, a matter that limited this tool to few research laboratories [13]. Nevertheless, ROA has been shown capable of providing rich information, especially about molecular structures, e.g. backbone, secondary and even tertiary structures [14-18]. In ROA, circularly polarized light is utilized, and chiroptical information about the examined molecule can be obtained. The detected signal is simply the intensity difference of right and left circularly polarized light. This may involve either measurement set-ups utilizing only incident circularly polarized (ICP) light, or only scattered circularly polarized (SCP) light, or the difference in both circularly polarized light of the incident and the scattered intensity, referred to as being dual circularly polarized (DCP). In our measurements we used the SCP setup. The theory of ROA has already been fully established, a few years after the phenomenon was reported [18], but a quantum-chemical calculation was first realized almost 20 years later [19], and the method became even more reliable once the development of the method for calculating frequency dependent polarizabilities [20] was found. Although ROA quantum-chemical calculations are still representing a challenge, the absolute configurations of CHFClBr [21, 22] and deuterated neopentane have already been achieved [23].

Experimentally, it has been demonstrated by e. g. Barron's group at Glasgow University, that ROA spectra could be measured for many kinds of molecules of life, e.g. proteins, carbohydrates, nucleic acids and viruses. Most importantly, ROA can be obtained from aqueous solutions, i.e. mimicking the biological environment of the samples [24-27]. However, due to the nature of ROA, its signal is 3-5 orders of magnitude weaker than the conventional Raman signal, and thus, it usually requires high concentrations, e.g. above mM concentrations, and long acquisition times, e.g. several hours to obtain ROA spectra without noise. It is worth mentioning here that the rapid development of combining ROA with SERS into SEROA, both experimentally [28-31] and theoretically [32-34] so that it could soon make this tool attractive even for industrial applications.

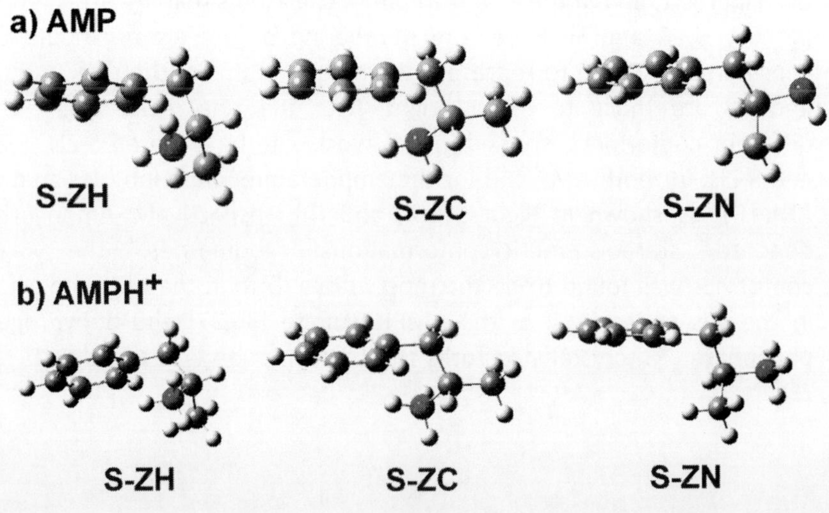

Figure 1. Calculated structures of lowest energy of a) AMP and b) $AMPH^+$ for S-ZH, S-ZC and S-ZN conformations in the gas phase. The Z-letter in this notation represents the general skeleton shape of the molecule, seen from the viewer side. C1-C6 are the atoms of the ring, and C7, C8 and C9 are those seen to the right. C7 is attached to the ring through C1, N is attached to C8 and C9 is that of the methyl group. The planar Z-letter therefore is made from the atoms C1-C7-C8 and the final atom, respectrively H or C9 or N bound to C8. As an example in S-ZC the final atom is C9.

NOMENCLATURE

We have earlier found the Raman spectra of AMP, obtained by quantum chemical calculations or experimentally to be sensitive to the internal rotational degree of freedom around the C7-C8 bond [9]. The rotational geometry can influence the structure of the molecule, so that changes can be seen in the vibrational spectrum, as it will be shown below for the ROA spectra. We studied the internal rotations in AMP, i.e. rotation of the bonds attached to the chiral C8 atom, as it can be seen in Figure 1. To help illustrating the presentation of this work, we will refer to the molecule by a notation that represents: 1) its enantiomer, e.g. S; 2) its skeleton shape, which when seen in the figure plan appears as the letter Z in Figures 1; and 3) the arrangement of the atoms that are attached to C8, i.e. N, C and H. Here, the numbering of the atoms should be considered as C1-C6 to represent the carbon atoms of the ring, and C7 and C8 are those to follow, right after the ring. Accordingly, the different conformers, studied in this work, can be denoted S-ZN, S-ZC and S-ZH, for both AMP and for the amphetammonium ion (designated $AMPH^+$), as shown in Figures 1(a) and (b), respectively. Among the denoted stereoiso-meric/conformational geometries, the S-ZC conformer was found to be the most stable form in the AMP molecule in the gas phase [35]. In the $AMPH^+$ sulfate [36,37] and di-hydrogen phosphate [38] crystal structures the conformation was found to be S-ZN.

2. EXPERIMENTAL

2.1. Sample Preparation

Samples of di-D-amphetammonium sulfate (di-D-$AMPH^+$ sulfate) and DL-amphetammonium sulfate (DL-$AMPH^+$ sulfate) were purchased from Sigma Aldrich. A concentration of 80 mM was prepared by dissolving 5.3 mg of di-D-$AMPH^+$ sulfate and 5.9 mg of DL-$AMPH^+$ sulfate in 180 μL and 200 μL of H_2O, respectively.

Two street drug powder samples (Drug A and Drug B), provided by the London Police, were prepared by directly dissolving them in water, similarly to the standard samples, to obtain concentrations of 60 and 64 mg/mL, respectively. It has been found that these samples contained impurities, which gave a high background level of fluorescence in the spectra [9]. This necessitated cleaning of the sample solutions by centrifugation and filtering, carried out by microspinning for 5 min at 1000 rpm in filter vials (Lida Microspin Filter, 0.2 μm PES, PP w/RCV + cap, Cat# 8508-00). By these operations, amounts of estimated 10 % were lost but the fluorescence was reduced by about a factor of 0.01. The solutions were then kept and measured in closed 2 mL glass vials.

2.2. ROA Spectral Acquisition

The ROA spectra were obtained by using a ChiralRAMAN (Biotools Inc., USA) instrument, which simultaneously provides Raman and ROA spectra of the sample. In this SCP-type of instrument, the right (I_R) and left (I_L) circularly polarized scattered light beams are subsequently measured under identical conditions. The sum of the intensities ($I_R + I_L$) represents the Raman intensity, whereas their difference ($I_R - I_L$) represents the raw ROA intensity. The dimensionless circular intensity difference (CID or Δ) is defined as Δ = (IR – IL)/(IR + IL). The denominator is the conventional Raman scattering intensity. The ROA spectra shown below were obtained using a laser source of wavelength 532 nm, a power of 300 mW at the sample and an acquisition time of 10 hours, and they are baseline corrected. To prevent heat deposition in the sample, two shutters were mounted in the beam path, one before and one after the sample, stepwise synchronized with the spectral acquisition time. The acquisition was stopped when no improvement in the signal to noise ratio (S/N) was found. The noise level was unfortunately quite high for the used thin solutions.

2.3. Quantum Chemical Calculations

The quantum chemical geometry optimizations were obtained by calculations using the Gaussian 03W program package [39]. The calculations were repeated by use of the Spartan program package [40,41] with the same methods and basis sets. The harmonic frequencies and the corresponding first order spectra were found by use of Gaussian, including all three types of internal rotational conformations (around the C7-C8 bond) for both AMP and $AMPH^+$, as shown in **Figure 1**. The AMP molecule has furthermore a quite marked energy dependence on the rotation around the C8-N bond. This behavior was studied by energy barrier calculations and the results are shown in **Figure 2**. In order to account properly for the electron correlation effects in the conjugated molecular system, the time-efficient density functional theory (DFT) approach was employed, including the B3LYP hybrid method, which incorporates a mixture of restricted Hartree-Fock and DFT exchange terms and the third order Becke parameterized gradient-corrected correlation functional of Lee, Yang and Parr. To represent orbitals basis sets of the 6-311G+(d,p) type were used.

The vibrational frequencies were computed from the second derivatives of the energy with respect to the Cartesian nuclear coordinates and then transforming to massweighted coordinates. Due to the fact that the surroundings, e.g. solvents, were ignored in these gas phase calculations, the wavenumber scales were—as often in such calculations—found somewhat higher than the experimental measurements. Empirical scale factors of the order of 0.95 has often been applied to obtain acceptable fitting to the experimental bands. In the present work we did not apply any empirical scale factor, and neither was any solvent nor continuum included. The band shape of the lines was modelled, using the Gaussian standard broadening procedure, in the far-from-resonance approximation at room temperature.

3. RESULTS AND DISCUSSION

3.1. Structures

The quantum chemical calculation results are reported in Tables 1-2 and in the figures. The optimized structures and the corresponding minimized energies of AMP and $AMPH^+$ are given in**Table 1** and **Figure 1**. Comparing the energy values, the S-ZC conformations of both AMP and $AMP\text{-}H^+$ clearly represent the most stable conformation, see **Figure 1**.

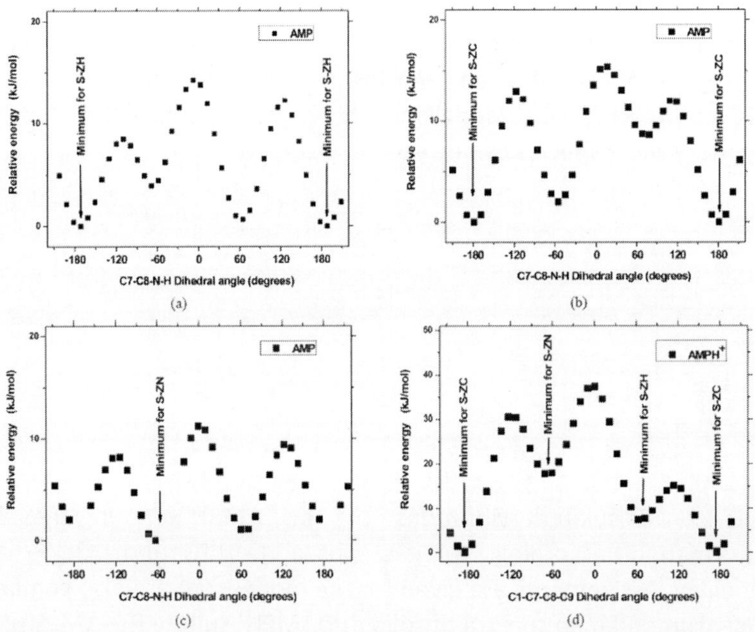

Figure 2. The AMP molecule - fixed in one of the minimum S-ZH, S-ZC or S-ZN conformations, respectively, has a rotational degree of freedom around the C8-N bond. Depending on preselected values of the dihedral angle C7-C8-N-H (abscissa), the molecule minimum energy varies considerably, as can be seen from plots (a, b and c). The amplitude variation is large when the amino group has contact with the aromatic ring (a and b) and smaller when the amino has no contact (c). For the ion $AMPH^+$—because of the 3-fold repetition symmetry of the NH_3^+ group around the C8-N bond—the situation is more simple: The minimum energy corresponds to the situation in which two ammonium protons approach the ring in the S-ZC conformation, see plot (d). All energy points shown correspond to conformations in the gas phase, totally minimized except for the fixing of the abscissa to the shown values.

Table 1. Minimum energies and dipole moments of the optimized structures of AMP and $AMPH^+$, calculated by use of 6-311G+(d,p)/B3LYP/DFT modelling. The corresponding calculated ROA spectra of the S-species can be seen in **Figure 5**.

Species	AMP		$AMPH^+$	
Conformation	Energy, totally or relative* Hartree/particle	Dipole Moment Debye	Energy, totally or relative* Hartree/particle	Dipole Moment Debye
S-ZH	−405.653504 or 0.002530 (or 6.64 kJ/mol)	1.11	−406.025836 or 0.002562 (or 6.73 kJ/mol)	7.89
S-ZC	−405.656034 or 0 Relatively most stable	1.20	−406.028398 or 0 Relatively most stable	7.54
S-ZN	−405.654668 or 0.001366 (or 3.59 kJ/mol)	1.26	−406.021738 or 0.006660 (or 17.49 kJ/mol)	11.85
R-ZN	−405.654668 or 0.001366 (or 3.59 kJ/mol)	1.26		

*Energies exclusive zero point vibrational corrections. For better comparison the energies are also given in kJ/mol, absolutely and relative to the S-ZN conformer of the lowest energy (1 Hartree/particle = 2625.5 kJ/mol).

Table 2. Calculated vibrations of the $AMPH^+$ ion in the S-ZN conformation according to gas phase 6-311G+(d,p)/B3LYP/ DFT modelling. Assignments are given for the modes that are also compared to measured Raman spectra of solid di-$DAMPH^+$ sulfate [$(D\text{-}AMPH)_2SO_4$]. The columns are giving mode number, wavenumber, Raman intensity, ROA intensity, assignment of the mode and tentative assignment of the measured Raman spectrum (wavenumber, band intensity, respectively).

Mode no.	Wave number (cm^{-1})	Raman Activity ($Å^4$/atomic mass unit)	ROA ICP_u/SCP_u 180°	Assignment[a]	Observed in Raman for Solid di-D-$(AMPH)_2SO_4$[b]
1	43.5	3.71	−152.9	C1-C7 rot	
2	68.8	0.81	54.0	C7-C8 rot	
3	96.1	2.80	−53.6	C1-C7-C8 wag	
4	210.1	0.25	4.6	C8-N twist, C8-C9 twist	
5	240.4	1.33	94.1	C8-C9 twist, ring wag	
6	244.8	1.30	−77.5	C8-C9 twist	
7	298.8	2.56	−18.5	C7-C8-N bend	255 m
8	344.2	0.12	−16.1	C2-C1-C7 ipl bend	
9	379.8	0.59	−69.0	CH_3 rock	342 w
10	412.1	0.06	20.3	ring twist	
11	418.7	1.94	−31.3	N-C8-C9 bend	
12	501.4	1.48	−7.6	skeleton & ring def	435 w
				sulfate ν_4 bend	
13	600.8	1.01	51.3	N-C8-C7 & ring ipl bend	466 w
14	634.5	4.23	−22.4	ring ipl def	
15	712.3	0.19	−4.2	ring C-H & ring oopl def	
				sulfate ν_2 bend	
16	745.0	10.92	32.4	ring oopl def & N-C8 str	
17	780.2	3.90	−71.8	ring oopl def & N-C8 str	
18	826.5	14.50	94.2	C1-C7 str & N-H bend & ring C-H bend	~502 w
19	855.0	0.40	21.9	ring C-H oopl def	
20	871.6	6.21	49.9	Chain C-C & C-N str	604 w
21	902.6	1.56	41.9	C-H & N-H def, C1-C7 & C7-C8 str	
22	934.2	0.84	−40.0	chain C-H def, ring C-H oopl def	623 m
23	939.6	0.65	46.8	NH_3 & CH_3 rock, ring C-H oopl def	
24	958.1	5.03	123.1	NH_3 & CH_3 rock, C8-C9 str	740 w
25	992.2	0.06	5.1	ring C-H oopl def	752 w
26	1017.3	33.07	6.6	ring skeleton ipl def	

27	1021.8	0.57	–2.0	ring C-H oopl def	826 m
28	1049.6	16.75	–17.0	ring C-C str & ring C-H ipl def	838 m
29	1070.4	2.11	55.2	skeleton & C-H def	
30	1091.5	0.42	–18.8	ring C-C str, C-H & N-H def	897 vw
31	1131.1	0.91	41.9	ring C-C str, C-H & N-H def	
32	1190.3	2.73	–3.4	ring C-H ipl def	914 vw
33	1198.1	2.09	–187.7	chain str & C-H & N-H def	942 w
34	1206.9	4.16	–26.1	ring C-H ipl def	
35	1218.0	21.74	169.2	C1-C7 str & ring C-H ipl def	
36	1261.9	2.83	–102.3	C7H_2 twist, C-H angle def & ring C-H ipl def	
				sulfate v_1 str	977 s
37	1336.4	5.10	–63.4	ring & chain C-C str & C-H angle def	1002 vs
38	1346.3	2.99	–46.9	ring & chain C-C str & C-H angle def	1033 m
39	1359.4	1.44	35.2	chain C-C str & ring C-H angle def	1066 vw
40	1383.8	4.16	–85.3	C7-C8 str & C-H def	1103 vw
41	1392.7	1.67	–2.0	CH_3 umbrella & chain C-H def	1158 w
42	1425.0	1.15	70.4	CH_3 umbrella & C-H bend	1181 w
43	1477.3	10.61	–48.6	C7H_2 sci & CH_3 def	1210 m
44	1486.5	1.53	107.4	ring C-C str, C-H & N-H bend	1246 vw
45	1490.9	0.95	–45.8	NH_3 umbrella & C-H bend	1258 vw
					1301 vw
					1334 w
46	1498.5	4.46	–8.7	CH_3 def	1367 w
47	1500.4	2.06	–5.2	NH_3 umbrella & chain C-H bend	1396 w
48	1527.5	0.23	19.4	ring ipl C-H bend	1453 wbr
49	1626.2	8.72	35.0	ring C-C str & ring ipl bend	1583 w
50	1640.6	33.06	142.4	ring C-C str & ring ipl bend	1605 m
51	1659.2	4.09	142.6	NH_3 bend	
52	1662.9	5.66	–144.2	NH_3 bend	
					2775 vw
53	3007.8	130.07	–340.3	C7H_2 sym str	2881 w
54	3032.3	156.89	39.3	C9H_3 sym str	2937 m
55	3051.5	60.59	637.2	C7H_2 asym str	
56	3083.6	39.40	–632.9	C8H str, C9H_3 str	
57	3102.8	47.53	709.7	C8H str, C9H_3 str	
58	3130.2	38.07	–568.7	C9H_3 asym str	2980 w
59	3149.6	58.59	157.6	ring C-H str	
60	3162.4	50.78	–240.4	ring C-H str	3040 w sh
61	3182.0	89.36	–13.6	ring C-H str	3058 vs
62	3191.4	58.38	56.6	ring C-H str	3069 s
63	3201.5	268.80	–43.2	ring C-H str	3168 vw
64	3395.7	130.16	–39.4	NH_3 sym str	3207 vw
65	3477.6	37.08	–247.6	NH_3 asym str	3227 vw
66	3485.8	50.47	–158.8	NH_3 asym str	3474 vw

[a] Assignment codes: asym = asymmetric, bend = bending, iph = in phase, ipl = in plane, ooph = out of phase, oopl = out of plane, rot = rotatory oscillation (also often called torsion or twist), str = stretching, sym = symmetric, twist = twisting. [b] Codes for band intensity: w = weak, m = medium, s = strong, v = very, br = broad, sh=shoulder.

When studying the geometry of different AMP conformers, it was found that rotation of the NH_2amino group around the C8-N bond had an appreciable influence on the minimum energy. We investigated this influence by fixing the AMP molecule in each of the minimum S-ZH, S-ZC or S-ZN conformations, respectively, and minimizing the energy under the constraint that the dihedral C7-C8-N-H angles should stay at preselected values. These results were obtained with the Spartan program [40] using the same basis sets, and giving identical results. The dependence of the molecule minimum energy versus the dihedral angle (abscissa) is shown in **Figure 2**, plots (a, b and c). A considerable (amplitude) variation can be seen. The energy is low when a proton of the amino group has a near contact with the aromatic ring (plots a and b) and smaller when the amino has no contact (c).

The $AMPH^+$ ion was found to behave somewhat differently, due to the 3-fold repetition symmetry of the ammonium NH_3^+ group around the C8-N bond. The situation is simpler: The minimum energy, see **Figure 2**, plot (d) corresponds to the situation in which two ammonium protons in the S-ZC conformation approach the aromatic ring.

We can compare this AMP calculation result to the results of Godfrey et al. [35]. These authors also found ZC as the most stable conformer in the gas phase: Their "structure I" with the dihedral angle of 174° was given as the most stable geometry both experimentally (millimetrewave rotational spectroscopy) and by means of their MP2/6-31G(d,p) modelling. This result compares well with our molecule, see **Figure 2**(b). From their spectroscopic experiments Godfrey et al. [35] also—as is to be expected—found small amounts of another comformation (named "structure II") with the dihedral angle of –54 (energy 1.4 kJ/mol). This agrees also well with our **Figure 2**(b). The explanation for the high stability of the ZC conformation seems to be due to the internal close contact between the aromatic electrons and one of the amino protons. This non-classical hydrogen bonding [35] feature is displayed in **Figure 3** (the distance between C1 and H was around 2.675 Å).

For the $AMPH^+$ ion in the gas phase, the agreement between model calculations and the experimental X-ray crystal structures is less obvious. We explain this in the following way: When the ion structure was optimized as a separate ion in the gas phase, the stabilization came from the close contact (around 2.675 Å) between C1 and one of the ammonium protons, see **Figure 3**. In the known crystal structures [36-38] the anions interfere with the $AMPH^+$ cations, making the ZN conformation favorable. The stabilization energy must come from the crystal lattice.

3.2. ROA Spectroscopy

In ROA spectroscopy, or generally in vibrational optical activity spectroscopy, the large number of probed vibrational transitions makes it unlikely that a change in conformation of a chiral molecule should result in oppositely signed bands in the entire ROA spectrum [42]. Therefore, it should be possible to achieve knowledge on the absolute configuration from associating measurements of the enantiomers with quantum chemical calculations.

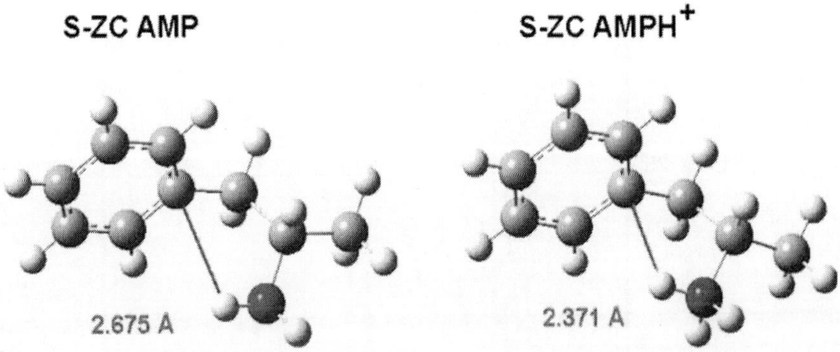

Figure 3. Comparison between the minimum calculated distance between the C1 and the amino H in the gas phase AMP molecule and the $AMPH^+$ion. The reason for the stabilisation of these conformations seem to be the internal close contact between the aromatic electrons and the protons. In the known crystal structures the anions interfere and make S-ZN $AMPH^+$ favorable.

When the ROA spectra were calculated by the Gaussian program for both AMP and $AMPH^+$ species the output came out in several ways, one of them given as the invariant ICP_u/SCP_u (180°) in units of 10^4 $Å^5$/AMU (AMU = atomic mass units). As mentioned in section 1, for ROA experiments there are three possible polarization schemes of measurement and calculation. These schemes are referred to as ICP, SCP or DCP, respecttively), depending on the experiment. Since we used the SCP_u setup and a collecting angle of 180°, where "u" denotes unpolarized scattering, the invariant ICP_u/SCP_u (180°) is the relevant one here.

As a check of the absolute configurations, we calculated the minimized energies of the two opposite enantiomers, R(–) and S(+), for example of the AMP ZN configuration. The results are included in**Table 1**. The optimized model of the S-ZN is the one shown in **Figure 1**; R-ZN looked exactly like the mirror image. The calculated corresponding ROA spectra of these AMP R-ZN and S-ZN conformers are given in **Figure 4**. As the theory predicts the spectra were completely opposite to each other, throughhout the whole wavenumber range (0 - 3500 cm^{-1}), Also, to our satisfaction, the minimum energy and dipole moment were observed with identical values (**Table 1**).

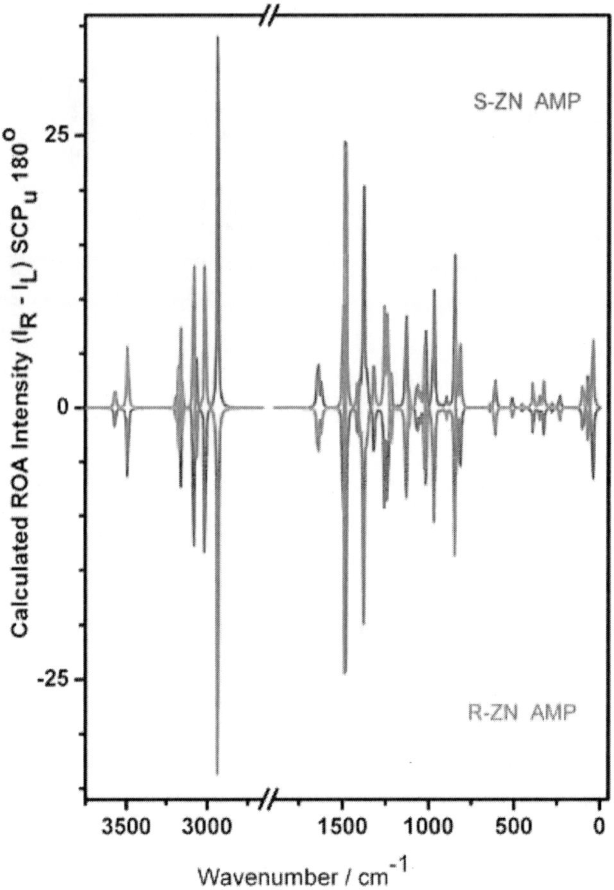

Figure 4. Quantum Chemical DFT/B3LYP/6-311G+(d,p) calculated ROA spectra for the S-ZN (red) and the R-ZN AMP molecule conformer in the gas phase (magenta). The region where no significant vibration is noticed has been omitted.

Calculated ROA spectra of the three different AMP and three different $AMPH^+$ species are compared in **Figure 5**. The spectra of all conformers of $AMPH^+$ and AMP differ considerably from each other in the whole wave-number range. Protonation of the amino-group has a large influence on the ROA spectra (compare the spectra of the same color). This is quite similar to the behaviour found for the Raman spectra [9]. Interestingly also the ROA spectra of AMP or $AMPH^+$ respectively, depend on the internal rotation around the C7-C8 bond. This can only be interpreted as a result of the conformational isomerism, as depicted in **Figure 1**. It means that, even within the same species i.e. AMP or $AMPH^+$, spectral differences arise as a result of different coupling schemes among the group vibrations depending on the geometry. Such a behavior has been seen before [43]. This reveals that such differences are exclusively attributable to the internal rotations, as any chirality difference within the same species would have appeared in opposition to each other, as seen in**Figure 4**.

To compare these theoretical results with experiments we note that most available samples are amphetamine salts. A measured Raman spectrum of the solid di-D-$AMPH^+$ sulfate is shown in **Figure 6**. The correspondence between this experimental Raman spectrum and a Raman spectrum calculated with a DFT/B3LYP/6-311G(d,p) model has been discussed previously [9]. In the present study the Raman and the ROA spectra for the $AMPH^+$ ion were calculated with a better model. Some of the results (for the S-ZN $AMPH^+$ ion) are reproduced in Table 2. The calculated ROA data can be seen in column 4 together with experimental data in the last column. Assignments for all 66 vibrations of the $AMPH^+$ ion in the S-ZN conformation are given in the 5^{th}column of **Table 2**, based on animated modes given by the Gaussian software [39]. These 66 modes are compared to the experimental data—in the last column—see also **Figure 6**. The assigning of these observed bands to the calculated modes has been done based on best wavenumber matching and also on the strengths of the peaks. Differences are noticed between the measured and the calculated wavenumber values of the modes. This is to be expected and is probably due to the insufficient modelling of the solid salt by an ion gas phase model, even though the calculated conformation has the same specific internal rotation (S-ZN) as found in the salt [36,37]. Differences may also be due to the sulfate (hydrogen bonded to the ammonium group) and the presence of fluorescing impurities.

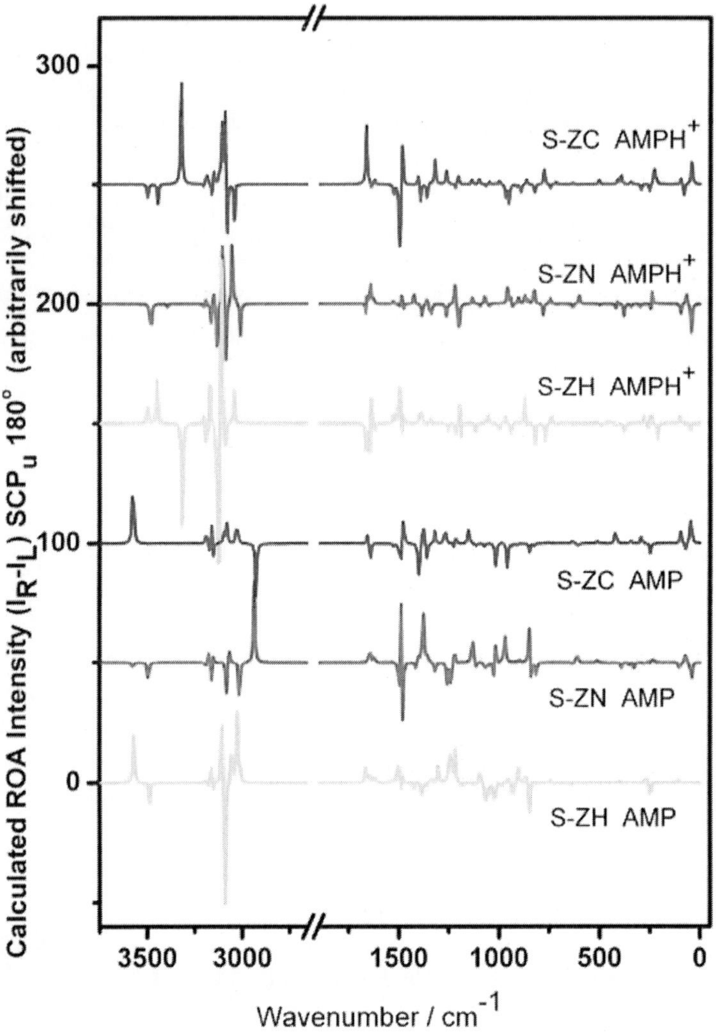

Figure 5. Calculated ROA spectra for three different conformations of $AMPH^+$ (above) and AMP (below) using quantum chemical DFT/B3LYP calculations. Gaussian 6-311G+(d,p) and 6-311G(d,p) split valence basis sets were used for AMP and $AMPH^+$, respectively. The differences due to internal rotation are obvious when comparing the spectra. The region where no significant vibration is noticed has been omitted.

To compare the calculated ROA results with experiments, we measured ROA spectra of amphetamine-H^+ sulfate standards purchased from Sigma-Aldrich and of two street "amphetamine" samples, Drug A and Drug B, dissolved in water. ROA spectra of Drug A and Drug B, depicted in red and blue, respectively, are compared in **Figure 7**. Unfortunately the signals were relatively weak compared to the noise. Remarkably however, these two samples seem to be different enantiomers of the same species, as seen most noticeably in the regions 1100-950 and 1650 - 1450 cm^{-1}. The spectral bands in these "finger-print" regions are mainly due to N-H angle deformation, ring C-C stretching and C-H in ring plane angle deformations, according to our calculations (see **Table 2**). The region around 1000 cm^{-1} is highly characteristic for $AMPH^+$, as it has been discussed before [9].

With regard to ROA spectra of the standard samples, the DL-$AMPH^+$ sulfate solution, as expected, did not show any ROA activity: Equal amounts of the R and S conformations cancel the ROA signal. In contrast to this the di-D-$AMPH^+$ sulfate standard solution gave an ROA spectrum that is shown in **Figure 8**, compared to the two street samples, Drugs A and B. Previously Raman spectra for the same samples were studied [9] and bands observed at 1006 cm^{-1} and 981 cm^{-1} have been assigned to the $AMPH^+$ and SO_4^{2-} ions, respectively (see also **Table 2**). It is worth mentioning that in spite of the fact that the SO_4^{2-} ion has no direct chirality, its 981 cm^{-1} band can still be seen in the ROA spectrum. This is attributed to an interionic effect. It is known that interionic interactions may introduce chirality into non-chiral molecules or ions bound to chiral species. Here, the sulfate ions must certainly be interacting with the chiral $AMPH^+$ ions by virtue of hydrogen bonds in the solution, somewhat similar to what was seen in the solid state [37,38]. The appearance of the signal in both of the spectra of Drugs A and B indicates that it is not likely to be an artefact.

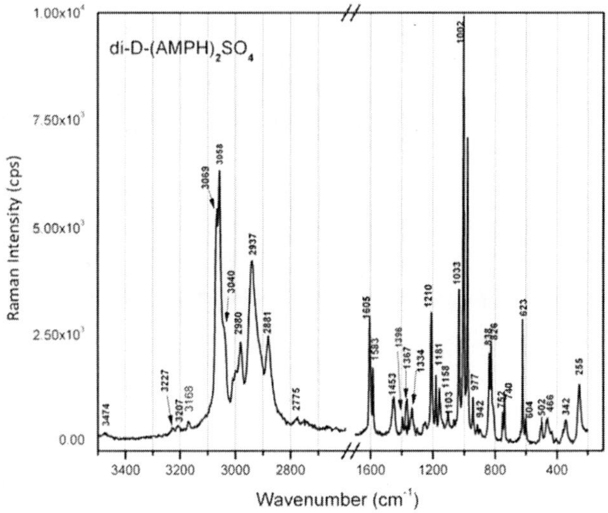

Figure 6. Raman spectrum of solid di-D-AMPH$^+$ sulfate, obtained on a LABRAM instrument with 514.5 nm laser light excitation [9]. The region where no significant vibration is noticed has been omitted.

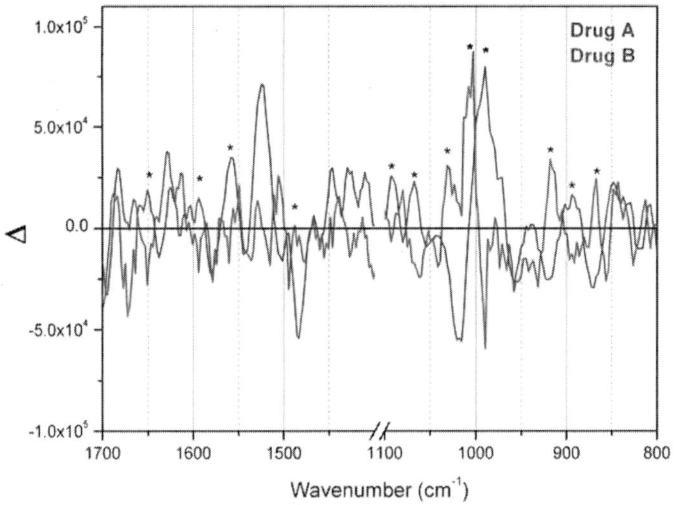

Figure 7. ROA spectra of street samples dissolved in water: Drug A (blue) and Drug B (red). It seems from these spectra, as indicated with asterisks, that many peaks occur with opposite sign, shape and intensity, signalling opposite chirality. This is obvious especially in the 1050-950 cm^{-1} region. Some regions have been omitted.

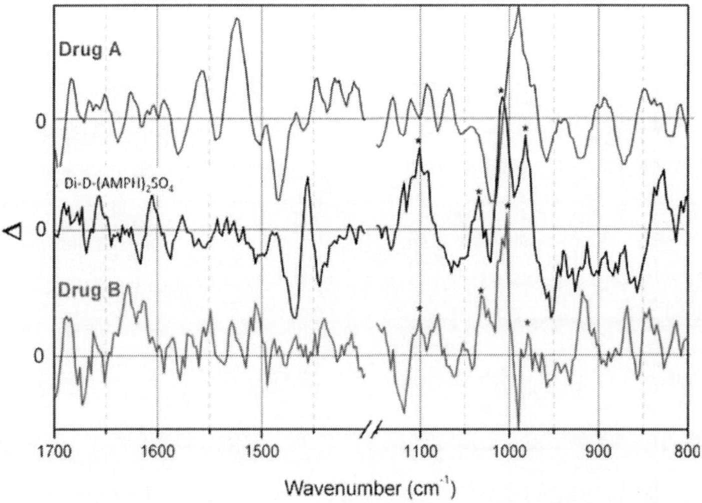

Figure 8. ROA spectra of street sample solutions (in water) of Drug A and Drug B, compared to a solution of a purchased standard di-D-AMPH$^+$sulfate sample. The peaks marked with asterisks show quite a resemblance between the standard sample (black) and one of the street samples, Drug B (red), especially in the 1100-800 cm^{-1} region. The three ordinate scale magnitudes can be judged by compareson to **Figure 7**. For clarity some regions have been omitted.

When comparing the spectra in **Figure 8**, strong similarities between the standard sample and one of the street samples (Drug B) can be noted (peaks marked with asterisks). This feature is most apparent in the lower wavenumber region (1100 - 800 cm^{-1}). Unfortunately the noise level was too high to give details, suggesting that more studies deserve to be carried out on stronger concentrations.

The measured ROA spectrum of the di-D-AMPH$^+$ sulfate is compared to the calculated results in**Figure 9** (see also **Figure 5**). It appears to be most satisfactorily modelled by the calculated S-ZN AMPH$^+$spectrum, especially when taking notice more to the shapes than to exact matching of the wavenumbers. This is not surpriseing as the S-ZN form from the crystal may still be stabilised in solution via formation of hydrogen bonds, etc. The similarity between the experimental di-D-AMPH$^+$ sulfate results and the AMPH$^+$ S-ZN modelling has also been found for the Raman and SERS spectra [9].

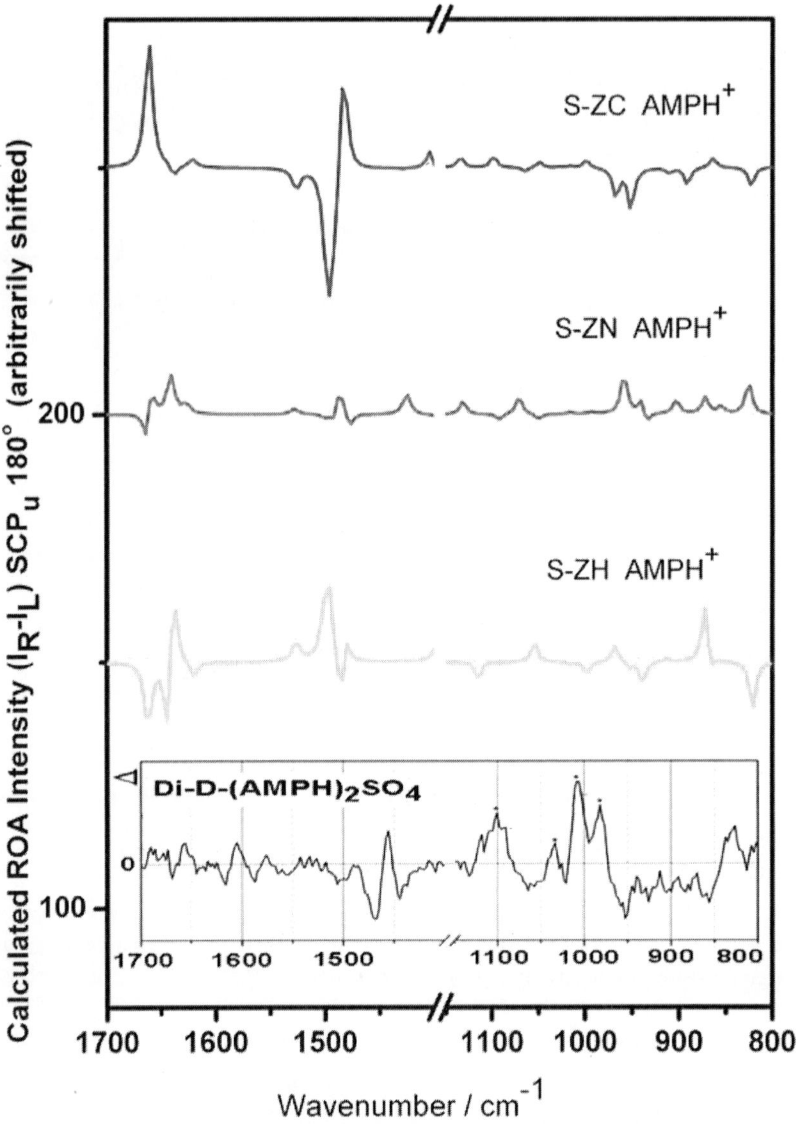

Figure 9. Calculated ROA spectra of $AMPH^+$ ions in different conformations, compared to a solution of standard di-D-$AMPH^+$ sulfate. The peaks marked with asterisks are the ones that resemble peaks in the street sample, Drug B.

4. CONCLUSIONS

The ROA spectra of chiral molecules can provide information about the absolute configuration, when one or both enantiomers are available. In this study we have obtained Raman and ROA spectra of different species of amphetamine (amphetamine and amphetamine-H^+), in which internal rotations and chirality were included. Spectra of street drug samples have been compared to standard samples, showing them to possibly be different enantiomers of the same compound even though they give almost identical Raman spectra [9]. Also the standard sample solution is likely to contain the $AMPH^+$ ion in the S-ZN conformation, interacting with the sulfate ions.

Quantum Chemical DFT model calculations (geometry minimizations followed by calculation of Raman optical activity spectra) indicate that obtained preliminary ROA spectra can be used to assign the S(+)-amphetamine molecule and the S(+)-amphetamine-H^+ ion to their different conformational states; the difference between these states being their internal rotation, i.e. the arrangements of the atoms or groups (H, CH_3 or NH_2/NH_3^+) bound to the C8 atom. This is the first time that ROA spectra of amphetamine compounds have been given. The spectra were used to characterize two street drug samples as being most likely opposite enantiomers of the same compound: Amphetamine-H^+ sulfate. This compound (purchased and used as a standard solution) was found to adopt the S-ZN conformation in aqueous solution with C8 adopting the S-chirality and with the NH_3^+ group completing the letter Z in our notation for the different conformations.

5. ACKNOWLEDGEMENTS

Dr. Thomas Nørbygaard is thanked for help and advice during the ROA measurements. Director Ib Henriksen's Foundation is thanked for maintenance of the Raman instrumentation. The Danish Fundamental Research Foundation as well as the Danish Agency for Science, Technology and Innovation (#09-065038/FTP) helped contribute funding for this project.

REFERENCES

1. E. Meyer, J. F. Van Bocxlaer, I. M. Dirinck, W. E. Lambert, L. Thienpont and A. P. De Leenheer, "Tissue Distribution of Amphetamine Isomers in a Fatal Overdose," Journal of Analytical Toxicology, Vol. 21, No. 3, 1997, pp. 236-239.

2. I. M. Dirinck, E. Meyer, J. F. Van Bocxlaer, W. E. Lambert and A. P. De Leenheer, "Application of Gas Chromatography-Fourier Transform Infrared Spectrometry to the Analysis of Amphetamine Analogues," Journal of Chromatography, Vol. 819, No. 1-2, 1998, pp. 155-159.

3. H. H. Maurer, T. Kraemer, D. Springer and R. F. Staack, "Chemistry, Pharmacology, Toxicology, and Hepatic Metabolism of Designer Drugs of the Amphetamine (Ecstasy), Piperazine, and Pyrrolidinophenone Types. A Synopsis," Therapeutic Drug Monitoring, Vol. 26, No. 2, 2004, pp. 127-131.

4. T. Kraemer and H. H. Maurer, "Determination of Amphetamine, Methamphetamine and Amphetamine-Derived Designer Drugs or Medicaments in Blood and Urine," Journal of Chromatography B: Biomedical Sciences and Applications, Vol. 713, No. 1, 1998, pp. 163-187.

5. F. T. Peters, T. Kraemer and H. H. Maurer, "Drug Testing in Blood: Validated Negative-Ion Chemical Ionization Gas Chromatographic-Mass Spectrometric Assay for Determination of Amphetamine and Methamphetamine Enantiomers and Its Application to Toxicology Cases," Clinical Chemistry, Vol. 48, No. 9, 2002, pp. 1472-1485.

6. H. Hegedüs, A. Gergely, T. Veress and F. Zsila, "Determination of the Enantiomeric Purity of Amphetamine after Derivatization with Sanger's Reagent (2,4-Dinitrofluorobenzene) by Simultaneous Dual Circular Dichroism and Ultraviolet Spectroscopy," Fresenius' Journal of Analytical Chemistry, Vol. 364, No. 8, 1999, pp. 749-752.

7. N. Purdie, "Applications of Circular Dichroism," In: N. Purdie and H. G. Brittain, Eds., Analytical, Elsevier, Amsterdam, 1994, pp. 241-278.

8. C. Weyermann, Y. Mimoune, F. Anglada, G. Massonnet, P. Esseiva and P. Buzzini, "Applications of a Transportable Raman Spectrometer for the in Situ Detection of Controlled Substances at Border Controls," Forensic Science International, Vol. 209, No. 1, 2011, pp. 21-28.

9. R. W. Berg, T. Nørbygaard, P. C. White and S. Abdali, "Ab Initio, Raman and SERS Spectral Analyses of Amphetamine Species," Applied Spectroscopy Reviews, Vol. 46, No. 2, 2011, pp.107-131.

10. W. Hug and G. A. Hangartner, "A Novel High-throughput Raman Spectrometer for Polarization Difference Measurements," Journal of Raman Spectroscopy, Vol. 30, No. 9, 1999, pp. 841-852.

11. L. A. Nafie, B. E. Brinson, X. Cao, D. A. Rice, O. M. Rahim, R. K. Dukor and N. J. Halas, "Near-Infrared Excited Raman Optical Activity," Applied Spectroscopy, Vol. 61, No. 10, 2007, pp. 1103-1106.

12. H. Lia and L. A. Nafie, "Simultaneous Acquisition of All Four Forms of Circular Polarization Raman Optical Activity: Results for α-Pinene and Lysozyme," Journal of Raman Spectroscopy, Vol. 43, 2012, pp. 89-94.

13. S. Abdali and E. W. Blanch, "Surface Enhanced Raman Optical Activity (SEROA), TUTORIAL REVIEW," Chemical Society Review, Vol. 37, No. 5, 2008, pp. 980- 992.

14. L. D. Barron and L. Hecht, "Vibrational Raman Optical Activity: From Fundamentals to Biochemical Applications," In: N. Berova, K. Nakanishi and R. Woody, Eds., Circular Dichroism: Principles and Applications, Chapter 23, 2nd Edition, Wiley-VCH, 2000, pp. 667-702.

15. L. D. Barron, L Hecht, I. H. McColl and E. W. Blanch, "Raman Optical Activity Comes of Age," Molecular Physics, Vol. 102, No. 8, 2004, pp. 731-744.

16. L. D. Barron, "Structure and Behaviour of Biomolecules from Raman Optical Activity," Current Opinion in Structural Biology, Vol. 16, No. 6, 2006, pp. 638-643.

17. L. D. Barron, F. Zhu, L. Hecht, G. E. Tranter and N. W. Isaacs, "Raman Optical Activity: An Incisive Probe of Molecular Chirality and Biomolecular Structure," Journal of Molecular Structure, Vol. 834-836, 2007, pp. 7-16.

18. L. D. Barron and A. D. Buckingham, "Rayleigh and Raman Scattering from Optically Active Molecules," Molecular Physics, Vol. 20, No. 6, 1971, pp. 1111-1119.

19. P. L. Polavarapu, "Ab Initio Raman and Raman Optical Activity Spectra," Journal of Physical Chemistry, Vol. 94, No. 12, 1990, pp. 8106-8112.

20. K. Ruud, T. Helgaker and P. Bour, "Gauge-Origin Independent Density-Functional Theory Calculations of Vibrational Raman Optical Activity," Journal of Physical Chemistry A, Vol. 106, No. 32, 2002, pp. 7448-7455.

21. J. Costante, L. Hecht, P. L. Polavarapu, A. Collet and L. D. Barron, "Absolute-Configuration of Bromochlorofluoromethane from Experimental and Ab-Initio Theoretical Vibrational Raman Optical-Activity," Angewandte Chemie International Edition in English, Vol. 36, No. 8, 1997, pp. 885-887.

22. P. L. Polavarapu, "The Absolute Configuration of Bromochlorofluoromethane," Angewandte Chemie International Edition in English, Vol. 41, No. 23, 2002, pp. 4544-4546.

23. J. Haesler, I. Schindelholz, E. Riguet, C. G. Bochet and W. Hug, "Absolute Configuration of Chirally Deuterated Neopentane," Nature, Vol. 446, No. 7135, 2007, pp. 526- 529.

24. L. D. Barron, L. Hecht, E. W. Blanch and A. F. Bell, "Solution Structure and Dynamics of Biomolecules from Raman Optical Activity," Progress in Biophysics and Molecular Biology, Vol. 73, 2000, pp. 1-49.

25. L. D. Barron, E. W.; Blanch, I. H. McColl, C. D. Syme, L. Hecht and K. Nielsen, "Structure and Behaviour of Proteins, Nucleic Acids and Viruses from Vibrational Raman Optical Activity," Spectroscopy, Vol. 17, 2003, pp. 101- 126.

26. L. D. Barron, "Molecular Light Scattering and Optical Activity," 2nd Edition, Cambridge University Press, Cambridge, 2004.

27. W. Hug, "Raman Optical Activity," In: J. M. Chalmers and P. R. Griffiths, Eds., Handbook of Vibrational Spectroscopy, Vol. 1, Wiley, New York, 2002.

28. S. Abdali, "Observation of SERS Effect in Raman Optical Activity, a New Tool for Chiral Vibrational Spectroscopy," Journal of Raman Spectroscopy, Vol. 37, 2006, pp. 1341-1345.

29. C. Johannessen, P. C. White and S. Abdali, "Resonance Raman Optical Activity and Surface Enhanced Resonance Raman Optical Activity Analysis of Cytochrome c," Journal of Physical Chemistry A, Vol. 111, No. 32, 2007, pp. 7771-7776.

30. C. Johannessen and S. Abdali, "Surface Enhanced Raman Optical Activity as an Ultra Sensitive Tool for Ligand Binding Analysis," Spectroscopy, Vol. 21, No. 3, 2007, pp. 143-149.

31. N. A., Brazhe, A. R. Brazhe, O. V. Sosnovtseva and S. Abdali, "Novel Chiroptical Analysis of Hemoglobin by Surface Enhanced Resonance Raman Optical Activity Spectroscopy," Chirality, Vol. 21, No. 1E, 2009, pp. 307- 312.

32. B. G. Janesko and G. E. Scuseria, "Surface Enhanced Raman Optical Activity of Molecules on Orientationally Averaged Substrates: Theory of Electromagnetic Effects," Journal of Chemical Physics, Vol. 125, No. 12, 2006, pp. 124704-124716.

33. L. Jensen, "Surface-Enhanced Vibrational Raman Optical Activity: A Time-Dependent Density Functional Theory Approach" Journal of Physical Chemistry A, Vol. 113, 2009, pp. 4437-4444.

34. R. Acevedo, R. Lombardini, N. J. Halas and B. R. Johnson, "Plasmonic Enhancement of Raman Optical Activity in Molecules near Metal Nanoshells," Journal of Physical Chemistry A, Vol. 113, No. 16, 2009, pp. 13173-13183.

35. P. D. Godfrey, S. J. McGlone and R. D. Brown, "The Shapes of Neurotransmitters by Millimetrewave Spectroscopy: Amphetamine," Journal of Molecular Structure, Vol. 599, No. 1-3, 2001, pp. 139-152.

36. R. Bergin and D. Carlström, "Crystal and Molecular Structure of Amphetamine Sulfate," Acta Crystallographica, Vol. B27, 1971, pp. 2146-2152.

37. K. Pogorzelec-Glaser, J. Kaszynska, A. Rachocki, J. Tritt-Goc, N. Pislewski and A. Pietraszko, "The Crystal Structure and Evidence of the Phase Transition in d-Amphetamine Sulfate, as Studied by X-Ray Crystallography, DSC and NMR Spectroscopy," New Journal of Chemistry, Vol. 33, No. 9, 2009, pp. 1894-1900.

38. H. Herbert, "X-Ray Structure of (+)-AmpH^+ $H_2PO_4^-$," Acta Crystallographica, Vol. B34, 1978, pp. 611-615. [Paper reference:1]

39. M. J. Frisch, G. W. Trucks, H. B. Schlegel, G. E. Scuseria, M. A. Robb, J. R. Cheeseman, J. A. Montgomery Jr., T. Vreven, K. N. Kudin, J. C. Burant, J. M. Millam, S. S. Iyengar, J. Tomasi, V. Barone, B. Mennucci, M. Cossi, G. Scalmani, N. Rega, G. A. Petersson, H. Nakatsuji, M. Hada, M. Ehara, K. Toyota, R. Fukuda, J. Hasegawa, M. Ishida, T. Nakajima, Y. Honda, O. Kitao, H. Nakai, M. Klene, X. Li, J. E. Knox, H. P. Hratchian, J. B. Cross, V. Bakken, C. Adamo, J. Jaramillo, R. Gomperts, R. E. Stratmann, O. Yazyev, A. J. Austin, R. Cammi, C. Pomelli, J. W. Ochterski, P. Y. Ayala, K. Morokuma, G. A. Voth, P. Salvador, J. J. Dannenberg, V. G. Zakrzewski, S. Dapprich, A. D. Daniels, M. C. Strain, O. Farkas, D. K. Malick, A. D. Rabuck, K. Raghavachari, J. B. Foresman, J. V.

Ortiz, Q. Cui, A. G. Baboul, S. Clifford, J. Cioslowski, B. B. Stefanov, G. Liu, A. Liashenko, P. Piskorz, I. Komaromi, R. L. Martin, D. J. Fox, T. Keith, M. A. Al-Laham, C. Y. Peng, A. Nanayakkara, M. Challacombe, P. M. W. Gill, B. Johnson, W. Chen, M. W. Wong, C. Gonzalez, and J. A. Pople, "Gaussian 03," Revision E.01, Gaussian, Inc., Wallingford CT, 2004. [Paper reference:2]

40. Spartan'10, version 1.1.0. Wavefunction, Inc. Irvine, CA. 2010. [Paper reference:1]

41. Y. Shao, L. F. Molnar, Y. Jung, J. Kussmann, C. Ochsenfeld, S. T. Brown, A. T. B. Gilbert, L. V. Slipchenko, S. V. Levchenko, D. P. O'Neill, R. A. DiStasio Jr, R. C. Lochan, T. Wang, G. J. O. Beran, N. A. Besley, J. M. Herbert, C. Y. Lin, T. Van Voorhis, S. H. Chien, A. Sodt, R. P. Steele, V. A. Rassolov, P. E. Maslen, P. P. Korambath, R. D. Adamson, B. Austin, J. Baker, E. F. C. Byrd, H. Dachsel, R J. Doerksen, A. Dreuw, B. D. Dunietz, A. D. Dutoi, T. R. Furlani, S. R. Gwaltney, A. Heyden, S. Hirata, C.-P. Hsu, G. Kedziora, R. Z. Khalliulin, P. Klunzinger, A. M. Lee, M. S. Lee, W. Z. Liang, I. Lotan, N. Nair, B. Peters, E. I. Proynov, P. A. Pieniazek, Y. M. Rhee, J. Ritchie, E. Rosta, C. D. Sherrill, A. C. Simmonett, J. E. Subotnik, H. L. Woodcock III, W. Zhang, A. T. Bell, A. K. Chakraborty, D. M. Chipman, F. J. Keil, A. Warshel, W. J. Hehre, H. F. Schaefer III, Jing Kong, A. I. Krylov, P. M. W. Gill and M. Head-Gordon, "Advances in Methods and Algorithms in a Modern Quantum Chemistry," Physical Chemistry Chemical Physics, Vol. 8, No. 27, 2006, 3172-3191.

42. P. L. Polavarapu, "Why IS IT IMPORtant to Simultaneously Use More Than One Chiroptical Spectroscopic Method for Determining the Structures of Chiral Molecules?" Chirality, Vol. 20, No. 5, 2008, pp. 664-672.

43. R. W. Berg, M. Deetlefs, K. R. Seddon, I. Shim, and J. Thompson, "Raman and Ab Initio Studies of Simple and Binary 1-Alkyl-3-methylimidazolium Ionic Liquids," Journal of Physical Chemistry B, Vol. 109, No. 40, 2005, pp. 19018-19025.

Chapter 9

Fast and Sensitive Chiral Analysis of Amphetamines and Cathinones in Equine Urine and Plasma Using Liquid Chromatography Tandem Mass Spectrometry

Caroline C. Wang, Petra Hartmann-Fischbach, Tim R. Krueger, Alisha Lester, Aaron Simonson, Terry L. Wells, Max O. Wolk, Nick J. Hidlay

Industrial Laboratories, Wheat Ridge, USA

ABSTRACT

A simple, rapid, sensitive and reproducible method for enantiomer analysis of methamphetamine, amphetamine, cathinone and methcathinone was developed and validated. The compounds were extracted from equine plasma and urine using a fast liquid-liquid extraction procedure. Only one milliliter plasma and one hundred microliter urine sample is needed for analysis. The extraction procedure had good recovery (>70%) and the matrix effect was negligible. Enantiomer differen- tiation and confirmation were achieved using liquid chromatography with chiral stationary phase and mass spectrometry detection. The method demonstrated excellent reproducibility with intra- day and inter-day precision of lower than 5%.

The lower limits of detection for all of the com- pounds studied here were at low pg/mL level for both plasma and urine. This is the first report of the analysis of four chiral compounds in equine plasma and urine. Routine application was demon- strated for (S)- and (R)-enantiomer differentiation.

Keywords: Amphetamines and Cathinones, Equine Plasma and Urine, Chiral Analysis, Liquid Chromatography Tandem Mass Spectrometry

1. INTRODUCTION

Methamphetamine, amphetamine, cathinone and methcathinone are powerful central nerve system (CNS) stimulants and are abused in many countries [1] -[8] . According to Uniform Classification Guidelines for Foreign Substances and Recommended Penalties and Model Rules from Association and Racing Commissioner International (RCI), methamphetamine, amphetamine, cathinone and methcathinone are all Class I drugs based on their ability to influence the outcome of a horse race. Class A Penalty will be imposed if any of these drugs are confirmed present at any level in post-race equine urine or plasma.

Amphetamine is a metabolite of methamphetamine [8] [9] . Cathinone and methcathinone both have a β-keto group and they are structurally close to amphetamine. These four compounds all contain a chiral center and have S and R enantiomers. The two enantiomers are non-superimposable mirror images of each other. In animal studies, the CNS stimulant activities increase in the order of (S)-amphetamine, (S)-cathinone, (S)-metham-pheta- mine and (S)-methcathinone [1] . Research results showed that the S-enantiomers of the four compounds demonstrated more CNS stimulant potency than the corresponding R-enantiomers due to the binding affinity differences to their receptor sites [9] -[13] . In the United States, (R)-methamphetamine is available in some over-the- counter nasal decongestant products, such as Vicks-Vapor inhaler and its generic equivalents. The illicitly manufactured methamphetamine consists mainly the S-enantiomer. Unambiguous identification of enantiomers can be extremely useful in clinical, forensic, and toxicological applications to distinguish illicit consumption, origin and the metabolism of the target compound [8] -[13] .

Over the years, gas chromatography (GC), capillary electrophoresis (CE), and high performance liquid chromatography (HPLC) have been used for enantiomer analysis [5] [8] [9] [12] -[25] . Chiral separations can be classified into three categories [15] . The first one is pre-column derivatization with a chiral derivatization reagent to generate diastereomers; the second one involves adding a chiral agent to the mobile phase to form adducts with the enantiomers; and the third one is a direct method using chiral stationary phase [20] [25] . GC methods involve complicated and time consuming pre-column derivatization steps [3] [8] [12] -[14] . Liquid chromatography mass spectrometry (LC-MS) has gained more and more popularity for drug analysis because it is generally faster, easy to use and has better sensitivity and specificity [22] [23] . Chiral additive in mobile phase is usually not compatible for mass spectrometry detection [20] [25] . Direct chiral separation using chiral stationary phase without previous derivatization is a convenient choice for LC-MS analysis. The published methods with this approach had poor sensitivity and very long acquisition time [17] [18] [23] . We are presenting a fast and sensitive liquid chromatography tandem mass spectrometry (LC-MS/MS) chiral analysis method that can be used for the differentiation of the enantiomers of four compounds after an easy extraction from equine plasma and urine. To the author's knowledge, this is the first report of this kind in racing industry.

2. EXPERIMENTAL

2.1. Chemicals & Reagents

S(+)-Methamphetamine, R(−)-Methamphetamine, S(+)-Amphetamine, R(−)-Amphetamine, S(−)-Cathinone, R(+)- Cathinone, S(−)-Methcathinone, and R(+)-Methcathinone were purchased from Cerilliant (Round Rock, TX, USA). Formic acid and ammonium formate were from Sigma-Aldrich (St. Louis, MO, USA). Potassium hydroxide (KOH), Methyl-tert butyl ether (MTBE), and LC-MS grademethanol and acetonitrile were obtained from Spectrum Chemical (Gardena, CA, USA).

All of the stock solutions were prepared at 1 mg/mL in methanol. The working standard solutions (1 µg/mL, 10 ng/mL and 1 ng/mL) were prepared by serial dilution of the eight stock solutions with acetonitrile. All solutions were stored at −20˚C in tightly sealed glass bottles. All drug standard solutions were allowed to equilibrate to room temperature for at least 30 minutes before use. No internal standard was used since it is a confirmation analysis and quantitation is not necessary.

2.2. Sample Preparations

Liquid-liquid extraction was used to extract cathinones and amphetamines from equine plasma and urine. Urine and plasma samples were prepared using similar procedures. The extraction was conducted using 1 mL of plasma or 0.1 mL urine mixed with 1 mL water. The mixture was then mixed thoroughly with 50 μL 1 M KOH to ensure that the samples were basic. Five milliliter of MTBE was added for liquid-liquid extraction. The tubes were gently shaken for 10 minutes on a rotorack and centrifuged at 3000 revolution per minute (RPM) for 10 minutes. The top organic layer was transferred to Pyrex disposable glass test tubes (16 × 100 mm), and the contents were dried at 40°C under nitrogen in a turbovap evaporator. The extracts were reconstituted with 100 μL solvent (water and methanol, volume ratio of 1:1) and transferred to polypropylene autosampler vials. For each LC-MS/MS analysis, ten microliters of the dissolved extract was used.

2.3. LC-MS/MS Conditions

The LC-MS/MS system comprised a Shimadzu liquid chromatography system and an AB Sciex 4000 Qtrap mass spectrometer. The LC system consisted of LC-20ADXR pumps, a SIL-20ACXR auto-sampler, a DGU-20A5 degasser and a CTO-20A column oven (Shimadzu Scientific Instruments, Columbia, MD, USA). Analyte separation was performed on an Astec Chirobiotic V2 column (2.1 × 150 mm, 5 micron particle size) from Sigma (St. Louis, MO, USA). Column oven temperature was maintained at 25°C. The mobile phase was a mixture of methanol and 50 mM ammonium formate/0.01% formic acid in LC-MS grade water (95/5, v/v). The isocratic total flow was 0.45 mL/min and the total analysis time was only6 minutes.

Qtrap 4000 (AB Sciex, Foster City, CA, USA) was used for mass spectrometry analysis. Positive ionspray voltage was set at 4000 volts. Ultra-pure nitrogen was used for ion source solvent evaporation and vacuum control. Gas 1, Gas 2, and curtain gas settings were 65, 45 and 40 psi, respectively. The ion source temperature was set at 400°C. Multiple-reaction-monitoring (MRM) was used for analysis due to its high sensitivity and specificity. The neat standards were infused using a syringe pump for optimization of ion source parameters. The quantifying ion is the most intense ion among all of the MRM transitions for one compound. The chromatographic peak areas of the quantifying ions are used for calculations of recovery, precision and matrix effect in the validation process. The other ions are qualifying ions that are used for ion chromatographic peak area ratio calculations. The quantifying ions, qualifying ions and the corresponding settings for declustering potential (DP), entrance potential (EP), collision energy (CE) and collision cell exit potential (CXP) for each compounds are listed in Table 1.

Table 1. MRM acquisition ions used and the corresponding electronic parameters for methamphetamine, amphetamine, cathinone and methcathinone.

		DP (volts)	EP (volts)	CE (volts)	CXP (volts)
Methamphetamine					
Quantifying ion	91	44	9	26	7.5
Qualifying ion	119	44	9	16	7.5
Qualifying ion	65	44	9	56	11
Amphetamine					
Quantifying ion	91	35	9	26	7.5
Qualifying ion	119	35	9	13	3.5
Qualifying ion	65	35	9	52	9
Cathinone					
Quantifying ion	117	39	10	34	9
Qualifying ion	105	39	10	26	11
Qualifying ion	89	39	10	59	7
Methcathinone					
Quantifying ion	131	49	14	29	10
Qualifying ion	130	49	14	44	10
Qualifying ion	105	49	14	33	8

2.4. Method Validation

Validation of this liquid-liquid extraction LC-MS/MS acquisition method was performed by checking specificity, extraction recovery, matrix effect, intra-day and inter-day precision, and limit of detection. Methamphetamine, amphetamine, cathinone and methcathinone are all RCI class 1 drugs, and positive confirmation of these drugs at any level in equine plasma or urine would be a violation. Since quantification is not necessary, the limit of quantification or linearity range was not assessed. Because each of the four compounds studied here has S and R enantiomers, eight analytes were evaluated.

Endogenous compounds and other matrix interferences could produce a false positive for analytes of interest. The method specificity was demonstrated by analysis of six different lots of blank equine plasma or urine samples. Each chromatogram was checked for peaks that might interfere with the detection of the eight analytes.

Extraction recovery was evaluated in three replicates. Plasma samples at concentration 0.1 ng/mL and urine samples at 1 ng/mL were extracted. Three blank plasma and urine samples were extracted in the same batch. After extraction, the blank plasma or urine extracts were spiked with the eight analytes to the corresponding concentration of 0.1 ng/mL (plasma) or 1 ng/mL (urine). Recovery was determined by comparing the average chromatographic peak areas between the samples spiked with the drug standards before and after extractions.

Ionization suppression or enhancement in electrospray ionization is usually from matrix effect. Triplicate samples at concentrations of 0.1 ng/mL (plasma) and 1 ng/mL (urine) were extracted and analyzed by this LC- MS/MS method. The same experiment was performed using deionized water. The plasma or urine matrix effect was calculated by comparing average chromatographic peak areas of the quantifying ions in plasma or urine with those in water. If the plasma or urine signal was stronger than that of water, it showed matrix enhancement, while a lower value indicated matrix suppression.

Intra-day precision was evaluated by analyzing six replicate plasma or urine samples at concentration of 0.1 ng/mL (plasma) or 1 ng/mL (urine) on the same day. For inter-day precision analysis, three sets of six replicate plasma or urine samples at the same concentrations as above were analyzed on three different days.

The lower limit of detection and lowest concentration at which the compounds can be confirmed were checked to find out the sensitivity of the method. Triplicate plasma samples at 2, 5, 10, 20, and 50 pg/mL were extracted and analyzed. Urine samples at concentrations of 10, 20, 50, 100, 200, and 500 pg/mL were also tested in triplicate.

3. RESULTS AND DISCUSSION

3.1. Method Development

The aim of our research was to develop and validate a simple, fast, sensitive and selective LC-MS/MS method for confirmation and enantiomer separation of amphetamines and cathinones extracted from equine blood or urine. Since more than 50% of the pharmaceutical drugs are chiral, enantioselective chromatography has gained more and more attention [14] [15] [26] . There are many types of commercial chiral columns with different stationary phases [25] [27] . These stationary phases include polysaccharide derivatives, macrocyclic antibodies, proteins, cyclodextrins and pirke-type. Efficiency of enantioseparation is mainly determined by the chiral discriminative power of the chiral stationary phase employed. Macrocyclic antibody Vancomycin-based CHIRO- BIOTIC V2 column has demonstrated separation of amine compounds and worked well for our applications.

The separation of chiral drugs was performed under isocratic conditions. Several mobile phase modifiers were studied in order to obtain chiral separation in LC and to maintain satisfactory electrospray ionisation perfor- mance in positive ionization mode. Methanol, acetonitrile, formic acid, acetic acid, ammonium formate and ammonium acetate were tested for mobile phases or additives. Methanol, formic acid and ammonium formate were chosen because narrower chromatographic peaks with shorter retention times were achieved with this mobile phase. Also, ammonium formate and formic acid were used in this method due to their solubility in high content organic mobile phases and their volatility for fast solvent evaporation inelectrospray. High percentage of organic solvent methanol also makes solvent evaporation easier and promotes better sensitivity. Figure 1shows the separation of the four compounds and the eight isomers showed their unique retention times. All of the analytes were eluted in 5 minutes. Even though the (S)- and (R)-enantiomers are not baseline resolved, the resolution was sufficient to unambiguously differentiate the two isomers.

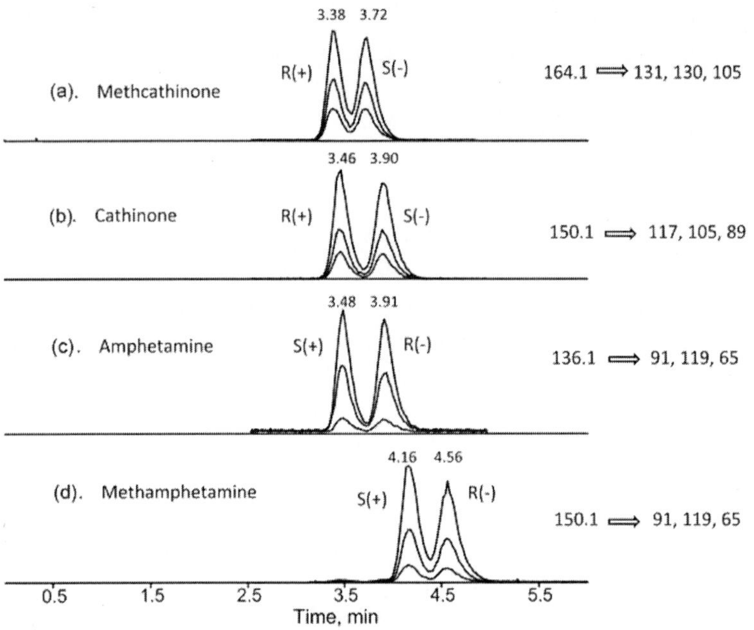

Figure 1. Chiral separation chromatograms of methcathinone, cathinone, amphetamine and methamphetamine extracted from a plasma sample spiked at 0.1 ng/mL.

3.2. Method Validation Results

Specificity testing was performed to make sure this method was free of endogenous compounds and other matrix interferences that could potentially produce a false positive signal and interfere with the analysis. Six different lots of blank equine plasma or urine samples were analyzed and the results indicated that the method is specific, because no interference peaks, capable of producing false positives, were observed in the MRM chromatograms.

A simple one step liquid-liquid extraction was used for sample processing. MTBE has a low boiling point and it evaporates quickly. Compared to the commonly used extraction solvent ethyl acetate, plasma and urine extracted with MTBE resulted in much cleaner extract, especially under basic conditions. The extraction recovery results for equine plasma and urine are listed in Table 2. Extraction recovery in plasma ranges from 84% to 100% and it is between 70% to 98% for urine. Urine samples had lower recovery compared to plasma. Even though cathinone has lowest extraction recovery among others (70% for urine and 84% for plasma), the results demonstrated that most of the drugs are extracted and recovered from both sample matrices.

Co-eluting compounds may cause ion suppressions or enhancements in the electrospray ionization process. These co-eluting compounds are extracted from the sample matrix together with the analytes, resulting in stronger or weaker signal. Triplicate plasma and urine extracts were compared with water extracts, which should be free of matrix effect (100%). In Table 2, matrix effect results showed slightly over 100% in general, which indicates both plasma and urine have some ion signal enhancements. This method is not a quantification method and the minor ion signal enhancement can be accepted.

Intra-day method precision was evaluated by analyzing six replicate plasma or urine samples on the same day. Inter-day method precision was evaluated by analyzing eighteen plasma or urine samples that were acquired on three different days. The precision of the method was determined by calculating the relative standard deviation (RSD) of peak areas of quantifying ions. The RSDs of allanalytes are below 5%, as listed in Table 2. The low RSDs indicated that the method had good precision for routine qualitative enantiomer analysis of metham-phe- tamine, amphetamine, cathinone and methcathinonein equine plasma and urine.

The lower limit of detection (LLOD) of this method in both equine plasma and urine is defined as the lowest concentration at which the compound of interest could be detected but not necessarily confirmed. It can be estimated as the lowest concentration at which all MRM products ions showed a signal-to-noise ratio ≥ 3. For medication violations, the racing industry commonly accepts confirmation criteria that include retention time and

Table 2. Urine and plasma validation results for methamphetamine, amphetamine, cathinone and methcathinone (S)- and (R)-enantiomers.

Urine validation results	Methamphetamine		Amphetamine		Cathinone		Methcathinone	
	S(+)	R(−)	S(+)	R(−)	R(+)	S(−)	R(+)	S(−)
Extraction recovery	94%	98%	86%	85%	70%	70%	85%	86%
Matrix effect	114%	106%	108%	109%	111%	113%	118%	117%
Precision RSD (intra-day) (6)	2.7%	3.7%	3.4%	2.3%	4.0%	4.4%	3.8%	3.2%
Precision RSD (inter-day) (6 + 6 + 6)	2.8%	4.0%	2.8%	3.2%	3.6%	3.7%	4.3%	3.3%
Lower limit of detection (pg/mL)	20	20	200	200	250	250	20	20
Lower limit of confirmation (pg/mL)	50	50	500	500	500	500	50	50
Plasma validation results	**Methamphetamine**		**Amphetamine**		**Cathinone**		**Methcathinone**	
	S(+)	R(−)	S(+)	R(−)	R(+)	S(−)	R(+)	S(−)
Extraction recovery	100%	97%	95%	98%	84%	84%	100%	94%
Matrix effect	109%	112%	118%	117%	98%	112%	113%	123%
Precision RSD (intra-day) (6)	3.7%	2.2%	4.3%	4.7%	3.5%	2.9%	3.8%	3.7%
Precision RSD (inter-day) (6 + 6 + 6)	4.5%	4.6%	4.8%	4.6%	3.9%	2.9%	4.3%	3.2%
Lower limit of detection (pg/mL)	2	2	20	20	10	10	2	2
Lower limit of confirmation (pg/mL)	5	5	50	50	25	25	5	5

spectral match, or comparison of the chromatographic peak area ratios of MRM signals for samples, calibrators and a neat standard. The lowest concentration at which the compounds can be confirmed was taken as the concentration at which the analyte responses were identifiable and discrete with a signal to noise ratio ≥ 10 for all MRM ionchromatogram peaks used. At this concentration, the product ion peak relative abundances should fall within the acceptable range when compared to the reference spectrum (Association of Official Racing Chemists (AORC) confirmation criteria: 10% absolute or 30% relative, whichever is greater) [28] . The results listed in Table 2 demonstrated that methamphetamine and methcathinone are more sensitive and they both could be detected as low as 2 pg/mL in plasma and 20 pg/mL in urine. In this method, urine sample volume used is only 0.1 mL. If more urine sample is used, the LLOD could be lower even though more matrix effect may be present. Amphetamine has relatively higher LLOD because MRM transition m/z 136 - 65 is not sensitive. However, a LLOD of 20 pg/mL in plasma and 200 pg/mL in urine are still the lowest numbers reported for amphetamine chiral analysis from equine samples. Overall, this method presented very good sensitivity coupled with short analysis time.

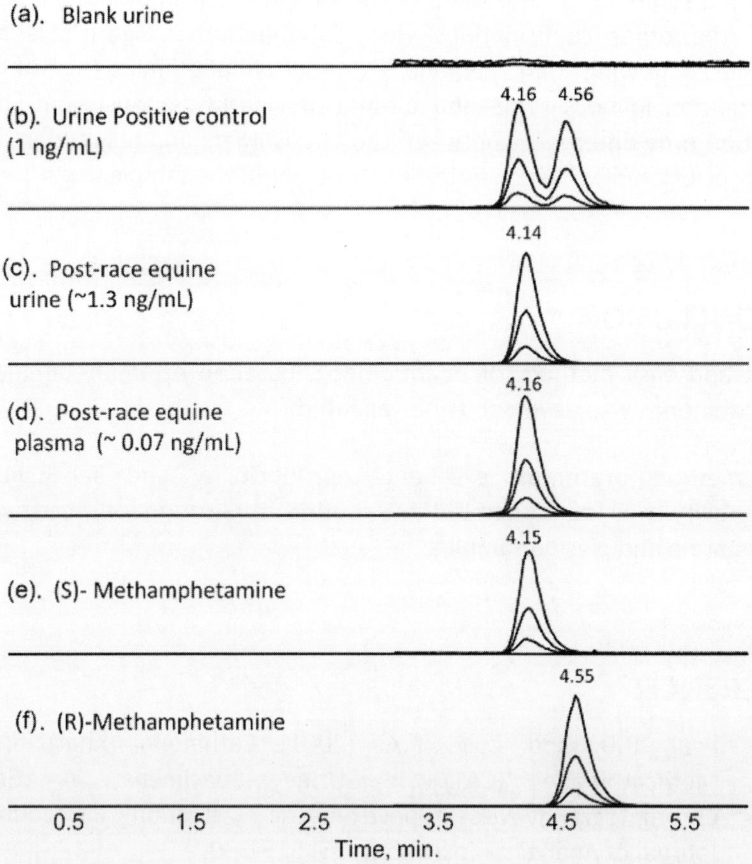

Figure 2. An example of (S)-methamphetamine identification in post-race horse urine and plasma samples. The three MRM transition traces are all shown. Product ion chromatograms of methamphetamine from analysis of (a) Blank urine; (b) Urine positive control; (c) Post-race equine urine sample; (d) The corresponding post-race equine plasma sample; (e) (S)-Me- thamphetamine standard; (f) (R)-Methamphetamine standard.

3.3. Race-Track Sample Applications

In the past two years, 12 equine urine samples and 6 plasms samples were confirmed positive for metham-phe- tamine. Only one plasma and one urine sample from the same horse were R-methamphetamine and all of the other confirmations were (S)-enantiomer. Figure 2 is an example showing an equine (S)-methamphetamine positive confirmation in both urine and plasma. It clearly demonstrated the retention time differences between the two isomers and resulted in an easy conclusion of which enantiomer is present in the samples.

4. CONCLUSION

A fast and easy method for enantiomer separation of amphetamines and cathinones was developed and validated.

This method presented excellent reproducibility and sensitivity. Applicability was demonstrated by routine application of post-race equine urine and plasma samples.

REFERENCES

1. Paul, B.D. and Cole, K.A. (2001) Cathinone (Khat) and Methcathinone (CAT) in Urine Specimens: A Gas Chromatography-Mass Spectrometric Detection Procedure. Journal of Analytical Toxicology, 25, 525-530.

2. Sporkert, F., Pragst, F., Bachus, R., Masuhr, F. and Harms, L. (2003) Determination of Cathinone, Cathine and Norephedrine in Hair of Yemenite Khat Chewers. Forensic Science International, 133, 39-46.

3. Strano-Rossi, S., Botre, F., Bermejo, A.M. and Tabernero, M.J. (2009) A Rapid Method for the Extraction, Enantiomeric Separation and Quantification of Amphetamines in Hair. Forensic Science International, 193, 95-100.

4. Yi, R., Zhao, S., Lam, G., Sandhu, J., Loganathan, D. and Morrissey, B. (2013) Detection and Elimination Profile of Cathinone in Equine after Norephedrine (Propalin®) Administration Using a Validated Liquid Chromatography—Tandem Mass Spectrometry Method. Analytical and Bioanalytical Chemistry, 405, 9711-9722.

5. Mikuma, T., Iwata, Y.T., Miyaguchi, H., Kuwayama, K., Tsujikawa, K., Kanamori, T. and Inoue, H. (2015) The Use of a Sulfonated Capillary on Chiral Capillary Electrophoresis/Mass Spectrometry of Amphetamine-Type Stimulants for Methamphetamine Impurity Profiling. Forensic Science International, 249, 59-65.

6. Pasin, D., Bidny, S. and Fu, S. (2015) Analysis of New Designer Drugs in Post-Mortem Blood Using High-Resolution Mass Spectrometry. Journal of Analytical Toxicology, 39, 163-171.

7. Gambaro, V., Arnoldi, S., Colombo, M.L., Dellacqua, L., Guerrini, K. and Roda, G. (2012) Determination of the Active Principles of Catha Edulis: Quali-Quantitative Analysis of Cathinone, Cathine, and Phenylpropanolamine. Forensic Science International, 217, 87-92.

8. Holler, J.M., Vorce, S.P., Bosy, T.Z. and Jacobs, A. (2005) Quantitative and Isomeric Determination of Amphetamine and Methamphetamine from Urine Using a Nonprotic Elution Solvent and R(-)-a-Methoxy-a-Trifluoromethylphenylacetic Acid Chloride Derivatization. Journal of Analytical Toxicology, 29, 652-657.

9. Makino, Y., Ohta, S. and Hirobe, M. (1996) Enantiomeric Separation of Amphetamine by High-Performance Liquid Chromatography Using Chiral Crown Ether-Coated Reversed-Phase Packing: Application to Forensic Analysis. Forensic Science International, 78, 65-70.

10. Glennon, R.A., Schechter, M.D. and Rosecrans, J.A. (1984) Discriminative Stimulus Properties of S(-)- and R(+)-Cathinone, (+)-Cathine and Several Structural Modifications. Pharmacology Biochemistry & Behavior, 21, 1-3.

11. Nielsen, J.A. and Schechter, M.D. (1985) Behavioral and Neurochemical Effects of (-)- and (±)-Cathinone: Dose- Response and Time-Course. Progress in Neuro-Psychopharmacology and Biological Psychiatry, 9, 739-743.

12. Mohr, S., Weib, J.A., Spreitz, J. and Schmid, M.G. (2012) Chiral Separation of New Cathinone- and Amphetamine-Related Designer Drugs by Gas Chromatography-Mass Spectrometry Using Trifluoroacetyl-L-Prolyl Chloride as Chiral Derivatization Reagent. Journal of Chromatography A, 1269, 352-359.

13. Rasmssen, L.B., Olsen, K.H. and Johansen, S.S. (2006) Chiral Separation and Quantification of R/S-Amphetamine, R/S-Methamphetamine, R/S-MDA, R/S-MDMA, and R/S-MDEA in Whole Blood by GC-EI-MS. Journal of Chromatography B, 842, 136-141.

14. Nystrom, I., Trygg, T., Woxler, P., Ahlner, J. and Kronstrand, R. (2005) Quantitation of R-(-)- and S-(+)-Amphetamine in Hair and Blood by Gas Chromatography-Mass Spectrometry: An Application to Compliance Monitoring in Adult-Attention Deficit Hyperactivity Disorder Treatment. Journal of Analytical Toxicology, 29, 682-688.

15. Mislanova, C. and Hutta, M. (2003) Role of Biological Matrices during the Analysis of Chiral Drugs by Liquid Chromatography. Journal of Chromatography B, 797, 91-109.

16. Guillarme, D., Bonvin, G., Badoud, F., Schappler, J., Rudaz, S. and Veuthey, J. (2010) Fast Chiral Separation of Drugs Using Columns Packed with Sub-2 μm Particles and Ultra-High Pressure. Chirality, 22, 320-330.

17. Kasprzyk-Hordern, B., Kondakal, V.V.R. and Baker, D.R. (2010) Enantiomeric Analysis of Drugs of Abuse in Waste-water by Chiral Liquid Chromatography Coupled with Tandem Spectrometry. Journal of Chromatography A, 1217, 4575-4586.

18. Bagnall, J.P., Evans, S.E., Wort, M.T., Lubben, A.T. and Kasprzyk-Hordern, B. (2012) Using Chiral Liquid Chromatography Quadrupole Time-of-Flight Mass Spectrometry for the Analysis

of Pharmaceuticals and Illicit Drugs in Surface and Wastewater at the Enantiomeric Level. Journal of Chromatography A, 1249, 115-129.

19. Mohr, S., Taschwer, M. and Schmid, M.G. (2012) Chiral Separation of Cathinone Derivatives Used as Recreational Drugs by HPLC-UV Using a Chiralpak AS-H Column as Stationary Phase. Chirality, 24, 486-492.

20. Schwaninger, A.E., Meyer, W.R. and Maurer, H.H. (2012) Chiral Drug Analysis Using Mass Spectrometric Detection Relevant to Research and Practice in Clinical and Forensic Toxicology. Journal of Chromatography A, 1269, 122-135.

21. Perera, R.W.H., Abraham, I., Gupta, S., Kowalska, P., Lightsey, D., Marathaki, C., Singh, N.S. and Lough, W.J. (2012) Screening Approach, Optimization and Scale-Up for Chiral Liquid Chromatography of Cathinones. Journal of Chromatography A, 1269, 189-197.

22. Newmeyer, M.N., Concheiro, M. and Huestis, M.A. (2014) Rapid Quantitative Chiral Amphetamine Liquid Chromatography-Tandem Mass Spectrometry: Method in Plasma and Oral Fluid with a Cost-Effective Chiral Derivatizing Reagent. Journal of Chromatography A, 1358, 68-74.

23. Wang, T., Shen, B., Shi, Y., Xiang, P. and Yu, Z. (2015) Chiral Separation and Determination of R/S-Methamphetamine and Its Metabolite R/S-Amphetamine in Urine Using LC-MS/MS. Forensic Science International, 246, 72-78.

24. Taschwer, M., Seidi, Y., Mohr, S. and Schmid, M.G. (2014) Chiral Separation of Cathinone and Amphetamine Derivatives by HPLC/UV Using Sulfated β-Cyclodextrin as Chiral Mobile Phase Additive. Chirality, 26, 411-418.

25. Ribeiro, A.R., Maia, A.S., Cass, Q.B. and Tiritan, M.E. (2014) Enantioseparation of Chiral Pharmaceuticals in Biomedical and Environmental Analyses by Liquid Chromatography: An Overview. Journal of Chromatography B, 968, 8-21.

26. Nguyen, L.A., He, H. and Pham-Huy, C. (2006) Chiral Drugs: An Overview. International Journal of Biomedical Science, 2, 85-100. [Paper reference:1]

27. Hamman, C., Wong, M., Aliagas, I., Ortwine, D.F., Pease, J., Schmid, D.E. and Victorino, J. (2013) The Evaluation of 2 Chiral Stationary Phase and the Utilization of Sub-2.0 µm Coated Polysaccharide Chiral Stationary Phases via Supercritical Fluid Chromatography. Journal of Chromatography A, 1305, 310-319.

28. The Association of Official Racing Chemists (2015) AORC Guidelines for the Minimum Criteria for Identification by Chromatography and Mass Spectrometry.

Chapter 10

Zinc Complexes of New Chiral Aminophenolate Ligands: Synthesis, Characterization and Reactivity toward Lactide

Pascal Binda[1*], Kimberly Rivers[1], Clifford Padgett[2]

[1]*Department of Chemistry and Forensic Science, Savannah State University, Savannah, GA, USA*

[2]*Department of Chemistry and Physics, Armstrong State University, Savannah, GA, USA*

ABSTRACT

The syntheses of a library of new chiral aminophenolate bidentate O,N-type ligands HOC_6H_4(2-R- 4-R′)$CH_2N(Me)CH(Me)C_6H_5$ [R = R′ = Bu^t, 1; R = R′ = Pen^t, 2; R = Bu^t, R′ = Me, 3; R = Me, R′ = Bu^t, 4; R = R′ = Me, 5] and tridentate O,N,O-type ligands HOC_6H_4(2,4-Bu^t)CH = NCH(R″)C_6H_5 [R″ = Me, 6; R″ = CH_2OMe, 7] are reported. These ligands were characterized by elemental analysis, nuclear magnetic resonance spectroscopy (^{1}H & ^{13}C), and single crystal X-ray diffraction. These ligands serve as chiral auxiliaries for inorganic chemists to design chiral metal-based complexes for asymmetric catalysis and stereoselective polymerization reactions. Three new heteroleptic zinc complexes based on these ligands have been synthesized in moderate yields via a ligand-exchange transamination reaction between homoleptic $[Zn(N(SiMe_3)_2)_2]$

and one equivalent of corresponding ligands to afford [L^3ZnN- $(SiMe_3)_2$] (3a), [$L^4ZnN(SiMe_3)_2$] (4a), and [$L^7ZnN(SiMe_3)_2$] (7a). Solvent-free polymerization of rac- lactide at 130˚C using these zinc compounds yielded atactic polylactides with M_w 10,000 g/mol and narrow polydispersity of 1.3.

Keywords: Chiral Ligands, Aminophenolate, Zinc, Lactide, Polymerization

1. INTRODUCTION

Due to the problems associated with conventional olefinic polymeric materials, the production of biodegradable plastics from renewable resources has been a large focus in chemistry and chemical engineering research within the last two decades [1] - [16] . Aliphatic polylactides (PLAs) and polycaprolactones (PCLs) are polyesters that have been studied intensively due to their biodegradable and bioassimilable properties and have found interesting applications in packaging, drug delivery and medical implantation devices [17] - [42] . In order to obtain well- defined polyester PLA and PCL materials with predetermined microstructure, the ring-opening polymerization (ROP) of cyclic monomers (lactide and caprolactone) initiated by single-site metal complexes has been employed for chain-growth polymerization through coordination-insertion mechanism [1] - [11] . This allows for a much higher polymerization control compared to step-growth direct condensation of lactic acid.

Well-defined metal complexes of the form LMX (L = multidentate ancillary ligand; M = central metal; X = initiating group) have been studied extensively to investigate the electronic and steric properties of the central metal and ancillary ligand and their effects on the polymerization process [4] , [43] - [70] . Metal-based initiators of aluminum, magnesium, zinc, tin, iron, titanium, zirconium, yttrium, and lanthanide metals have been employed with reactivity increasing with metal size due to increase in electropositivity, while polymerization control decreases in the same order. As the reactivity and selectivity of a metal catalyst are largely determined by the auxiliary ligands [71] - [74] , ligand design has been a central focus in ROP of cyclic esters, with aminophenolate ligands receiving great attention due to the potential to fine tune the steric and electronic properties by varying the substituent groups and pendant side-arms to afford different donor atoms, as well as their inexpensive synthetic strategies [67] - [70] , [75] - [80] . Given their widespread application, it is somewhat surprising that the chiral variants of aminophenolate ligands are relatively lacking in the literature. The physical, mechanical, and thermal properties of PLA depend to a great extent on the polymer's tacticity (isotactic, syndiotactic, heterotactic and atactic). It is believed that isotactic and heterotactic PLAs produced from rac-LA will produce materials with superior properties. Thus controlling the microstructure of PLA produced from rac-LA has received great attention [6] , [81] - [87] and chiral catalysts can provide a better stereo-control.

Zinc complexes are efficient catalysts for ROP of lactides with moderate reactivities compared to the highly electropositive lanthanide metals and have recently received much attention due to its flexible coordination chemistry, substitutional lability, Lewis acidity and non-toxicity [88] - [101] . With moderate reactivity of zinc allowing for more polymerization control, attaching chiral aminophenolate ancillary ligands with varying substituents and pendant arms may induce high isotactic/heterotactic selectivity in the ROP of rac-lactide. To the best of our knowledge, only Wang and Ma have reported the diastereoselective synthesis of chiral aminophenolate zinc complexes with multiple stereogenic centers and their isoselective polymerization of rac-lactide [101] . Herein we report the synthesis and characterization of new chiral aminophenolate zinc complexes with varying substituents and pendant donor arms containing one stereogenic center, and their reactivity toward racemic lactide.

2. EXPERIMENTAL PROCEDURE

2.1. Materials and Measurements

All air- or moisture-sensitive reactions were carried out under a dry nitrogen atmosphere, employing standard Schlenk line and glovebox techniques. Solvents were dried over sodium/benzophenone and distilled under nitrogen. Racemic lactide was purchased from Aldrich, stored under an inert atmosphere, and used as received. Deuterated solvents were purchased from Alfa Aesar and used as received. 2,4-Di-tert-butylphenol, 2,4-dime- thylphenol, 2,4-di-tert-pentylphenol, 37 wt% formaldehyde, and D(+)-alpha-methylbenzylamine were purchased from Acros Organic and used as received. 3,5-Di-tert-butyl-2-hydroxybenzaladehyde was purchased from Alfa Aesar and used as received. (R)-(+)-N-α-dimethylbenzylamine, (R)-(?)-2-methoxy-1-phenylethylamine, and 2- tert-butyl-4-methylphenol were purchased from Aldrich while 4-tert-butyl-2-methylphenol was purchased from Fluka and used as received. All ^{1}H and ^{13}C NMR spectra were recorded on a JEOL-300 NMR spectrometer and referenced to $CDCl_3$, C_6D_6, C_7D_8, or C_4D_8O. Elemental analyses (sealed ampoules under inert atmosphere for air-sensitive compounds) were performed by Midwest Microlab Incorporated in Indianapolis, IN. Melting points were obtained on a Mel-Temp apparatus and are uncorrected. Optical rotations were recorded on a Rudolph Autopol III polarimeter with sodium D-line (589 nm) at room temperature. GC-MS analyses were performed on Bruker Scion 436-GC systems at 50˚C with electron impact ionization (70 eV). Gel permeation chromatography (GPC) analysis was performed using Tosoh EcoSEC HLC-8320 GPC instrument and calibrated to polystyrene standards. Single crystals were analyzed at Armstrong State University in Savannah, GA using Rigaku XtaLAB mini X-ray diffractometer.

2.2. Synthesis of Chiral Ligands

(R)-(+)-(2,4-Di-tert-butyl-1-hydroxylbenzyl)-N-α-dimethylbenzylamine ($L^{1}H$)

2,4-Di-tert-butylphenol (3.054 g, 14.80 mmol), 37 wt% formaldehyde (0.444 g, 14.80 mmol), and (R)-(+)-N- α-dimethylbenzylamine (2.000 g, 14.80 mmol) were dissolved in ethanol (5 mL). The resulting solution was heated at reflux for 18 h and then cooled to room temperature. Solvent and water were removed using high vacuum Schlenk line to obtain pale yellow oily solid. Recrystallization from ethanol at −10˚C (freezer) yielded an off-white solid, which was dried under high vacuum at 40˚C (4.858 g, 92.8%). Mp: 73.4˚C - 73.6˚C; $[\alpha]_D$ + 0.301 (c = 0.04, toluene). Elemental analysis: (Found: C 81.55, H 9.94, N 4.07. $C_{24}H_{35}NO$ requires C 81.535, H 9.98, N 3.96. ^{1}H NMR (300 MHz; $CDCl_3$; 298 K) 1.29 (s, 9H, $Ar^{t}Bu$), 1.51 (s, 9H, $Ar^{t}Bu$), 1.55 (d, 3H, J = 6.87 Hz, ArCH(Me)NMe), 2.23 (s, 3H, ArCH(Me)NMe), 3.77 (br, 2H, $ArCH_2N$), 3.89 (q, 1H, J = 6.87 Hz, ArCH- (Me)NMe), 6.90 (s, 1H, ArH), 7.27 (s, 1H, ArH),

7.34 - 7.41 (br, 5H, ArH), 11.32 (br, 1H, ArOH). $^{13}C\{H\}$ NMR (75 MHz; $CDCl_3$; 298 K) 17.3 ($ArCMe_3$), 29.8 ($ArCMe_3$), 31.9 ($ArCMe_3$), 34.3 ($ArCMe_3$), 35.0 (ArCH(Me)NMe), 36.7 (ArCH(Me)NMe), 59.1 (ArCH(Me)NMe), 61.6 ($ArCH_2N$), 121.4, 122.8, 123.6, 127.6, 128.4, 128.5, 135.5, 140.5, 154.7 (all ArC). GC-MS m/z calcd for $C_{24}H_{35}NO$: 353.55; found 353.4.

(R)-(+)-(2,4-Di-tert-pentyl-1-hydroxylbenzyl)-N-α-dimethylbenzylamine (L^2H)

2,4-Di-tert-pentylphenol (1.734 g, 7.40 mmol), 37 wt% formaldehyde (0.222 g, 7.40 mmol), and (R)-(+)-N- α-dimethylbenzylamine (1.000 g, 7.40 mmol) were dissolved in ethanol (5 mL). The resulting solution was hea- ted at reflux for 18 h and then cooled to room temperature. Solvent and water were removed using high vacuum Schlenk line to obtain colorless oil. Recrystallization from ethanol at −10°C (freezer) yielded a white, oily solid that was dried under high vacuum at room temperature to afford a colorless oil (2.115 g, 74.9%); $[\alpha]_D$ + 0.224 (c = 0.04, toluene). Elemental analysis: (Found: C 81.51, H 10.17, N 3.78. $C_{26}H_{39}NO$ requires C 81.84, H 10.30, N 3.67%). ^1H NMR (300 MHz; $CDCl_3$; 298 K) 0.69 (t, 3H × 2, J = 7.56 Hz, $ArCMe_2CH_2Me$), 1.27 (s, 6H, $ArCMe_2CH_2Me$), 1.42 (s, 6H, $ArCMe_2CH_2Me$), 1.52 (d, 3H, J = 6.87 Hz, ArCH(Me)NMe), 1.61 (q, 2H, J = 7.56 Hz, $ArCMe_2CH_2Me$), 1.94 (q, 2H, J = 7.56 Hz, $ArCMe_2CH_2Me$), 2.18 (s, 3H, ArCH(Me)NMe), 3.73 (br, 2H, $ArCH_2N$), 3.85 (q, 1H, J = 6.87 Hz, ArCH(Me)NMe), 6.76 (s, 1H, ArH), 7.09 (s, 1H, ArH), 7.26 - 7.39 (br, 5H, ArH), 11.15 (br, 1H, ArOH). $^{13}C\{H\}$ NMR (75 MHz; $CDCl_3$; 298 K) 9.3 ($ArCMe_2CH_2Me$), 9.7 ($ArCMe_2$- CH_2Me), 18.7 ($ArCMe_2CH_2Me$), 27.7 ($ArCMe_2CH_2Me$), 28.7 ($ArCMe_2CH_2Me$), 33.0 ($ArCMe_2CH_2Me$), 36.5 ($ArCMe_2CH_2Me$), 37.3 (ArCH(Me)NMe), 38.5 (ArCH(Me)NMe), 59.1 (ArCH(Me)NMe), 61.3 ($ArCH_2N$), 121.1, 124.2, 124.9, 127.6, 128.4, 128.5, 133.7, 138.6, 154.4 (all ArC).

(R)-(+)-(2-Tert-butyl-4-methyl-1-hydroxylbenzyl)-N-α-dimethylbenzylamine (L^3H)

2-Tert-butyl-4-methylphenol (2.430 g, 14.80 mmol), 37 wt% formaldehyde (0.444 g, 14.80 mmol), and (R)- (+)-N-α-dimethylbenzylamine (2.000 g, 14.80 mmol) were dissolved in ethanol (5 mL). The resulting solution was heated at reflux for 18 h and then cooled to room temperature. Solvent and water were removed using high vacuum Schlenk line to obtain a white solid. Recrystallization from ethanol at −10°C (freezer) yielded a white powder that was dried under high vacuum at room temperature (4.010 g, 92.0%). Yellow single crystals suitable for X-ray crystallography were grown from the supernatant solution at room temperature. Mp: 62.9°C - 63.2°C; $[\alpha]_D$ + 0.232 (c = 0.04, toluene). Elemental analysis: (Found: C 81.01, H 9.33, N 4.55. $C_{21}H_{29}NO$ requires C 80.98, H 9.385, N 4.50%). ^{1}H NMR (300 MHz; $CDCl_3$; 298 K) 1.49 (s, 9H, Ar^{t}Bu), 1.54 (d, 3H, J = 6.87 Hz, ArCH(Me)NMe), 2.19 (s, 3H, ArCH(Me)NMe), 2.30 (s, 3H, ArMe), 3.71 (br, 2H, $ArCH_2N$), 3.89 (q, 1H, J = 6.87 Hz, ArCH(Me)NMe), 6.70 (s, 1H, ArH), 7.05 (s, 1H, ArH), 7.33 - 7.43 (br, 5H, ArH), 11.31 (br, 1H, ArOH). ^{13}C{H} NMR (75 MHz; $CDCl_3$; 298 K) 17.2 ($ArCMe_3$), 20.9 (ArMe), 29.7 ($ArCMe_3$), 34.7 (ArCH- (Me)NMe), 36.5 (ArCH(Me)NMe), 58.7 (ArCH(Me)NMe), 61.3 ($ArCH_2N$), 122.2, 126.7, 127.1, 127.6, 128.4, 128.5, 136.3, 140.4, 154.8 (all ArC).

(R)-(+)-(4-Tert-butyl-2-methyl-1-hydroxylbenzyl)-N-α-dimethylbenzylamine (L^4H)

4-Tert-butyl-2-methylphenol (1.215 g, 7.40 mmol), 37 wt% formaldehyde (0.222 g, 7.40 mmol), and (R)-(+)- N-α-dimethylbenzylamine (1.000 g, 7.40 mmol) were dissolved in ethanol (3 mL). The resulting solution was heated at reflux for 18 h and then cooled to room temperature. Solvent and water were removed using high vacuum Schlenk line to obtain a white, oily solid. Recrystallization from ethanol was unsuccessful as only a colorless oil was obtained. Compound was purified by column chromatography (silica gel 100 mesh, hexane/ethyl acetate = 9:1) to afford a colorless oil. The oil was dissolved in hot methanol and allowed to cool to room temperature to yield a white powder, that was dried under high vacuum at 60°C (4.858 g, 92.8%). Mp: 90.4°C - 90.6°C; $[\alpha]_D$+ 0.304 (c = 0.04, toluene). Elemental analysis: (Found: C 80.88, H 9.29, N 4.61. $C_{21}H_{29}NO$ requires C 80.98, H 9.385, N 4.50%). ^{1}H NMR (300 MHz; $CDCl_3$; 298 K) 1.30 (s, 9H, Ar^{t}Bu), 1.56 (d, 3H, J = 6.87 Hz, ArCH(Me)NMe), 2.24 (s, 3H, ArCH(Me)NMe), 2.29 (s, 3H, ArMe), 3.65 (br, 2H, $ArCH_2N$), 3.82 (q, 1H, J = 6.87 Hz, ArCH(Me)NMe), 6.81 (s, 1H, ArH), 7.09 (s, 1H, ArH), 7.32 - 7.40 (br, 5H, ArH), 11.31 (br, 1H, ArOH). ^{13}C{H} NMR (75 MHz; $CDCl_3$; 298 K) 16.1 (ArMe), 17.9 ($ArCMe_3$), 31.7 ($ArCMe_3$), 34.0 (ArCH- (Me)NMe), 37.4 (ArCH(Me)NMe), 58.6 (ArCH(Me)NMe), 63.0 ($ArCH_2N$), 120.7, 123.0, 123.7, 126.7, 127.7, 128.2, 128.6, 141.1, 141.3, 153.7 (all ArC).

(R)-(+)-(2,4-Di-methyl-1-hydroxylbenzyl)-N-α-dimethylbenzylamine (L^5H)

2,4-Di-methylphenol (4.52 g, 37 mmol), 37 wt% formaldehyde (1.11 g, 37 mmol), and (R)-(+)-N-α-dime- thylbenzylamine (5.00 g, 37 mmol) were dissolved in methanol (20 mL). The resulting solution was heated at reflux for 18 h and then cooled to room temperature. Solvent and water were removed using high vacuum Schlenk line to obtain a pale yellow, oily solid. Recrystallization from ethanol at −10°C (freezer) yielded an off-white solid, which later became pale yellow oil upon warming to room temperature. The oil was dried under high vacuum at room temperature (9.45 g, 94.8%); $[\alpha]_D$ + 0.252 (c = 0.04, toluene). Elemental analysis: (Found: C 79.65, H 8.38, N 5.09. $C_{18}H_{23}NO$ requires C 80.256, H 8.606, N 5.200. ^1H NMR (300 MHz; $CDCl_3$; 298 K) 1.59 (d, 3H, J = 6.87 Hz, ArCH(Me)NMe), 2.23 (s, 3H, ArMe), 2.29 (s, 3H, ArMe), 2.39 (s, 3H, ArCH(Me)- NMe), 3.70 (br, 2H, $ArCH_2N$), 3.87 (q, 1H, J = 6.87 Hz, ArCH(Me)NMe), 6.65 (s, 1H, ArH), 6.97 (s, 1H, ArH), 7.38 - 7.47 (br, 5H, ArH), 11.02 (s, 1H, ArOH). $^{13}C\{H\}$ NMR (75 MHz; $CDCl_3$; 298 K) 15.9 (ArMe), 17.6 (ArMe), 20.6 (ArCH(Me)NMe), 37.3 (ArCH(Me)NMe), 58.3 (ArCH(Me)NMe), 62.9 ($ArCH_2N$), 114.8, 121.1, 124.6, 126.7, 127.7, 128.1, 128.7, 130.5, 140.9, 153.8 (all ArC). GC-MS m/z calcd for $C_{18}H_{23}NO$: 269.39; found 269.3.

(R)-(+)-α-Methyl-2-benzyl-imino-methyl-2,4-Di-tert-butyl-phenol (L^6H)

3,5-Di-tert-butyl-2-hydroxybenzaldehyde (5.000 g, 21.340 mmol), and D(+)-alpha-methylbenzylamine (2.586 g, 21.340 mmol) were dissolved in ethanol (100 mL). The resulting solution was heated at reflux for 18 h and then cooled to room temperature. Crystallization from the saturated methanol solution at room temperature yielded yellow crystals (6.354 g, 88.2%). Mp: 93.8°C - 94.1°C; $[\alpha]_D$ + 0.513 (c = 0.02, toluene). Elemental analysis: (Found: C 81.92, H 9.16, N 4.24. $C_{23}H_{31}NO$ requires C 81.85, H 9.26, N 4.15%). ^1H NMR (500 MHz; $CDCl_3$; 298 K) 1.34 (s, 9H, Ar^tBu), 1.50 (s, 9H, Ar^tBu), 1.69 (d, 3H, J = 6.50 Hz, ArCH(Me)N), 4.59 (q, 1H, J = 6.50 Hz, ArCH(Me)N), 7.12 (s, 1H, ArH), 7.29 (s, 1H, ArH), 7.38 - 7.44 (br, 5H, ArH), 8.49 (s, 1H, ArCH = N), 13.88 (s, 1H, ArOH). $^{13}C\{H\}$ NMR (125 MHz; $CDCl_3$; 298 K) 24.9 ($ArCMe_3$), 29.5 ($ArCMe_3$), 31.5 ($ArCMe_3$), 34.1 ($ArCMe_3$), 35.1 (ArCH(Me)N), 68.5 (ArCH(Me)N), 118.0, 126.0, 126.5, 127.2, 128.6, 136.7, 140.1, 144.1, 158.0 (all ArC), 164.6 (ArCH = N).

(R)-(−)-α-Methylene-β-methoxy-2-benzyl-imino-methyl-2,4-Di-tert-butyl-phenol (L^7H)

3, 5-Di-tert-butyl-2-hydroxybenzaldehyde (1.550 g, 6.613 mmol), and (R)-(?)-2-methoxy-1-phenylethylamine (1.000 g, 6.613 mmol) were dissolved in ethanol (100 mL). The resulting solution was heated at reflux for 18 h and then cooled to room temperature. Solvent and water were removed using high vacuum Schlenk line to obtain a yellow solid. Recrystallization from ethanol at −10˚C (freezer) yielded a yellow solid (2.317 g, 95.3%); $[\alpha]_D$ −0.298 (c = 0.02, toluene). Yellow single crystals suitable for X-ray crystallography were grown from the supernatant solution at room temperature. Mp: 67.1˚C - 67.3˚C. Elemental analysis: (Found: C 78.47, H 8.94, N 4.00. $C_{24}H_{33}NO_2$ requires C 78.43, H 9.05, N 3.81%). ^1H NMR (300 MHz; $CDCl_3$; 298 K) 1.33 (s, 9H, Ar^tBu), 1.51 (s, 9H, Ar^tBu), 3.39 ($ArCH(N)CH_2OMe$), 3.76 (br, 2H, $ArCH(N)CH_2OMe$), 4.56 (br, 1H, $ArCH(N)CH_2$- OMe), 7.14 (s, 1H, ArH), 7.29 - 7.44 (br, 6H, ArH), 8.46 (s, 1H, ArCH = N), 11.69 (br, 1H, ArOH). $^{13}C\{H\}$ NMR (75 MHz; $CDCl_3$; 298 K) 29.6 ($ArCMe_3$), 31.6 ($ArCMe_3$), 34.3 ($ArCMe_3$), 35.2 ($ArCMe_3$), 59.0 (ArCH- $(N)CH_2OMe$), 59.4 ($ArCH(N)CH_2OMe$), 73.7 ($ArCH(N)CH_2OMe$), 118.1, 126.5, 127.3, 127.8, 128.8, 136.7, 140.0, 140.2, 140.6, 158.1 (all ArC), 166.8 (ArCH = N). GC-MS m/z calcd for $C_{24}H_{33}NO_2$: 337.51; found 337.6.

2.3. Synthesis of Chiral Zinc Complexes

$[L^3ZnN(SiMe_3)_2]$ (3a)

To a colorless toluene solution (10 mL) of $Zn[N(SiMe_3)_2]_2$ (1.545 g, 4.000 mmol) at −20˚C, a colorless hexane solution (20 mL) of ligand L^3 (1.246 g, 4.000 mmol) was added drop wise under nitrogen. The resulting reaction mixture was stirred gently (4 h) as it warmed to 12˚C to afford a clear pale yellow solution of 3a. Volatiles were removed in vacuo without heating to afford a yellow foam-like oily solid that was washed with hexanes and dried under high vacuum to afford 3a (1.15 g, 53.6%); Mp: 97.1˚C - 97.4˚C; $[\alpha]_D$ + 0.056 (c = 0.01, toluene). Elemental analysis: (Found: C 60.38, H 8.61, N 5.29. $C_{27}H_{46}N_2OZnSi_2$ requires C 60.48, H 8.65, N 5.22%). ^1H NMR (300 MHz; C_4D_8O; 298 K) 0.02 - 0.008 (br, 18H, $N(SiMe_3)_2$), 1.26 (s, 9H, Ar^tBu), 1.40 (br, 3H, ArMe), 2.02 (br, 3H, ArCH(Me)NMe), 2.16 (br, 1H, ArCH(Me)NMe), 2.40 (s, 3H, ArCH(Me)NMe), 4.39 (br, 2H, $ArCH_2N$), 6.21 (s, 1H, ArH), 6.85 (s, 1H, ArH), 7.32 - 7.46 (br, 5H, ArH).

$[L^4ZnN(SiMe_3)_2]$ (4a)

To a colorless toluene solution (10 mL) of $Zn[N(SiMe_3)_2]_2$ (1.545 g, 4.000 mmol) at −20˚C, a colorless hexane solution (20 mL) of ligand L^4 (1.246 g, 4.000 mmol) was added drop wise under nitrogen. The resulting reaction mixture was stirred gently (4 h) as it warmed to 12˚C to afford a clear pale yellow solution of 4a. Volatiles were removed in vacuo without heating to afford a pale-yellow (off white) solid which was washed twice with hexanes and dried under high vacuum to afford 4a (1.10 g, 51.3%); Mp: 119.8˚C - 120.1˚C; $[\alpha]_D$ + 0.068 (c = 0.01, toluene). Elemental analysis: (Found: C 60.40, H 8.61, N 5.07. $C_{27}H_{46}N_2OZnSi_2$ requires C 60.48, H 8.65, N 5.22%). ^1H NMR (300 MHz; C_4D_8O; 298 K) 0.04 (s, 18H, $N(SiMe_3)_2$), 1.12 (s, 9H, Ar^tBu), 1.21 (br, 3H, ArMe), 1.46 (br, 3H, ArCH(Me)NMe), 2.20 (br, 1H, ArCH(Me)NMe), 2.29 (s, 3H, ArCH(Me)NMe), 4.51 (br, 2H, $ArCH_2N$), 6.48 (s, 1H, ArH), 7.00 - 7.16 (br, 5H, ArH), 7.39 (s, 1H, ArH).

$[L^7ZnN(SiMe_3)_2]$ (7a)

To a colorless THF solution (10 mL) of $Zn[N(SiMe_3)_2]_2$ (1.545 g, 4.000 mmol) at −20˚C, a clear yellow THF solution (15 mL) of ligand L^7 (1.470 g, 4.000 mmol) was added drop wise under nitrogen. The resulting reaction mixture was stirred gently (4 h) as it warmed to 12˚C to afford a clear yellow solution of 7a that was put in a freezer (−56˚C) to grow crystals. Yellow crystals of 7a were obtained at −56˚C that later dissolved at room temperature. Volatiles were removed in vacuo without heating to afford a yellow oily solid that was recrystallized from a THF/hexane mixture at −56˚C and dried under high vacuum to afford 7a (1.40 g, 53.5%); Mp: 211.9˚C - 212.3˚C, $[\alpha]_D$−0.052 (c = 0.01, toluene). Elemental analysis: (Found: C 62.21, H 8.49, N 4.58. $C_{34}H_{48}N_2O_3ZnSi_2$requires C 62.41, H 7.39, N 4.28%). ^1H NMR (300 MHz; C_4D_8O; 298 K) 0.04 (s, 18H, $N(SiMe_3)_2$), 1.30 (s, 9H, Ar^tBu), 1.45 (s, 9H, Ar^tBu), 3.09 ($ArCH(N)CH_2OMe$), 4.12 (br, 2H, ArCH(N)- CH_2OMe), 4.81 (br, 1H, $ArCH(N)CH_2OMe$), 6.84 (s, 1H, ArH), 6.95 (br, 5H, ArH),8.06 (s, 1H, ArCH = N).

2.4. Polymerization Procedure

Appropriate amount of zinc compound and racemic lactide were measured and put in an oven-dried Schlenk flask. The flask was subjected to heating at 130˚C. After appropriate reaction time, the polymerization reaction was quenched with 1 ml of acidified methanol and the polymer was isolated and analyzed.

3. RESULTS AND DISCUSSION

3.1. Synthesis of Chiral Ancillary Ligands

The chiral ligands L^1H-L^5H (Figure 1) were synthesized via Mannich condensation reactions using inexpensive substituted phenols, formaldehyde and (R)-(+)-N-α-dimethylbenzylamine in refluxing ethanol (Scheme 1). Meanwhile, the chiral Schiff base ligand L^6H and L^7H were synthesized through condensation reactions of 3, 5-Di-tert-butyl-2-hydroxybenzaldehyde with the corresponding chiral amine, (R)-(+)-N-α-dimethylbenzylamine and (R)-(?)-2-methoxy-1-phenylethylamine, respectively (Scheme 2). The synthesized ligands were characterized using NMR, elemental analysis, and GC-MS to ascertain the structures. X-ray crystallography of single crystals of ligands L^3H and L^7H indeed supported NMR spectra and elemental analysis.

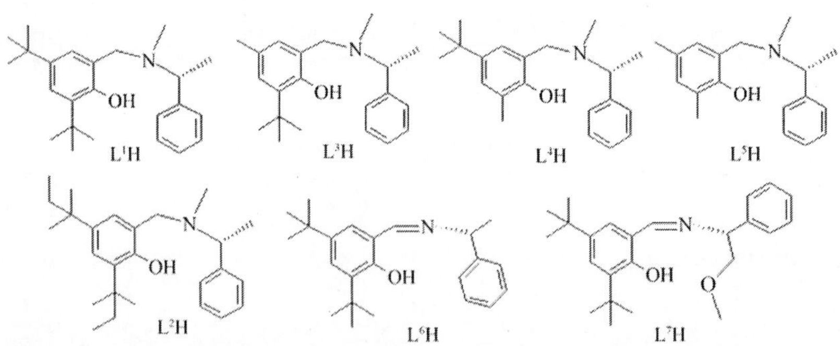

Figure 1. New chiral [ON] and [ONO] aminophenolate ligands.

The use of different phenolic substituents (methyl, butyl and pentyl) will provide a library of compounds suitable for metal catalytic investigations in polymerization reactions. Attachment of synthesized ligands to zinc, calcium, tin and palladium metals would offer new research opportunities in asymmetric synthesis and metal catalyzed ring-opening polymerization of lactones. There is great interest in investigating the effect of one stereogenic center in conjunction with phenolic bulky substituent on catalytic selectivity. The [ON] ligands are expected to be bidentate with the possibility of having a tridentate coordination via the phenyl pendant arms while the [ONO] ligand has an additional coordinating oxygen atom.

3.2. Synthesis of Zinc Complexes

Three new zinc compounds 3a, 4a, and 7a have been synthesized in moderate yields, via acid-base transamination reactions employing one equivalent of the zinc precursor, $Zn(N(SiMe_3)_2)_2$, and one equivalent of the ligands L^3H, L^4H and L^7H in toluene and THF to afford $[L^3ZnN(SiMe_3)_2]$ (3a) $[L^4ZnN(SiMe_3)_2]$ (4a) and $[L^7ZnN(SiMe_3)_2]$ (7a) (Scheme 3). Compounds 3a and 4a were synthesized in toluene while 7a was synthesized in THF. The synthesized zinc compounds have been fully characterized by NMR spectroscopy, elemental analysis and melting point (see experimental). ^1H NMR spectroscopy of compounds 3a and 4a in d_8-toluene (C_7D_8) revealed two distinct ligand environments (in approximate equal ratio); likely caused by molecular dimerization to satisfy the coordinatively unsaturated zinc metal. The silylamide ligand was represented by two peaks of approximate equal intensity. However, NMR spectroscopy of 3a and 4a in the presence of a donor solvent such as

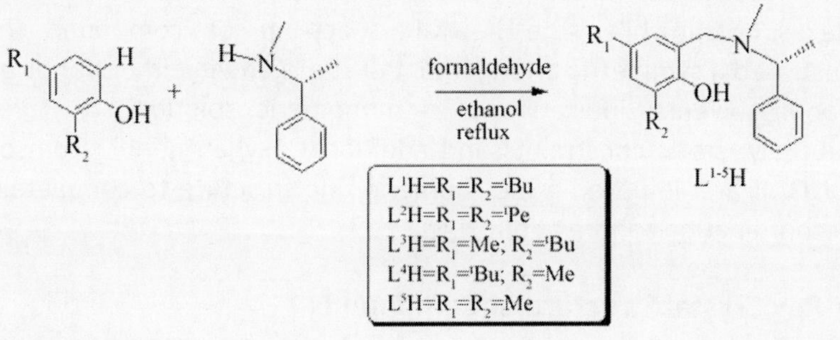

Scheme 1. Synthesis of ligands L^1H-L^5H via Mannich condensation reactions.

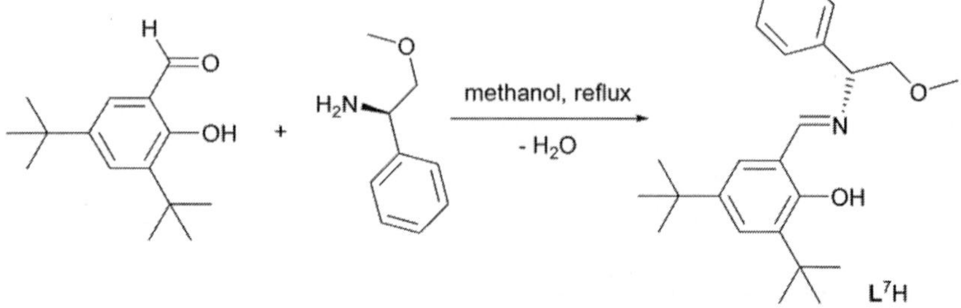

Scheme 2. Synthesis of chiral Schiff base ligand L^7H via condensation reaction.

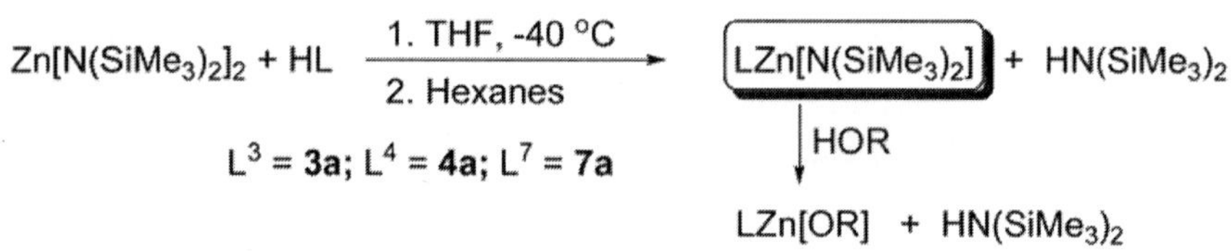

Scheme 3. General synthesis of metal catalysts via ligand exchange reactions.

d8-THF (C_4D_8O), revealed only one chemical environment consistent with a symmetrical, coordinately saturated monomeric zinc center. It is difficult to be certain of the exact nature of the asymmetry without solid state structural data. However, it was very difficult to isolate good single crystals for X-ray determination due to the extreme solubility of the zinc complexes. Meanwhile, the ^1H NMR spectrum of compound 7a demonstrated a symmetric arrangement of the ligand in either donor or non-donor solvents; indicative of a monomeric solution structure. Undoubtedly, steric constraints and additional oxygen donor atom of the [ONO] ligand imposed a mo- nomeric zinc structure to completely fill the coordination sphere about zinc.

3.3. X-Ray Crystal Structure of Compounds

The results of the single crystal X-ray structure determination of ligands L^3H, and L^7H are consistent with the formulation proposed by elemental analysis data and NMR spectroscopic analysis. Ligand L^7H crystallized in the monoclinic space group $P2_1$ with two molecules in the asymmetric unit, while L^3H crystallized in the orthorhombic space group $P2_12_12_1$ with a single molecule in the asymmetric unit (see Figure 2 and Table 1). The solid state structures also confirmed the configuration of chiral centers for the ligands as indicated in Figure 1. Due to the extreme solubility of the zinc complexes in donor (THF) and non-donor solvents (hexane and toluene), it was very difficult to isolate good single crystals for X-ray determination.

3.4. Polymerization of Lactide Using Zinc Complexes

Compounds 3a, 4a, and 7a were treated with rac-lactide under different reaction times and conditions and the results are summarized in Table 2. Except where noted, all polymerization reactions were performed solvent free at 130°C and quantitative conversion (based on ^1H NMR spectroscopy) was achieved (see Table 2). Entry 1 is the

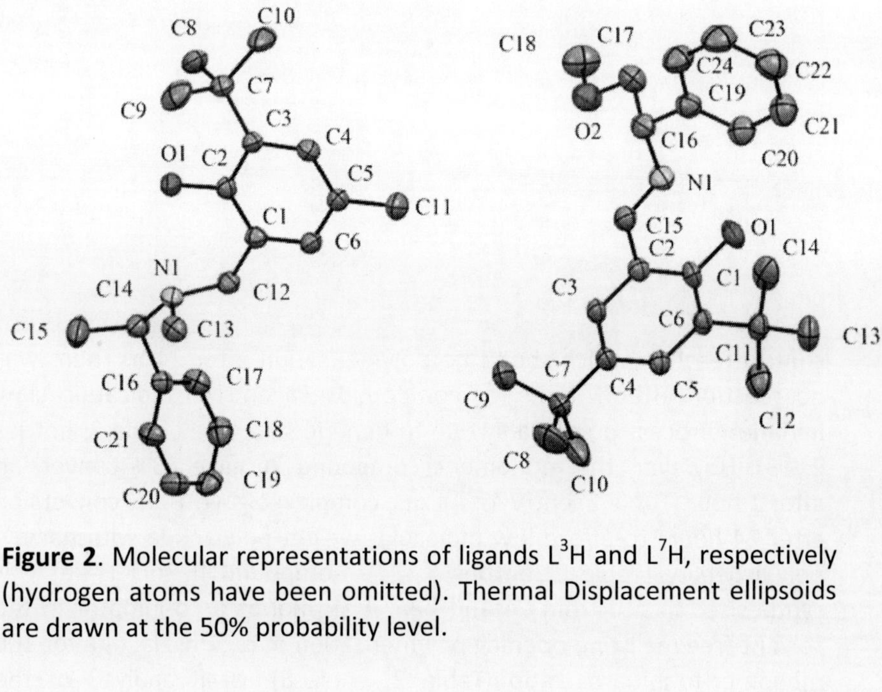

Figure 2. Molecular representations of ligands L^3H and L^7H, respectively (hydrogen atoms have been omitted). Thermal Displacement ellipsoids are drawn at the 50% probability level.

Table 1. Crystallographic data of ligands L^3H and L^7H.

	L^3H	L^7H
Chemical structure	$C_{21}H_{29}NO$	$C_{24}H_{33}NO_2$
Space group	$P2_12_12_1$	$P2_1$
Cell lengths: a, b, c (Å)	8.8192(8), 9.1586(9), 23.020(2)	10.653(6), 9.423(3), 22.096(6)
Cell volume: V (Å^3)	1859.36	2217.09
Z	4	4
Cell angles: α, β, γ (°)	90.000, 90.000, 90.000	90.000, 91.699(13), 90.000
R-Factor (%)	5.32	5.5

Table 2. Polymerization of rac-Lactide using zinc complexes.

Entry	Initiator	Co-initiator	[LA]/[I]^a	Time (h)	Conv. (%)^b	M_n (10^3)^c	M_w (10^3)^c	PDI^c
1	–	–	1000^d	24	0	–	–	–
2	$L^3ZnN(SiMe_3)_2$ 3a	–	1000^d	1	0	–	–	–
3	$L^4ZnN(SiMe_3)_2$ 4a	–	1000^d	1	0	–	–	–
4	$L^7ZnN(SiMe_3)_2$ 7a	–	1000^d	1	53	–	–	–
5	$L^3ZnN(SiMe_3)_2$ 3a	–	1000^d	24	100	7.4	9.9	1.34
6	$L^4ZnN(SiMe_3)_2$ 4a	–	1000^d	24	100	7.0	8.9	1.27
7	$L^7ZnN(SiMe_3)_2$ 7a	–	1000^d	24	100	8.9	11.8	1.29
8	$L^7ZnN(SiMe_3)_2$ 7a	$PhCH_2OH$	100^d	24	100	–	–	–

^{a}Monomer to initiator ratio. ^{b}Conversion: determined by ^1H NMR (integration of the methyl resonances of LA and PLA). ^{c}M_n and M_w/M_n (PDI) of polymer determined by SEC with calibration to polystyrene standards. ^{d}Bulk polymerization at 130°C.

control reaction which shows no polymerization after 24 h. There was no reaction after 1 hour for compounds 3a and 4a indicating slow initiation process presumably due to dimeric structure (Table 2, entries 2 - 3). However, the monomeric compound 7a gave 53% conversion after 1 hour (Table 2, entry 4). All zinc complexes gave 100% conversion after 24 hours to afford low molecular weight polylactide with narrow polydispersity (Table 2, entries 5 - 7). Compound [L^7ZnOCH_2Ph] was synthesized in-situ from 7a and benzyl alcohol as a co-initiator in the solvent-free melt ring-opening polymerization of racemic lactide for 100 monomer-to-initiator ratio (Table 2, entry 8). NMR analysis of the polymer obtained shows the initiating group as part of the polylactide without ligand L^7. All polymerization reactions were quenched with acidified methanol and polylactide was isolated as amorphous solids indicative of atactic polymer.

3.5. Reactivity of Zinc Complexes with Lactide

We observed moderate catalytic reactivity of rac-LA with the newly synthesized chiral zinc complexes with no stereo-control, probably due to the harsh reaction conditions with temperatures of 130°C. No reactivity was observed with the zinc complexes when polymerization was conducted in either toluene or THF at 80°C after 24 hours for 1000:1 lactide-to-initiator ratio. Furthermore, increasing the amount of initiator to 100:1 under the same conditions did not yield any polymer. Due to the small size of zinc metal, in order to effectively carryout chain-growth polymerization of LA via coordination-insertion mechanism, most researchers have been successful at a temperature of 130°C [88] - [101] . Even though this is not somewhat surprising, it is hypothesized that attaching a larger metal such as calcium or lanthanum to the newly synthesized chiral aminophenolate ligands would provide better catalytic reactivity at milder conditions with better polymerization control.

The new chiral zinc complexes gave polymer molecular weights lower than expected due to extensive transesterification as a result of extended reaction times beyond complete polymerization reaction. It should be noted that transesterification backbiting reactions has been reported as a major cause of obtaining low molecular weight polyester chains during active polymerization process that is allowed to run over long periods without quenching the reaction [68] [70] [75] . In addition, some rac-lactide molecules were sublimed during the solvent-free bulk polymerization reactions at 130°C resulting in low M_n. Having the tert-butyl group at the ortho (3a) or para (4a) positions of the phenolate did not make any significant difference in reactivity with lactide due to small metal size.

4. CONCLUSION

We have reported new heteroleptic zinc amido complexes supported by newly synthesized chiral multidentate monoanionic amino phenolate ligands with varying steric and electronic demands. Zinc complexes were found to have moderate catalytic activity towards ring-opening polymerization of racemic lactide at 130°C to afford atactic polymers with molecular weight of 10,000 g/mol and a narrow polydispersity index of 1.3. The newly synthesized chiral aminophenolate ligands are suitable chiral auxiliaries for inorganic chemists to design metal-based complexes for asymmetric catalysis and stereoselective polymerization reactions.

ACKNOWLEDGEMENTS

The authors are grateful to Savannah State University's president's mini grant and US Department of Defense Army Research Office Award No. 67208-RT-REP for partial financial supports, and to Xiaolin Liu of Clemson University for help with GPC analysis.

REFERENCES

1. Wu, X.-Y., Ren, Z.-G. and Lang, J.-P. (2014) Ni(II) Tetraphosphine Complexes as Catalysts/Initiators in the Ring Opening Polymerization of ε-Caprolactone. Dalton Transactions, 43, 1716-1723.

2. Stanlake, L.J.E., Beard, J.D. and Schafer, L.L. (2008) Rare-Earth Amidate Complexes. Easily Accessed Initiators for ε-Caprolactone Ring-Opening Polymerization. Inorganic Chemistry, 47, 8062-8068.

3. Celiz, A.D. and Scherman, O.A. (2008) Controlled Ring-Opening Polymerization Initiated via Self-Complementary Hydrogen-Bonding Units. Macromolecules, 41, 4115-4119.

4. O'Keefe, B.J., Hillmyer, M.A. and Tolman, W.B. (2001) Polymerization of Lactide and Related Cyclic Esters by Discrete Metal Complexes. Journal of the Chemical Society, Dalton Transactions, 2215-2224.

5. Coates, G.W. (2002) Polymerization Catalysis at the Millennium: Frontiers in Stereoselective, Metal-Catalyzed Polymerization. Journal of the Chemical Society, Dalton Transactions, 467-475.

6. Dechy-Cabaret, O., Martin-Vaca, B. and Bourissou, D. (2004) Controlled Ring-Opening Polymerization of Lactide and Glycolide. Chemical Reviews, 104, 6147-6176.

7. Hou, Z. and Wakatsuki, Y. (2002) Recent Developments in Organolanthanide Polymerization Catalysts. Coordination Chemistry Reviews, 231, 1-22.

8. Saruul, P., Sriene, F., Somers, D.A. and Samac, D.A. (2002) Production of a Biodegradable Plastic Polymer, Poly-β-Hydroxybutyrate, in Transgenic Alfalfa. Crop Science, 42, 919-927.

9. Cameron, P.A., Gibson, V.C., Redshaw, C., Segal, J.A., White, A.J.P. and Williams, D.J. (2002) Synthesis and Characterisation of Neutral and Cationic Alkyl Aluminium Complexes Bearing N,O-Schiff Base Chelates with Pendant Donor Arms. Journal of the Chemical Society, Dalton Transactions, 415-422.

10. Tsuji, H. (2005) Poly(lactide) Stereocomplexes: Formation, Structure, Properties, Degradation, and Applications. Macromolecular Bioscience, 5, 569-597.

11. Wu, J., Yu, T.-L., Chen, C.-T. and Lin, C.-C. (2006) Recent Developments in Main Group Metal Complexes Catalyzed/Initiated Polymerization of Lactides and Related Cyclic Esters. Coordination Chemistry Reviews, 250, 602-626.

12. Kricheldorf, H.R., Boettcher, C. and Tonnes, K.-U. (1992) Polylactones: 23. Polymerization of Racemic and Meso D,L-Lactide with Various Organotin Catalysts-Stereochemical Aspects. Polymer, 33, 2817-2824.

13. Chabot, F., Vert, M., Chapelle, S. and Grange, P. (1983) Configurational Structures of Lactic Acid Stereocopolymers as Determined by 13C and 1H nmr. Polymer, 24, 53-59.

14. Jikei, M., Takeyama, Y., Yamadoi, Y., Shinbo, N., Matsumoto, K., Motokawa, M., Ishibashi, K. and Yamamoto, F. (2015) Synthesis and Properties of Poly(L-lactide)-Poly(ε-caprolactone)

Multiblock Copolymers by the Self-Polycon- densation of Diblockmacromonomers. Polymer Journal, 47, 657-665.

15. Haba, O. and Itabashi, H. (2014) Ring-Opening Polymerization of a Five-Membered Lactone Transfused to a Cyclohexane Ring. Polymer Journal, 46, 89-93.

16. Bero, M., Kasperczyk, J. and Jedlinski, Z. (1990) Coordination Polymerization of Lactides, 1. Structure Determination of Obtained Polymers. Die Makromolekulare Chemie, 191, 2287-2296.

17. Pltel, R.H., Hodgson, L.M. and Williams, C. (2008) Biocompatible Initiators for Lactide Polymerization. Polymer Reviews, 48, 11-63.

18. Joseph, J.G. (2006) Polymers for Tissue Engineering, Medical Devices, and Regenerative Medicine. Concise General Review of Recent Studies. Polymers for Advanced Technologies, 17, 395-418.

19. Fukushima, K. and Kimura, Y. (2006) Stereocomplexed Polylactides (Neo-PLA) as High-Performance Bio-Based Polymers: Their Formation, Properties, and Application. Polymer International, 55, 626-642.

20. Albertsson, A.-C. and Varma, I.K. (2003) Recent Developments in Ring Opening Polymerization of Lactones for Biomedical Applications. Biomacromolecules, 4, 1466-1486.

21. Ikada, Y. and Tsuji, H. (2000) Biodegradable Polyesters for Medical and Ecological Applications. Macromolecular Rapid Communications, 21, 117-132.

22. Isogai, N., Asamura, S., Hagishi, T., Ikada, Y., Morita, S., Hillyer, J. and Landis, W.J. (2004) Tissue Engineering of an Auricular Cartilage Model Utilizing Cultured Chondrocyte-Poly(L-Lactide-ε-Caprolactone) Scaffolds. Tissue Engineering, 10, 673-687.

23. Benicewicz, B.C. and Hoyt, A.E. (1992) Liquid Crystal Polyester Thermosets. US Patent, US5114612 A.

24. Daniels, A.U., Chang, M.K. and Adriano, K.P. (1990) Mechanical Properties of Biodegradable Polymers and Composites Proposed for Internal Fixation of Bone. Journal of Applied Biomaterials, 1, 57-78.

25. Athanasiou, K.A., Niederauer, G.G. and Agrawal, C.M. (1996) Sterilization, Toxicity, Biocompatibility, and Clinical Applications of Polylactic Acid/Polyglycolic Acid Copolymers. Biomaterials, 17, 93-102.

26. Langer, R. (1998) Drug Delivery and Targeting. Nature, 392, 5-10.

27. Uhrich, K.E., Cannizzaro, S.M., Langer, R.S. and Shakesheff, K.M. (1999) Polymeric Systems for Controlled Drug Release. Chemical Reviews, 99, 3181-3198.

28. Jacoby, M. (2001) Applying Engineering, Materials, and Chemistry Principles, Researchers Produce Safe, Smart, and Effective Implantable Devices. Chemical & Engineering News, 79, 30-35.

29. Panyam, J. and Labhasetwar, V. (2003) Biodegradable Nanoparticles for Drug and Gene Delivery to Cells and Tissue. Advanced Drug Delivery Reviews, 55, 329-347.

30. Mu, L. and Feng, S. (2003) A Novel Controlled Release Formulation for the Anticancer Drug Paclitaxel (Taxol): PLGA Nanoparticles Containing Vitamin E TPGS. S. Journal of Controlled Release, 86, 33-48.

31. Kellomaki, M., Niiranen, H., Puumanen, K., Ashammakhi, N., Waris, T. and Tormala, P. (2000) Bioabsorbable Scaffolds for Guided Bone Regeneration and Generation. Biomaterials, 21, 2495-2505.

32. Ito, H., Minami, A., Tanino, H. and Matsuno, T. (2002) Fixation with Poly-L-lactic Acid Screws in Hip Osteotomy: 68 Hips Followed for 18 - 46 Months. Acta Orthopaedica Scandinavica, 73, 60-64.

33. Waris, E., Ninkovic, M., Harpf, C., Ninkovic, M. and Ashammakhi, N. (2004) Self-Reinforced Bioabsorbable Miniplates for Skeletal Fixation in Complex Hand Injury: Three Case Reports. The Journal of Hand Surgery, 29A, 452-457.

34. Gilding, D.K. and Reed, A.M. (1979) Biodegradable Polymers for Use in Surgery—Polyglycolic Acid/Polylactic Acid Homo- and Copolymers. Polymer, 20, 1459-1464.

35. Benicewicz, B.C. and Hopper, P.K. (1990) Review: Polymers for Absorbable Surgical Sutures—Part I. Journal of Bioactive and Compatible Polymers, 5, 453-472.

36. Lunt, J. (1998) Large-Scale Production, Properties and Commercial Applications of Polylactic Acid Polymers. Polymer Degradation and Stability, 59, 145-152.

37. Caldorera-Moore, M., Nicholas A. and Peppas, N.A. (2009) Micro- and Nanotechnologies for Intelligent and Responsive Biomaterial-Based Medical Systems. Advanced Drug Delivery Reviews, 16, 1391-1401.

38. Slager, J. and Domb, A.J. (2003) Biopolymer Stereocomplexes. Advanced Drug Delivery Reviews, 55, 549-583.

39. Gollwitzer, H., Ibrahim, K., Meyer, H., Mittelmeier, W., Busch, R. and Stemberger, A. (2003) Antibacterial Poly(D,L- lactic Acid) Coating of Medical Implants Using a Biodegradable Drug Delivery Technology. Journal of Antimicrobial Chemotherapy, 51, 585-591.

40. Lendlein, A. and Kelch, S. (2002) Shape-Memory Polymers. Angewandte Chemie International Edition, 41, 2034-2057.

41. Lendlein, A. and Langer, R. (2002) Biodegradable, Elastic Shape-Memory Polymers for Potential Biomedical Applications. Science, 296, 1673-1676.

42. Aoyagi, T., Miyata, F. and Nagase, Y. (1994) Preparation of Cross-Linked Aliphatic Polyester and Application to Thermos-Responsive Materials. Journal of Controlled Release, 32, 87-96.

43. Radano, C.P., Baker, G.L. and Smith, M.R. (2000) Stereoselective Polymerization of a Racemic Monomer with a Racemic Catalyst: Direct Preparation of the Polylactic Acid Stereocomplex from Racemic Lactide. Journal of the American Chemical Society, 122, 1552-1553.

44. Darensbourg, D.J., Choi, W., Karroonnirum, O. and Bhuvanesh, N. (2008) Ring-Opening Polymerization of Cyclic Monomers by Complexes Derived from Biocompatible Metals. Production of Poly(Lactide), Poly(Trimethylene Carbonate), and Their Copolymers. Macromolecules, 41, 3493-3502.

45. Ovitt, T.M. and Coates, G.W. (2002) Stereochemistry of Lactide Polymerization with Chiral Catalysts: New Opportunities for Stereocontrol Using Polymer Exchange Mechanisms. Journal of the American Chemical Society, 124, 1316-1326.

46. Kasperczyk, J.E. (1995) Microstructure Analysis of Poly(Lactic Acid) Obtained by Lithium Tert-Butoxide as Initiator. Macromolecules, 28, 3937-3939.

47. Rajashekhar, B., Roymuhury, S.K., Chakraborty, D. and Ramkumar, V. (2015) Group 4 Metal Complexes of Trost's Semi-Crown Ligand: Synthesis, Structural Characterization and Studies on the Ring-Opening Polymerization of Lactides and ε-Caprolactone. Dalton Transactions, 44, 16280-16293.

48. Thakur, K.A.M., Kean, R.T., Zell, M.T., Padden, B.E. and Munson, E.J. (1998) An Alternative Interpretation of the HETCOR NMR Spectra of Poly(Lactide). Chemical Communications, No. 17, 1913-1914.

49. Thakur, K.A.M., Kean, R.T., Hall, E.S., Kolstad, J.J. and Lindgren, T.A. (1997) High-Resolution 13C and 1H Solution NMR Study of Poly(Lactide). Macromolecules, 30, 2422-2428.

50. Zell, M.T., Padden, B.E., Paterick, A.J., Thakur, K.A.M., Kean, R.T., Hillmyer, M.A. and Munson, E.J. (2002) Unambiguous Determination of the 13C and 1H NMR Stereosequence Assignments of Polylactide Using High-Resolution Solution NMR Spectroscopy. Macromolecules, 35, 7700-7707.

51. Ovitt, T.M. and Coates, G.W. (2000) Stereoselective Ring-Opening Polymerization of rac-Lactide with a Single-Site, Racemic Aluminum Alkoxide Catalyst: Synthesis of Stereoblockpoly(Lactic Acid). Polymer Chemistry, 38, 4686-4692.

52. Cheng, M., Attygalle, A.B., Lobkovsky, E.B. and Coates, G.W. (1999) Single-Site Catalysts for Ring-Opening Polymerization: Synthesis of Heterotactic Poly(Lactic Acid) from rac-Lactide. Journal of the American Chemical Society, 121, 11583-11584.

53. Ovitt, T.M. and Coates, G.W. (1999) Stereoselective Ring-Opening Polymerization of meso-Lactide: Synthesis of Syndiotactic Poly(Lactic Acid). Journal of the American Chemical Society, 121, 4072-4073.

54. Chisholm, M.H., Iyer, S.S., McCollum, D.G., Pagel, M. and Werner-Zwanziger, U. (1999) Microstructure of Poly (Lactide). Phase-Sensitive HETCOR Spectra of Poly(meso-Lactide), Poly(rac-Lactide), and Atactic Poly(Lactide). Macromolecules, 32, 963-973.

55. Chisholm, M.H., Gallucci, J.C. and Phomphrai, K. (2005) Comparative Study of the Coordination Chemistry and Lactide Polymerization of Alkoxide and Amide Complexes of Zinc and Magnesium with a β-Diiminato Ligand Bearing Ether Substituents. Inorganic Chemistry, 44, 8004-8010.

56. Zhong, Z., Dijkstra, P.J. and Feijen, J. (2003) Controlled and Stereoselective Polymerization of Lactide: Kinetics, Selectivity, and Microstructures. Journal of the American Chemical Society, 125, 11291-11298.

57. Cai, C.-X., Amgoune, A., Lehmann, C.W. and Carpentier, J.-F. (2004) Stereoselective Ring-Opening Polymerization of Racemic Lactide Using Alkoxy-Amino-Bis(Phenolate) Group 3 Metal Complexes. Chemical Communications, No. 3, 330-331.

58. Coates, G.W. (2000) Precise Control of Polyolefin Stereochemistry Using Single-Site Metal Catalysts. Chemical Reviews, 100, 1223-1252.

59. Nimitsiriwat, N., Marshall, E.L., Gibson, V.C., Elsegood, M.R.J. and Dale, S.H. (2004) Unprecedented Reversible Migration of Amide to Schiff Base Ligands Attached to Tin: Latent Single-Site Initiators for Lactide Polymerization. Journal of the American Chemical Society, 126, 13598-13599.

60. Chisholm, M.H., Eilerts, N.W., Huffman, J.C., Iyer, S.S., Pacold, M. and Phomphrai, K. (2000) Molecular Design of Single-Site Metal Alkoxide Catalyst Precursors for Ring-Opening Polymerization Reactions Leading to Polyoxygenates. 1. Polylactide Formation by Achiral and Chiral Magnesium and Zinc Alkoxides, (η3-L)MOR, Where L = Trispyrazolyl- and Trisindazolylborate Ligands. Journal of the American Chemical Society, 122, 11845-11854.

61. Cai, C.X., Toupet, L., Lehmann, C.W. and Carpentier, J.-F. (2003) Synthesis, Structure and Reactivity of New Yttrium Bis(Dimethylsilyl)Amido and Bis(Trimethylsilyl)Methyl Complexes of a Tetradentatebis(Phenoxide) Ligand. Journal of Organometallic Chemistry, 683, 131-136.

62. Chamberlain, B.M., Cheng, M., Moore, D.R., Ovitt, T.M., Lobkovsky, E.B. and Coates, G.W. (2001) Polymerization of Lactide with Zinc and Magnesium β-Diiminate Complexes: Stereocontrol and Mechanism. Journal of the American Chemical Society, 123, 3229-3238.

63. Kowalski, A., Duda, A. and Penczek, S. (1998) Polymerization of L,L-Lactide Initiated by Aluminum Isopropoxide Trimer or Tetramer. Macromolecules, 31, 2114-2122.

64. Dove, A.P., Gibson, V.C., Marshall, E.L., White, A.J.P. and Williams, D. (2001) A Well Defined Tin(II) Initiator for the Living Polymerisation of Lactide. Chemical Communications, No. 3, 283-284.

65. Grunova, E., Kirillov, E., Roisnel, T. and Carpentier, J.-F. (2008) Group 3 Metal Complexes of Salen-like FluorousDialkoxy-Diimino Ligands: Synthesis, Structure, and Application in Ring-Opening Polymerization of rac-Lactide and rac-β-Butyrolactone.Organometallics, 27, 5691-5698.

66. Binda, P.I., Delbridge, E.E., Dugah, D.T., Skelton, B.W. and White, A.H. (2008) Synthesis and Structural Characterization of Some Potassium Complexes of Some Bis(Phenolate) Ligands and Some Novel Heterobimetallic Binuclear Arrays Formed with Trivalent Lanthanoid Ions. Zeitschrift für Anorganische und Allgemeine Chemie, 634, 325-334.

67. Delbridge, E.E., Dugah, D.T., Nelson, C.R., Skelton, B.W. and White, A.H. (2007) Synthesis, Structure and Oxidation of New Ytterbium(II) Bis(Phenolate) Compounds and Their Catalytic Activity towards ε-Caprolactone. Dalton Transactions, No. 1, 143-153.

68. Binda, P.I. and Delbridge, E.E. (2007) Synthesis and Characterisation of Lanthanide Phenolate Compounds and Their Catalytic Activity towards Ring-Opening Polymerisation of Cyclic Esters. Dalton Transactions, No. 41, 4685-4692.

69. Kerton, F.M., Whitwood, A.C. and Willans, C.E. (2004) A High-Throughput Approach to Lanthanide Complexes and Their Rapid Screening in the Ring Opening Polymerisation of Caprolactone. Dalton Transactions, No. 15, 2237-2244.

70. Binda, P.I., Delbridge, E.E., Abrahamson, H.B. and Skelton, B.W. (2009) Coordination of Substitutionally Inert Phenolate Ligands to Lanthanide(II) and (III) Compounds—Catalysts for Ring-Opening Polymerization of Cyclic Esters. Dalton Transactions, No. 15, 2777-2787.

71. Miura, M. (2004) Rational Ligand Design in Constructing Efficient Catalyst Systems for Suzuki-Miyaura Coupling. Angewandte Chemie International Edition, 43, 2201-2203.

72. Katz, B.A., Cass, R.T., Liu, B., Arze, R. and Collins, N. (2005) Functional Characterization of Novel Human and Mouse Equilibrative Nucleoside Transporters (hENT3 and mENT3) Located in Intracellular Membranes. The Journal of Biological Chemistry, 270, 31210-31218.

73. Falciola, C.A. and Alexakis, A. (2008) Copper-Catalyzed Asymmetric Allylic Alkylation. European Journal of Organic Chemistry, No. 2008, 3765-3780.

74. Heitbaum, M., Glorius, F. and Escher, I. (2006) Asymmetric Heterogeneous Catalysis. Angewandte Chemie International Edition, 45, 4732-4762.

75. Dugah, D.T., Skelton, B.W. and Delbridge, E.E. (2009) Synthesis and Characterization of New Divalent Lanthanide Complexes Supported by Amine Bis(Phenolate) Ligands and Their Applications in the Ring Opening Polymerization of Cyclic Esters. Dalton Transactions, No. 8, 1436-1445.

76. Xu, X., Ma, M., Yao, Y., Zhang, Y. and Shen, Q. (2005) Synthesis, Characterisation of Carbon-Bridged (Diphenolato)Lanthanide Complexes and Their Catalytic Activity for Diels-Alder Reactions. European Journal of Inorganic Chemistry, 2005, 676-684.

77. Lendlein, A., Schmidt, A.M., Schroeter, M. and Langer, R. (2005) Shape-Memory Polymer Networks from Oligo(ε-Caprolactone)Dimethacrylates. Journal of Polymer Science Part A: Polymer Chemistry, 43, 1369-1381.

78. Amgoune, A., Thomas, C.M., Roisnel, T. and Carpentier, J.F. (2005) Ring-Opening Polymerization of Lactide with Group 3 Metal Complexes Supported by Dianionic Alkoxy-Amino-Bisphenolate Ligands: Combining High Activity, Productivity, and Selectivity. Chemistry—A European Journal, 12, 169-179.

79. Guo, H., Zhou, H., Yao, Y., Zhang, Y. and Shen, Q. (2007) Synthesis and Structural Characterization of Novel Mixed-Valent Samarium and Divalent Ytterbium and Europium Complexes Supported by Amine Bis(Phenolate) Ligands. Dalton Transactions, No. 32, 3555-3561.

80. Zats, G.M., Arora, H., Lavi, R., Yufit, D. and Benisvy, L. (2011) Phenolate and Phenoxyl Radical Complexes of Cu(II) and Co(III), Bearing a New Redox Active N,O-Phenol-Pyrazole Ligand. Dalton Transactions, 40, 10889-10896.

81. Li, W., Xue, M., Tu, J., Zhang, Y. and Shen, Q. (2012) Syntheses and Structures of Lanthanide Borohydrides Supported by a Bridged Bis(Amidinate) Ligand and Their High Activity for Controlled Polymerization of ε-Caprolactone, L-Lactide and rac-Lactide. Dalton Transactions, 41, 7258-7265.

82. Chisholm, M.H. and Zhou, Z. (2004) New Generation Polymers: The Role of Metal Alkoxides as Catalysts in the Production of Polyoxygenates. Journal of Materials Chemistry, 14, 3081-3092.

83. Darensburg, D.J. and Karroonnirun, O. (2010) Ring-Opening Polymerization of Lactides Catalyzed by Natural Amino-Acid Based Zinc Catalysts. Inorganic Chemistry, 49, 2360-2371.

84. Tsuji, H. and Ikada, Y. (1999) Stereocomplex Formation between Enantiomeric Poly(Lactic Acid)s. XI. Mechanical Properties and Morphology of Solution-Cast Films. Polymer, 40, 6699-6708.

85. Spinu, M., Jackson, C. and Keating, M.Y. (1996) Stereoselective Polymerization with Single-Site Catalysts. Journal of Macromolecular Science, Part A: Pure and Applied Chemistry, A33, 1497-1530.

86. Sarasua, J.-R., Prud'homme, R.E., Wisniewski, M., Le Borgne, A. and Spassky, N. (1998) Crystallization and Melting Behavior of Polylac Tides. Macromolecules, 31, 3895-3905.

87. Kobayashi, K., Sumitomo, H. and Itoigawa, T. (1987) Maltopentaose- and Maltoheptaose-Carrying Styrene Macromers and Their Homopolymers. Macromolecules, 20, 906-908.

88. Wheaton, C.A., Hayes, P.G. and Ireland, B.J. (2009) Complexes of Mg, Ca and Zn as Homogeneous Catalysts for Lactide Polymerization. Dalton Transactions, No. 25, 4832-4846.

89. Wang, L. and Ma, H. (2010) Zinc Complexes Supported by Multidentate Aminophenolate Ligands: Synthesis, Structure and Catalysis in Ring-Opening Polymerization of rac-Lactide. Dalton Transactions, 39, 7897-7910.

90. Song, S., Zhang, X., Ma, H. and Yang, Y. (2012) Zinc Complexes Supported by Claw-Type Aminophenolate Ligands: Synthesis, Characterization and Catalysis in the Ring-Opening Polymerization of rac-Lactide. Dalton Transactions, 41, 3266-3277.

91. 91. Drouin, F., Oguadinma, P.O., Whitehorne, T.J.J., Prud'homme, R.E. and Schaper, F. (2010) Lactide Polymerization with Chiral β-Diketiminate Zinc Complexes. Organometallics, 29, 2139-2147.

92. Labourdette, G., Lee, D.J., Patrick, B.O., Ezhova, M.B. and Mehrkhodavandi, P. (2009) Unusually Stable Chiral Ethyl Zinc Complexes: Reactivity and Polymerization of Lactide. Organometallics, 28, 1309-1319.

93. Borner, J., Vieira, I.S., Pawlis, A., Doring, A., Kuckling, D. and Pawlis, S.H. (2011) Mechanism of the Living Lactide Polymerization Mediated by Robust Zinc Guanidine Complexes. Chemistry—A European Journal, 17, 4507-4512.

94. Borner, J., Floke, U., Huber, K., Doring, A., Kuckling, D. and Pawlis, S.H. (2009) Lactide Polymerisation with Air- Stable and Highly Active Zinc Complexes with Guanidine-Pyridine Hybrid Ligands. Chemistry—A European Journal, 15, 2362-2376.

95. Garcés, A., Sánchez-Barba, L.F., Alonso-Moreno, C., Fajardo, M., Fernández-Baeza, J., Otero, A., Lara-Sánchez, A., López-Solera, I. and Rodriguez, A.M. (2010) Hybrid Scorpionate/Cyclopentadienyl Magnesium and Zinc Complexes: Synthesis, Coordination Chemistry, and Ring-Opening Polymerization Studies on Cyclic Esters. Inorganic Chemistry, 49, 2859-2871.

96. Gao, B., Duan, R., Pang, X., Li, X., Qu, Z., Shao, H., Wang, X. and Chen, X. (2013) Zinc Complexes Containing Asymmetrical N,N,O-Tridentate Ligands and Their Application in Lactide Polymerization. Dalton Transactions, 42, 16334-16342.

97. Tschan, M.J.-T., Guo, J., Raman, S.K., Brulé, E., Roisnel, T., Marie-Noelle Rager, M.-N., Legay, R., Durieux, G., Rigaud, B. and

Thomas, C.M. (2014) Zinc and Cobalt Complexes Based on Tripodal Ligands: Synthesis, Structure and Reactivity toward Lactide. Dalton Transactions, 43, 4550-4564.

98. Hens, A., Mondal, P. and Rajak, K.K. (2013) Synthesis, Structure and Spectral Properties of O,N,N Coordinating Ligands and Their Neutral Zn(II) Complexes: A Combined Experimental and Theoretical Study. Dalton Transactions, 43, 14905-14915.

99. Ikpo, N., Saunders, L.N., Walsh, J.L., Smith, J.M.B., Dawe, L.N. and Kerton, F.M. (2011) Zinc Complexes of Piperazinyl-Derived Aminephenolate Ligands: Synthesis, Characterization and Ring-Opening Polymerization Activity. European Journal of Inorganic Chemistry, 2011, 5347-5359.

100. Mou, Z., Liu, B., Wang, M., Xie, H., Li, P., Li, L., Li, S. and Cui, D. (2014) Isoselective Ring-Opening Polymerization of rac-Lactide Initiated by Achiral Heteroscorpionate Zwitterionic Zinc Complexes. Chemical Communications, 50, 11411-11414.

101. Wang, H. and Ma, H. (2013) Highly Diastereoselective Synthesis of Chiral Aminophenolate Zinc Complexes and Isoselective Polymerization of rac-Lactide. Chemical Communications, 49, 8686-8688.

Chapter 11

Synthesis of Tertiary and Quaternary Amine Derivatives from Wood Resin as Chiral NMR Solvating Agents

Tiina Laaksonen, Sami Heikkinen and Kristiina Wähälä *

Department of Chemistry, University of Helsinki, A.I. Virtasen aukio 1, P. O. Box 55, FI-00014, Helsinki 00100, Finland

ABSTRACT

Chiral tertiary and quaternary amine solvating agents for NMR spectroscopy were synthesized from the wood resin derivative (+)-dehydroabietylamine (**2**). The resolution of enantiomers of model compounds [Mosher's acid (**3**) and its *n*-Bu_4N salt (**4**)] (guests) by (+)-dehydroabietyl-*N*,*N*-dimethylmethanamine (**5**) and its ten different ammonium salts (hosts) was studied. The best results with **3** were obtained using **5** while with **4** the best enantiomeric resolution was obtained using (+)-dehydroabietyl-*N*,*N*-dimethylmethanaminium bis(trifluoromethane-sulfonimide) (**6**). The compounds **5** and **6** showed a 1:1 complexation behaviour between the host and guest. The capability of **5** and**6** to recognize the enantiomers of various α-substituted carboxylic acids and their *n*-Bu_4N salts in enantiomeric excess (ee) determinations was demonstrated. A modification of the RES-TOCSY NMR pulse sequence is described, allowing the enhancement of enantiomeric discrimination when the resolution of multiplets is insufficient.

Keywords: chiral resolution; chiral solvating agent; (+)-dehydroabietylamine; NMR spectroscopy

1. INTRODUCTION

Wood resin is a natural product that after losing its volatile components hardens and is then called rosin. Resin functions in wood as a protective agent against micro-organisms and as a reserve nutrient supply [1]. Resin, a mixture of compounds (e.g., resin acids, fatty acids, sitosterol) can be collected from the tree itself, but can be also obtained from the pulp industry where it is a by-product of pulp milling [2]. For example, pine resin is a mixture of resin acids (*ca.* 90%) and neutral compounds (*ca.* 10%). The most abundant resin acid in pine rosin is abietic acid (**1**, Figure 1), amounting up to 90%. Rosin can be derivatized to an amine mixture (known as Rosin Amine D) containing 60% of (+)-dehydroabietylamine (**2**, Figure 1) [3,4,5], able to resolve chiral carboxylic acids by crystallization [6,7]. We have previously reported [8] that neutral and ammonium forms of secondary amines derived from dehydroabietylamine may be used in the chiral recognition of enantiomers of certain carboxylic acids. To evaluate the corresponding tertiary amines for chiral recognitions we have examined in the present study the behaviour of dehydroabietylamine (**2**)-derived tertiary amines and their ammonium salts as chiral solvating agents (CSAs) that can be used in the discrimination of enantiomers of both aromatic and aliphatic carboxylic acids by NMR. In particular, it was of interest to develop ionic CSAs to see if the ionic functionality would provide improved enantiomeric resolution.

Especially in medicinal and biological chemistry, where enantiopurity is important, analytical applications such as NMR spectroscopy for determining the enantiomeric purity are highly useful. In NMR, enantiomeric excess (ee) may be determined up to the level of 99% but generally for ee values over 95% more sensitive chromatographic methods (e.g., chiral HPLC and GC) have been used [9,10,11,12]. Compared to the most commonly used method HPLC, the minimal sample preparation, ease of use and fast analysis make CSAs an optimal tool for expedient ee determinations.

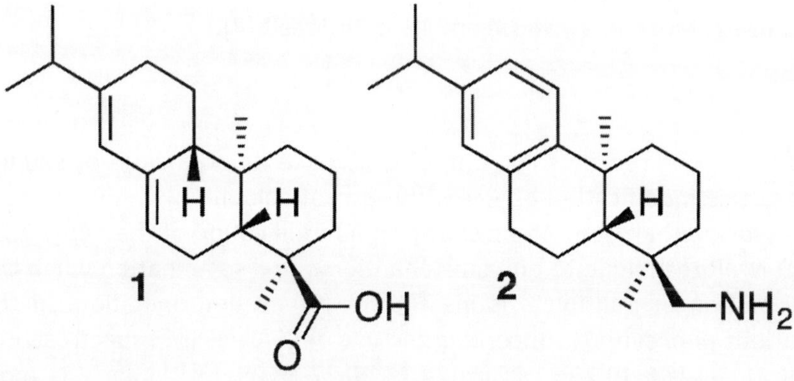

Figure 1. Abietic acid (**1**) and (+)-dehydroabietylamine (**2**).

Enantiomeric resolution by CSAs is based on the formation of a diastereomeric complex (or diastereomeric salt) [13,14]. There are several factors that may have an effect on the complex formation. It is known in the literature that the ability of CSAs (host) to bind a chiral compound (guest) is affected by the deuterated solvent used, the possible anion of the chiral host [15], concentration, host:guest ratio, temperature and the functional groups of the host and guest [13,14]. Since polar solvents can solvate ions and protic solvents can interfere in hydrogen bond formation, it is preferable to use non-polar or weakly polar aprotic NMR solvents such as $CDCl_3$ in recognition studies, especially when the analyte and CSA used are ionic (or when the formation of a diastereomeric salt pair is expected) [13]. The most frequently used compound to test the discrimination ability of a CSA, especially an ionic one, is Mosher's acid (**3**, 3,3,3-trifluoro-2-methoxy-2-phenyl-propanoic acid, Figure 2) and its sodium or potassium salt. In our enantiomeric discrimination tests, also Mosher's acid *n*-Bu_4N salt (**4**, Figure 2) was employed.

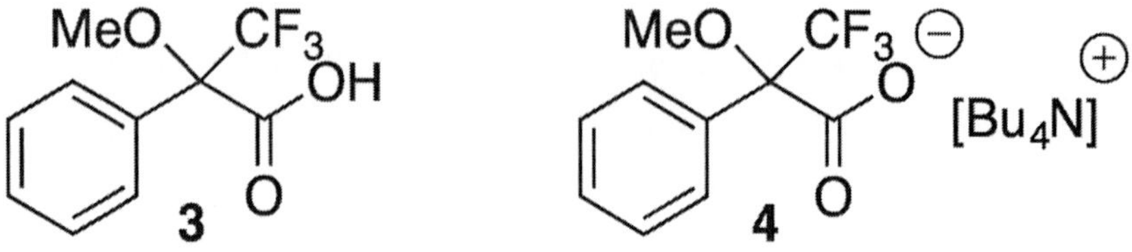

Figure 2. Mosher' s acid (**3**) and its *n*-Bu_4N salt (**4**).

With **4** being readily soluble in $CDCl_3$, unlike its potassium or sodium salt, this modification obviates the use of solubilizing additives such as crown ethers [16]. We also report a modification of the RES-TOCSY 2D-NMR technique to enhance enantiomeric discrimination when the resolution of multiplets is insufficient for ee determination. In the various publications concerning the use of CSAs in NMR spectroscopy, all [17,18,19,20,21,22,23,24,25,26,27,28,29,30] or most [31,32,33,34,35,36] of the racemic carboxylic acids or salts studied contain an aromatic moiety, and acids lacking an aromatic ring are largely ignored or deemed [37] poorly resolvable at best. As described in the following, our new ionic and non-ionic tertiary amine CSA agents enable efficient enantiomeric resolution and the determination of ee values of racemic carboxylic acids or salts, including those that lack an aromatic ring.

2. RESULTS AND DISCUSSION

Starting material **2** was purchased as 60% grade. It was converted to its acetate salt, which was then purified by crystallisation. Pure (+)-dehydroabietyl acetate was then treated with NaOH solution to release **2** in pure form. The synthesis of CSAs based on **2** consists of two steps (Scheme 1). First, **2** is reacted with formaldehyde and formic acid to form **5** (63.8%). This tertiary amine is then quaternized with an alkyl halide under microwave irradiation. Three different alkyl halides were used: methyl iodide to obtain an uncrowded ammonium terminus (**7a**, 82.9%), 2-hydroxyethyl bromide to give hydrogen bonding capability (**8a**, 59.4%), and benzyl bromide to provide a bulky group at the ammonium terminus (**9a**, 46.5%). It is known that the more delocalised and bulky anions can enhance binding between the cationic CSA and (ionic or non-ionic) chiral substrate due to a weaker binding between the cation and anion of CSA [23]. To tune the binding properties of **7a**, **8a** and **9a**, anion exchange was performed with NH_4BF_4 or $LiNTf_2$ to obtain **7b**, **8b**, **9b** or **7c**, **8c**, **9c**, respectively, in high yield (89.9%–97.8%). The delocalization and increased size of the anion also affect the physical properties of the ionic CSAs [23]. The melting points of ionic compounds decrease when the anion is bulky and/or weakly coordinating. Molar rotations for compounds were also determined. Alternatively, compound **5** may be protonated with bis(trifluoromethane)-sulfonimide ($HNTf_2$) to give **6**. Table 1 presents the collected physical property data of the compounds synthesized.

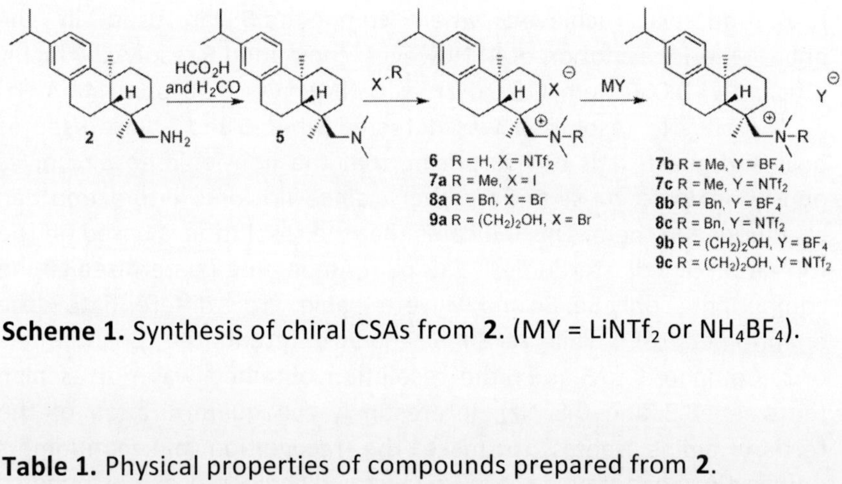

Scheme 1. Synthesis of chiral CSAs from **2**. (MY = $LiNTf_2$ or NH_4BF_4).

Table 1. Physical properties of compounds prepared from **2**.

CSA	R	X	mp (°C)	$[\alpha]_D^{23}$ [(a)]	$[M]_D^{23}$ [(b)]
5	-	-	liquid at rt.	+52.05 [(c)]	+161.71
6	H	NTf_2	114.2	+7.45	+44.29
7a	Me	I	250.3	+20.91	+95.19
7b	Me	BF_4	246.8	+19.93 [(d)]	+82.77
7c	Me	NTf_2	46.6	+7.79	+47.41
8a	Bn	Br	188.6	+7.19	+34.83
8b	Bn	BF_4	179.9	+2.28	+11.18
8c	Bn	NTf_2	48.8	+1.70	+11.67
9a	$(CH_2)_2OH$	Br	213.5	+16.45 [(e)]	+72.12
9b	$(CH_2)_2OH$	BF_4	188.5	+18.73	+83.43
9c	$(CH_2)_2OH$	NTf_2	viscous liquid at rt.	+6.56	+41.90

(a) $[\alpha]_D^{23}$ = deg cm^3·g^{-1}·dm^{-1}, c = 1.0 g·cm^{-3}, $CHCl_3$; (b) Molar rotation calculated from $[\alpha]_D^{23} \times M/100$, where M is the molar mass; (c) Temperature 22 °C; (d) Solvent $CHCl_3$ + 3% MeOH; (e) Solvent MeOH.

To investigate the ability of the synthesized compounds **5–9c** to resolve ionic and non-ionic racemic carboxylic acids both**3** and **4** were used as model compounds as 22.0 mM solutions in $CDCl_3$. Compounds **5–9c** (1.0 eq or 2.0 eq) were dissolved in 0.5 mL (1.0 eq) of the prepared solution and ^{1}H- and ^{19}F-NMR spectra were recorded (Supplementary Material Figures S1 and S2). Both 1:1 and 2:1 host:guest molar ratios were studied since according to literature, the magnitude of non-equivalence (Δδ) increases when the amount of host is higher than that of the guest [13,14]. Compounds **5** and **6** gave the best results both in 1:1 and 2:1 host:guest ratios (Table 2). The former efficiently resolved the enantiomers of **3** according to ^{1}H- and ^{19}F-NMR. The magnitude of non-equivalence was 0.036 ppm (18.1 Hz) in ^{1}H-NMR and 0.12 ppm (58.5 Hz) in ^{19}F-NMR. Only very weak resolution was achieved when compound **5** was used in the enantiomeric resolution of **4**. However, compound **6** resolved **4** highly efficiently, 0.030 ppm (15.0 Hz) in ^{1}H-NMR and 0.10 ppm (48.3 Hz) in ^{19}F-NMR. No resolution was detected when **6** and **3** were used as host and guest. It is not surprising that the non-ionic host resolves poorly an ionic guest and *vice versa* since no ionic interaction can exist between them. This indicates that the resolution is based on the formation of a diastereomeric salt pair. Among the quaternized amine compounds only **8a**, **8c** and **9c** were able to differentiate the enantiomers of **4** while **7c**, **8b**, **8c** and **9c** differentiated enantiomers of **3**. Compared to **5** and **6** the resolution obtained was not as high (between 8.3 and 0.8 Hz). Interestingly the quaternization of the tertiary amine seems to make the recognition of enantiomers unfeasible. This may be due to a crowding in the active bonding site, *i.e.*, ammonium terminus, caused by the side chain (methyl, benzyl, 2-hydroxyethyl) so that the guest cannot get close enough. In regard to this it is surprising that **7a–c** (max. 1.3 Hz) are less effective than **8a–c** (max. 8.3 Hz) and **9a–c** (max. 8.2 Hz). This may be caused not only by the crowding but also by the failure of the methyl group (**7a–c**) to give specific enough resolution between the enantiomers compared e.g., to benzyl (**8a–c**) and hydroxyethyl (**9a–c**) groups. When the concentration of CSA was increased (host:guest ratio 2:1) no significant increase in the Δδ was observed although in the case of **5** Δδ was increased by 3.5 Hz in ^{1}H-NMR and 13.2 Hz in ^{19}F-NMR. Interestingly, in the case of **6** Δδ decreased in^{1}H-NMR by 1.9 Hz although it increased in ^{19}F-NMR by 5.9 Hz.

Table 2. Determination of the magnitude of non-equivalence (Δδ) with **3** and **4** as model compounds in the presence of different **2**-based CSAs, using both ^{1}H (500 MHz) and ^{19}F-NMR (470 MHz) in $CDCl_3$ at 27 °C (-indicates resolution not detected).

CSA	Host:Guest	3 (ppm, (Hz))		4 (ppm, (Hz))	
		^{1}H	^{19}F	^{1}H	^{19}F
5	1:1	0.036 (18.1)	0.12 (58.5)	0.0018 (0.9)	-
	2:1	0.042 (21.6)	0.15 (71.7)	-	-
6	1:1	-	-	0.030 (15.0)	0.10 (48.3)
	2:1	-	-	0.026 (13.1)	0.12 (54.2)
7a	1:1	-	-	-	-
	2:1	-	-	-	-
7b	1:1	-	-	-	-
	2:1	-	-	-	-
7c	1:1	0.027 (1.3)	-	-	-
	2:1	-	-	-	-
8a	1:1	-	-	-	-
	2:1	-	-	-	0.015 (6.8)
8b	1:1	0.0015 (0.8)	-	-	-
	2:1	-	-	-	-
8c	1:1	0.0017 (0.9)	-	0.0037 (1.9)	-
	2:1	-	-	0.010 (5.1)	0.018 (8.3)
9a	1:1	-	-	-	-
	2:1	-	-	-	-
9b	1:1	-	-	-	-
	2:1	-	-	-	-
9c	1:1	0.0017 (0.9)	-	0.0052 (2.6)	-
	2:1	-	-	0.016 (8.2)	-

The discrimination ability of the best performing CSAs **5** and **6** was further investigated by titration to find the optimum conditions. Since **5** gave best resolution for **3**, and **6** for **4**, **3** was titrated by **5** and **4** was titrated by **6**. The guest solution (0.5 mL, 2.0 mM) was measured into an NMR tube and titrated with the host solution (46.6 mM). NMR spectra were recorded and Δδ **3** a **4** (both in ^{1}H- and ^{19}F-NMR) shown in Figure 3a,b. Results from ^{1}H- and ^{19}F-NMR spectra suggest that a maximum resolution with **5** and **6** is obtained when the concentrations of host and guest are the same (2.0 mM) indicating a 1:1 complexation of host and guest (Job's plot in Supplementary material Figures S8 and S12). According to the results both enantiomers of **3** interact with **5** (and both enantiomers of **4** with **6**). This can be detected from the chemical shift changes experienced by both the *S* and *R* enantiomers (Figure 3c,d) during the titration.

The possibility of using compounds **5** and **6** in enantiomeric excess (ee) measurements by NMR spectroscopy was also tested using solutions of racemic **3** and *S*-**3** (as well as **4** and *S*-**4**) (2.0 mM). Mixtures of enantiomerically enriched samples were prepared in an NMR tube (0.5 mL, 1.0 eq) and CSA (46.6 mM, 22.5 µL, 1.0 eq) was added. A clear correlation was detected between the expected and measured ee% values, when just one equivalent of host with respect to the guest in a $CDCl_3$ solution was used (Figure 4). Line shape fitting was used for ee estimation to enhance accuracy.

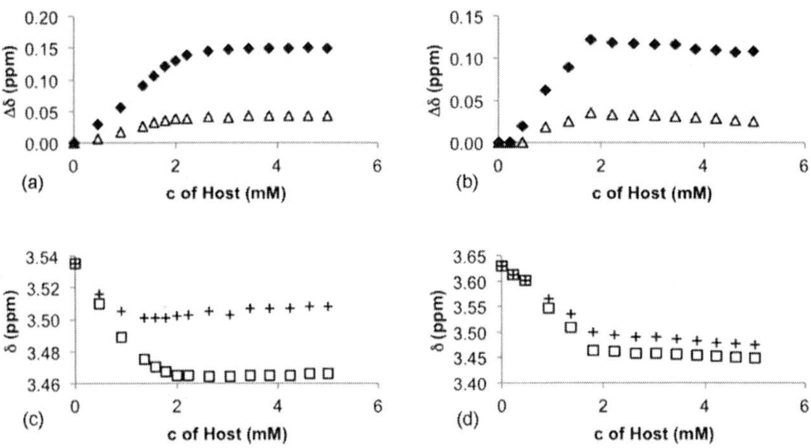

Figure 3. The magnitude of non-equivalence (Δδ): (**a**) of **3** with **5** (white triangle: ^{1}H-NMR and black diamond: ^{19}F-NMR) and (**b**) of **4** with **6** (white triangle: ^{1}H-NMR and black diamond: ^{19}F-NMR). The change of chemical shifts of *S* and *R* enantiomers: (**c**) of **3** as a function of the concentration of **5** (white square: *R* enantiomer and plus sign:*S* enantiomer) at ^{1}H-NMR; and (**d**) of **4** as a function of the concentration of **6** (white square: *R* enantiomer and plus sign: *S* enantiomer) at ^{1}H-NMR.

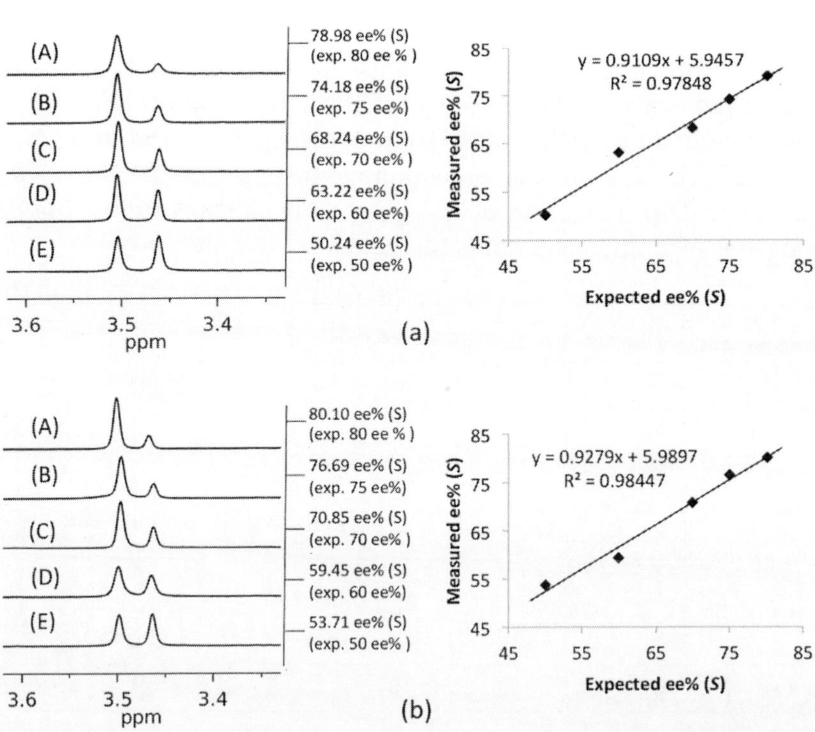

Figure 4. Determination of enantiomeric purities of (**a**) **3** in the presence of **5** and (**b**) **4**in the presence of **6** by ^{1}H-NMR (500 MHz) in $CDCl_3$ at 27 °C. (Expected ee% (*S*): (A) 80, (B) 75, (C) 70, (D) 60, (E) 50).

The resolution of various racemic aromatic or non-aromatic α-substituted carboxylic acids **10a–16a**, or their *n*-Bu_4N salts**10b–16b**, by **5** and **6** was tested (Table 3). In general, **5** and **6** are able to discriminate the corresponding guest and no major differences between the resolution of aromatic and non-aromatic carboxylic acids were detected. Especially **5** gave excellent resolution for the non-aromatic carboxylic acids **13a**, **15a** and **16a**. According to the results, the best enantiomeric resolutions are obtained with racemic carboxylic acids bearing an electronegative atom (e.g., O, N, Br) at the α site. Therefore, it is interesting that compound **5** cannot discriminate the chiral proton in **12a**, nor does **6** discriminate the chiral proton in **12b**. This indicates that not only the polarity but also the size of the α-group (e.g., **14a,b**) and/or crowding at the α site

Table 3. The magnitude of non-equivalences (Δδ) of five racemic carboxylic acids in the presence of **5** and their *n*-Bu_4N salts in the presence of **6** (^1H-NMR (500 MHz) in $CDCl_3$ at 27 °C). The experiment was performed by adding a solution containing CSA (46.6 mM, 22.5 µL, 1.0 eq) to a solution of the guest (2.0 mM, 0.5 mL, 1.0 eq) (- indicates resolution was not detected).

Cmpd.	Racemic Carboxylic Acid		Δδ ppm	Δδ Hz	Cmpd.	*n*-Bu_4N Salt of Racemic Carboxylic Acid		Δδ ppm	Δδ Hz
10a	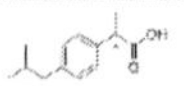	Me CH	0.0023 -	1.1 -	10b	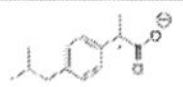	Me CH	- -	- -
11a	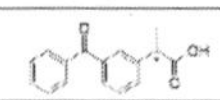	Me CH	0.0059 0.0047	3.0 2.4	11b	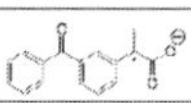	Me CH	0.0041 0.0021	2.0 1.0
12a	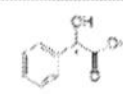	CH	-	-	12b	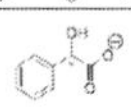	CH	-	-
13a	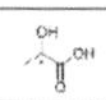	CH Me	0.0081 0.022	4.1 11.1	13b	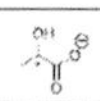	CH Me	0.0068 0.017	3.4 8.6
14a	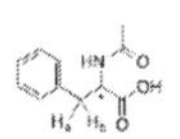	CH NH Me H_a H_b	0.012 0.013 0.0028 0.072 0.027	6.1 6.5 1.4 36.2 13.4	14b	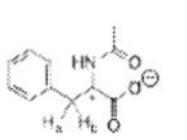	CH NH Me H_a [(a)] H_b [(a)]	0.012 0.014 0.0039 0.065 0.036	6.0 6.8 1.9 32.5 17.8
15a	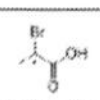	CH Me	- 0.023	- 11.5	15a	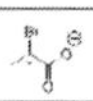	CH Me	- 0.002	- 0.9
16a	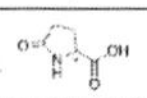	CH NH	0.016 0.020	7.9 10.2	16b	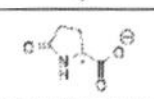	CH NH	0.003 0.020	1.4 10.0

[(a)] Due to overlapping with protons of $[n\text{-}Bu_4N]^+$ values are from HSQC/NOESY experiment.

(e.g., **3** and **4**) may have an effect. Intriguingly both **5** and **6** discriminate the prochiral CH_2 protons of the *R* and *S* enantiomers of **14a** and **14b**. The resolution of carboxylic acids containing an electropositive (methyl group) at the α-site (**10** and **11**, **a** and **b**) was less efficient. In **14b** the CH_2 peaks overlapped with those of **6**. This was overcome by using the 2D NMR techniques HSQC and NOESY (Supplementary Material Figures S17 and S18). Also other 2D experiments such as HMBC may be utilized among 1D experiments such as selective TOCSY as well as carbon selective 1D-HSQC when an overlap of CSA and substrate signals occurs. When the peaks are not baseline resolved (e.g., in case of **13a** and **14a**), certain specialised NMR techniques are available. Obviously, traditional line shape fitting of an ordinary 1D ^1H spectrum can significantly enhance the accuracy of estimated ee values. Other possiblities for ee determination include pure shift experiments [38,39], *J*-resolved techniques [40] and the recently published RES-TOCSY [41]. Naturally, the use of 2D methods for reliable ee determination requires, that relevant, quantification-affecting NMR properties in the presence of chiral auxiliary for both enantiomers remain essentially similar (*cf.* Supplementary Material Figure S6). In the current study, the RES-TOCSY pulse sequence was modified to incorporate only one selective pulse (selective refocusing pulse) and gradients for coherence selection. The resulting 2D spectrum is phase sensitive, which allows the extraction of 1D traces with line shapes as encountered in the normal ^{1}H spectrum. A more detailed description of the aforementioned pulse sequence as well as the actual pulse sequence code are given in Supplementary Material (Figures S15–S23). The use of this modified RES-TOCSY to enhance multiplet resolution in an indirectly detected dimension is demonstrated for compounds**13a** and **14a** in Figure 5.

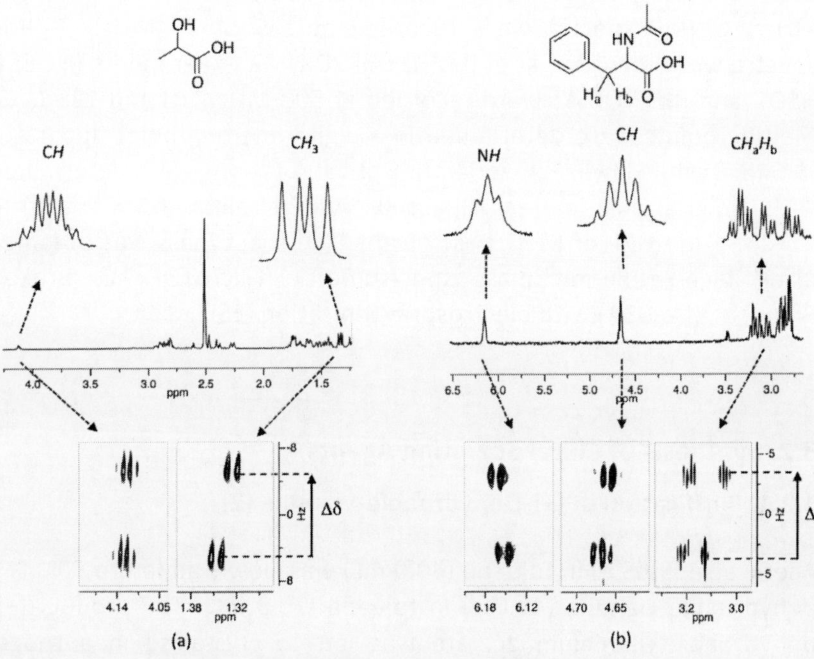

Figure 5. RES-TOCSY experiment performed on **(a) 13a** (Δδ 11.1 Hz, CH_3) and **(b) 14a**(Δδ 6.1 Hz, CH) with CSA **5** showing the resolution of *R* and *S* enantiomer in an indirect dimension.

3. EXPERIMENTAL SECTION

3.1. General Methods

All reagents and solvents were obtained from commercial suppliers and were used without further purification unless otherwise stated. (+)-Dehydroabietylamine was purchased (Sigma Aldrich, St. Louis, MO, USA) as 60% grade and purified using a method described in the literature [42] with slight modifications (see below). Flash chromatography was performed using 40–63 mesh silica gel. Microwave oven reactions were performed in closed vessel using the CEM Focused Microwave™ Synthesis System with an external infrared temperature control system (CEM, Matthews, NC, USA). NMR spectra were recorded using UNITY INOVA 500 (500 MHz ^{1}H-frequency) and Mercury Plus 300 (300 MHz ^{1}H-frequency) instruments (Varian, Palo Alto, CA, USA) at 27 °C. ^{1}H-NMR spectra were recorded at 500 MHz, ^{13}C-NMR spectra were recorded at 125 or 75 MHz, ^{19}F-NMR spectra were recorded at 470 MHz. All 2D NMR experiments (NOESY, HSQC and RES-TOCSY) were recorded at 500 MHz (^{1}H) and 125 (^{13}C). Melting points were determined in a digital melting point apparatus (B 545, Büchi, Flawil, Switzerland). Optical rotations were determined with a digital polarimeter (DIP-1000, JASCO, Halifax, NS, Canada) at 22–23 °C in $CHCl_3$ or MeOH as solvent. The exact mass was obtained using high-resolution mass spectrometry (MicroTOF LC, Bruker, Billerica, MA, USA) with electrospray ionisation (ESI).

3.2. Synthesis of Chiral Solvating Agents

3.2.1. Purification of (+)-Dehydroabietylamine (2)

Acetic acid (9.65 g) in toluene (30.0 mL) was slowly added to 60% (+)-dehydroabietylamine (42.0 g) in toluene (70.0 mL). The product (+)-dehydroabietylaminium acetate was left to crystallise in a fridge, filtered, washed with hexane and recrystallised from MeOH. The salt (21.0 g) was dissolved in hot water and 10% NaOH solution (28.0 mL) was added. (+)-Dehydroabietylamine was extracted by Et_2O and the organic phase was washed with water until neutral. The organic phase was dried over Na_2SO_4. The solvent was evaporated and (+)-dehydroabietylamine was dried under vacuum; mp 44.2 °C (lit. 44–45 °C) [43]; HRMS-ESI (*m/z*) calc. for $C_{20}H_{32}N$ $[M + H]^+$ 286.2529 found

286.2540; [α]22D +44.35 (*c* 1.0, $CHCl_3$) (lit. +58.0, *c* 0.2, DMSO, 20 °C) [43]; ^{1}H-NMR (500 MHz, $CDCl_3$) δ ppm 0.85 (s, 3H, CH_3), 1.22 (s, 3H, CH_3), 1.22 (d, *J* = 6.98 Hz, 6H, 2× CH_3), 1.33 (m, 2H, CH_2), 1.39 (m, 1H, C*H*H), 1.52 (dd, *J* = −11.75, 3.31 Hz, 1H, C*H*), 1.69 (m, 2H, CH_2), 1.74 (m, 2H, CH_2), 2.29 (dt, *J* = −13.14, 1.72 Hz, 1H, CH*H*), 2.40 (d, *J* = −13.46 Hz, 1H, C*H*H), 2.61 (d, *J* = −13.46 Hz, 1H, CH*H*), 2.82 (sep, *J*= 6.98 Hz, 1H, C*H*), 2.88 (m, 2H, CH_2), 6.89 (d, *J* = 1.94 Hz, 1H, CH_{Ar}), 6.99 (dd, *J* = 8.08, 1.94 Hz, 1H, CH_{Ar}), 7.18 (d, *J* = 8.08 Hz, 1H, CH_{Ar}); ^{13}C-NMR (125 MHz, $CDCl_3$) δ ppm 18.8 (CH_2), 18.9 (CH_3), 18.895 (CH_2), 24.1 H_3), 24.130 (CH_3), 25.4 (CH_3), 30.3 (CH_2), 33.6 (*C*H), 35.355 (CH_2), 37.4 (*C*), 37.527 (*C*), 38.7 (CH_2), 45.0 (*C*H), 53.9 (CH_2), 123.9 (CH_{Ar}), 124.4 (CH_{Ar}), 126.9 (CH_{Ar}), 134.8 (C_{Ar}), 145.7 (C_{Ar}), 147.6 (C_{Ar}).

3.2.2. Synthesis of (+)-Dehydroabietyl-*N,N*-dimethylmethanamine (5)

Formic acid (3.96 mL, 0.105 mol, 5.0 eq) was added to **2** (6.0 g, 0.021 mol, 1.0 eq) at 0 °C. Formaldehyde (37% H_2O solution, 3.81 mL, 0.048 mol, 2.3 eq) was added dropwise and the reaction mixture was refluxed for 4 h. The reaction mixture was cooled to rt. and made basic by adding NaOH solution (2.0 M). The product was extracted with diethyl ether. The organic phase was washed with water until neutral, dried over Na_2SO_4, concentrated and dried in vacuum. The product was purified by column chromatography (2:3 DCM:EtOAc). Colorless liquid (4.2 g 63.8%); HRMS-ESI (*m/z*) calc. for $C_{22}H_{36}N$ [M + H]$^+$ 314.2842, found 314.2840; [α]22D +52.05 (*c* 1.0, $CHCl_3$); ^{1}H-NMR (500 MHz, $CDCl_3$) δ ppm 0.85 (s, 3H, CH_3), 1.22 (s, 3H, CH_3), 1.23 (d, *J* = 6.91 Hz, 6H, 2× CH_3), 1.34 (m, 1H, C*H*H), 1.43 (td, *J* = −13.21, 4.15 Hz, 1H, C*H*H), 1.56 (td,*J* = −13.21, 4.15 Hz, 1H, CH*H*), 1.65 (m, 2H, CH_2), 1.701 (m, 1H, C*H*), 1.704 (m, 1H, C*H*H), 1.79 (m, 1H, CH*H*), 1.95 (d, *J* = −14.25 Hz, 1H, C*H*H), 2.26 (m, 1H, CH*H*), 2.28 (s, 6H, 2× CH_3), 2.29 (d, *J* = −14.25 Hz, 1H, CH*H*), 2.83 (sep, *J*= 6.91 Hz, 1H, C*H*), 2.88 (m, 2H, CH_2), 6.88 (d, *J* = 1.90 Hz, 1H, CH_{Ar}), 6.98 (dd, *J* = 8.14, 1.90 Hz, 1H, CH_{Ar}), 7.18 (d, *J* = 8.14 Hz, 1H, CH_{Ar});^{13}C-NMR (75 MHz, $CDCl_3$) δ ppm 19.0 (CH_3), 19.1 (CH_2), 19.3 (CH_2), 24.2 (2× CH_3), 25.8 (CH_3), 30.3 (CH_2), 33.6 (*C*H), 36.6 (CH_2), 37.6 (*C*), 38.6 (CH_2), 38.9 (*C*), 44.3 (*C*H), 49.3 (2× CH_3), 71.2 (CH_2), 123.8 (CH_{Ar}), 124.3 (CH_{Ar}), 126.9 (CH_{Ar}), 134.9 (C_{Ar}), 145.5 (C_{Ar}), 147.9 (C_{Ar}).

3.2.3. Synthesis of (+)-Dehydroabietyl-*N*,*N*-dimethylmethanaminium bis(trifluoromethanesulfon-imide) (6)

$HNTf_2$ (89.7 mg, 1.0 eq) was added at 0 °C to the tertiary amine **5** (0.1 g, 0.319 mmol, 1.0 eq) in DCM (0.5 mL). After stirring for 1 h at rt water was added. The layers were separated and the organic phase washed with water (3 × 2.0 mL). The organic solvent was evaporated and the product dried under vacuum. White solid (0.18 g, 93.3%;); mp 114.2 °C; HRMS-ESI (*m/z*) calc. for $C_{22}H_{36}N$ $[M - NTf_2]^+$314.2842, found 314.2834; calc. for $C_2F_6NO_4S_2$ $[NTf_2]$ 279.9167, found 279.9170; [α]23D+7.45 (*c* 1.0, $CHCl_3$); ^{1}H-NMR (500 MHz, $CDCl_3$) δ ppm 1.16 (s, 3H, CH_3), 1.21 (d, *J* = 6.88 Hz, 6H, 2× CH_3), 1.24 (s, 3H, CH_3), 1.33 (m, 1H, *C*HH), 1.37 (dd, *J* = −12.67, 2.07 Hz, 1H, C*H*), 1.43 (m, 1H, *C*HH), 1.65 (dt, *J* = −13.45, 7.69 Hz, 1H, *C*HH), 1.67 (dt, *J* = −13.45, 7.69 Hz, 1H, CH*H*), 1.79 (m, 2H,CH_2), 1.84 (m, 1H, CH*H*), 2.34 (dt, *J* = −13.27, 2.97 Hz, 1H, CH*H*), 2.82 (sep, *J* = 6.88 Hz, 1H, C*H*), 2.85 (m, 1H, *C*HH), 2.94 (d, *J* = −13.22 Hz, 1H, *C*HH), 2.95 (m, 1H, CH*H*), 3.01 (s, 6H, 2× CH_3), 3.28 (d, *J* = −13.22 Hz, 1H,CH*H*), 6.88 (d, *J* = 1.65 Hz, 1H, CH_{Ar}), 6.99 (dd, *J* = 8.14, 1.65 Hz, 1H, CH_{Ar}), 7.14 (d, *J* = 8.14 Hz, 1H, CH_{Ar}); ^{13}C-NMR (125 MHz, $CDCl_3$) δ ppm 17.6 (CH_3), 18.1 (CH_2), 19.5 (CH_2), 24.1 (2× CH_3), 25.4 (CH_3), 29.7 (CH_2), 33.6 (*C*H), 35.9 (CH_2), 37.7 (*C*), 37.7 (CH_2), 37.7(*C*), 47.4 (CH), 48.4 (2× CH_3), 73.3 (CH_2), 119.8 (q, *J* = 319.79, CF_3), 124.1 (CH_{Ar}), 124.4 (CH_{Ar}), 126.9 (CH_{Ar}), 133.7 (C_{Ar}), 146.2 (C_{Ar}), 146.3 (C_{Ar}).

3.2.4. Synthesis of (+)-Dehydroabietyl-N,N,N-trimethylmethanaminium iodide (7a)

The tertiary amine **5** (0.15 g, 0.479 mmol, 1.0 eq), iodomethane (0.68 g 0.30 mL, 4.79 mmol, 10.0 eq, caution toxic) and $CHCl_3$ (1.0 mL) were measured into a microwave tube. The reaction was irradiated in microwave oven at 120 W, 30 min, 47 °C. Et_2O was added and the product was collected by filtration and washed with Et_2O. The product was dried in vacuum. White solid (0.18 g, 82.9%); mp 250.3 °C (lit. 249–252 °C) [44]; HRMS-ESI (*m/z*) calc. for $C_{23}H_{38}N$ $[M - I]^+$ 328.2999, found 328.2988; [α]23D = +20.91 (*c* 1.0, $CHCl_3$) (lit. +22.0, *c* 1.20, $CHCl_3$, 20 °C) [44]; ^{1}H-NMR (500 MHz, $CDCl_3$) δ ppm 1.19 (d, *J* = 7.01 Hz, 6H, 2× CH_3), 1.23 (s, 3H, CH_3), 1.33 (s, 3H, CH_3), 1.40 (dd, *J* =

−12.32, 1.87 Hz, 1H, C*H*), 1.42 (m, 1H, C*H*H), 1.73 (m, 1H, C*H*H), 1.74 (m, 2H, CH_2), 1.86 (m, 1H, C*H*H), 2.00 (m, 1H, CH*H*), 2.05 (m, 1H, CH*H*), 2.30 (dt, *J* = −13.03 Hz, 1H, CH*H*), 2.80 (sep, *J* = 7.01 Hz, 1H, C*H*), 2.94 (m, 2H, CH_2), 3.39 (d, *J* = −14.04 Hz, 1H, C*H*H), 3.57 (s, 9H, 3× CH_3), 3.94 (d, *J* = −14.04 Hz, 1H, CH*H*), 6.88 (d, *J* = 1.75 Hz, 1H, CH_{Ar}), 6.96 (dd, *J* = 8.20, 1.75 Hz, 1H, CH_{Ar}), 7.09 (d, *J* = 8.20 Hz, 1H, CH_{Ar}); ^{13}C-NMR (125 MHz, $CDCl_3$) δ ppm 18.6 (CH_2), 20.06 (CH_3), 20.08 (CH_2), 24.18 (CH_3), 24.22 (CH_3), 25.8 (CH_3), 29.9 (CH_2), 33.7 (CH), 37.7 (CH_2), 38.2 (*C*), 39.3 (CH_2), 40.9 (*C*), 48.1 (CH), 56.9 (3× CH_3), 78.7 (CH_2), 123.8 (CH_{Ar}), 124.2 (CH_{Ar}), 127.2 (CH_{Ar}), 134.4 (C_{Ar}), 146.3 (C_{Ar}), 146.8 (C_{Ar}).

3.2.5. Synthesis of *N*-Benzyl-1-(+)-dehydroabietyl-*N*,*N*-dimethylmethanaminium bromide (8a)

The tertiary amine **1** (0.3 g, 0.956 mmol, 1.0 eq) and benzyl bromide (0.491 g, 0.341 mL, 2.87 mmol, l.3 eq) were measured into a microwave tube and EtOAc (1.0 mL) was added. The reaction was irradiated in the oven at 170 W, 13 min, 80 °C. The crystalline solid formed was filtered and washed with EtOAc. White solid (0.27 g, 59.4%;); mp 188.6 °C (lit. 225–231 °C) [44]; HRMS-ESI (*m/z*) calc. for $C_{29}H_{42}N$ $[M - Br]^+$ 404.3312, found 404.3310; [α]23D +7.19 (*c* 1.0, $CHCl_3$) (lit. +11.0, *c* 1.07, $CHCl_3$, 20 °C) [44]; ^{1}H-NMR (500 MHz, $CDCl_3$) δ ppm 1.20 (d, *J* = 7.00 Hz, 6H, 2× CH_3), 1.21 (s, 3H, CH_3), 1.32 (m, 1H, C*H*), 1.33 (s, 3H, CH_3), 1.34 (m, 1H, C*H*H), 1.59 (m, 1H, C*H*H), 1.70 (m, 2H, CH_2), 1.82 (m, 1H, C*H*H), 1.99 (m, 1H, CH*H*), 1.99 (m, 1H, CH*H*), 2.26 (dt, *J* = −12.88, 3.00 Hz, 1H, CH*H*), 2.80 (sep, *J* = 7.00 Hz, 1H, C*H*), 2.85 (m, 1H, C*H*H), 2.93 (m, 1H, CH*H*), 3.32 (s, 3H, CH_3), 3.33 (d, *J* = −14.11 Hz, 1H, C*H*H), 3.42 (s, 3H, CH_3), 4.08 (d, *J* = −14.11 Hz, 1H, CH*H*), 5.23 (d, *J* = −12.44 Hz, 1H, C*H*H), 5.33 (d, *J* = −12.44 Hz, 1H, CH*H*), 6.86 (d, *J* = 1.59 Hz, 1H, CH_{Ar}), 6.96 (dd, *J* = 8.23, 1.59 Hz, 1H, CH_{Ar}), 7.07 (d, *J* = 8.23 Hz, 1H, CH_{Ar}), 7.37 (m, 1H, CH_{Ar}), 7.40 (m, 1H, CH_{Ar}), 7.70 (d, *J* = 7.14 Hz, 1H, CH_{Ar}); ^{13}C-NMR (125 MHz, $CDCl_3$) δ ppm 18.5 (CH_2), 19.9 (CH_2), 20.1 (CH_3), 24.0 (CH_3), 24.1 (CH_3), 25.6 (CH_3), 29.8 (CH_2), 33.5 (CH), 37.6 (CH_2), 38.1 (*C*), 39.6 (CH_2), 40.6 (*C*), 48.4 (CH), 51.4 (CH_3), 51.6 (CH_3), 71.9 (CH_2), 75.9 (CH_2), 123.7 (CH_{Ar}), 124.1 (CH_{Ar}), 127.0 (CH_{Ar}), 127.7 (C_{Ar}), 129.2 (CH_{Ar}), 130.8 (CH_{Ar}), 133.8 (CH_{Ar}), 134.3 (C_{Ar}), 146.1 (C_{Ar}), 146.8 (C_{Ar}).

3.2.6. Synthesis of 2-Hydroxy-*N*-(+)-dehydroabietyl-*N*,*N*-dimethylethanaminium bromide (9a)

The tertiary amine **5** (0.3 g, 0.956 mmol, 1.0 eq) and benzyl bromide (0.359 g, 0.204 mL, 2.87 mmol, 3.0 eq) were measured into a microwave tube and $CHCl_3$ was added. The mixture was irradiated in the oven at 120 W, 2 h, 110 °C. The solvent was evaporated and product washed with Et_2O (3 mL × 3). The product was purified by column chromatography (1:9 MeOH:DCM). White powder (0.20 g, 46.5%); mp 213.5 °C; HRMS-ESI (*m/z*) calc. for $C_{24}H_{40}NO$ $[M - Br]^+$ 358.3104, found 358.3095; [α]23D +16.45 (*c* 1.0, MeOH); ^{1}H-NMR (500 MHz, CD_3OD) δ ppm 1.71 (d, *J* = 6.91 Hz, 6H, 2× CH_3), 1.79 (s, 3H, CH_3), 1.88 (s, 3H, CH_3), 1.97 (m, 1H, C*H*H), 1.99 (dd, *J* = −11.85, 2.49 Hz, 1H, C*H*), 2.25 (m, 1H, C*H*H), 2.31 (m, 1H, C*H*H), 2.37 (m, 1H, CH*H*), 2.40 (m, 1H, C*H*H), 2.47 (m, 1H, CH*H*), 2.63 (dt, *J* = −11.93 Hz, 1H, CH*H*), 2.89 (dt, *J* = −12.68 Hz, 1H, CH*H*), 3.31 (sep, *J* = 6.91 Hz, 1H, C*H*), 3.43 (m, 1H, C*H*H), 3.48 (ddd, *J* = −17.37, 7.17, 2.13 Hz, 1H, CH*H*), 3.83 (s, 6H, 2× CH_3), 3.91 (d, *J* = −14.01 Hz, 1H, C*H*H), 4.16 (m, 2H, CH_2), 4.27 (d, *J* = −14.01 Hz, 1H, CH*H*), 4.56 (m, 2H, CH_2), 7.39 (d, *J* = 1.94 Hz, 1H, CH_{Ar}), 7.48 (dd, *J* = 8.27, 1.94 Hz, 1H, CH_{Ar}), 7.66 (d, *J* = 8.27 Hz, 1H, CH_{Ar}); ^{13}C-NMR (125 MHz, CD_3OD) δ ppm 19.5 (CH_2), 19.9 (CH_3), 20.6 (CH_2), 24.5 (2× CH_3), 25.9 (CH_3), 30.8 (CH_2), 34.8 (*C*H), 38.9 (*C*), 39.2 (CH_2), 39.7 (CH_2), 41.6 (*C*), 49.6 (*C*H), 54.3 (CH_3), 54.6 (CH_3), 57.1 (CH_2), 70.3 (CH_2), 79.0 (CH_2), 124.7 (CH_{Ar}), 124.9 (CH_{Ar}), 127.7 (CH_{Ar}), 135.3 (C_{Ar}), 147.2 (C_{Ar}), 148.3 (C_{Ar}).

3.2.7. General Procedure for Anion Exchange

Anion exchange reactions were performed as described in the literature [32]. $LiNTf_2$ or NH_4BF_4 solution (1.0 M in H_2O, 1.0 eq) was added to CSA (1.0 eq, in DCM) at rt. and stirred for 1 h. Phases were separated and the organic phase was washed with water, concentrated and dried in vacuum.

(+)-Dehydroabietyl-N,N,N-trimethylmethanaminium tetrafluoroborate (**7b**). White solid (0.085 g, 93.3%); mp 246.8 °C; HRMS-ESI (*m/z*) calc. for $C_{23}H_{38}N$ $[M - BF_4]^+$ 328.2999, found 328.2990; [α]23D = +19.93 (*c* 1.0, $CHCl_3$ + 3% MeOH); ^{1}H-NMR (500 MHz, $CDCl_3$ + 3% CD_3OD) δ ppm 1.21 (d, *J* = 7.02 Hz, 6H, 2× CH_3), 1.25

(s, 3H, CH_3), 1.31 (s, 3H, CH_3), 1.40 (dd, *J* = −11.63, 2.60 Hz, 1H, C*H*), 1.43 (m, 1H, C*H*H), 1.64 (m, 1H, C*H*H), 1.76 (m, 2H, CH_2), 1.89 (m, 2H, CH_2), 2.00 (dt, *J* = −13.10, 2.87 Hz, 1H, CH*H*), 2.32 (dt, *J* = −12.83, 2.60 Hz, 1H, CH*H*), 2.81 (sep, *J* = 7.03 Hz, 1H, C*H*), 2.91 (m, 1H, C*H*H), 2.96 (ddd, *J* = −17.17, 7.06, 1.86 Hz, 1H, CH*H*), 3.22 (d, *J* = −14.33 Hz, 1H, C*H*H), 3.34 (s, 9H, 3× CH_3), 3.67 (d, *J* = −14.33 Hz, 1H, CH*H*), 6.89 (d, *J* = 2.23 Hz, 1H, CH_{Ar}), 6.98 (dd, *J* = 8.22, 2.23 Hz, 1H, CH_{Ar}), 7.11 (d, *J* = 8.22 Hz, 1H, CH_{Ar}); ^{13}C-NMR (125 MHz, $CDCl_3$, +3% CD_3OD) δ ppm 18.4 (CH_2), 19.5 (CH_3), 19.6 (CH_2), 23.9 (CH_3), 24.0 (CH_3), 25.6 (CH_3), 29.6 (CH_2), 33.5 (*C*H), 37.6 (CH_2), 38.0 (*C*), 38.8 (CH_2), 40.6 (*C*), 47.9 (*C*H), 56.5 (3× CH_3), 78.8 (CH_2), 123.6 (CH_{Ar}), 124.1 (CH_{Ar}), 126.9 (CH_{Ar}), 134.1 (C_{Ar}), 146.1 (C_{Ar}), 146.6 (C_{Ar}).

(+)-Dehydroabietyl-N,N,N-trimethylmethanaminium bis(trifluoromethanesulfonimide) (**7c**). White solid (0.13 g, 97.3%); mp 46.6 °C; HRMS-ESI (*m/z*) calc. for $C_{23}H_{38}N$ [M − NTf_2]$^+$ 328.2999, found 328.3011; calc. for $C_2F_6NO_4S_2$ [NTf_2] 279.9167, found 279.9169; [α]23D = +7.79 (*c* 1.0, $CHCl_3$); ^{1}H-NMR (500 MHz, $CDCl_3$) δ ppm 1.21 (d, *J* = 7.04 Hz, 6H, 2× CH_3), 1.26 (s, 3H, CH_3), 1.31 (s, 3H, CH_3), 1.39 (dd, *J* = −12.30, 2.70 Hz, 1H, C*H*), 1.42 (m, 1H, C*H*H), 1.60 (m, 1H, C*H*H), 1.76 (m, 2H, CH_2), 1.83 (m, 2H, CH_2), 1.99 (m, 1H, CH*H*), 2.33 (dt, *J* = −13.31, 3.12 Hz, 1H, CH*H*), 2.82 (sep, *J* = 7.04 Hz, 1H, C*H*), 2.87 (m, 1H, C*H*H), 2.98 (dd, *J* = −17.20, 6.70 Hz, 1H, CH*H*), 3.11 (d, *J* = −14.21 Hz, 1H, C*H*H), 3.29 (s, 9H, 3× CH_3), 3.53 (d, *J* = −14.21 Hz, 1H, CH*H*), 6.89 (d, *J* = 1.88 Hz, 1H, CH_{Ar}), 6.99 (dd, *J* = 8.21, 1.88 Hz, 1H, CH_{Ar}), 7.11 (d, *J* = 8.21 Hz, 1H, CH_{Ar}); ^{13}C-NMR (125 MHz, $CDCl_3$) δ ppm 18.4 (CH_2), 19.4 (CH_3), 19.6 (CH_2), 24.0 (CH_3), 24.1 (CH_3), 25.6 (CH_3), 29.5 (CH_2), 33.6 (*C*H), 37.6 (CH_2), 38.1 (*C*), 38.9 (CH_2), 40.7 (*C*), 47.9 (*C*H), 56.7 (3× CH_3), 79.3 (CH_2), 119.9 (q, *J* = 320.54, CF_3), 123.7 (CH_{Ar}), 124.2 (CH_{Ar}), 127.1 (CH_{Ar}), 134.0 (C_{Ar}), 146.3 (C_{Ar}), 146.5 (C_{Ar}).

N-Benzyl-1-(+)-dehydroabietyl-N,N-dimethylmethanaminium tetrafluoroborate (**8b**). White solid (0.19 g, 92.6%); mp 179.9 °C; HRMS-ESI (*m/z*) calc. for $C_{29}H_{42}N$ [M − BF_4]$^+$ 404.3312, found 404.3311; [α]23D = +2.28 (*c* 1.0, $CHCl_3$); ^{1}H-NMR (500 MHz, $CDCl_3$) δ ppm 1.206 (d, *J* = 6.86 Hz, 6H, 2× CH_3), 1.209 (s, 3H, CH_3), 1.29 (s, 3H, CH_3), 1.33 (m, 1H, C*H*), 1.39 (m, 1H, C*H*H), 1.54 (m, 1H, C*H*H), 1.70 (m, 2H, CH_2), 1.82 (m, 2H, CH_2), 1.98 (dt, *J* = −12.28 Hz, 1H, CH*H*), 2.28 (dt, *J* = −12.77 Hz, 1H, CH*H*), 2.81 (sep, *J* = 6.86 Hz, 1H, C*H*), 2.83 (m, 1H, C*H*H), 2.92 (m, 1H, CH*H*), 3.14 (s, 3H, CH_3), 3.17 (d, *J* = −12.75 Hz,

1H, C*H*H), 3.21 (s, 3H, C*H*$_3$), 3.71 (d, *J* = −12.75 Hz, 1H, CH*H*), 4.69 (d, *J* = −12.75 Hz, 1H, C*H*H), 4.73 (d, *J* = −12.75 Hz, 1H, CH*H*), 6.86 (d, *J* = 1.87 Hz, 1H, C*H*$_{Ar}$), 6.97 (dd, *J* = 8.17, 1.87 Hz, 1H, C*H*$_{Ar}$), 7.08 (d, *J* = 8.17 Hz, 1H, C*H*$_{Ar}$), 7.39 (m, 1H, C*H*$_{Ar}$), 7.42 (m, 1H, C*H*$_{Ar}$), 7.55 (m, 1H, C*H*$_{Ar}$); ^{13}C-NMR (75 MHz, CDCl$_3$) δ ppm 18.5 (*C*H$_2$), 19.7 (*C*H$_2$), 19.8 (*C*H$_3$), 24.08 (*C*H$_3$), 24.11 (*C*H$_3$), 25.6 (*C*H$_3$), 29.8 (*C*H$_2$), 33.6 (*C*H), 37.6 (*C*H$_2$), 38.1 (*C*), 39.2 (*C*H$_2$), 40.6 (*C*), 48.4 (*C*H), 51.3 (*C*H$_3$), 51.6 (*C*H$_3$), 73.1 (*C*H$_2$), 76.2 (*C*H$_2$), 123.7 (*C*H$_{Ar}$), 124.1 (*C*H$_{Ar}$), 127.0 (*C*H$_{Ar}$), 127.4 (*C*$_{Ar}$), 129.3 (*C*H$_{Ar}$), 130.9 (*C*H$_{Ar}$), 133.6 (*C*H$_{Ar}$), 134.3 (*C*$_{Ar}$), 146.2 (*C*$_{Ar}$), 146.8 (*C*$_{Ar}$).

N-Benzyl-1-(+)-dehydroabietyl-N,N-dimethylmethanaminium bis(trifluoromethanesulfonimide) (**8c**). Colorless glass (0.27 g, 89.9%); mp 48.8 °C; HRMS-ESI (*m/z*) calc. for $C_{29}H_{42}N$ [M − NTf$_2$]$^+$ 404.3312 found 404.3323 calc. for $C_2F_6NO_4S_2$ [NTf$_2$] 279.9167, found 279.9166; [α]23D = +1.70 (*c* 1.0, CHCl$_3$); ^{1}H-NMR (500 MHz, CDCl$_3$) δ ppm 1.22 (d, *J* = 6.93 Hz, 6H, 2× C*H*$_3$), 1.24 (s, 3H, C*H*$_3$), 1.31 (s, 3H, C*H*$_3$), 1.37 (m, 1H, C*H*), 1.41 (m, 1H, C*H*H), 1.53 (m, 1H, C*H*H), 1.74 (m, 2H, C*H*$_2$), 1.84 (m, 2H, C*H*$_2$), 2.00 (dt, *J* = −12.37, 3.29 Hz, 1H, CH*H*), 2.31 (dt, *J* = −12.83, 2.82 Hz, 1H, CH*H*), 2.82 (m, 1H, C*H*H), 2.83 (sep, *J* = 6.93 Hz, 1H, C*H*), 2.97 (dd, *J* = −17.75, 6.68 Hz, 1H, CH*H*), 3.10 (d, *J* = −14.00 Hz, 1H, C*H*H), 3.11 (s, 3H, C*H*$_3$), 3.17 (s, 3H, C*H*$_3$), 3.59 (d, *J* = −14.00 Hz, 1H, CH*H*), 4.50 (d, *J* = −12.54 Hz, 1H, C*H*H), 4.56 (d, *J* = −12.54 Hz, 1H, CH*H*), 6.89 (d, *J* = 2.05 Hz, 1H,C*H*$_{Ar}$), 6.99 (dd, *J* = 8.16, 2.05 Hz, 1H, C*H*$_{Ar}$), 7.11 (d, *J* = 8.16 Hz, 1H, C*H*$_{Ar}$), 7.469 (m, 1H, C*H*$_{Ar}$), 7.472 (m, 1H, C*H*$_{Ar}$), 7.51 (m, 1H, C*H*$_{Ar}$); ^{13}C-NMR (75 MHz, CDCl$_3$) δ ppm 18.4 (*C*H$_2$), 19.7 (*C*H$_2$), 19.8 (*C*H$_3$), 24.06 (*C*H$_3$), 24.09 (*C*H$_3$), 25.6 (*C*H$_3$), 29.6 (*C*H$_2$), 33.6 (*C*H), 37.6 (*C*H$_2$), 38.2 (*C*), 39.3 (*C*H$_2$), 40.8 (*C*), 48.3 (*C*H), 51.6 (*C*H$_3$), 51.9 (*C*H$_3$), 73.6 (*C*H$_2$), 76.8 (*C*H$_2$), 119.9 (q, *J* = 320.36, *C*F$_3$), 123.7 (*C*H$_{Ar}$), 124.3 (*C*H$_{Ar}$), 126.7 (*C*$_{Ar}$), 127.0 (*C*H$_{Ar}$), 129.6 (*C*H$_{Ar}$), 131.4 (*C*H$_{Ar}$), 133.3 (*C*H$_{Ar}$), 134.0 (*C*$_{Ar}$), 146.3 (*C*$_{Ar}$), 146.6 (*C*$_{Ar}$).

2-Hydroxy-N-(+)-dehydroabietyl-N,N-dimethylethanaminium tetrafluoroborate (**9b**). White solid (0.093 g, 91.3%); mp 188.5 °C; HRMS-ESI (*m/z*) calc. for $C_{24}H_{40}NO$ [M − BF$_4$]$^+$ 358.3104, found 358.3117; [α]23D = +18.73 (*c* 1.0, CHCl$_3$); ^{1}H-NMR (500 MHz, CDCl$_3$) δ ppm 1.20 (d, *J* = 6.93 Hz, 6H, 2× C*H*$_3$), 1.24 (s, 3H, C*H*$_3$), 1.30 (s, 3H, C*H*$_3$), 1.38 (m, 1H, C*H*), 1.42 (m, 1H, C*H*H), 1.60 (m, 1H, C*H*H), 1.73 (m, 2H, C*H*$_2$), 1.85 (m, 2H, C*H*$_2$), 2.01 (dt, *J* = −12.20 Hz, 1H, CH*H*), 2.29

(dt, *J* = −13.03 Hz, 1H, CH*H*), 2.80 (sep, *J* = 6.93 Hz, 1H, C*H*), 2.93 (m, 2H, CH_2), 3.18 (d, *J* = −14.31 Hz, 1H, C*H*H), 3.24 (s, 3H, CH_3), 3.25 (s, 3H, CH_3), 3.60 (br s, 2H, CH_2), 3.64 (d, *J* = −14.31 Hz, 1H, CH*H*), 4.07 (br s, 2H, CH_2), 6.88 (d, *J* = 1.75 Hz, 1H, CH_{Ar}), 6.97 (dd, *J* = 8.11, 1.75 Hz, 1H, CH_{Ar}), 7.09 (d, *J* = 8.11 Hz, 1H, CH_{Ar}); ^{13}C-NMR (75 MHz, $CDCl_3$) δ ppm 18.5 (CH_2), 19.62 (CH_2), 19.64 (CH_3), 24.08 (CH_3), 24.11 (CH_3), 25.7 (CH_3), 29.7 (CH_2), 33.6 (CH), 37.7 (*C*), 38.2 (CH_2), 39.1 (CH_2), 40.7 (*C*), 48.2 (CH), 53.7 (CH_3), 53.9 (CH_3), 56.8 (CH_2), 69.3 (CH_2), 78.3 (CH_2), 123.7 (CH_{Ar}), 124.1 (CH_{Ar}), 127.0 (CH_{Ar}), 134.3 (C_{Ar}), 146.2 (C_{Ar}), 146.8 (C_{Ar}).

2-Hydroxy-N-(+)-dehydroabietyl-N,N-dimethylethanaminium bis(trifluoromethanesulfonimide) (**9c**). Viscous colorless liquid (0.14 g, 97.8%); HRMS-ESI (*m/z*) Calc. for $C_{24}H_{40}NO$ [M − NTf_2]$^+$ 358.3104, found 358.3105; calc. for $C_2F_6NO_4S_2$ [NTf_2] 279.9167, found 279.9164; [α]23D = +6.56 (c 1.0, $CHCl_3$); ^{1}H-NMR (500 MHz, $CDCl_3$) δ ppm 1.21 (d, *J* = 6.80 Hz, 6H, 2× CH_3), 1.26 (s, 3H, CH_3), 1.31 (s, 3H, CH_3), 1.39 (m, 1H, C*H*), 1.43 (m, 1H, C*H*H), 1.59 (m, 1H, C*H*H), 1.82 (m, 2H, CH_2), 2.01 (dt, *J* = −12.52, 2.59 Hz, 1H, CH*H*), 2.33 (dt, *J* = −12.93, 2.99 Hz, 1H, CH*H*), 2.82 (sep, *J* = 6.80 Hz, 1H, C*H*), 2.87 (m, 1H, C*H*H), 2.97 (ddd, *J* = −17.65, 6.80, 1.81 Hz, 1H, CH*H*), 3.18 (d, *J* = −14.05 Hz, 1H, C*H*H), 3.26 (s, 3H, CH_3), 3.27 (s, 3H, CH_3), 3.61 (br s, 2H, CH_2), 3.62 (d, *J* = −14.05 Hz, 1H, CH*H*), 4.09 (br s, 2H, CH_2), 6.89 (d, *J* = 1.87 Hz, 1H, CH_{Ar}), 6.99 (dd, *J* = 8.15, 1.87 Hz, 1H, CH_{Ar}), 7.11 (d, *J* = 8.15 Hz, 1H, CH_{Ar}); ^{13}C-NMR (75 MHz, $CDCl_3$) δ ppm 18.4 (CH_2), 19.66 (CH_2), 19.70 (CH_3), 24.05 (CH_3), 24.11 (CH_3), 25.6 (CH_3), 29.5 (CH_2), 33.6 (CH), 37.6 (CH_2), 38.2 (*C*), 39.3 (CH_2), 40.8 (*C*), 48.2 (CH), 54.0 (CH_3), 54.2 (CH_3), 56.8 (CH_2), 69.6 (CH_2), 78.7 (CH_2), 119.9 (q, *J* = 320.27, CF_3), 123.7 (CH_{Ar}), 124.3 (CH_{Ar}), 127.0 (CH_{Ar}), 134.0 (C_{Ar}), 146.3 (C_{Ar}), 146.6 (C_{Ar}).

3.2.8. Synthesis of Guests

N-Acetylation of phenylalanine was performed according to the literature [45]. *n*-Bu_4N salts were prepared by adding tetrabutylammonium hydroxide (1.0 M in MeOH, 1.0 eq) to the racemic acid (1.0 eq) in MeOH. After stirring for 1–3 h, the solvent was evaporated and the product was dried under vacuum.

4. CONCLUSIONS

A number of new chiral tertiary and quaternary amine solvating agents (CSAs) based on (+)-dehydroabietylamine were synthesized and found to resolve racemic Mosher's acid and its *n*-Bu_4N salt by ^{1}H-NMR and ^{19}F-NMR spectrocopy. Optimum conditions for the enantiomeric resolution with the CSAs were determined by titration. The CSAs are also useful in the determination of ee values of enantiomerically enriched mixtures. Both non-ionic and ionic CSAs resolve racemic carboxylic acids equally well. Best results were obtained with racemic carboxylic acids containing a large electronegative group at the α-position. A modification of the RES-TOCSY NMR pulse sequence was used, allowing the enhancement of enantiomeric discrimination when the resolution of multiplets is insufficient. In future work, the development of different**2**-based CSAs will be continued.

ACKNOWLEDGMENTS

T.L. is grateful for the University of Helsinki and the Finnish Concordia Fund for the support.

AUTHOR CONTRIBUTIONS

T.L. conceived and designed the experiments; T.L. performed the experiments, except the modification of RES-TOCSY pulse sequence and measurement of RES-TOCSY experiments which were done by S.H.; T.L. analyzed the data, except the data from RES-TOCSY which was analysed by S.H.; T.L., S.H. and K.W. wrote the paper.

CONFLICTS OF INTEREST

The authors declare no conflict of interest.

REFERENCES

1. Nuopponen, M.; Willfor, S.; Jääskeläinen, A.; Sundberg, A.; Vuorinen, T. A UV resonance Raman (UVRR) spectroscopic study on the extractable compounds of Scots pine (Pinus sylvestris) wood Part I: Lipophilic compounds. Spectrochim. Acta A Mol. Biomol. Spectrosc. 2004, 60, 2953–2961.

2. Qin, M.; Hannuksela, T.; Holmbom, B. Physico-chemical characterization of TMP resin and related model mixtures.Colloids Surfaces A Physicochem. Eng. Asp. 2003, 221, 243–254.

3. Cheney, L.C. Penicillin Salts of Amines Derived from Rosin. U.S. Patent 2585436, 12 February 1952.

4. Nolan, M.O.; Bond, H.W. Results of laboratory screening tests of chemical compounds for molluscicidal activity. III. Derivatives of abietic acid. Am. J. Trop. Med. Hyg. 1955, 4, 152–155. [PubMed]

5. Rosscup, R.J.; Liehe, H.J. Lubricant Comprising a Lubricating Oil and a Ureido Compound. U.S. Patent 3015625, 2 January 1962.

6. Gottstein, W.J.; Cheney, L.C. Dehydroabietylamine. A new resolving agent. J. Org. Chem. 1965, 30, 2072–2073.

7. Bolchi, C.; Fumagalli, L.; Moroni, B.; Pallavicini, M.; Valoti, E. A short entry to enantiopure 2-substituted 1,4-benzodioxanes by efficient resolution methods. Tetrahedron Asymmetry 2003, 14, 3779–3785.

8. Laaksonen, T.; Heikkinen, S.; Wähälä, K. Synthesis and applications of secondary amine derivatives of (+)-dehydroabietylamine in chiral molecular recognition. Org. Biomol. Chem. 2015.

9. Bergmann, H.; Grosch, B.; Sitterberg, S.; Bach, T. An enantiomerically pure 1,5,7-trimethyl-3-azabicyclo[3.3.1]nonan-2-one as 1H-NMR shift reagent for the ee determination of

chiral lactams, quinolones, and oxazolidinones. J. Org. Chem. 2004, 69, 970–973.

10. Heo, K.S.; Hyun, M.H.; Cho, Y.J.; Ryoo, J.J. Determination of optical purity of 3,5-dimethoxybenzoyl-leucine diethylamide by chiral chromatography and 1H- and 13C-NMR spectroscopy. Chirality 2011, 23, 281–286.

11. Grimm, S.H.; Allmendinger, L.; Hoefner, G.; Wanner, K.T. Enantiopurity Determination of the Enantiomers of the Triple Reuptake Inhibitor Indatraline. Chirality 2013, 25, 923–933.

12. Suzuki, M.; Deschamps, J.R.; Jacobson, A.E.; Rice, K.C. Chiral Resolution and Absolute Configuration of the Enantiomers of the Psychoactive "Designer Drug" 3,4-Methylenedioxypyrovalerone. Chirality 2015, 27, 287–293.

13. Uccello-Barretta, G.; Balzano, F. Chiral NMR Solvating Additives for Differentiation of Enantiomers. Top. Curr. Chem.2013, 341, 69–131. [PubMed]

14. Wenzel, T.J. Discrimination of Chiral Compounds Using NMR Spectroscopy; John Wiley & Sons: Hoboken, NJ, USA, 2007; p. 549.

15. Kumar, V.; Olsen, C.E.; Schäffer, S.J.C.; Parmar, V.S.; Malhotra, S.V. Synthesis and Applications of Novel Bis(ammonium) Chiral Ionic Liquids Derived from Isomannide. Org. Lett. 2007, 9, 3905–3908.

16. De Rooy, S.L.; Li, M.; Bwambok, D.K.; El-Zahab, B.; Challa, S.; Warner, I.M. Ephedrinium-based protic chiral ionic liquids for enantiomeric recognition. Chirality 2011, 23, 54–62.

17. Satishkumar, S.; Periasamy, M. Chiral recognition of carboxylic acids by Troeger's base derivatives. Tetrahedron Asymmetry 2009, 20, 2257–2262.

18. Jain, N.; Mandal, M.B.; Bedekar, A.V. Roof shape amines: synthesis and application as NMR chiral solvating agents for

discrimination of α-functionalized acids. Tetrahedron 2014, 70, 4343–4354.

19. Yang, X.; Wang, G.; Zhong, C.; Wu, X.; Fu, E. Novel NMR chiral solvating agents derived from (1R,2R)-diaminocyclohexane: Synthesis and enantiodiscrimination for chiral carboxylic acids. Tetrahedron Asymmetry 2006,17, 916–921.

20. Winkel, A.; Wilhelm, R. New chiral ionic liquids based on imidazolinium salts. Tetrahedron Asymmetry 2009, 20, 2344–2350.

21. Periasamy, M.; Dalai, M.; Padmaja, M. Chiral trans-1,2-diaminocyclohexane derivatives as chiral solvating agents for carboxylic acids. J. Chem. Sci. 2010, 122, 561–569.

22. Liu, L.; Ye, M.; Hu, X.; Yu, X.; Zhang, L.; Lei, X. Chiral solvating agents for carboxylic acids based on the salen moiety. Tetrahedron Asymmetry 2011, 22, 1667–1671.

23. Kumar, V.; Pei, C.; Olsen, C.E.; Schaeffer, S.J.C.; Parmar, V.S.; Malhotra, S.V. Novel carbohydrate-based chiral ammonium ionic liquids derived from isomannide. Tetrahedron Asymmetry 2008, 19, 664–671.

24. Heckel, T.; Winkel, A.; Wilhelm, R. Chiral ionic liquids based on nicotine for the chiral recognition of carboxylic acids. Tetrahedron Asymmetry 2013, 24, 1127–1133.

25. Gonzalez, L.; Altava, B.; Bolte, M.; Burguete, M.I.; Garcia-Verdugo, E.; Luis, S.V. Synthesis of Chiral Room Temperature Ionic Liquids from Amino Acids—Application in Chiral Molecular Recognition. Eur. J. Org. Chem. 2012,26, 4996–5009.

26. Chaudhary, A.R.; Yadav, P.; Bedekar, A.V. Application of optically active aminonaphthols as NMR solvating agents for chiral discrimination of mandelic acid. Tetrahedron Asymmetry 2014, 25, 767–774.

27. Ashraf, S.A.; Pornputtkul, Y.; Kane-Maguire, L.A.P.; Wallace, G.G. Facile synthesis of a chiral ionic liquid derived from 1-phenylethylamine. Aust. J. Chem. 2007, 60, 64–67.

28. Altava, B.; Barbosa, D.S.; Isabel Burguete, M.; Escorihuela, J.; Luis, S.V. Synthesis of new chiral imidazolium salts derived from amino acids: Their evaluation in chiral molecular recognition. Tetrahedron Asymmetry 2009, 20, 999–1003.

29. Kannappan, J.; Jain, N.; Bedekar, A.V. Synthesis and applications of exo N-((1R,2R,4R)-1,7,7-trimethylbicyclo[2.2.1]heptan-2-yl)benzamides as NMR solvating agents for the chiral discrimination of 1,1'-binaphthyl-2,2'-diyl hydrogenphosphates and α-substituted acids. Tetrahedron Asymmetry 2015, 26, 1102–1107.

30. Gospodarowicz, K.; Holynska, M.; Paluch, M.; Lisowski, J. Novel chiral hexaazamacrocycles for the enantiodiscrimination of carboxylic acids. Tetrahedron 2012, 68, 9930–9935.

31. Tabassum, S.; Gilani, M.A.; Wilhelm, R. Imidazolinium sulfonate and sulfamate zwitterions as chiral solvating agents for enantiomeric excess calculations. Tetrahedron Asymmetry 2011, 22, 1632–1639.

32. Foreiter, M.B.; Gunaratne, H.Q.N.; Nockemann, P.; Seddon, K.R.; Stevenson, P.J.; Wassell, D.F. Chiral thiouronium salts: Synthesis, characterisation and application in NMR enantio-discrimination of chiral oxoanions. New J. Chem.2013, 37, 515–533.

33. Bozkurt, S.; Durmaz, M.; Naziroglu, H.N.; Yilmaz, M.; Sirit, A. Amino alcohol based chiral solvating agents: Synthesis and applications in the NMR enantiodiscrimination of carboxylic acids. Tetrahedron Asymmetry 2011, 22, 541–549.

34. Wang, W.; Ma, F.; Shen, X.; Zhang, C. New chiral auxiliaries derived from (S)-α-phenylethylamine as chiral solvating agents for carboxylic acids. Tetrahedron Asymmetry 2007, 18, 832–837.

35. Pena, C.; Gonzalez-Sabin, J.; Alfonso, I.; Rebolledo, F.; Gotor, V. Cycloalkane-1,2-diamine derivatives as chiral solvating agents. Study of the structural variables controlling the NMR enantiodiscrimination of chiral carboxylic acids. Tetrahedron 2008, 64, 7709–7717.

36. Gualandi, A.; Grilli, S.; Savoia, D.; Kwit, M.; Gawronski, J. C-hexaphenyl-substituted trianglamine as a chiral solvating agent for carboxylic acids. Org. Biomol. Chem. 2011, 9, 4234–4241.

37. Tanaka, K.; Fukuda, N. "Calixarene-like" chiral amine macrocycles as novel chiral shift reagents for carboxylic acids.Tetrahedron Asymmetry 2009, 20, 111–114.

38. Perez-Trujillo, M.; Castanar, L.; Monteagudo, E.; Kuhn, L.T.; Nolis, P.; Virgili, A.; Williamson, R.T.; Parella, T. Simultaneous 1H- and 13C-NMR enantiodifferentiation from highly-resolved pure shift HSQC spectra. Chem. Commun. 2014, 50, 10214–10217.

39. Aguilar, J.A.; Faulkner, S.; Nilsson, M.; Morris, G.A. Pure shift 1H-NMR: A resolution of the resolution problem?Angew. Chem. Int. Ed. Engl. 2010, 49, 3901–3903.

40. Chaudhari, S.R.; Suryaprakash, N. Chiral discrimination and the measurement of enantiomeric excess from a severely overcrowded NMR spectrum. Chem. Phys. Lett. 2013, 555, 286–290.

41. Lokesh, N.; Chaudhari, S.R.; Suryaprakash, N. RES-TOCSY: A simple approach to resolve overlapped 1H-NMR spectra of enantiomers. Org. Biomol. Chem. 2014, 12, 993–997.

42. Cheney, L.C. Purification of Dehydroabietylamine. U.S. Patent 2787637, 2 April 1957.

43. Su, G.; Huo, L.; Huang, W.; Wang, H.; Pan, Y. Synthesis and crystal structure of 2-dehydroabietyl-5-ethylsulfanyl-1,2,3,4-tetrazole. Chin. J. Struct. Chem. 2009, 28, 693–698.

44. Wang, H.; Tang, L.; Pan, Y.; Liang, M. Synthesis of novel chiral quaternary ammonium salt from rosin. Chem. J. Internet 2004, 6, 56.

45. Stella, S.; Chadha, A. Resolution of N-protected amino acid esters using whole cells of Candida parapsilosis ATCC 7330. Tetrahedron Asymmetry 2010, 21, 457–460.

Chapter 12

Syntheses of Four Enantiomers of 2,3-*Diendo*- and 3-*Endo*-aminobicyclo[2.2.2]oct-5-ene-2-*exo*-carboxylic Acid and Their Saturated Analogues

Márta Palkó [1], Mikko M. Hänninen [2], Reijo Sillanpää [2] and Ferenc Fülöp [1,3,*]

[1]*Institute of Pharmaceutical Chemistry, University of Szeged, Szeged H-6720, Eötvös utca 6, Hungary*

[2]*Department of Chemistry, University of Jyväskylä, Turku FIN-40014, Finland*

[3]*Stereochemistry Research Group of the Hungarian Academy of Sciences, University of Szeged, Szeged H-6720, Eötvös utca 6, Hungary*

ABSTRACT

Ethyl 2,3-*diendo*-3-aminobicyclo[2.2.2]oct-5-ene-2-carboxylate ((±)-**1**) was resolved with *O,O*'-dibenzoyltartaric acid via diastereomeric salt formation. The efficient synthesis of the enantiomers of 2,3-*diendo*-3-aminobicyclo[2.2.2]oct-5-ene-2-carboxylic acid ((+)-**7** and (−)-**7**), 3-*endo*-aminobicyclo[2.2.2]oct-5-ene-2-*exo*-carboxylic acid ((+)-**5** and (−)-**5**), *cis*- and *trans*-3-aminobicyclo[2.2.2]octane-2-carboxylic acid ((+)-**6**, (−)-**6**, (+)-**8** and (−)-**8**) was achieved via isomerization, hydrogenation and hydrolysis of the corresponding esters (−)-**1** and (+)-**1**. The stereochemistry and relative configurations of the synthesized compounds were determined by NMR spectroscopy (based on the ^{3}J(H,H) coupling constants) and X-ray crystallography.

Keywords: bicyclic β-amino acid derivatives; constrained chiral β-amino acids; resolution; continuous flow hydrogenations

1. INTRODUCTION

In the past decade, the number of investigations on β-amino acids, in both racemic and optically active forms, has risen exponentially as a consequence of their increasing chemical and biological importance. β-Amino acids and their derivatives possess noteworthy pharmacological effects. For example, the first natural alicyclic β-amino acid, (1*R*,2*S*)-2-aminocyclopentanecarboxylic acid (cispentacin) exhibits antifungal activity [1,2,3,4]. Alicyclic β-amino acids can also be used as building blocks of modified analogues of pharmacologically active peptides [5,6,7,8,9,10].

While a range of stereoselective syntheses of enantiomerically enriched small (three- or four-membered: [11,12,13] and medium (five- to eight-membered) cyclic [14,15,16,17] and sterically hindered bicyclic norbornane and norbornene β-amino acids [18,19] or their derivatives have been reported, relatively few examples cocerning the synthesis and applications of enantiomerically enriched bicyclo[2.2.2]octane β-amino acid derivatives have been described [20,21,22,23,24].

Many attractive techniques are available for the production of enantiomerically pure amino acids. Resolution via diastereomeric salt formation, for instance, is still useful for the production of enantiomerically pure compounds on a laboratory scale. Resolution with an equivalent of the resolving agent (Pasteur's method) is the most convenient in work with small amounts of the racemate (DL). In resolution with one equivalent of the resolving agent (R), diastereomers are separated (DL+2R → DR+LR), while when half an equivalent of resolving agent and half an equivalent of achiral acid or base (I) are used (Pope-Peacheay's method [25,26,27,28], a diastereomeric salt is separated from a salt with an achiral agent (DL+R+I → DR+LI). The role of the achiral acid or base is to form a highly soluble salt with the enantiomer remaining in the solution. If there is a large difference in stability of the resulting diastereomeric salt and the enantiomer remaining in solution, the resolutions may be performed with half an equivalent of resolving agent and the achiral auxiliary material is omitted (DL+R → DR+L). A synthesis of racemic 2,3-*diendo*-3-aminobicyclo[2.2.2]oct-5-ene-2-carboxylic acid has been published [29], but its C-2 epimer and their enantiomers have not yet been examined. Our present aim was to synthetize of the title alicyclic β-amino acid enantiomers. This report focuses on the resolution of racemic 2,3-*diendo*-3-aminobicyclo[2.2.2]oct-5-ene-2-carboxylic acid derivatives by diastereomeric salt formation.

2. RESULTS AND DISCUSSION

To find the most suitable resolving agent for (±)-**1**, three kinds of commercially available acidic resolving agents were examined. The solvent in each resolution experiment was EtOH. We first used half an equivalent of *L*-tartaric acid, and *S*-mandelic acid as the resolving agent for (±)-**1**, but surprisingly poor results were obtained. We next focused our attention on *O,O*'-dibenzoyltartaric acid (DBTA) as a resolving agent which is often used in gram-scale productions. In the first experiments of the Pope-Peacheay resolutions, 0.7 equivalent of aqueous HCl (achiral acid), 0.5 equivalent of DBTA as resolving agent and 1 equivalent of (±)-**1** were mixed with the solvent, and the mixture was heated at 70 °C. The solution was subsequently stirred and further cooled to room temperature. After stirring for 2 h, the solids were collected. Finally, this protocol was repeated without HCl. As the ^{1}H-NMR spectra of the salt-pairs were identical, the diastereomeric purity of the salt obtained in each resolution experiment was determined as the diastereomeric excess (*de*%), based on the enantiomeric excess (*ee*%) of **1** in the salt. The experimental results are listed in Table 1.

Table 1. Resolutions of (±)-**1** with chiral acids.

Entry	Resolving agent	Yield (%)	*de* [b] (%)	S factor [c]
1	*L*-tartaric acid	23	48	0.22
2	*S*-mandelic acid	30	45	0.27
3	L-DBTA [a]	47	70	0.66
4	L-DBTA	45	84	0.76

[a] In the presence of 0.7 equivalent of aq. HCl; [b] The *de* of the salt was determined via the *ee* of ester **1** liberated from the salt; [c] The efficiency factor S is used to indicate how effective a resolution is: S-factor = 2 × yield × *de* [30].

Recrystallization of the L-DBTA salt containing (+)-**1** with 84% *de* in EtOH furnished enantiomer (+)-**1** with 96% *de*. Similarly, enantiomer (−)-**1** with D-DBTA was obtained from the mother liquor in 98% *de* (Scheme 1).

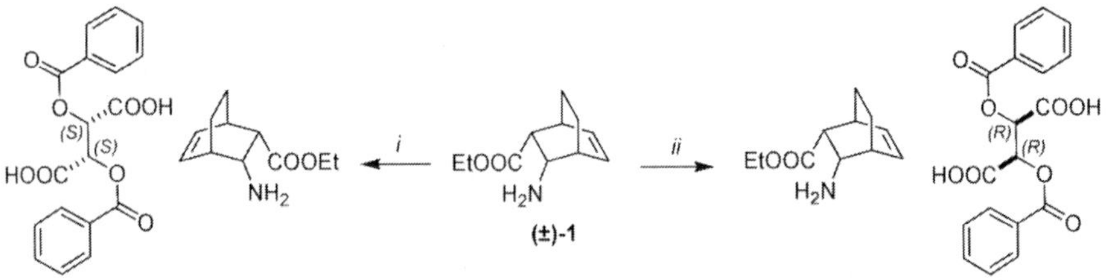

Scheme 1. Resolution of ester **1** with DBTA.

The C-2 isomerization of (−)-**1** with NaOEt in EtOH at 70 °C resulted in amino ester (+)-**2**. Compounds (−)-**1** and (+)-**2**were also transformed into amino ester enantiomers (−)-**3** and (−)-**4** with H_2 in the presence of Pd/C. Continuous flow hydrogenations were carried out in a ThalesNano H-cube™ system. For each run, 150 mg of catalyst was added to in a tubular catalyst cartridge with an inner diameter of 4 mm and a length of 30 mm. The catalyst was rinsed for 0.5 h with a flow of EtOH 1 mL min^{-1}, followed by pretreatment with H_2 for 0.5 h in the same solvent. The reactant was dissolved in EtOH and this solution was delivered to the hydrogenation system via a conventional HPLC pump, through the mixer of the apparatus, where

H_2 was mixed into the liquid flow under a pressure of 1 MPa. The catalyst cartridge holder was equipped with an externally controlled cooling jacket. The mixture was pumped through the catalyst bed so as to obtain an ascending flow of the reaction components. After one reaction cycle, samples of 1 mL were taken from the product flow and analysed by GC analysis: complete conversion was observed.

When subjected to microwave irradiation in H_2O at 150 °C for 1 h, ester (−)-**1**, (+)-**2**, (−)-**3**, and (−)-**4** gave amino acids (+)-**5**, (−)-**6**, (−)-**7** and (−)-**8** (Scheme 2). All the reactions were first optimized for the racemic compounds. The whole syntheses were repeated, starting from racemic amino ester (±)-**1** and enantiomer (+)-**1**.

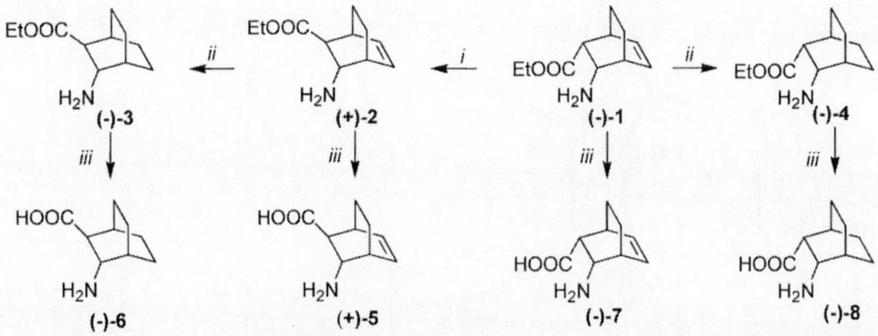

Scheme 2. Synthesis of amino acid enantiomers (+)-**5**, (−)-**6**, (−)-**7** and (−)-**8**.

X-ray investigations revealed the absolute configurations of (−)-**1** and (−)-**2**. Amino esters (−)-**1** and (−)-**2** were transformed into ureas (+)-**9** and (−)-**10** upon reaction with (*S*)-(−)-α-methylbenzyl isocyanate (Scheme 3). The X-ray structures clearly showed the 1*S*,2*R*,3*S*,4*R* configuration of (−)-**1** (Figure 1) and the 1*R*,2*R*,3*R*,4*S* configuration of (−)-**2**(Figure 2).

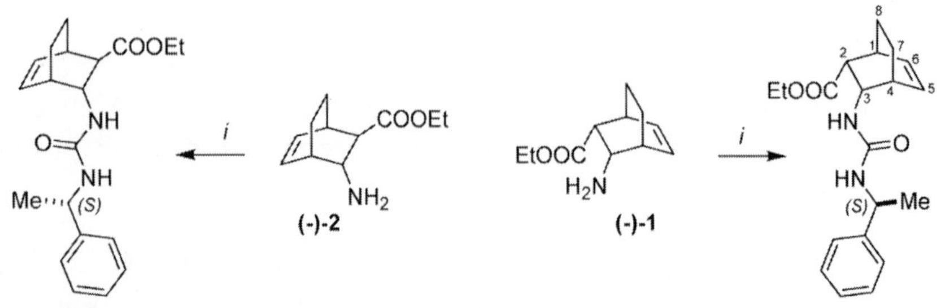

Scheme 3. Synthesis of ureas (+)-**9** and (–)-**10**.

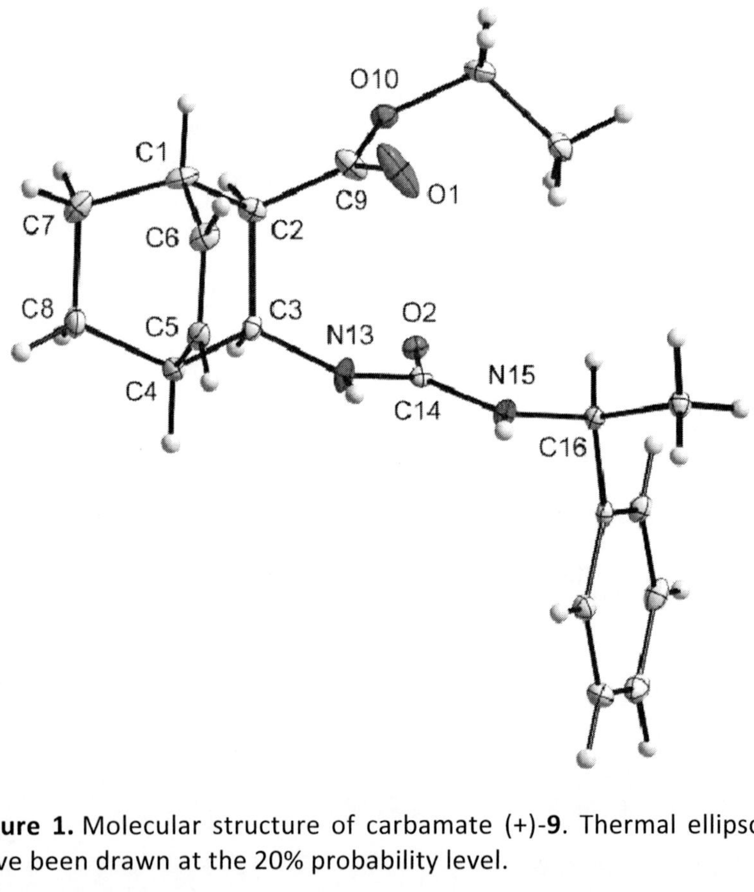

Figure 1. Molecular structure of carbamate (+)-**9**. Thermal ellipsoids have been drawn at the 20% probability level.

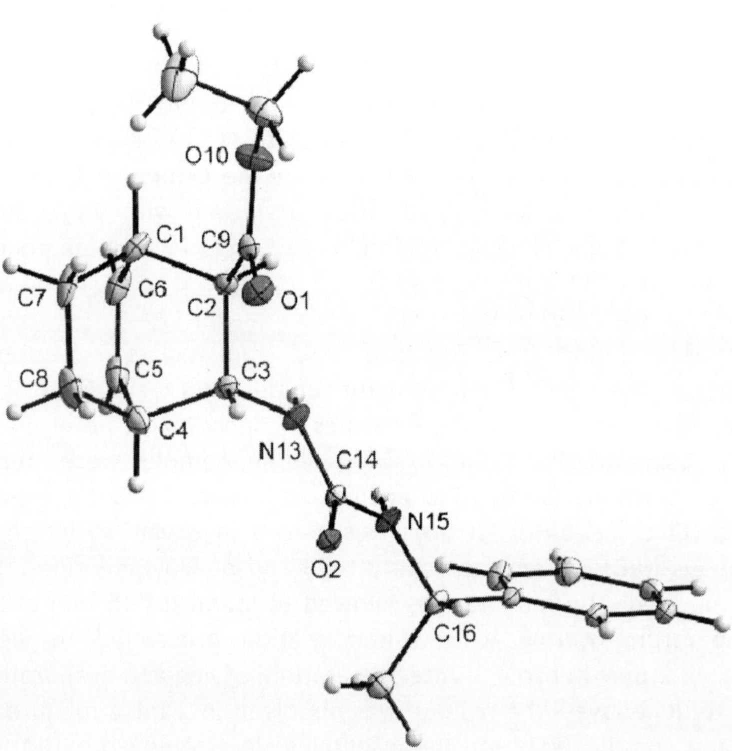

Figure 2. Molecular structure of carbamate (–)-**10**. Thermal ellipsoids have been drawn at the 20% probability level.

3. EXPERIMENTAL

3.1. General

The chemicals were purchased from Aldrich (Budapest, Hungary) or Fluka (Budapest, Hungary) The ^{1}H-NMR spectra were recorded at 400 MHz and the ^{13}C-NMR spectra at 100 MHz on a Bruker AM 400 spectrometer at ambient temperature (27 °C) in DMSO-d_6. Chemical shifts are given in δ (ppm) relative to TMS as internal standard. Elemental analyses were performed with a Perkin-Elmer CHNS-2400 Ser II Elemental Analyzer. Melting points were measured with a Hinotek X-4 melting point apparatus and are uncorrected. Optical rotations were measured with a Perkin-Elmer 341 polarimeter. Microwave reactions were performed in a CEM Discover LabMate MW reactor. Continuous hydrogenations were carried out in an H-

Cube high-pressure continuous-flow system purchased from Thales Nanotechnology Inc. Racemic ethyl 2,3-*diendo*-3-aminobicyclo[2.2.2]oct-5-ene-2-carboxylate (±)-**1** was prepared by a literature method [29]. The *ee* values for the esters (−)-**1**, (+)-**1**, (−)-**4** and (+)-**4** were determined after acylation with Ac_2O in the presence of base by using Perkin-Elmer GC instrumentation equipped with CP-Chirasil L-Val columns [31]. All analyses for derivatized amino esters were performed with N_2 as carrier gas; the column temperature and inlet pressure were adjusted to an optimized program. The injector and detector temperature were set at 250 °C and 270 °C, respectively. The *ee* values of **2** and **3** were determined by HPLC, using a Daicel Chiralcel ODH column. Samples were prepared for *ee* determination by HPLC analysis as follows: (+)-**2**·HCl, (−)-**2**·HCl, (+)-**3**·HCl or (−)-**3**·HCl (10 mg) was placed in a vial, to which 1 M aqueous NaOH (1 mL), toluene (1 mL) and benzoyl chloride (15 μL) were added. The mixture was allowed to stand for 15 min at room temperature, during which *N*-benzoylation proceeded to yield *N*-benzoyl-**2** or *N*-benzoyl-**3**. After separation, drying and evaporation of the toluene layer, the residue was dissolved in 2 mL a mixture of *n*-hexane and IPA (8:2) and the insolubles were removed by filtration. The filtrate (2 μL) was injected into the HPLC apparatus. The analytical conditions were as follows: (a) eluent: a mixture of *n*-hexane and IPA (8:2), flow rate: 0.25 mL min^{-1}, detection at 233 nm, retention times: (−)-**2**: 26.1 min, (+)-**2**: 34.3 min; (b) a mixture of *n*-hexane and IPA (95:5), flow rate: 0,25 mL min^{-1}, detection at 233 nm, retention times: (−)-**3**: 33.48 min, (+)-**3**: 35.2 min.

3.2. Determination of de Values of O,O'-dibenzoyltartaric Acid (DBTA) Salts of 1

The *de* values of the salts were determined from the *ee* values of esters **1**. Samples were prepared for *ee* determination by GC analysis as follows: diastereomeric salt (5 mg) was dissolved in CH_2Cl_2 (50 μL). The sample was acylated with Ac_2O (15 μL) and a mixture of 4-dimethylaminopyridine (DMAP) and pyridine (1:9) (15 μL) was added. After shaking for 2–3 s, the derivatized samples were analysed on GC CP-Chirasil L-Val columns (30 m) with the temperature held at 140 °C for 5 min and then raised to 160 °C at 10 °C min^{-1}, flow rate: 2 mL min^{-1}, retention times: (−)-1: 6.96 min, (+)-1: 7.11 min.

3.3. A Typical Resolution Procedure

A mixture of racemic ester base **1** (10.98 g, 5 mmol), (–)-DBTA (0.94 g, 2.5 mmol) and EtOH (9 mL) in a 50 mL flask was heated under stirring at 70 °C to obtain a clear solution. The solution was gradually cooled to 20 °C during about 30 min, and the precipitated diastereomeric salt was filtered off and washed with Et_2O (10 mL) to yield white crystals, which were dried at room temperature to afford the (1*S*,2*R*,3*S*,4*R*)-(–)-1.(–)-DBTA salt (0.92 g, *de* 84%). The product was recrystallized from EtOH (yield 0.7 g, *de* 96%). The mother liquor was evaporated down and, 2 N NaOH solution (10 mL) was added to the residue. The mixture was extracted with CH_2Cl_2 (3 × 20 mL). The combined organic phase was dried (Na_2SO_4) and the solvent was evaporated off. (+)-DBTA (0.48 g, 1.3 mmol) and EtOH (6 mL) were added to the ester residue (+)-**1** (0.5 g, 1.6 mmol, *ee* 57%) followed by heating under stirring at 70 °C to give a clear solution. The solution was gradually cooled to 20 °C during about 30 min, and the precipitated diastereomeric salt was filtered off and washed with Et_2O (10 mL) to yield white crystals, which were dried at room temperature to afford the (1*R*,2*S*,3*R*,4*S*)-(+)-**1**.(+)-DBTA salt (0.7 g, *de* 92.5%). The crystals were recrystallized from EtOH (yield 0.5 g, *de* 98%)

Ethyl (1S,2R,3S,4R)-3-aminobicyclo[2.2.2]oct-5-ene-2-carboxylate (–)-**1**. (–)-**1**·(–)-DBTA salt, mp 186–188 °C, $[\alpha]_D^{20}$ = –59.9 (c, 0.5, EtOH), *de* = 96%.; (–)-**1**.HCl salt mp 192–194 °C, $[\alpha]_D^{20}$ = –14.8 (c, 0.6, EtOH), *ee* = 96%. The ^{1}H- and ^{13}C-NMR spectroscopic and elemental analysis data on the enantiomeric derivative were in accordance with those for racemic (±)-**1**·HCl [26].

Ethyl (1R,2S,3R,4S)-3-aminobicyclo[2.2.2]oct-5-ene-2-carboxylate (+)-**1**. (+)-**1**·(+)DBTA salt, mp 189–190 °C, $[\alpha]_D^{20}$ = +63.5 (c, 0.5, EtOH), *de* = 98%.; (+)-**1**.HCl salt, mp 192–194 °C, $[\alpha]_D^{20}$ = +15.3 (c, 0.6, EtOH), *ee* = 98%. The ^{1}H- and ^{13}C-NMR spectroscopic and elemental analysis data on the enantiomeric derivative were in accordance with those for racemic (±)-**1**·HCl [26].

3.4. Isomerization of Amino Esters (–)-1 and (+)-1

Freshly prepared NaOEt (280 mg, 4 mmol) was added to a solution of the free base of (–)-**1** or (+)-1 (394 mg, 2 mmol) in dry EtOH (12 mL), and the mixture was heated for 2 h at 70 °C. It was then concentrated under reduced pressure, taken up in CH_2Cl_2 and washed with H_2O (2 × 20 mL). The combined organic phase was dried (Na_2SO_4), the solvent was evaporated off, the residue was dissolved in EtOH containing 22% HCl (2 mL), and the solution was stirred for 10 min at room temperature. After removal of the solvent, amino ester hydrochloride **2** was obtained, which was recrystallized from EtOH/Et_2O.

Ethyl (1S,2S,3S,4R)-3-aminobicyclo[2.2.2]oct-5-ene-2-carboxylate hydrochloride (+)-**2**. White crystals (256 mg, 55%), mp 220 °C (with sublimation), $[\alpha]_D^{20}$ = +47.9 (c, 0.5, EtOH), *ee* = 98%. ^{1}H-NMR: δ = 0.98–1.09 (m, 1H, H-8), 1.18–1.26 (t, *J* = 7.1 Hz, 3H, CH_3), 1.18–1.38 (m, 3H, H-7, H-7, H-8,), 2.282.32 (m, 1H, H-2), 2.82–2.91 (m, 2H, H-1, H-4), 3.64 (t, *J* = 3.2 Hz, 1H, H-3), 4.8–4.23 (m, 2H, OCH_2), 6.18 (t, *J* = 7.1Hz, 1H, H-5) 6.53 (t, *J* = 7.5 Hz 1H, H-6) 7.95 (bs, 3H, NH_3^+) ppm. ^{13}C-NMR: δ = 14.9, 19.9, 23.0, 33.3, 33.4, 49.3, 51.7, 61.6, 130.9, 136.6, 172.4 ppm. Anal. Calcd for $C_{11}H_{18}ClNO_2$ (231,74): C, 57.02; H, 7.83; Cl 15,30; N, 6,04. Found: C, 56.81; H, 8.04; N, 6.05.

Ethyl (1R,2R,3R,4S)-3-aminobicyclo[2.2.2]oct-5-ene-2-carboxylate hydrochloride (–)-**2**. White crystals (263 mg, 56%), mp 178–180 °C, $[\alpha]_D^{20}$ = –43 (c, 0.4, EtOH), *ee* = 98%. The ^{1}H- and ^{13}C-NMR spectroscopic data on the enantiomeric derivative were consistent with the data on the antipode (+)-**2**. Anal. Calcd for $C_{11}H_{18}ClNO_2$ (231.74): C, 57.02; H, 7.83; Cl 15.30; N, 6.04. Found: C, 56.94; H, 8.11; N, 6.12.

3.5. General Procedure for Hydrogenation of Amino Esters (–)-1 (+)-1, (–)-2 and (+)-2 over Pd/C Catalyst in a Fixed-Bed Reactor

Free amino ester (–)-**1**, (+)-**1**, (–)-**2** or (+)-**2** (98 mg, 5 mmol) was dissolved in dry EtOH (100 mL) to form a 0.05 M solution. This solution was hydrogenated in the ThalesNano H-cube™ system, using a 10% Pd/C catalyst at a flow rate of 1 mL min^{-1} at 50 °C and a H_2 pressure of 50 bar. The EtOH was removed under vacuum. The residue was dissolved in EtOH containing 22% HCl (2 mL) and the solution was stirred for 10 min at room temperature. After removal of the solvent, the amino ester hydrochloride was obtained.

Ethyl (2S,3S)-3-aminobicyclo[2.2.2]octane-2-carboxylate Hydrochloride (–)-**3**. An oil (90 mg, 91%), $[\alpha]_D^{20}$ = –17.5 (c, 1.0, MeOH),*ee* = 99%. ^{1}H-NMR: δ = 1.21 (t, *J* = 7.2, 3H, CH_3) 1.25–1.86 (m, 9H, H-5, H-5, H-6, H-6, H-7, H-7, H-8, H-8, H-2), 1.90–1.95 (m, 1H, H-4), 2.54–2.58 (m, 1H, H-4), 3.54–3,64 (m, 1H, H-3), 4.06–4.21 (m, 2H, OCH_2), 8.16 (bs, 3H, NH_3^+) ppm. ^{13}C-NMR: δ = 14.7, 18.6, 21.0, 24.5, 25.3, 27.8, 28.8, 47.9, 50.5, 61.58, 166.4 ppm. Anal. Calcd for $C_{11}H_{20}ClNO_2$ (233.74): C, 56.52; H, 8.62; Cl 15.17; N, 5.99. Found: C, 56.21; H, 8.39; N, 5.93.

Ethyl (2R,3R)-3-aminobicyclo[2.2.2]octane-2-carboxylate Hydrochloride (+)-**3**. An oil (90 mg, 91%), $[\alpha]_D^{20}$ = +15,4 (c, 0.9, MeOH), *ee* = 99%. The ^{1}H- and ^{13}C-NMR spectroscopic data on the enantiomeric derivative were consistent with the data on the antipode (–)-**3**. Anal. Calcd for $C_{11}H_{20}ClNO_2$ (233.74): C, 56.52; H, 8.62; Cl 15.17; N, 5.99. Found: C, 56.29; H, 8.88; N, 6.14.

Ethyl (2R,3S)-3-aminobicyclo[2.2.2]octane-2-carboxylate Hydrochloride (–)-**4**. White crystals (86 mg, 86%,), mp 195-196 °C,$[\alpha]_D^{20}$ = –31.5 (c, 0.6, EtOH), *ee* = 99%. ^{1}H-NMR: δ = 1.22 (t, *J* = 7.1, 3H, CH_3) 1.29–1.98 (m, 10H, H-5, H-5, H-6, H-6, H-7, H-7, H-8, H-8, H-1, H-4), 3.00 (dd, *J* = 5.1, *J* = 1.1 H-2), 3.47 (d, *J* = 4.6 1H, H-3), 4.03–4.23 (m, 2H, OCH_2), 8.00 (bs, 3H, NH_3^+) ppm. ^{13}C-NMR: δ = 14.9, 18.7, 21.2, 24.5, 25.2, 28.0, 28.7, 43.4, 48.8, 61.4, 172.8 Anal. Calcd for $C_{11}H_{20}ClNO_2$ (233.74): C, 56.52; H, 8.62; Cl 15.17; N, 5.99. Found: C, 56.76; H, 8.49; N, 6.17. The *ee* values for esters (–)-**4** and (+)-**4** were determined after derivatization with Ac_2O in the presence of DMAP and pyridine (1:9) by using Perkin-Elmer GC instrumentation equipped with CP-Chirasil L-Val columns (30 m) with the temperature held at 140 °C for 5 min and then raised to 160 °C at 10 °C min^{-1}, flow rate: 1 mL min^{-1}, retention times: (–)-**4**: 9.62 min; (+)-**4**: 9.97 min.

Ethyl (2S,3R)-3-aminobicyclo[2.2.2]octane-2-carboxylate Hydrochloride (+)-**4**. White crystals (81 mg, 81%,), mp 193–

194°C, $[\alpha]_D^{20}$ = +30.1 (c, 0.4, EtOH) *ee* = 99%. The ^{1}H- and ^{13}C-NMR spectroscopic data on the enantiomeric derivative were consistent with the data on the antipode (−)-**4**. Anal. Calcd for $C_{11}H_{20}ClNO_2$ (233.74): C, 56.52; H, 8.62; Cl 15.17; N, 5.99. Found: C, 56.81; H, 8.75; N, 6.21.

3.6. General Procedure for Hydrolyses of Amino Esters ***1–4***

The individual amino ester enantiomers **1–4** (198 mg, 1 mmol) were dissolved in water (4 mL) in a 10 mL pressurized reaction vial, and the solution was stirred at 100 °C for 60 min at max. 150 W microwave irradiation. The solvent was evaporated off, and the crude amino acid was recrystallized from H_2O/acetone to afford a white crystalline product.

(1S,2S,3S,4R)-3-Aminobicyclo[2.2.2]oct-5-ene-2-carboxylic Acid (+)-**5**. White crystals (80 mg, 46%), mp 245–260 °C (dec.), $[\alpha]_D^{20}$ = +51 (c, 0.3, H_2O). ^{1}H-NMR: δ = 0.95–1.55 (m, 4H, H-7, H-7, H-8, H-8), 2.13–2.21 (m, 1H, H-2), 2.75–2.85 (m, 1H, H-1) 2.85–2.95 (m, 1H, H-4), 3.63 (t, *J* = 3.0 Hz, 1H, H-3), 3.76 (bs, 3H, NH_3^+) 6.17 (t, *J* = 7.1 Hz, 1H, H-5) 6.52 (t, *J* = 7.4 Hz 1H, H-6) ppm. ^{13}C-NMR: δ = 20.0, 23.2, 33.3, 33,6, 49.9, 52.0, 130.9, 136.8, 173.9 ppm. Anal. Calcd for $C_9H_{13}NO_2$ (167.09): C, 64.65; H, 7.84; N, 8.38. Found: C, 64.71; H, 7.98; N, 8.45.

(1R,2R,3R,4S)-3-Aminobicyclo[2.2.2]oct-5-ene-2-carboxylic Acid (−)-**5**. White crystals (96 mg, 56%), mp 270–277 °C (dec.), $[\alpha]_D^{20}$ = −64 (c, 0.5, H_2O). The ^{1}H- and ^{13}C-NMR spectroscopic data on the enantiomeric derivative are consistent with the data of the antipode (+)-**5**. Anal. Calcd for $C_9H_{13}NO_2$ (167.09): C, 64.65; H, 7.84; N, 8.38. Found: C, 64.83; H, 7.99; N, 8.61.

(2S,3S)-3-Aminobicyclo[2.2.2]octane-2-carboxylic Acid (−)-**6**. White crystals (116 mg, 67%), mp 255–260 °C (dec.), $[\alpha]_D^{20}$ =−35.4 (c, 0.5, H_2O). ^{1}H-NMR: δ = 1.39–1.75 (m, 8H, H-5, H-5, H-6, H-6, H-7, H-7, H-8, H-8), 1.87–1.91 (m, 1H, H-4), 2.07–2.11 (m, 1H, H-1) 2.34 (d, *J* = 6.1, 1H, H-2), 3.90 (d, *J* = 6.1 Hz, 1H, H-3). ^{13}C-NMR: δ = 18.4, 20.9, 24.2, 25.5, 28.1, 29.2, 51.0, 52.9, 180.9 ppm. Anal. Calcd for

$C_9H_{15}NO_2$ (169.11): C, 63.88; H, 8.93; N, 8.28. Found: C, 64.07; H, 9.11; N, 8.08.

(2R,3R)-3-Aminobicyclo[2.2.2]octane-2-carboxylic Acid (+)-**6**. White crystals (100 mg, 58%), mp 255–260 °C (dec.), $[\alpha]_D^{20}$ = +35.1 (c, 0.4, H_2O). The ^{1}H- and ^{13}C-NMR spectroscopic data on the enantiomeric derivative were consistent with the data on the antipode (–)-**6**. Anal. Calcd for $C_9H_{15}NO_2$ (169.11): C, 63.88; H, 8.93; N, 8.28. Found: C, 64.12; H, 9.05; N, 8.41.

(1S,2R,3S,4R)-3-Aminobicyclo[2.2.2]oct-5-ene-2-carboxylic Acid (–)-**7**. White crystals (96 mg, 56%), mp 215–219 °C (dec.), $[\alpha]_D^{20}$ = –3 (c, 0.4, H_2O). The ^{1}H- and ^{13}C-NMR spectroscopic and elemental analysis data on the enantiomeric derivative were in accordance with those for racemic (±)-**7** [29].

(1R,2S,3R,4S)-3-Aminobicyclo[2.2.2]oct-5-ene-2-carboxylic Acid (+)-**7**. White crystals (88 mg, 51%), mp 220–221 °C (dec.), $[\alpha]_D^{20}$ = +3.2 (c, 0.4, H_2O) The ^{1}H- and ^{13}C-NMR spectroscopic and elemental analysis data on the enantiomeric derivative were in accordance with those for racemic (±)-**7** [29].

(2R,3S)-3-Aminobicyclo[2.2.2]octane-2-carboxylic Acid (–)-**8**. White crystals (92 mg, 54%), mp 223–230 °C (dec.), $[\alpha]_D^{20}$ = –49 (c, 0.3, H_2O). The ^{1}H- and ^{13}C-NMR spectroscopic and elemental analysis data on the enantiomeric derivative were in accordance with those for racemic (±)-**8** [29].

(2S,3R)-3-Aminobicyclo[2.2.2]octane-2-carboxylic Acid (+)-**8**. White crystals (83 mg, 48%), mp 236–240 °C (dec.), $[\alpha]_D^{20}$ = +46.5 (c, 0.3, H_2O). The ^{1}H- and ^{13}C-NMR spectroscopic and elemental analysis data on the enantiomeric derivative were in accordance with those for racemic (±)-**8** [29].

*3.7. Syntheses of Ureas (+)-**9** and (–)-**10***

Amino ester base (–)-**1** or (–)-**2** (100 mg, 0.33 mmol) was dissolved in dry Et_2O (20 mL) and a 10% excess of (*S*)-(–)-1-phenylethyl isocyanate

(50 mg, 0.34 mmol) was added. The mixture was allowed to stand for 24 h at room temperature. After evaporation, the resulting crystalline urea adducts were recrystallized from iPr_2O.

Ethyl (1S,2R,3S,4R)-3-[3-(1-(S)-phenylethyl)ureido]bicyclo[2.2.2]oct-5-ene-2-carboxylate (+)-**9**. White crystals (92 mg, 82%), mp 195–200 °C, $[\alpha]_D^{20}$ = +8 (c, 0.3, EtOH). ^{1}H-NMR: δ = 0.99–1.07 (m 1H, H-7) 1.11–1.20 (m, 1H, H-7) 1.16 (t, *J* = 7.2, 3H, CH_3) 1.23 (d, *J* = 7.1 (3H, CH_3) 1.43–1.53 (m, 2H, H-8), 2.44 (m, 1H, H-1) 2.66 (m, 1H, H-4) 2.96 (d, *J* = 9.8, 1H, H-2) 3.90–4.06 (m, 2H, OCH_2) 4.3 (td, *J* = 10.1, *J* = 1.5, 1H, H-3) 4.68 (m, 1H, CH) 5.34 (d, *J* = 10.4 H, NH) 6.12 (t, *J* = 7.2, 1H, H-5, 6.47 (t, *J* = 7.4, 1H, H-6) 6.54 (d, *J* = 8.1 1H, NH) 7.16–7.32 (m, 5H, Ar) ^{13}C-NMR: δ = 14.8, 22.7, 24.4, 25.3, 32.6, 36.9, 49.3, 51.3, 51.4, 60.4, 126.5, 127.2, 129.0, 130.5, 137.1, 146.6, 157.0, 173.0. Anal. Calcd for $C_{20}H_{26}N_2O_3$ (342.43): C 70.15, H 7.65; N 8.18. Found C 70.22, H 7.92, N 8.12.

Ethyl (1R,2R,3R,4S)-3-[3-(1-(S)-phenylethyl)ureido]bicyclo[2.2.2]oct-5-ene-2-carboxylate (–)-**10**. White crystals (108 mg, 96%), a white solid, mp. 130–135 °C, $[\alpha]_D^{20}$ = –101 (c, 0.2, EtOH) ^{1}H-NMR: δ = 0.92–1.06 (m 1H, H-7) 1.19–1.23 (m, 1H, H-7) 1.16 (t, *J*= 7.1, 3H, CH_3) 1.28 (d, *J* = 6.9 (3H, CH_3) 1.36–1.52 (m, 2H, H-8), 1.95 (m, 1H, H-2) 2.58 (m, 1H, H-1) 2.70 (m, 1H, H-4) 4,08–4.23 (m, 3H, OCH_2, H-3) 4.64 (m, 1H, CH) 5.54 (d, *J* = 7.9 H, NH) 6.12–6,21 (m, 2H, H-5, NH), 6.44 (t, *J* = 7.3, 1H, H-6) 7.14–7.35 (m, 5H, Ar) ^{13}C-NMR: δ = 14.9, 20.3, 23.3, 24.3, 33.6, 36.0, 49.3, 51.5, 53.1, 60.8, 126.6, 127.3, 129.1, 132.8, 135.7, 146.5, 157.3, 173.8, Anal. Calcd for $C_{20}H_{26}N_2O_3$ (342.43): C 70.15, H 7.65, N 8.18. Found C 70.31, H 7.79, N 8.27.

3.8. Racemic Compounds

All the reactions were first optimized for the racemic compounds. The ^{1}H- and ^{13}C-NMR spectroscopic and elemental analysis data on the racemic derivatives were in accordance with those for enantiomers.

Data on racemates (±)–**2**-(±)-**8**

Ethyl 3-endo-aminobicyclo[2.2.2]oct-5-ene-2-exo-carboxylate hydrochloride (±)-**2**: White crystals, mp 227–229 °C.

Ethyl trans-3-aminobicyclo[2.2.2]octane-2-carboxylate hydrochloride (±)-**3**: White crystals, mp 130–133 °C.

Ethyl cis-3-aminobicyclo[2.2.2]octane-2-carboxylate hydrochloride (±)-**4**: White crystals, mp 189–191 °C.

3-endo-Aminobicyclo[2.2.2]oct-5-ene-2-exo-carboxylic acid (±)-**5**: White crystals, mp 250–255 °C.

trans-3-Aminobicyclo[2.2.2]octane-2-carboxylic acid (±)-**6**: White crystals, mp 255–260 °C.

2,3-Diendo-3-aminobicyclo[2.2.2]oct-5-ene-2-carboxylic acid (±)-**7**: White crystals, mp 228–231 °C, Lit. mp 204–208 °C [29].

cis-3-Aminobicyclo[2.2.2]octane-2-carboxylic acid (±)-**8**: White crystals, mp 208–210, Lit. mp 232–235 °C [32].

3.9. X-Ray Crystallographic Studies

The crystallographic data on compounds (+)-9 and (–)-10 were collected at 123 K with an Agilent SuperNova dual wavelength diffractometer equipped with an Atlas CCD area detector with the use of Cu-Kα radiation and the CrysAlisPro program package [33]. The empirical absorption correction was performed with the SCALE3 ABSPACK scaling algorithm as implemented in the CrysAlisPro program [33]. The crystal data along with selected refinement details for compounds (+)-**9** and (–)-**10** are presented in Table 2.

The structures were solved by direct methods with the SHELXS-97 [34] program or the SIR-97 [35] program, and the full-matrix least squares refinements on F^2 were performed with the SHELXL-9728 program. Figures were drawn with Diamond 3 [36]. For all compounds, the heavy atoms were refined anisotropically. The CH hydrogen atoms were included at the calculated distances with fixed displacement parameters from their host atoms (1.2 or 1.5 times the host atom). The NH hydrogens were located from the electron density map and refined isotropically. The absolute configurations of the compounds were determined from the Flack parameters.

Detailed crystallographic data for compound (+)-**9** (CCDC 918507) and (–)-**10** (CCDC 918508) is deposited at the Cambridge Crystallographic Data Centre. These data can be obtained free of charge viahttp://www.ccdc.cam.ac.uk/conts/retrieving.html (or from the CCDC, 12 Union Road, Cambridge CB2 1EZ, UK; Fax: +44 1223 336033; E-mail: deposit@ccdc.cam.ac.uk).

Table 2. Crystallographic data for compounds (+)-**9** and (–)-**10**.

Compound	(+)-9	(–)-10
Formula	$C_{20}H_{26}N_2O_3$	$C_{20}H_{26}N_2O_3$
Mr	342.43	342.43
Crystal system	orthorhombic	orthorhombic
Space group (no.)	$P2_12_12_1$(19)	$P2_12_12_1$ (19)
a (Å)	12.0973(2)	8.9562(3)
b (Å)	17.4189(2)	18.4189(6)
c (Å)	17.5471(2)	22.9915(3)
α (°)	90	90
β (°)	90	90
γ (°)	90	90
V (Å)	3697.55(9)	3792.75(18)
Z	8	8
Dc (g cm^{-3})	1.230	1.199
T (K)	123	123
$\mu(CuK_\alpha)$	0.665	0.648
Observed reflections	6269	6726
R_{int}	0.0279	0.0213
Parameters	467	477
Flack's parameter	0.05(17)	0.0(2)
R_1 [a]	0.0406 (0.0386) [b]	0.0521 (0.0480)[b]
wR_2 [c]	0.0991 (0.0969)	0.1266 (0.1230)

[a] $R_1 = \Sigma||Fo| - |Fc||/\Sigma|Fo|$; [b] Values in parentheses for reflections with $I > 2\sigma(I)$; [c] $wR_2 = \{\Sigma[w(F2o - F2c)2]/\Sigma[w(F2o)2]\}^{1/2}$ and $w = 1/[\sigma2(F2o) + (aP)2 + (bP)]$, where $P = (2F2c + F2o)/3$.

4. CONCLUSIONS

In conclusion, we have successfully synthetized all four enantiomers of 2,3-*diendo*-3-aminobicyclo[2.2.2]oct-5-ene-2-carboxylic acid and 3-*endo*-aminobicyclo[2.2.2]oct-5-ene-2-*exo*-carboxylic acid and their saturated analogues in a simple scalable protocol. The prepared compounds are highly likely to be useful and well applicable in synthetic chemistry and drug research, with the creation of diverse libraries of conformationally constrained compounds.

ACKNOWLEDGMENTS

The authors thank István Mándity for his kind assistance in the H-Cube experiments. Their thanks are also due to the Hungarian Research Foundation (OTKA grants TS 04888 and T 034901) and TAMOP-4.2.2.A-II/1/KONV-2012-0035 for financial support.

CONFLICTS OF INTEREST

The authors declare no conflict of interest.

REFERENCES

1. Konishi, M.; Nishio, M.; Saitoh, K.; Miyaki, T.; Oki, T.; Kawaguchi, H. Cispentacin: A new antifungal antibiotic I. Production, isolation, physico-chemical properties and structure. J. Antibiot. 1989, 42, 1749–1755.

2. Oki, T.; Hirano, M.; Tomatsu, K.; Numata, K.; Kamei, H. Cispentacin, a new antifungal antibiotic II. In vitro and in vivo antifungal activities. J. Antibiot. 1989, 42, 1756–1762.

3. Kuhl, A.; Hahn, M.G.; Dumić, M.; Mittendorf, J. Alicyclic β-amino acids in medicinal chemistry. Amino Acids 2005, 29, 89–100.

4. Pou, A.; Moyano, A. Stereoselective organocatalytic approach to α,β-disubstituted β-amino acids: A sort enantioselective synthesis of Cispentacin. Eur. J. Org. Chem. 2013, 3103–3111.

5. Martinek, T.A.; Fülöp, F. Peptidic foldamers: Ramping up diversity. Chem. Soc. Rev. 2012, 41, 687–702.

6. Horne, W.S. Peptide and peptoid foldamers in medicinal chemistry. Expert Opin. Drug Disc. 2011, 6, 1247–1262.

7. Sathe, M.; Thavaselvam, D.; Srivastava, A.K.; Kaushik, M.P. Synthesis and antimalarial evaluation of cyclic β-amino acid-containing dipeptides. Molecules 2008, 13, 432–443.

8. Keresztes, A.; Szücs, M.; Borics, A.; Kövér, K.E.; Forró, E.; Fülöp, F.; Tömböly, C.; Péter, A.; Páhi, A.; Fábián, G.; et al. New endomorphin analogues containing alicyclic β-amino acids: Influence on bioactive conformation and pharmacological profile. J. Med. Chem. 2008, 51, 4270–4279.

9. Horne, W.S.; Gellman, S.H. Foldamers with heterogeneous backbones. Acc. Chem. Res. 2008, 41, 1399–1408.

10. Seebach, D.; Gardiner, J. β-Peptidic peptidomimetics. Acc. Chem. Res. 2008, 41, 1366–1375.

11. Martín-Vilà, M.; Muray, E.; Aguado, G.P.; Alvarez-Larena, A.; Branchadell, V.; Minguillón, C.; Giralt, E.; Ortuño, R.M. Enantioselective synthetic approaches to cyclopropane and cyclobutane β-amino acids: Synthesis and structural study of a conformationally constrained β-dipeptide. Tetrahedron-Asymmetr. 2000, 11, 3569–3584.

12. Gauzy, C.; Pereira, E.; Faure, S.; Aitken, D.J. Synthesis of (+)-(1S,2R) and (–)-(1R,2S)-2-aminocyclobutane-1-carboxylic acids. Tetrahedron Lett. 2004, 45, 7095–7097.

13. Fernandez, C.; Pereira, E.; Faure, S.; Aitken, D.J. Expedient preparation of all isomers of 2-aminocyclobutanecarboxylic acid in enantiomerically pure form. J. Org. Chem. 2009, 74, 3217–3220.

14. Forró, E.; Fülöp, F. The first direct enzymatic hydrolysis of alicyclic β-amino esters: A route to enantiopure cis andtrans β-amino acids. Chem. Eur. J. 2007, 13, 6397–6401.

15. Priego, J.; Flores, P.; Ortiz-Nava, C.; Escalante, J. Synthesis of enantiopure cis- and trans-2-aminocyclohexane-1-carboxylic

acids from octahydroquinazolin-4-ones. Tetrahedron-Asymmetr. 2004, 15, 3545–3549.

16. Forró, E.; Fülöp, F. Vapour-assisted enzymatic hydrolysis of β-lactams in a solvent-free system. Tetrahedron-Asymmetr.2008, 19, 1005–1009.

17. Palkó, M.; Benedek, G.; Forró, E.; Wéber, E.; Hänninen, M.; Sillanpää, R. Synthesis of mono- and dihydroxy-substituted 2-aminocyclooctanecarboxylic acid enantiomers. Tetrahedron-Asymmetr. 2010, 21, 957–961.

18. Bolm, C.; Schiffers, I.; Atodiresei, I.; Hackenberger, P.R. An alkaloid-mediated desymmetrization of meso-anhydrides via a nucleophilic ring opening with benzyl alcohol and its application in the synthesis of highly enantiomerically enriched β-amino acids. Tetrahedron-Asymmetr. 2003, 14, 3455–3467.

19. Forró, E.; Fülöp, F. Synthesis of enantiopure 1,4-ethyl- and 1,4-ethylene-bridged cispentacin by lipase-catalyzed enantioselective ring opening of β-lactams. Tetrahedron-Asymmetr. 2004, 15, 573–575.

20. Todorov, P.T.; Wesselinova, D.W.; Pavlov, N.D.; Martinez J.; Calmes, M.; Naydenova, E.D. Cytotoxic activity of new racemic and optically active N-phosphonoalkyl bicyclic β-amino acids against human malignant cell lines. Amino Acids 2012, 43, 1445–1450.

21. André, C.; Calmes, M.; Escale, F.; Amblard, M.; Martinez, J.; Songis, O. New 1,3-amino alcohols derived from enantiopure bridgehead β-aminobicyclo[2.2.2]oct-5-ene-2-carboxylic acids. Amino Acids 2012, 43, 415–421.

22. Calmes, M.; Escale, F.; Didierjean, C.; Martinez, J. Synthesis of enantiopure trans-N-Boc-3-aminobicyclo[2.2.2]octane-2-carboxylic acids and their bicyclic 1,3-amino alcohol derivatives via the [4+2] cycloaddition of 1,3-cyclohexadiene to a chiral β-nitroacrylate. Chirality 2011, 23, 245–249.

23. Ruebsam, F.; Murphy, D.E.; Tran, C.V.; Li, L.S.; Zhao, J.; Dragovich, P.S.; McGuire, H.M.; Xiang, A.X.; Sun, Z.; Ayida, B.K.; et al. Discovery of tricyclic 5,6-dihydro-1H-pyridin-2-ones as novel, potent, and orally bioavailable inhibitors of HCV NS5B polymerase. Bioorg. Med. Chem. Lett. 2009, 19, 6404–6412.

24. Bunue, E.; Cativiela, C.; Diaz-de-Villages, M.D.; Galvez, J.A. A new conformationally restricted aspartic acid analogue with a bicyclo[2.2.2]octanes skeleton. Acta Cryst. C 1996, 52, 2292–2294.

25. Pope, W.J.; Peachey, S.J. The application of powerful optically active acids to the resolution of externally compensated basic substances. Resolution of tetrahydroquinaldine. J. Chem. Soc. Trans. 1899, 75, 1066–1093.

26. Sakurai, R.; Yuzawa, A.; Sakai, K. Practical resolution of 3-aminopyrrolidine via diastereomeric salt formation with (S)-2-methoxy-2-phenylacetic acid. Tetrahedron-Asymmetr. 2008, 19, 1622–1625.

27. Faigl, F.; Fogassy, E.; Nógrádi, M.; Pálovics, E.; Schindler, J. Strategies in optical resolution: A practical guide.Tetrahedron-Asymmetr. 2008, 19, 519–536.

28. Leeman, M.; Kaptein, B.; Kellogg, R.M. Nucleation inhibition in attrition-enhanced Pope-Peachey type of diastereomeric resolutions. Tetrahedron-Asymmetr. 2009, 20, 1363–1364.

29. Palkó, M.; Sohár, P.; Fülöp, F. Synthesis and transformations of di-endo-3-aminobicyclo-[2.2.2]oct-5-ene-2-carboxylic acid derivatives. Molecules 2011, 16, 7691–7705.

30. Fogassy, E.; Lopata, A.; Faigl, F.; Darvas, F.; Ács, M.; Tőke, L. A quantitative approach to optical resolution.Tetrahedron Lett. 1980, 21, 647–650.

31. Forró, E. New gas chromatographic method for the enantioseparation of β-amino acids by a rapid double derivatization technique. J. Chromatogr. A 2009, 1216, 1025–1029.

32. Moriconi, E.I.; Crawford, W.C. Reaction of chlorosulfonyl isocyanate with bridge bi- and tricyclic olefins. J. Org. Chem. 1968, 33, 370–378.

33. Agilent. CrysAlis PRO, Agilent Technologies UK Ltd. Yarnton, UK, 2011.

34. Sheldrick, G.M. A short history of SHELX. Acta Crystallogr. A 2008, 64, 112–122.

35. Altomare, A.; Burla, M.C.; Camalli, M.; Cascarano, G.L.; Giacovazzo, C.; Guagliardi, A.; Moliterni, A.G.G.; Polidori, G.; Spagna, R. SIR97: A new tool for crystal structure determination and refinement. J. Appl. Cryst. 1999, 32, 115–119.

36. Pennington, W.T. DIAMOND-visual crystal structure information system. J. Appl. Cryst. 1999, 32, 1028–1029.

Chpater 13

VCD Studies on Chiral Characters of Metal Complex Oligomers

Hisako Sato *[,1,†] **and Akihiko Yamagishi** [2,†]

[1]*Department of Chemistry, Graduate School of Science and Engineering, Ehime University, Matsuyama 790-8577, Japan*

[2]*Department of Chemistry, Toho University, Funabashi 274-8510, Japan*

ABSTRACT

The present article reviews the results on the application of vibrational circular dichroism (VCD) spectroscopy to the study of stereochemical properties of chiral metal complexes in solution. The chiral characters reflecting on the vibrational properties of metal complexes are revealed by measurements of a series of β-diketonato complexes with the help of theoretical calculation. Attention is paid to the effects of electronic properties of a central metal ion on vibrational energy levels or low-lying electronic states. The investigation is further extended to the oligomers of β-diketonato complex units. The induction of chiral structures is confirmed by the VCD spectra when chiral inert moieties are connected with labile metal ions. These results have demonstrated how VCD spectroscopy is efficient in revealing the static and dynamic properties of mononuclear and multinuclear chiral metal complexes, which are difficult to clarify by means of other spectroscopes.

Keywords: chiral; multi-nuclear metal complex; vibrational circular dichroism; chiral induction; β-diketonato; tecton; supramolecule; circular dichroism; DFT calculation; catalysis; low-lying electronic states

1. INTRODUCTION

Chiral metal complexes have been attracting continuous interest from the fundamental areas of coordination chemistry [1–13]. They constitute an important element in asymmetric catalyses, non-linear optics, chiral sensing and biological probes. Their functions are even more enhanced by coupling the stereochemical properties with the electronic and magnetic ones. Among a variety of chiral elements employed in these attempts, the ΔΛ isomerism of tris(chelated) octahedral complexes have played a unique role as a chiral source [12]. It is characterized by a rigid helical structure with D_3 symmetry. The helical property is amplified by connecting chiral octahedral motifs to form multinuclear complexes.

In order to investigate the chiral properties of metal complexes, a number of spectroscopic methods are applied, such as X-ray analyses, NMR and electronic circular dichroism (ECD) measurements [3]. These methods help us to obtain the static and dynamic details of chiral metal complexes in solid and solution. As far as our knowledge is concerned, however, relatively little attention has been paid to vibrational circular dichroism spectroscopy as a measure for such purposes.

In recent years, we have been pursuing the possible utility of the vibrational circular dichroism (VCD) spectroscopy to chiral transition metal complexes [14–25]. VCD measures the differential absorption of left *versus* right circularly polarized IR radiation for molecular vibration transitions [26–29]. In comparison to the ECD spectra, the VCD spectra often provide more detailed information as to the stereochemical characters of chiral metal complexes [26–49]. This is because the method possesses the following advantages over other spectroscopes:

1. The VCD spectrum typically contains many well resolved vibrational bands, whereas ECD tends to show fairly broad band contour. This makes VCD assignment considerably more conclusive than ECD.

2. Most of 3N-6 normal vibrations, which are all well resolved as stated above, are obtained from a single measurement and can be utilized to analyze the chiral character in the molecular vibrations of a given molecule.

3. Even a molecule with no electronic absorption in the UV-visible region can be a target. This property is particularly useful for analyzing such a metal complex as having perfluoro groups [16,18,50,51].

4. The DFT modeling of VCD spectra in the ground electronic state is more reliable than for ECD. Moreover the program is commercially available.

The following sections describe how to analyze the chiral structures of metal complexes and their oligomers in solution by making use of the above advantages [14–24].

2. VCD APPLICATION TO CHIRAL MONONUCLEAR METAL COMPLEXES

2.1. Effects of Electronic Properties of Central Metal Ions on Vibrational Energy Levels

The VCD spectroscopy was applied to a series of β-diketonato complexes, [M(III)(acac)$_3$] (acac = acetylacetonato; M(III) = Cr(III), Co(III), Ru(III), Rh(III), Ir(III) and Al(III)) and [M(III)(acac)$_2$(dbm)] (dbm = dibenzoylmethanato; M(III) = Cr(III), Co (III) and Ru(III)) [14,15]. It was first noticed that the β-diketonato complexes gave very large VCD signals in comparison to the bipyridine, diamine or cyclometalated complexes. The properties made us to obtain the accurate results for a wide range of complexes within short time (less than 10,000 scans). The optical antipodes gave the mirror-imaged spectra in the region of

1700–1000 cm^{-1}, confirming the validity and reliability of measurements.

The VCD results showed how the electronic properties of a central metal ion affect the vibrational energy levels and the appearance of low-lying electronic states. The positions of VCD peaks assigned to C–O stretches (1500–1300 cm^{-1}) remarkably depend on a central metal ion for both [M(III)(acac)$_3$] (Chart 1a) and [M(III)(acac)$_2$(dbm)] (Chart 1b). In case of Δ-[M(III)(acac)$_3$], for example, the order of frequency of two C–O stretches (E and A_2 symmetries) is determined as follows: E (negative sign) > A_2 (positive sign) for M(III) = Co, Rh and Ir, while A_2 (positive sign) > E (negative sign) for M(III) = Cr and Ru. In case of Δ-[M(III)(acac)$_2$(dbm)], the order of frequency of three C–O stretches (A, B and B symmetries) is determined as follows: A (negative sign) > B (positive sign) > B (positive sign) for Co(III), B (positive sign) > A (negative sign) > B (negative sign) for Cr(III) and A (negative sign) > B (positive sign) > B (negative sign) for Ru(III). The results imply that the energy levels of C–O stretches are delicately affected by the electronic configuration of a central metal ion. Since no such detailed information is obtained from the IR spectra alone, the VCD spectrum is a unique method to probe the effect of a central metal ion on interligand cooperative vibrational modes.

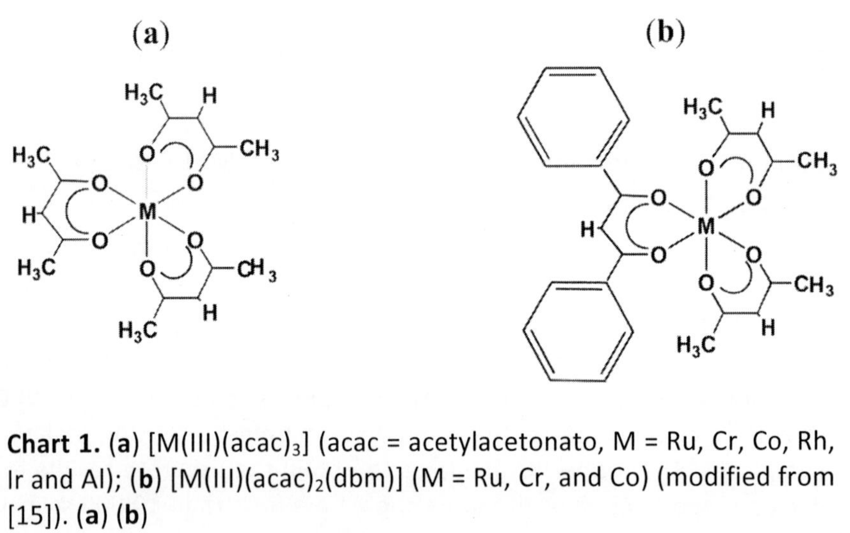

Chart 1. (**a**) [M(III)(acac)$_3$] (acac = acetylacetonato, M = Ru, Cr, Co, Rh, Ir and Al); (**b**) [M(III)(acac)$_2$(dbm)] (M = Ru, Cr, and Co) (modified from [15]). (**a**) (**b**)

It is a general belief that magnetic field perturbation (MFP) theory gives reliable reports on VCD results for the closed-shell systems but not for the open-shell systems. In order to interpret the VCD spectra of paramagnetic metal ions theoretically, the more accurate treatment is required [27,30]. For example, the open-shell density functional theory (DFT) calculations with M06 exchange-correlation functional and all electron Douglas-Kroll second order scalar relativistic correction (DK2) are performed to interpret the vibrational circular dichroism (VCD) spectra of four kinds of tris(acetylacetonato)metal(III), [M(III)(acac)$_3$] (acac = acetylacetonato, M = Ru, Cr, Co and Rh) [20]. It is deduced that the experimental spectra are well reproduced by the calculation with harmonic approximation in case of [Co(III)(acac)$_3$] (d6; S = 0), [Rh(III)(acac)$_3$] (d6; S = 0) and [Ru(III)(acac)$_3$] (d5; S = 1/2). In case of [Cr(III)(acac)$_3$] (d3; S = 3/2), however, anharmonic effects should be taken into account to predict the accurate vibrational frequencies of closely located modes. We found experimentally that the order of closely locating vibrational energy levels is dependent on a metal ion in case of the same type of metal complex (or [M(acac)$_3$]). For example, the relative position of two stretching vibrations of C–O bonds (A_2 and E symmetries) is opposite for Co(III) and Cr(III) complexes. From the theoretical treatment, this was caused by the anharmonic effects.

Time-dependent density functional theory (TDDFT) calculations are performed to estimate the contribution of excited states in the VCD spectra. As a consequence, the presence of the low-lying excited states is predicted for [Ru(III)(acac)$_3$] alone, which agrees with the experimental observation.

These calculations implied that the more accurate treatment is needed in order to take into account the following factors: (i) the anharmonic effects of molecular vibrations, (ii) the contribution of relativistic effects particularly to a complex with a heavy metal ion and (iii) the contribution of low-lying excited states particularly in case of a paramagnetic ion.

2.2. Identification of Geometrical and Diastereomeric Isomers of Octahedral Complexes

The VCD spectroscopy is applied to identify the isomers of mixed-ligand Co(III) complexes. The spectra were measured on the chloroform solutions of a series of Co(III) complexes, $[Co(tfac)_n(acac)_{3-n}]$ (n = 0 ~ 3, tfac = 1,1,1-trifluoro-2,4-pentanedionato; acac = acetylacetonato) [18]. All of seven pairs of optical antipodes gave mirror-imaged spectra over the whole wavenumber range (1000~1800 cm^{-1}), confirming the reliability of measurements. The obtained spectra are compared among the geometrical isomers of bis(tfac) and tris(tfac) complexes. As a result, the difference among the isomers is manifested most remarkably in C–O stretches and C–C–C bending in cooperation with C–CF_3 stretching. Distinct differences are observed in the VCD spectra among the geometrical isomers of the same ligand composition. Such discrimination is hardly possible by their IR spectra alone.

The structural identification of the diamagnetic Co(III) isomers is performed in conjunction with DFT calculations. In the case of bis(tfac) complexes, the theory is successful in predicting the spectral feature of the band in both C–O stretches and C–C–C bending in cooperation with C–CF_3 stretching.

As another attempt, a complete series of mixed ligand Ru(III) complexes, which are expressed by the formula of Δ- or Λ-[Ru((−)- or (+)-tfac)$_n$(acac)$_{3-n}$] (n = 1, 2 and 3, (−)- or (+)-tfac = (−)- or (+)-3-trifluoroacetylcamphorato and acac = acetylacetonato) (Chart 2), were prepared in a pure diastereomeric form [16]. The separation of these diastereomers was accomplished chromatographically by rational use of two antipodal chiral columns. The separated complexes were identified by means of mass spectra, ^{1}H-NMR, electronic circular dichroism and partly X-ray diffraction analyses. When a pair of Δ- and Λ-$[Ru(acac)_3]$ (n = 0) is added to this group, they constitute *the complete series* of mixed ligand complexes including ligand chirality under the condition of no mixing of chiral ligands.

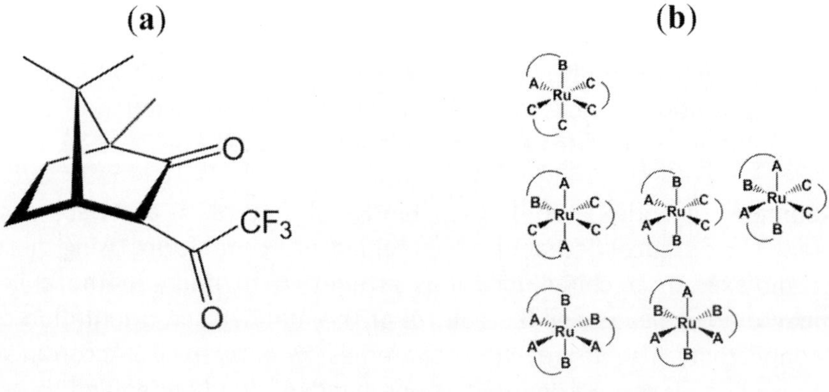

Chart 2. (**a**) (−)-tfac = (−)-3-trifluoroacetylcamphorato); (**b**) Δ- or Λ-[Ru((−)- or (+)-tfac)$_n$(acac)$_{3-n}$] (n = 1, 2 and 3, (−)- or (+)-tfac = (−)- or (+)-3-trifluoroacetylcamphorato and acac = acetylacetonato) (modified from [16]).

The VCD spectra of their $CDCl_3$ solutions were recorded in the wavenumber region of 1000~1800 cm^{-1}. The results provide a benchmark for examining systematically the effects of the stereochemical properties on VCD spectra such as the degree of ligand substitution, ΔΛ configurations, geometrical isomerism and ligand chirality. As a result, the geometrical isomers of trans- or cis-[Ru((−)- or (+)-tfac)$_2$(acac)] and mer- or fac-[Ru((−)- or (+)-tfac)$_3$] are clearly differentiated by their VCD signals, which is hardly possible from their IR spectra alone. Notably the main spectral features are predicted by the VCD theory based on the magnetic field perturbation (MFP). This is surprising since the present theory is shown to be effective to reproduce the vibrational details even for open-shell metal complexes.

3. VCD APPLICATION TO OLIGOMERS OF CHIRAL METAL COMPLEXES IN SOLUTION

3.1. Induction of Chiral Structures in Multinuclear Complexes

The VCD spectroscopy is extended to the study of chiral multinuclear complexes in solutions. Heterometallic oligomers were prepared by connecting bis(β-diketonato)ruthenium(III) moieties to a labile metal ion through bis-β-diketonato bridging ligands [19,21,22,52,53]. The main attention is focused on the possibility of the induction of chiral coordination structures around the labile metal ion.

Complex ligands, [Ru(III)(acac)$_n$(taetH)$_{3-n}$] (acacH = acetylacetone, taetH$_2$ = tetraacetylethane), are obtained as a chiral form. Using these complexes as a chiral unit, it is attempted to build-up the chiral macromolecules under the control of the number and orientation of connectivity. The approach is denoted as *chiral tectonics*. Accordingly these complexes are denoted as one-handed, two-handed and three-handed tectons for 2, 1 and 0 (Chart 3), respectively.

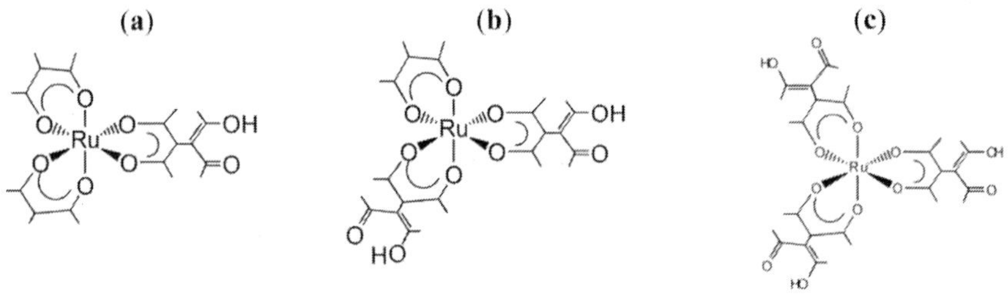

Chart 3. (**a**) one-handed, (**b**) two-handed and (**c**) three-handed tectons (modified from [19,52]).

As the first application of chiral tectons, three units of chiral one-handed tecton, Δ- or Λ- [Ru(acac)$_2$(taetH)], are assembled around an aluminum(III) ion to form a star-shaped tetranuclear complex, [{Ru(acac)$_2$(taet)}$_3$Al(III)] [52]. The remarkable features appear in case of [{Δ-Ru(III)(acac)$_2$(taet)}$_3$Al(III)]. A fresh chloroform solution of a [{Δ-Ru(III)(acac)$_2$(taet)}$_3$Al(III)], gives three single distinct peaks due to CH_3 protons in ^{1}H NMR spectra. As time elapses, each single peak begins to split into two composites in about an hour. In addition, the ECD (electronic circular dichroism) spectrum of a freshly prepared chloroform solution of [{Δ-Ru(III)(acac)$_2$(taet)}$_3$Al(III)] is measured. The spectrum changes in an hour, accompanied by the decrease of the positive peak around 320 nm with the simultaneous increase of the positive peak at 275 nm. The final spectrum is nearly identical to that of Δ-[Ru(III)(acac)$_2$(taetH)]. It is concluded that the central labile core of Al(III) in [{Δ-Ru(III)(acac)$_2$(taet)}$_3$Al(III)] takes initially the coordination structure analogous to Λ-[{Δ-Ru(III)(acac)$_2$(taet)}$_3$Al(III)] and that it epimerizes slowly to a diastereomeric mixture of Λ- and Δ-[{Δ-Ru(III)(acac)$_2$(taet)}$_3$Al(III)]. In other words, the coordination sphere around the central Al(III) is locked as a chiral form antipodal to the peripheral parts in the solid state [52]. This example exhibits that the incorporation of a labile metal ion introduces dynamical aspects through rapid ligand substitution processes. An attempt at obtaining the VCD evidence for chiral locking in a solid state is now under progress.

As another application, heterometallic oligomers are formed by reacting one or two-handed chiral tecton, Δ- or Λ-[Ru(III)(acac)$_n$(taetH)$_{3-n}$] (n = 2 or 1, respectively), with labile Ni(II) ions in a solution [19]. These chiral tectons react with Ni^{2+} ions in the presence of excess *N,N,N′,N′*- tetramethylethylenediamine (tmen) in methanol or methanol/chloroform. In case of one-handed tecton, a trinuclear complex, [{Ru(III)(acac)$_2$(taet)}$_2$Ni(II)(tmen)] (Chart 4a), is formed at the ratio of Ni(II)/Ru(III) = 0.5. No chirality is induced in the coordination spheres of labile Ni(II) connectors.

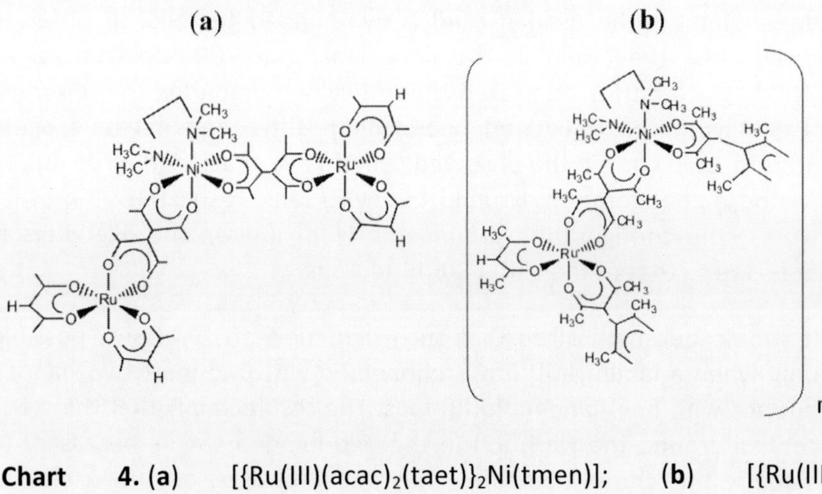

Chart 4. (**a**) [{Ru(III)(acac)$_2$(taet)}$_2$Ni(tmen)]; (**b**) [{Ru(III)(acac)(taet)$_2$Ni(II) (tmen)}*n*{Ni(II)(tmen)}](ClO$_4$)$_2$ (modified from [19]).

In case of two-handed tecton, a soluble oligomer, [{Ru(III)(acac)(taet)$_2$Ni(II)(tmen)}$_n$Ni(II)(tmen)]$^{2+}$ (n~4) (Chart 4b), is produced around Ni(II)/Ru(III) = 1.0. The ECD and VCD spectra are measured in order to examine the possibility of chiral induction in the produced oligomers. When the reaction is monitored by ECD, a new peak appears in the region of 300~400 nm, where the portion of –[(taet)Ni(II)(tmen)(taet)]-in the oligomers has an electronic absorption. The sign of the peak reverses, depending on the ΔΛ configuration of the two-handed tecton. Since the peaks exist in the wavelength region corresponding to the electronic absorption bands due to [Ni(acac)$_2$tmen], it is suggested that the peak is caused by the chiral octahedral coordination around Ni(II) ion. Since no CD spectrum is reported for [Ni(acac)$_2$tmen] because of its labile properties, it is unknown which of the absolute configuration, Δ or Λ, the Ni(II) ions take in the oligomers.

The VCD spectra of a 4:1 (*v*/*v*) CD_3Cl/CD_3OD solution containing chiral [Ru(III)(acac)(taetH)$_2$], Ni(ClO$_4$)$_2$ and tmen at a ratio of 1:1:10 were measured. The spectra correspond to either {Δ-[{Ru(III)(acac)(taet)$_2$Ni(II)(tmen)}*n*{Ni(II)(tmen)}](ClO$_4$)$_2$or {Λ-[{Ru(III)(acac)(taet)$_2$Ni(II) (tmen)}$_n${Ni(II)(tmen)}](ClO$_4$)$_2$. The new VCD signal is observed around 1250 cm^{-1}, where the chiral two-handed tectons show no absorption peak. The sign of the peak inverses, depending on the used Λ- and Δ-two-handed tectons. In order to make clear the origin of the new peak, the VCD spectrum of Λ-[Ni(acac)$_2$(tmen)] is calculated theoretically. Comparing the observed results with the calculated ones, the positive and negative peaks around 1250 cm^{-1} in the observed spectra are concluded to be due to Λ- and Δ-configurations around the Ni(II) ions, respectively. In other words, the configuration around the Ni(II) ions in the oligomers is opposite to that of the chiral Ru(III) tectons.

It should be emphasized that such induction of chirality is possible only when a labile Ni(II) ion is connected with the inert two-handed but not with one-handed Ru(III) ions. The results imply that the steric control around the Ni(II) ion in the two-handed way is necessary to stabilize its chiral structure. The VCD spectroscopy is useful in analyzing these chiral oligomeric species in solution.

3.2. Chiral Structures of Microdomains in Multinuclear Complexes

The VCD spectroscopy enables us to characterize the nature of the microdomains in supramolecules. In order to exemplify such application, a star-burst type tetranuclear complexes, Δ-(or Λ-)[{Δ-(or

Λ-)Ru(III)(acac)$_2$(taet)}$_3$Ru(III)], was synthesized by reacting three-handed tecton (Chart 3c) with bis-chelated Ru(III) units [53]. As a result, three bis(acetylacetonato)Ru(III) moieties are connected with one tris(chelated)Ru(III) core.

The molecule is characterized by the dual structure consisting of the central core ((taet)$_3$Ru(III)) and the peripheral region ({Ru(III)(acac)$_2$}$_3$). The net chirality due to the ΔΛ isomerism of four chiral Ru(III) moieties is manifested in the peak intensity of ECD spectra. It remains to be clarified, however, how to characterize spectroscopically the homo- or hetero-connectivity between the tris(chelated) central core and the bis(chelated) peripheral moieties. VCD spectroscopy is applied to study the stereochemical properties of a star-burst type tetranuclear Ru(III) complex, Δ- (or Λ-)[{Δ- (or Λ-)-Ru(III)(acac)$_2$(taet)}$_3$Ru(III)] (acac = acetylacetonato; taet = tetraacetylethanato) (Chart 5) [22].

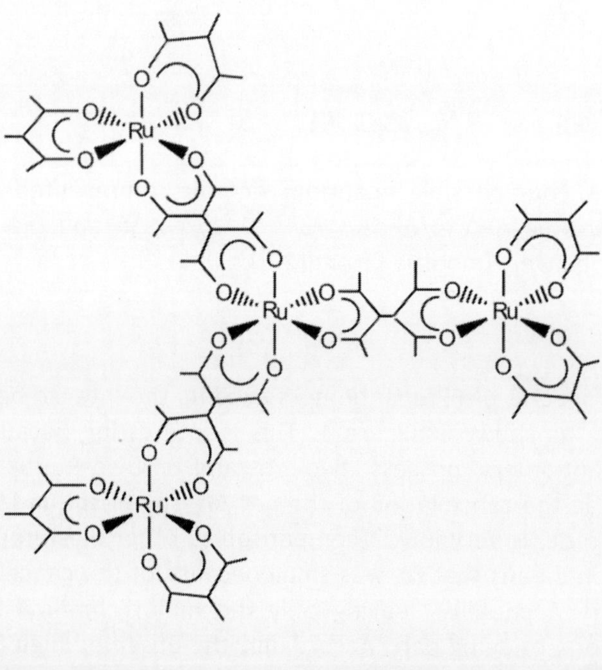

Chart 5. Star-burst type tetranuclear complexes, Δ-(or Λ-)[{Δ-(or Λ-)Ru(III)(acac)$_2$(taet)}$_3$Ru(III)] from three-handed tecton (modified from [22]).

By comparing the VCD spectra of eight diastereomeric enantiomers (Scheme 1), it is shown that the spectra reflect the homo- or hetero-chiral nature of the bridging part connecting the central core and the peripheral region. The sign of the band of 1500~1550 cm^{-1} is positive for P1 and negative for P2 for all diastereomers. In other words, the band has the positive sign for the Λ-rich peripheries, while it has the negative sign for the Δ-rich peripheries. In this sense, the peak around 1340 cm^{-1} reflects the net chiral characters of the three peripheral moieties.

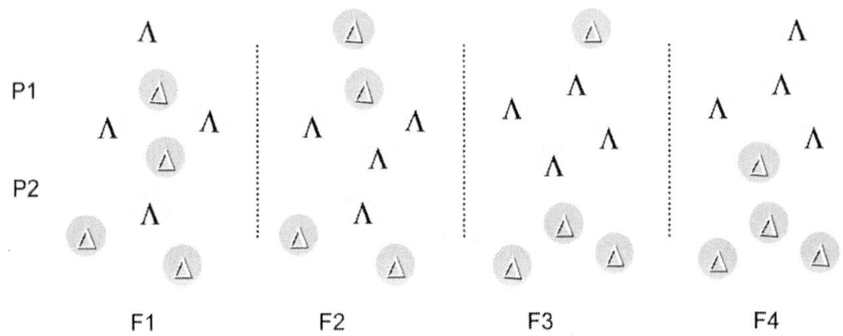

Scheme 1. Four possible enantiomeric pairs represented by (F1) Δ–ΛΛΛ/Λ–ΔΔΔ F2 Δ–ΛΛΔ/Λ–ΔΔΛ F3 Λ–ΛΛΔ/Δ–ΔΔΛ and (F4 Λ–ΛΛΛ/Δ–ΔΔΔ, respectively (modified from [22]).

The VCD spectra of F2 enantiomers exhibits the intense peak around 1340 cm^{-1} as shown in Figure 1. This is interesting because the F2-type enantiomers possess two Λ- and two Δ-Ru(III) elements, resulting in the cancellation of the net ΔΛ isomerism. In fact, its ECD spectrum (Δε) is very low in comparison to other diastereomers. The expression means that Δε was small because of the cancelling out of the main ΔΛ chirality, leaving only the minor chirality due to the chirality of a bridging part. Accordingly the observed high intensity in VCD spectra is suspected to reflect the local chirality in the molecules. The band at 1340 cm^{-1} is assigned to the C–C–C stretches of acetylacetonato groups.

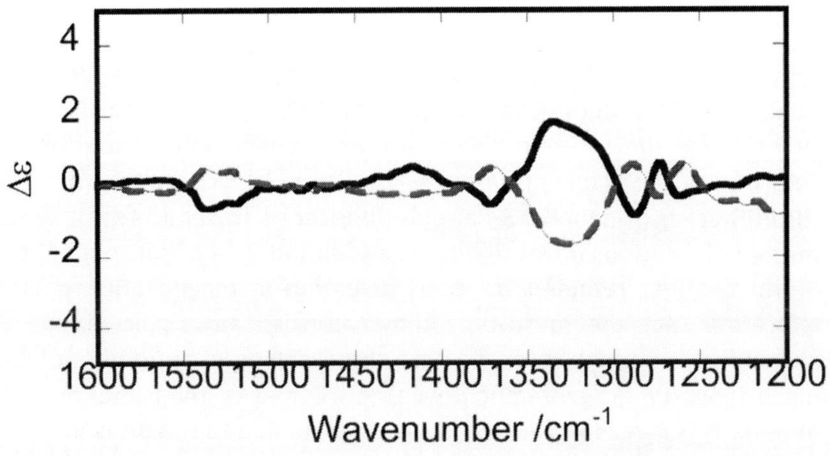

Figure 1. The vibrational circular dichroism spectra of the optically resolved enantiomers of F2 in $CDCl_3$. Solid and dotted lines correspond to P1 and P2 as shown in Scheme 1, respectively, (modified from [22]).

3.3. Axial Chirality in a Dimer Bridged with Non-Symmetric Bis(β-diketonato)

The multi-nuclear complexes appearing in the previous section possess Δ- or Λ-tris-β-diketonato parts as a chiral unit, while the bridging parts are achiral since they are connected by symmetric bis(β-diketonato) ligand with D_{2d} symmetry. In this section, we report the chiral induction of a bridging part by use of an non-symmetrical β-diketonato ligand, in which the twisting of two β-diketonato planes causes C_2 symmetry [21,24].

As the precursor of such a ligand, 1,2-diacetyl-1,2-dibenzoylethane ($dabeH_2$), is used (Chart 6a). The meso-type and racemic diastereomers of dinuclear complex, ΔΛ- and ΔΔ- (or ΛΛ)-[Ru(III)$(acac)_2$(dabe)Ru(III)$(acac)_2$] (Chart 6b), are obtained. From the ^{1}H-NMR spectra of these complexes in $CDCl_3$, the two tris-β-diketonato moieties in the bridging part are unequivalent for the meso-type dimer, while they are equivalent for the racemic dimers as shown in Scheme 2. The results are rationalized by assuming that the bridging part ($dabe^{2-}$) is chiral (denoted as *S*-dabe and *R*-dabe tentatively). Based on this assumption, the meso-type dimer is assigned to ΔΛ-[Ru(III)(acac)$_2$(*S*-dabe or *R*-dabe)Ru(III)(acac)$_2$] (meso-type), while the racemic dimers are assigned to either ΔΔ- (or ΛΛ-)[Ru(III)(acac)$_2$(*S*-dabe or *R*-dabe)Ru(III)(acac)$_2$] or ΔΔ- (or ΛΛ-)[Ru(III)(acac)$_2$(*R*-dabe or *S*-dabe)Ru(III)(acac)$_2$] (racemic type). When methanol solutions of these dimers are eluted on a chiral column, the more and less retained fractions give mirror-imaged ECD spectra, indicating that the meso-type dimer consists of a pair of optical antipodes. It should be noted that the resolved enantiomers of the meso-type dimer give much weaker CD peaks than the racemic dimers. This is reasonable, since the chirality due to the ΔΛ isomerism of two tris-β-diketonato parts are cancelled out, leaving the chirality of the bridging part alone for the meso-type dimer.

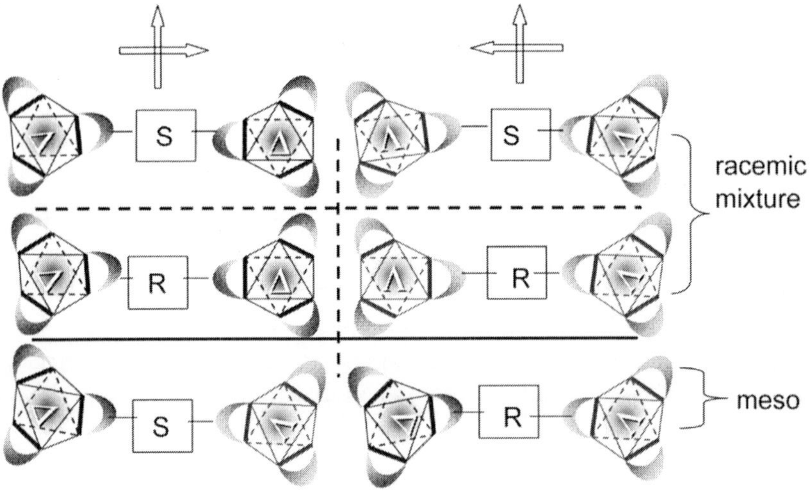

Scheme 2. ΔΔ- (or ΛΛ-)[Ru(III)(acac)$_2$(*S*-dabe or *R*-dabe)Ru(III)(acac)$_2$] or ΔΔ- (or ΛΛ-)[Ru(III)(acac)$_2$(*R*-dabe or *S*-dabe)Ru(III)(acac)$_2$] (racemic type) and ΔΛ-[Ru(III)(acac)$_2$(*S*-dabe or *R*-dabe)Ru(III)(acac)$_2$] (meso-type) with non-symmetrical orthogonal bridging ligands.

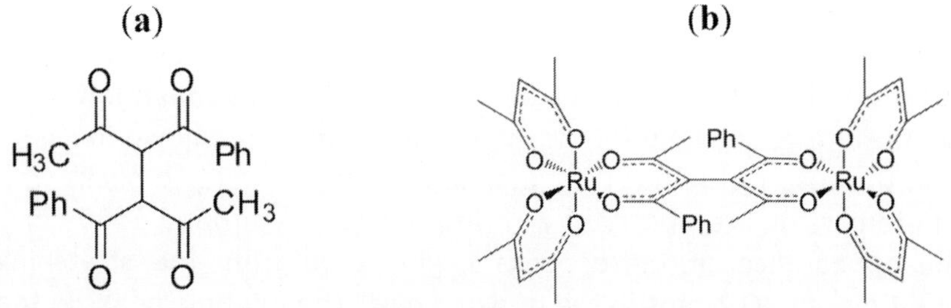

Chart 6. Structures of (**a**) 1,2-diacetyl-1,2-dibenzoylethane (dabeH_2) and (**b**) [Ru(III)$(acac)_2$(dabe)Ru(III)$(acac)_2$] (modified from [21]).

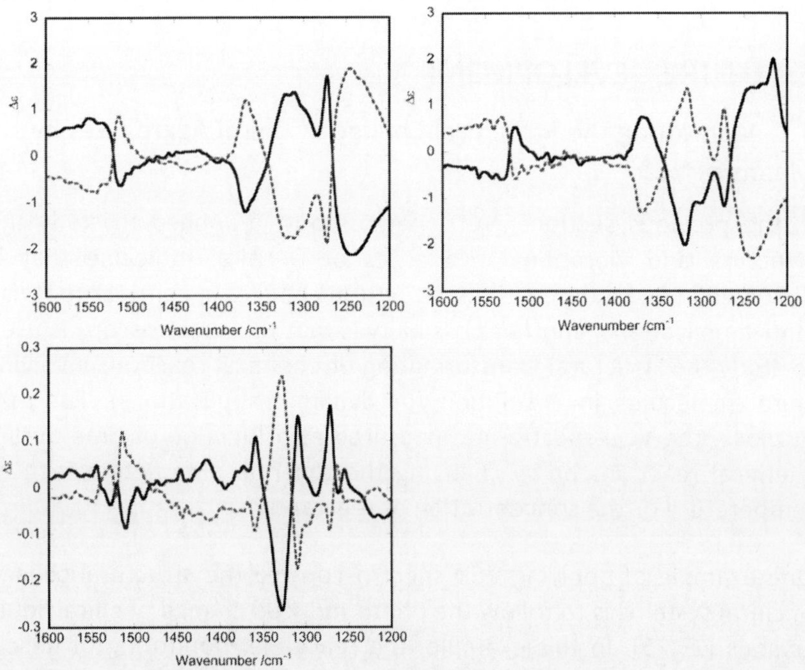

Figure 2. The vibrational circular dichroism spectra of the optically resolved enantiomers of racemic types (upper left and right) and meso-type (under) in $CDCl_3$. Solid and dotted lines correspond to less and more retained enantiomers, respectively. It should be noted that the peak intensity for the meso-type dimers is ten times lower than that for the racemic dimers (modified from [21]).

When the VCD spectra are measured on these dimers as a $CDCl_3$ solution, the intensities of VCD peaks are also much lower for the meso-type dimer than for the racemic dimers as shown in Figure 2. In the case of the meso-type dimer, the triple multiple peaks with different signs are observed with lower intensity around 1550 cm^{-1}. The appearance of these peaks might come from the stretching vibration of C–O bonds in the bridging part. The multiple peaks in the region of 1300–1400 cm^{-1} give a clue to determining the *RS* configuration of the bridging part. More detailed theoretical analyses to determine the absolute configuration from the VCD spectra are now in progress.

4. FUTURE DEVELOPMENT

4.1. Monitoring the Structural Change of Chiral Aggregates by Means of VCD

In the previous sections, VCD spectroscopy is applied to study the structure and vibrational properties of a chiral molecule that is dissolved in a solution with no structural change. In contrast to those static applications, another possibility is that the spectroscopy is used to study the structural transformation or chemical reactions involving chiral molecules in a solution (or dynamic applications). For that purpose, the VCD spectra are measured as a function of time during chemical reactions or by changing the external parameters such as temperature or the concentration of reactants.

One example of applying VCD spectroscopy to the structural change of chiral systems is to follow the photo-induced change of chiral liquid crystals [13,25]. In this example, the real time monitoring of helical rewind process in chiral nematics liquid crystals is performed by use of VCD spectroscopy. As a result, it is revealed that the rewinding of supramolecular helices is monitored *in situ* in a chiral nematic phase under the illumination of UV light (365 nm). Here the change is caused by the photoracemization of a doped chromium(III) complex. It should be noted that the rewinding process of the helix is visualized as the change of the spectral shape at each of the four vibrational peaks. This is the first application of VCD spectroscopy to dynamical systems.

4.2. VCD Application to Asymmetric Reactions in Solutions

As another example of dynamical applications, the VCD spectra were measured as a function of time for the asymmetric reactions involving chiral metal complexes. A nickel(II) complex with (*R*)- or (*S*)-2,2′-bis(salicylideneamino)-1,1′-binaphthyl was synthesized and its crystal structure was determined. In a solid, the nickel complex forms a binuclear species consisting of two Ni(II) ions and homochiral two ligand dianions. Each Ni(II) ion has trans-N_2O_2 square-planar coordination sphere. In a solution, the same complex transforms its coordination structures among square-planar, tetrahedral and octahedral ones, depending on solvent and/or temperature [54]. The complex is possible to catalyze the asymmetric syntheses such as epoxidation [55]. On these systems, it is now attempted to apply the VCD spectroscopy *in situ* to follow each step in achieving the discrimination and generation of chirality.

5. SUMMARY

In the present paper, the results of our recent application of the vibrational circular dichroism (VCD) spectroscopy to investigate the stereochemical properties of chiral metal complexes in a solution. Attention has mainly been paid to the following aspects of mononuclear and multinuclear metal complexes: (1) the effects of electronic configuration of a central metal ion on the vibrational properties, (2) the identification of geometric and diastereomeric isomers of metal complexes, (3) the chiral structures induced on linking homo- or hetero-metallic ions, (4) the chiral characters of micro-domains in multi-nuclear metal complexes and lastly (5) the future development of the VCD method to the dynamical processes involving chiral metal complexes.

REFERENCES

1. Amouri, H.; Gruselle, M. Chirality in Transion Metal Chemsitry; Wiley: West Sussex, UK, 2008; pp. 121–232.

2. Riehl, J.P.; Kaizaki, S. Absolute Chiral Structures of Inorganic Compounds. In Physical Inorganic Chemistry; Bakac, A., Ed.; Wiley: Hoboken, NJ, USA, 2010; pp. 143–197.

3. Kaizaki, S. Applications of Electronic Circular Dichroism to Inorganic Sterochemsitry. In Comprehensive Chiroptical Spectroscopy; Berova, N., Polavarapu, P.L., Nakanishi, K., Woody, R.W., Eds.; Wiley: Hoboken, NJ, USA, 2012; Volume 2, pp. 451–471.

4. Canary, J.W.; Dai, Z. Dynamic Stereochemistry and Chiroptical Spectroscopy of Metallo-Organic Compounds. InComprehensive Chiroptical Spectroscopy; Berova, N., Polavarapu, P.L., Nakanishi, K., Woody, R.W., Eds.; Wiley: Hoboken, NJ, USA, 2012; Volume 2, pp. 251–287.

5. Nafie, L.A. Infrared Vibrational Optical Activity: Measurement and Instrumentation. In Comprehensive Chiroptical Spectroscopy; Berova, N., Polavarapu, P.L., Nakanishi, K., Woody, R.W., Eds.; Wiley: Hoboken, NJ, USA, 2012; Volume 1, pp. 115–146.

6. Knof, U.; von Zelewsky, A. Predetermined Chirality at Metal Centers. Angew. Chem. Int. Ed 1999, 38, 302–322.

7. Swiegers, G.F.; Malefetse, T.J. New Self-Assembled Structural Motifs in Coordination Chemistry. Chem. Rev 2000, 100, 3483–3537.

8. Hembury, G.A.; Borovkov, V.V.; Inoue, Y. Chirality-Sensing Supramolecular Systems. Chem. Rev 2008, 108, 1–69.

9. Gupta, K.C.; Sutar, A.K. Catalytic Activities of Schiff Base Transition Metal Complexes. Coord. Chem. Rev 2008, 252, 1420–1450.

10. Meggers, E. Chiral Auxiliaries as Emerging Tools for the Asymmetric Synthesis of Octahedral Metal Complexes.Chem. Eur. J 2010, 16, 752–758.

11. Cook, T.R.; Zheng, Y.-R.; Stang, P.J. Metal-Organic Frameworks and Self-Assembled Supramolecular Coordination Complexes: Comparing and Contrasting the Design, Synthesis, and Functionality of Metal-Organic Materials. Chem. Rev. 2012.

12. Sato, H.; Yamagishi, A. Application of the Isomerism of Octahedral Metal Complexes as a Chiral Source in Photochemistry. J. Photochem. Photobiol. C: Photochem. Rev 2007, 8, 67–84.

13. Sato, H.; Yamagishi, A. Application of Δ- and Λ-isomerism of Octahedral Metal Complexes for Inducing Chiral Nematic Phases. Int. J. Mol. Sci 2009, 10, 4559–4574.

14. Sato, H.; Taniguchi, T.; Monde, K.; Nishimura, S.-I.; Yamagishi, A. Dramatic Effects of d-Electron Configurations on Vibrational Circular Dichroism Spectra of Tris(acetylacetonato)metal(III). Chem. Lett 2006, 35, 364–365.

15. Sato, H.; Taniguchi, T.; Nakahashi, A.; Monde, K.; Yamagishi, A. Effects of Central Metals Ions on Vibrational Circular Dichroism Spectra of Tris-(β-diketonato)Metal(III) Complexes. Inorg. Chem 2007, 46, 6755–6766.

16. Sato, H.; Mori, Y.; Fukuda, Y.; Yamagishi, A. Syntheses and Vibrational Circular Dichroism Spectra of the Complete Series of [Ru((-)- or (+)-tfac)n(acac)3-n] (n = 0 ~ 3, tfac = 3-trifluoroacetylcamphorato and acac = acetylacetonato).Inorg. Chem 2009, 48, 4354–4361.

17. Sato, H.; Dai Shirotani, D.; Yamanari, K.; Kaizaki, S. Vibrational Circular Dichroism of Δ-SAPR- 8- tetrakis ((+)-heptafluorobutyrylcamphorato) lanthanide(III) Complexes with an Encapsulated Alkali Metal Ion. Inorg. Chem 2010,49, 356–358.

18. Sato, H.; Uno, H.; Nakano, H. Identification of Geometrical Isomers Using Vibrational Circular Dichroism Spectroscopy:

A Series of Mixed-Ligand Complexes of Diamagnetic Co(III) Ions. Dalton Trans 2011, 40, 1332–1337.

19. Sato, H.; Nakao, A.; Yamagishi, A. Formation of Chiral Heterometallic Oligomers by Combination of Inert Ru(III) Tectons and Labile Ni(II) Connectors. New J. Chem 2011, 35, 1823–1828.

20. Mori, H.; Yamagishi, A.; Sato, H. Theoretical Study on Vibrational Circular Dichroism Spectra of Tris(acetylacetonato)metal(III) Complexes: Anharmonic Effects and Low-lying Excited States. J. Chem. Phys 2011, 135, 84506–84512.

21. Sato, H.; Takase, R.; Mori, Y.; Yamagishi, A. Can a meso-type dinuclear complex be chiral?: Dinuclear β-diketonato Ru(III) complexes. Dalton Trans 2012, 41, 747–751.

22. Sato, H.; Sato, F.; Taniguchi, M.; Yamagishi, A. Chirality Effects on Core-periphery Connection in a Star-burst Type Tetranuclear Ru(III) Complex: Application of Vibrational Circular Dichroism Spectroscopy. Dalton Trans 2012, 41, 1709–1712.

23. Shirotani, D.; Sato, H.; Yamanari, K.; Kaizaki, S. Chiroptical Spectra of Tetrakis (+)-3- heptafluorobutylrylcamphorate Ln(III) Complexes with an Encapsulated Alkali Metal Ion: Electronic Circular Dichroism in the 4f-4f Transitions of a Series of the Cs-Ln Complexes. Dalton Trans 2012, 41, 10557–10567.

24. Sato, H.; Mori, Y.; Kitazawa, T.; Yamagishi, A. Inversion of Axial Chirality in Coordinated Bis-β-diketonato Ligands.Dalton Trans 2013, 42, 232–237.

25. Taniguchi, T.; Monde, K.; Nishimura, S.-I.; Yoshida, J.; Sato, H.; Yamagishi, A. Rewinding of Helical Systems by Use of Cr(III) Complex as a Photoresponsive Chiral Dopant. Mol. Cryst. Liq. Cryst 2006, 460, 107–116.

26. Stephen, P.J.; Lowe, M.A. Vibrational Circular Dichroism. Ann. Rev. Phys. Chem 1985, 36, 213–241.

27. He, Y.; Cao, X.; Nafie, L.A.; Freedman, T.B. Ab Initio VCD Calculation of a Transition-Metal Containing Molecule and a New Intensity Enhancement Mechanism for VCD. J. Am. Chem. Soc 2001, 123, 11320–11321.

28. Freedman, T.B.; Cao, X.; Dukor, R.K.; Nafie, L.A. Absolute Configuration Determination of Chiral Molecules in the Solution State using Vibrational Circular Dichroism. Chirality 2003, 15, 743–758.

29. Bieri, M.; Gautier, C.; Bürgi, T. Probing Chiral Interfaces by Infrared Spectroscopic Methods. Phys. Chem. Chem. Phys2007, 9, 671–685.

30. Johannessen, C.; Thulstrup, P.W. Vibrational Circular Dichroism Spectroscopy of a Spin-Triplet Bis-(biuretato) Cobaltate(III) Coordination Compound with Low-Lying Electronic Transitions. Dalton Trans 2007, 36, 1028–1033.

31. Amstrong, W.; Cotton, F.A.; Petrovic, A.G.; Polavarapu, P.L.; Warnke, M.M. Resolution of Enantiomers in Solution and Determination of the Chirality of Extended Metal Atom Chains. Inorg. Chem 2007, 46, 1535–1537.

32. Stephens, P.J.; Devlin, F.J.; Pan, J.-J. The Determination of the Absolute Configurations of Chiral Molecules using Vibrational Circular Dichroism (VCD) Spectroscopy. Chirality 2008, 20, 643–663.

33. Polavarapu, P.L. Why is It Important to Simultaneously Use More Than One Chiroptical Spectroscopic Method for Determining the Structures of Chiral Molecules? Chirality 2008, 20, 664–672.

34. Mukhopadhyay, P.; Wipf, P.; Beratan, D.N. Optical Signatures of Molecular Dissymmetry: Combining Theory with Experiments To Address Stereochemical Puzzles. Acc. Chem. Res 2009, 42, 809–819.

35. Nicu, V.P.; Austschbach, J.; Baereends, E.J. Enhancement of IR and VCD Intensities due to Charge Transfer. Phys. Chem. Chem. Phys 2009, 11, 1526–1538.

36. Nic, V.P.; Baerends, E.J. Robust Normal Modes in Vibrational Circular Dichroism Spectra. Phys. Chem. Chem. Phys2009, 11, 6107–6118.

37. Han, Z.-B.; Ji, J.-W.; An, H.-Y.; Zhang, W.; Zhang, G.-X.; Yang, L.-G. Two 3D Chiral Coordination Polymers with 4-connected 66 Topological Net: Synthesis, Structure and Magnetic Properties. Dalton Trans 2009, 38, 9807–9811.

38. Merten, C.; Amkreutz, M.; Hartwig, A. Determining the Structure of α-phenylethyl Isocyanide in Chloroform by VCD Spectroscopy and DFT Calculations—Simple Case or Challenge? Phys. Chem. Chem. Phys 2010, 12, 11635–11641.

39. Wu, T.; Li, C.-H.; Li, Y.-Z.; Zhang, Z.-G.; You, Z.-Z. Synthesis, Structure and Chiroptical Study of Chiral Macrocyclic Imine nickel(II) Coordination Compounds Derived from Camphor. Dalton Trans 2010, 39, 3227–3232.

40. Soioshonok, V.A.; Ono, T.; Ueki, H.; Vanthuyne, N.; Balaban, T.S.; Bürch, J.; Fliegi, H.; Klopper, W.; Naubron, J.-V.; Bui, T.T.T.; et al. Ridge-Tile-like Chiral Topology: Synthesis, Resolution, and Complete Chiroptical Characterization of Enantiomers of Edge-Sharing Binuclear Square Planar Complexes of Ni(II) Bearing Achiral Ligands. J. Am. Chem. Soc 2010, 132, 10477–10483.

41. Sadlej, J.; Dobrowolski, J.C.; Joanna, E.; Rode, J.E. VCD Spectroscopy as a Novel Probe for Chirality Transfer in Molecular. Chem. Soc. Rev 2010, 39, 1478–1488.

42. Szilvágyi, G.; Majer, Z.; Vass, E.; Hollósi, M. Conformational Studies on Chiral Rhodium complexes by ECD and VCD spectroscopy. Chirality 2011, 23, 294–299.

43. Chamayou, A.-C.; Lüdeke, S.; Brecht, V.; Freedman, T.B.; Nafie, L.A.; Janiak, C. Chirality and Diastereoselection of Δ/Λ-configured Tetrahedral Zinc Complexes through Enantiopure Schiff Base Complexes: Combined Vibrational Circular Dichroism, Density Functional Theory, 1H NMR, and X-ray Structural Studies. Inorg. Chem 2011, 50, 11363–11374.

44. Zhang, K.; Cao, K.-S.; Wang, G.; Peng, Y.-X.; Chu, Z.-L.; Huang, W. Reversible Color Changes of Chiral Double Salts of d-(+)-camphoric Diammonium and Transition-Metal Sulfates via Gain and Loss of Crystalline and Coordination Water Molecules. Inorg. Chim. Acta 2011, 378, 224–230.

45. Yang, G.; Xu, Y. Vibrational Circular Dichroism Spectroscopy of Chiral Molecules. Top. Curr. Chem 2011, 298, 189–236.

46. Merten, C.; Hiller, K.; Xu, Y. Effects of Electron Configuration and Coordination Number on the Vibrational Circular Dichroism Spectra of Metal Complexes of Trans-1,2-diaminocyclohexane. Phys. Chem. Chem. Phys 2012, 14, 12884–12891.

47. Dezhahang, Z.; Merten, C.; Poopari, M.R.; Xu, Y. Vibrational Circular Dichroism Spectroscopy of Two Chiral Binaphthyl Diphosphine Ligands and their Palladium Complexes in Solution. Dalton Trans 2012, 41, 10817–10824.

48. Wu, T.; Zhang, X.-P.; Li, C.-H.; Bouř, P.; Li, Y.-Z.; You, X.-Z. Vibrational and Electronic Circular Dichroism Monitoring of Copper(II) Coordination with a Chiral Ligand. Chirality 2012, 24, 451–458.

49. Luber, S.; Reiher, M. Prediction of Raman Optical Activity Spectra of Chiral 3-Acetylcamphorato-Cobalt Complexes.Chem. Phys. Chem 2010, 11, 1876–1887.

50. Monde, K.; Miura, N.; Hashimoto, M.; Taniguchi, T.; Inabe, T. Conformational Analysis of Chiral Helical Perfluoroalkyl Chains by VCD. J. Am. Chem. Soc 2006, 128, 6000–6001.

51. Sato, H.; Yajima, T.; Yamagishi, A. Molecular Origin for Helical Winding of Fibrils Formed by Perfluorinated Gelators.Chem. Commun 2011, 47, 3736–3738.

52. Sato, H.; Furuno, Y.; Fukuda, Y.; Okamoto, K.; Yamagishi, A. Crystallization Induced Chiral Locking of a Central Labile Core in a Star-shaped Tetra-nuclear Complex. Dalton Trans 2008, 37, 1283–1285.

53. Fujimoto, N.; Mori, Y.; Yamagishi, A.; Sato, H. Molecular Recognition of Star-burst Tetranuclear Ru(III) Complexes on a Chirally Modified Clay Surface. Chem. Commun 2010, 46, 5473–5475.

54. Saito, M.; Sato, H.; Mori, Y.; Fukuda, Y. Structure and Enantio-Differentiating Behaviors of Nickel(II) Complexes with Chiral Schiff Base Ligands Derived from 1,1′-Binaphthyl-2,2′-diamine. Bull. Chem. Soc. Jpn 2009, 82, 1266–1273.

55. Che, C.-M.; Huang, J.-S. Metal Complexes of Chiral Binaphthyl Schiff-base Ligands and their Application in Stereoselective Organic Transformations. Coord. Chem. Rev 2003, 242, 97–113.

Chapter 14

Aplisulfamines, New Sulfoxide-Containing Metabolites from an *Aplidium*Tunicate: Absolute Stereochemistry at Chiral Sulfur and Carbon Atoms Assigned Through an Original Combination of Spectroscopic and Computational Methods

Anna Aiello [1], Ernesto Fattorusso [1], Concetta Imperatore [1], Paolo Luciano [2], Marialuisa Menna [1,*] and Rocco Vitalone [1]

[1]*The NeaNat Group, Dipartimento di Chimica delle Sostanze Naturali, Università degli Studi di Napoli "Federico II", Via D. Montesano 49, 80131 Napoli, Italy*

[2]*C.S.I.A.S. (Centro Servizi Interuniversitario di Analisi Strumentale), Università degli Studi di Napoli "Federico II", Via D. Montesano 49, 80131 Napoli, Italy*

ABSTRACT

Two new sulfoxide-containing metabolites, aplisulfamines A (**1**) and B (**2**), have been isolated from an*Aplidium* sp. collected in the Bay of Naples. Their planar structure and geometry of a double bond were readily determined by using standard methods, mainly NMR spectroscopy. An original approach was used to assign the absolute configuration at the three contiguous chiral centers present in the structures of both aplisulfamines, two at carbon and one at sulfur. This involved Electronic Circular Dichroism (ECD) studies, *J*-based configuration analysis and Density Functional Theory (DFT) calculations and represents an interesting integration of modern techniques in stereoanalysis, which could contribute to the enhancement of theoretical protocols recently applied to solve stereochemical aspects in structure elucidation.

Keywords: ascidian; sulfoxide; stereochemical analysis; computational methods; ECD

1. INTRODUCTION

The occurrence of sulfoxides in nature is limited, being confined mostly to peptide derivatives containing methionine- or β,β-dimethylmethionine S-oxides [1,2], podolactones [3], compounds from onions and other *Allium* species [4], as well as few marine secondary metabolites [5,6,7,8]. As a part of our ongoing search for new and/or bioactive metabolites from Mediterranean ascidians, two novel natural sulfoxides, aplisulfamines A (**1**) and B (**2**), have been isolated from the tunicate*Aplidium* sp. collected in the Bay of Naples. We here report the isolation and structure determination of these two unique compounds (Figure 1). Particularly, an original approach was used to solve the absolute configuration at the three contiguous chiral centers of the molecules, two at carbon and one at sulfur. This represented an interesting integration of modern techniques in stereoanalysis and involved ECD studies, J-based configuration analysis and Density Functional Theory (DFT) calculations. Aplisulfamines A and B were tested for their cytotoxic and/or antiproliferative effects on cancer cells as well as for their antimicrobic properties; in both cases, the new metabolites did not show significant activity.

2. RESULTS AND DISCUSSION

Specimens of *Aplidium* sp. (150 g dry wt.) collected at Pozzuoli (Naples, Italy) were homogenized and extracted with MeOH. The concentrated extract was partitioned between H_2O and EtOAc and the organic layer was dried and then subjected to silica gel MPLC (hexane→EtOAc→MeOH). Fractions eluted with EtOAc/MeOH 9:1 were separated and purified by repeated RP-HPLC's to give **1** (9.0 mg) (t_R = 11.7 min) and **2** (3.0 mg) (t_R = 13.9 min).

HRESI mass spectrum (positive ions) of **1** revealed two pseudomolecular ion peaks at *m/z* 300.2351 and 322.2171 corresponding to $[M + H]^+$ (calculated value: 300.2356) and $[M + Na]^+$ (calculated value: 322.2175), respectively. The molecular formula $C_{17}H_{33}NOS$ was thus established for **1** which corresponded to two unsaturation degrees. The ^{13}C NMR spectrum (CD_3OD) evidenced the presence of 4 olefin carbons (3 methines and 1 methylene), which accounted for the two unsaturation degrees implied by the molecular formula. Therefore, **1** must be acyclic.

^1H-NMR spectrum exhibited a number of well resolved signals, which were associated to the bonding carbons by analysis of HSQC spectrum (Table 1).

Inspection of COSY and TOCSY spectra revealed that most of the proton signals belong to a single spin system, corresponding to the whole linear tetradeca-6,13-diene skeleton of **1**. The *trans* geometry of C6 double bond was indicated by the large coupling constant between H6 and H7 as well as by the ^{13}C chemical shift of C5 and C8 allylic carbons (Table 1) [9,10,11]. In addition to signals of the above spin system, NMR spectra showed signals indicative of the presence of three methyl groups. Chemical shift values (δ_H 2.43; δ_C 30.4) of one of them were consistent with those of a methyl sulfoxide group; this agreed with a facile loss of 64 amu observed in the ESI MS/MS spectrum of **1**, attributable to expulsion of CH_3SOH from the pseudomolecular ion at *m/z* 300.12. HMBC correlations were observed between the protons of this methyl group (Me-15) and C2 (δ 58.2), as well as between the methine proton signal at δ 3.31(H2) and C15; this allowed to locate the methyl sulfoxide functionality at C2. The remaining two methyls were assigned to those of an *N,N*-dimethylamino group (δ_H 2.29, 6H, s; δ_C 41.0) linked at C3; this was consistent with the long-range coupling observed between the N-flanking methyl protons and C3.

The most challenging task in the structure elucidation of aplisulfamine A (**1**) was the assignment of its configurational pattern, since **1** contains three adjacent stereocenters in a conformationally flexible system. This sterochemical problem was solved by combination of NMR and ECD experiments assisted by computational studies through a three stage-approach involving the sequential assignment of: (i) sulfur absolute configuration; (ii) relative configuration of the C2-C3 segment; (iii) relative configuration of the S-C2 segment.

The assignment of the absolute configuration at sulfur was achieved by ECD studies. Mislow *et al.* have shown that a correlation exists between the absolute configuration of methyl alkyl sulfoxides and their optical activity in terms of the signs and rotational strengths of appropriate Cotton effects [12]. In the absence of strongly perturbing groups, as in the case of alkyl allyl or diallyl sulfoxides [13], a negative Cotton effect, centered at the absorption band near in the region 220–230 nm in acetonitrile, correlates with the ***R*** configuration. This rule was found to still be applicable when the alkyl group itself is also chiral [14] as in the case of aplisulfamine A (**1**).

Therefore, by application of Mislow's rule [12], the *R* configuration could be assigned to the sulfur atom in **1** because of the negative sign of the Cotton effect observed in its ECD spectrum (Figure 2).

The relative configuration of C2-C3-segment of **1** was then assigned through a *J*-based NMR configurational analysis according to the method proposed by Murata and coworkers [15]. This method has proved particularly useful for the stereochemical analysis of acyclic structures with adjacent stereogenic carbons bearing hydroxy, alkoxy or ethyl substituents and, successively, it has been extended to chlorine- and nitrogen-containing systems [16,17,18].

We could now extend its application to a sulfoxide-substituted chain, due to the existence of a staggered dominant conformation in C2-C3 segments as evidenced by the large $^{3}J_{H2\text{-}H3}$ value (9.2 Hz). Evaluation of the complete set of homo- and hetero-nuclear *J* values pointed to the two rotamers with an H/H anti orientation among the six staggered rotamers of the two possible relative configurations (threo and erythro) of the stereopair (Figure 3).

In this case the unassisted knowledge of coupling constants does not allow discrimination between the two conformers with opposite relative configuration and additional spatial information, typically dipolar effects, is required [15]. A strong correlation between protons on C1 and C4 was observed in the ROESY spectrum of **1**, indicative of a gauche orientation for Me-1 and CH_2-4 (Figure 3). This dipolar coupling allowed the threo stereochemical relationship (2*S*, 3*S* or 2*R*, 3*R*) for the pair of vicinal asymmetric carbons C2 and C3 to be assigned. Two stereoisomers of **1** met with the whole results so far reported, (2*S*,3*S*,*E*)- and (2*R*,3*R*,*E*)-*N*,*N*-dimethyl-2-[(*R*)-methylsulfinyl]tetradeca-6,13-dien-3-amine.

The assignment of the relative configuration of S-C2 segment allowed the right selection between the two alternatives. For this task we started from the analysis of ROESY spectra; strong dipolar couplings of Me-15 with Me-1 and H3 were observed in **1**, while no ROE correlation was present with H2. This suggested the presence, around the S-C2 bond, of a preferential rotamer in which Me-15 is gauche to Me-1 and H3, and anti to H2. This information turned out a key datum in the light of the results of a conformational analysis carried out on models A and B (Figure 4), which paralleled the functionalized part of the two alternative stereoisomers of **1**.

Through a DFT (Density Functional Theory) approach we have identified a series of conformers resulting from rotation around the S(O)-C2 bond in models A and B.

In order to generate a rational number of conformations for this highly flexible substance, the torsion angles C2-C3 have been fixed on the basis of the size of $^3J_{H2\text{-}H3}$ coupling constant and the conformational explorations for the O-S-C2-C1 dihedral angles were achieved within a dihedral angle range from +48° to −48°. This systematic search afforded 12 rotamers around S-C2 bond for each stereoisomeric structures A and B; they were geometrically optimized at DFT level using a B3LYP functional and 6-31G(d) basis set. Then, the relative energies of all conformations were calculated with respect to the dihedral angle O-S-C2-C1 and equilibrium room-temperature Boltzmann populations obtained thence. All DFT calculations were carried out using the GAUSSIAN 03 program.

As shown in Figure 5, structure A is characterized by a sole dominant rotamer (96.6% of total population) while, for structure B, five of the 12 rotamers have energies within 3 kcal/mol of the lowest energy conformation and are significantly populated (39.4%, 34.4%, 17.2%, 6.2%, and 2.4%). However, only the lowest energy conformer of model A meets with ROESY spatial information obtained for **1.** In this structure, Me-15 is gauche to both Me-1 and H3 while it is anti to H2 (Figure 6). Notwithstanding the appearance of the Newman model of rotamer A1, actually in this conformation the steric interactions between C15, C3, and C1 are probably reduced due to the features of the S-C bonds (C15-S and C2-S). They are indeed longer (≈1.8 Å) when compared to C-C bonds (≈1.5 Å), lowing the torsional barrier that would normally be expected. So, relative configuration of S-C2 segment in **1** was believed to be the same as model A, suggesting the conclusive stereostructure of aplisulfamine A to be (2*S*,3*S*,*E*)-*N*,*N*-dimethyl-2-[(*R*)-methylsulfinyl]tetradeca-6,13-dien-3-amine.

Quantum-mechanical prediction of both ^{13}C NMR chemical shifts and ECD spectra of models A and B strongly corroborated the proposed stereochemistry. Briefly (more details are reported in Supporting Information), ^{13}C NMR chemical shifts of the lowest energies conformers of the models A and B were calculated, using the MPW1PW91 functional and the 6-31G(d, p) basis set.

Chemical shift values for structure B were obtained considering the Boltzmann weighted GIAO (Gauge Including Atomic Orbitals) average derived from the energies of single conformers. The calculated values were compared to the experimental ones relevant to the C1/C5 segment of 1. Mean absolute error (MAE) values obtained for each stereoisomer indicated the best fit with the experimental data relevant to the C1/C5 segment of 1 for model A (1.40 *versus* 3.43 of model B) [19].

The ECD spectra of model A and model B were also simulated. The excitation energies as well as the oscillator and rotatory strengths of the electronic excitation were calculated for the lowest energies conformational families of each structure using the TDDFT methodology [20]. The theoretical curves of models A and B *versus* the experimental one of aplisulfamine A are reported in Figure 7; their courses, all with a negative sign, strongly supported the stereochemistry assignment at sulfur in **1**.

Spectral data obtained for compound **2** were nearly identical to those of **1**; the ESI mass spectrum (positive ion mode) of aplisulfamine B (**2**) exhibited the same pseudomolecular and fragment ions present in the spectrum of **1**, thus indicating that the two compounds were isomers with the molecular formula of $C_{17}H_{33}NOS$. Comparison of their ^{13}C and ^{1}H NMR spectra showed few differences, the only major being associated with the resonances relevant to the most functionalized part of the molecules (see Table 1).

Analysis of 2D NMR data of **2** revealed it possessed the same *N*,*N*-dimethyl-2-[methylsulfinyl]tetradeca-6,13-dien-3-amine planar structure of **1**; the *trans* geometry was also assigned to C6 double bond on the basis of $J_{H6\text{-}H7}$ value (15.1 Hz) and the chemical shifts of C5 and C8 allylic carbons. This information led to the conclusion that **1** and **2** were diastereoisomers differing in the absolute configuration of one or two of the chiral atoms.

The assignment of absolute stereochemistry of **2** was achieved following the same procedure as described for **1**. On the basis of the positive sign of the Cotton effect in the ECD curve (Figure 2), the *S* absolute configuration was assigned to the sulfur atom in **2**, opposite to that in **1**. Furthermore, the *threo* relative stereochemistry was assigned to C2-C3 segment through evaluation of the homo- and hetero-nuclear *J* values and ROESY data of **2** (see Supporting Information).

The results obtained from these first two stages of the configurational analysis of **2** already led to establish its absolute stereochemistry to be (2*S*, 3*S*, S*S*), discarding the alternative (2*R*, 3*R*, S*S*) configuration since it was enantiomeric to that of**1**. Moreover, conformational analysis performed on models A and B (Figure 5) as well as DFT calculations of their ^{13}C NMR chemical shifts strongly supported the proposed stereochemistry. Indeed, the finding of **2** constituted good evidence that arguments on which we have based the relative configuration of S-C2 segment assignment in **1** were sound. In fact, as expected, the ROESY spectrum of **2** showed correlations between Me-15 (δ 2.20)and Me-1, H2 and H3 (Figure 8), according with the structure of the lowest energy rotamers of model B (Figure 4) which is enantiomeric to the configuration proposed for **2**. Furthermore, comparison of theoretical ^{13}C NMR chemical shifts of models A and B with the experimental ones of the C1/C5 fragment of **2** gave a MAE value of 2.72 for model B *versus* 3.91 for model A.

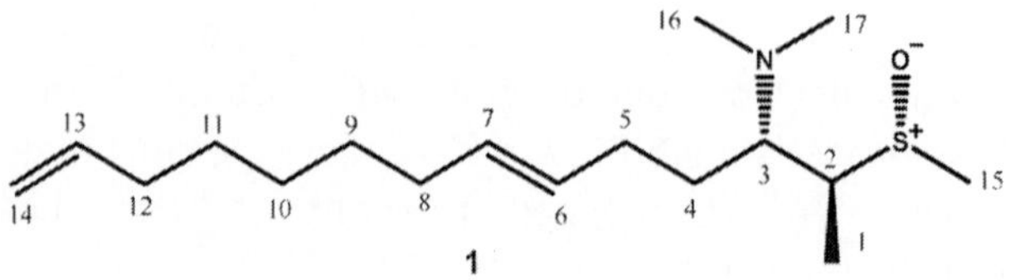

1

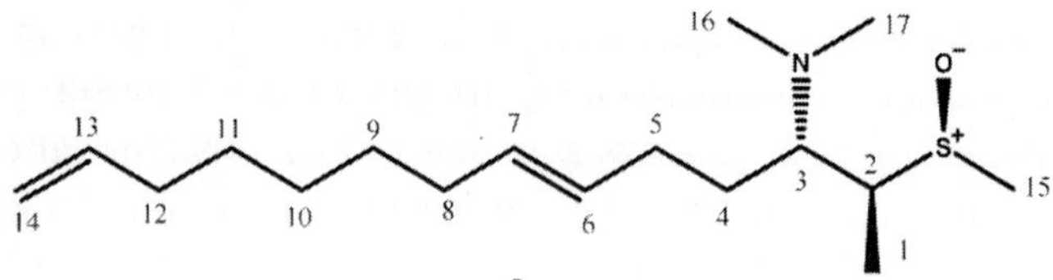

2

Figure 1. Structures of compounds **1** and **2**.

Table 1. ^{1}H and ^{13}C NMR (CD_3OD) of **1** and **2**.

POS	1		2	
	δ_C[a]	δ_H (mult, *J* in Hz)[b]	δ_C[a]	δ_H (mult, *J* in Hz)[b]
1	7.8	1.25 (d, 6.8)	9.4	1.06 (d, 6.6)
2	58.2	3.31(dq, 9.2,6.8)	60.0	2.91(dq, 10.6,6.6)
3	65.2	2.64(m)	65.2	2.81 (dt, 10.6,4.4)
4a	28.8	1.43[c]	25.2	1.70 [c]
4b		1.78 (m)		1.90 (m)
5	32.5	2.12(m)	31.2	2.17 (m)
6	130.6	5.42(bdt 15.2, 6.2)	132.7	5.41(bdt 15.1, 6.5)
7	132.4	5.47(bdt 15.1, 6.2)	132.7	5.47(bdt 15.1, 6.5)
8	33.5	2.00(m)	34.6	2.02 (m)
9	30.5	1.38 [c]	30.0	1.40 [c]
10	29.7	1.33 [c]	30.0	1.40 [c]
11	30.0	1.39 [c]	30.0	1.40 [c]
12	34.9	2.05(q 6.7)	31.1	2.04 (m)
13	140.0	5.80(ddt, 17.1, 10.2, 6.7)	138.8	5.80(ddt, 17.1, 10.2, 6.7)
14a	114.7	4.92 (bdd, 10.2, 2.0)	114.7	4.92 [c]
14b		4.98 (bdd, 17.1, 2.0)		4.98(bdd, 17.1, 2.0)
15	30.4	2.43 (s)	40.0	2.20 (s)
16/17	41.0	2.29 (s)	38.0	2.63 (s)

[a] Spectrum recorded in CD_3OD at 125 MHz. [b] Spectrum recorded in CD_3OD at 500 MHz. [c] Partially overlapped by other signals.

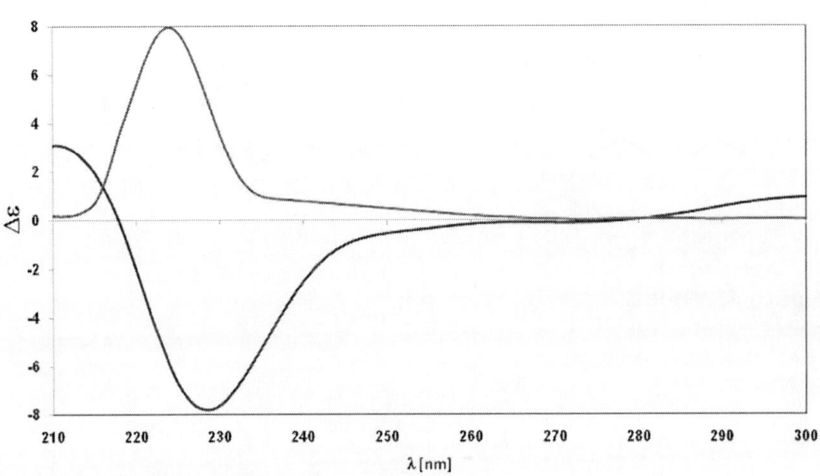

Figure 2. ECD curves of compounds **1** (blue) and **2** (green).

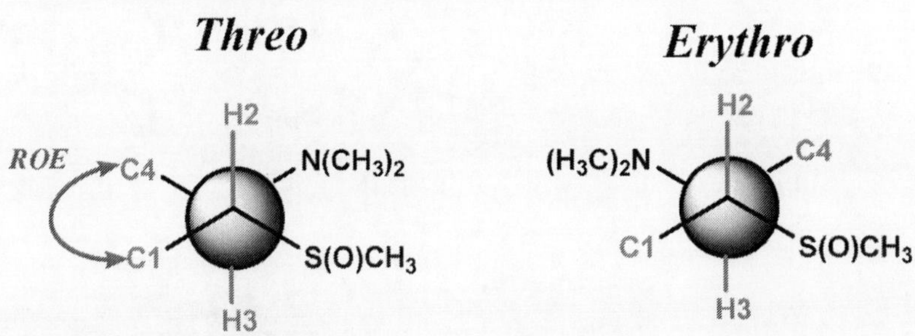

	anti	**1**	*anti*
$^{3}J_{H2\text{-}H3}$	large	9.2	large
$^{3}J_{H2\text{-}C4}$	small	1.9	small
$^{3}J_{C1\text{-}H3}$	small	2.0	small
$^{2}J_{C3\text{-}H2}$	large	-3.9	large

Figure 3. $^{3}J_{H\text{-}H}$ and $^{2,3}J_{C\text{-}H}$ (Hz) values of C2-C3 segment of **1**.

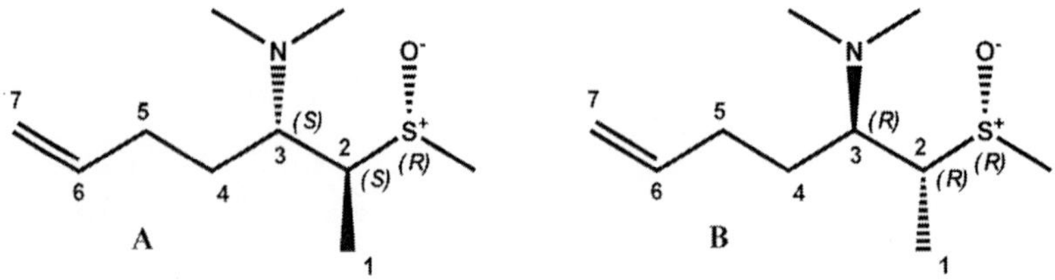

Figure 4. Models A and B.

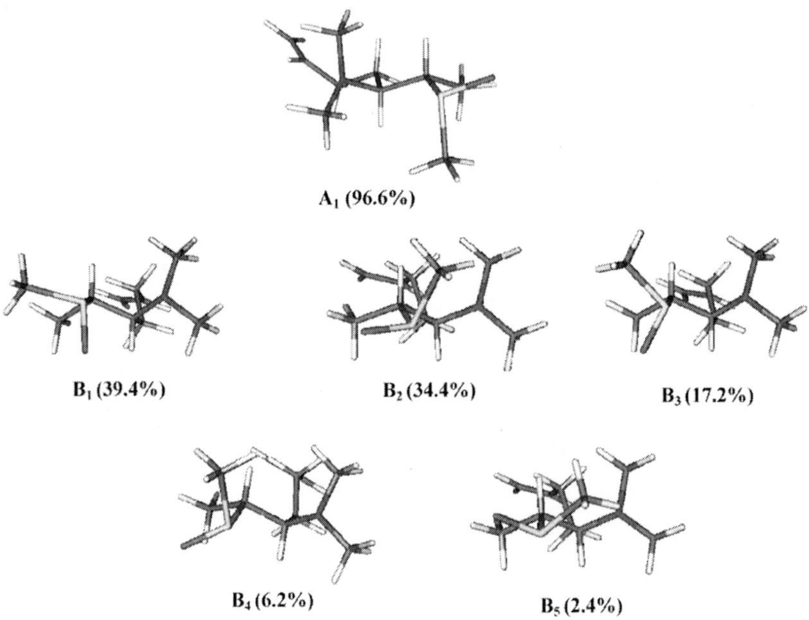

Figure 5. Dominant rotamers of models A and B with the relevant Boltzmann populations.

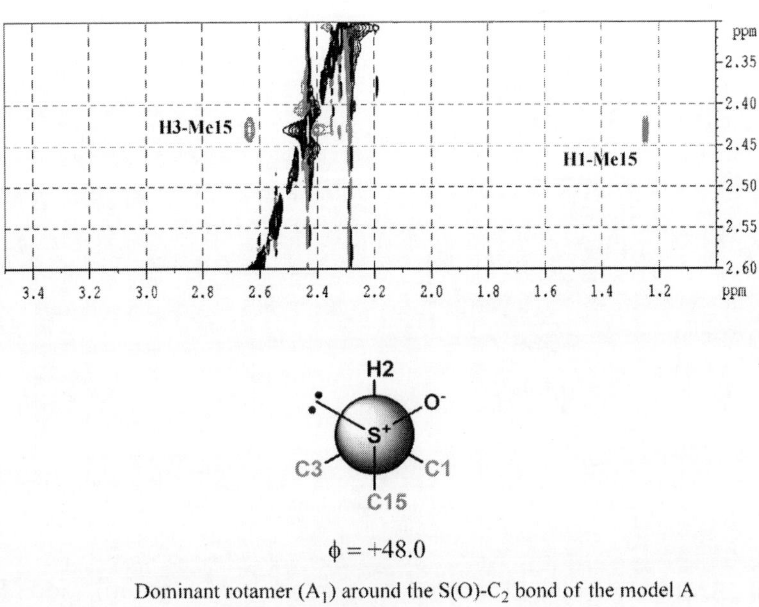

Figure 6. Key ROE correlations of compound **1**.

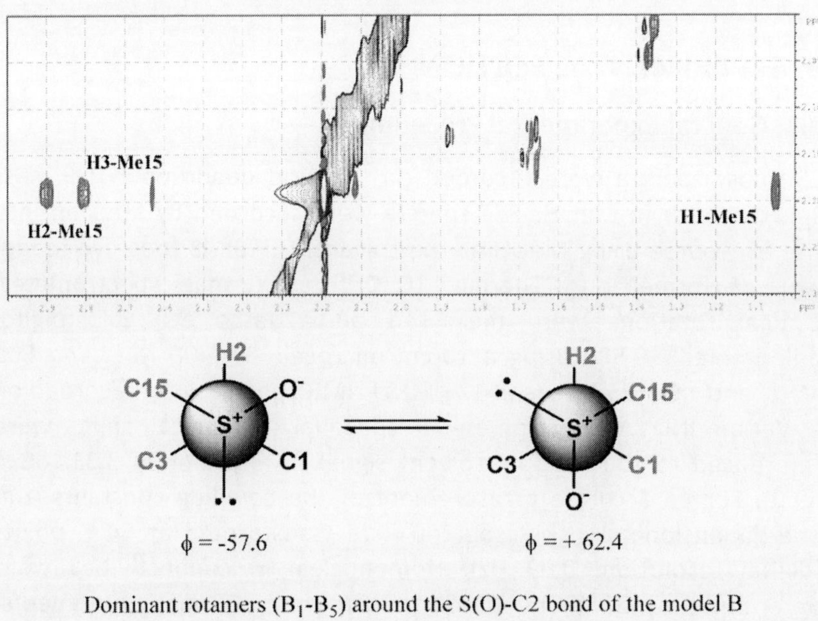

Figure 7. Key ROE correlations of compound **2**.

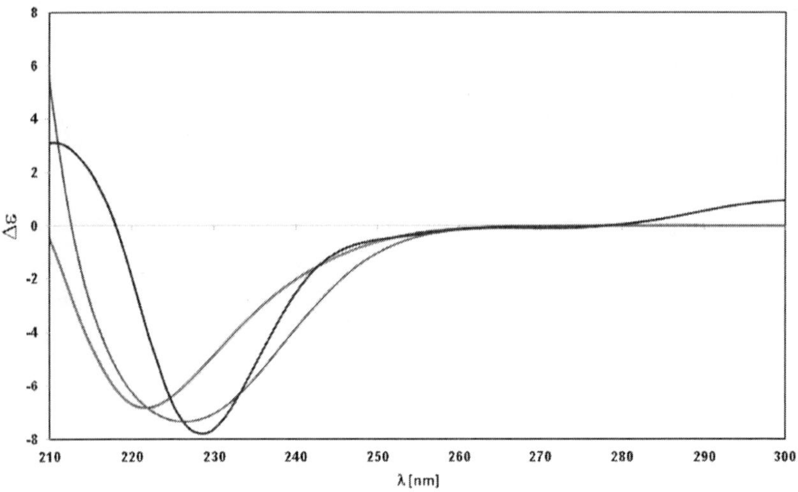

Figure 8. Theoretical ECD curves of models A (green) and B (red) *vs.* experimental ECD curve of aplisulfamine A (blue).

3. EXPERIMENTAL SECTION

3.1. General Experimental Procedures

ESI mass spectra were recorded on a hybrid quadrupole-TOF mass spectrometer in MeOH. The spectra were recorded by infusion into the ESI source using MeOH as the solvent. HRESIMS (positive mode) were performed on a Thermo LTQ Orbitrap XL mass spectrometer. Optical rotations were measured on a Jasco DIP 370 digital polarimeter. at 589 using a 10-cm microcell. ^{1}H (700 MHz and 500 MHz) and ^{13}C (175 MHz and 125 MHz) NMR spectra were recorded on a Varian INOVA spectrometer respectively; chemical shifts were referenced to the residual solvent signal (CD3OD: δH = 3.31, δC = 49.0). For an accurate measurement of the coupling constants, the one-dimensional ^{1}H NMR spectra were transformed at 64 K points (digital resolution: 0.09 Hz). Homonuclear ^{1}H connectivities were determined by COSY and TOCSY (mixing time 100 ms) experiments. Through-space ^{1}H connectivities were evidenced using a ROESY experiment with a mixing time of 500 ms. Two and three bond ^{1}H-^{13}C connectivities were determined by gradient 2D HMBC experiments optimized for a $^{2,3}J$of 8 Hz. $^{3}J_{H\text{-}H}$ values were extracted from 1D ^{1}H

NMR and 2D E.COSY spectra. For the E.COSY spectrum 32 scans per t1 value were acquired with a t1max of 65 ms. $^{2,3}J_{C\text{-}H}$ values were obtained from phase-sensitive PFG-PS-HMBC spectra and ^{13}C coupled and decoupled HSQC-TOCSY according the following conditions. The PFG-PS-HMBC spectrum was recorded using 2K points in ω2, setting the delay for long-range coupling evolution (Δ) at 50 ms, with 32 scans/t1 (t1max 15.2 ms). Zero-filling (8 K × 1 K) was carried out in ω2 and ω1, respectively, to obtain a digital resolution of 0.9 Hz in ω2. The ^{13}C coupled and decoupled HSQC-TOCSY were recorded using 2K points in ω2, setting the mixing time 80 ms and $^{1}J_{CH}$ of 140 Hz, with 120 scans/t1 (t1max 9.7 ms). Zero-filling (8 K × 1 K) was carried out in ω2 and ω1, respectively, to obtain a digital resolution of 0.5 Hz in ω2; the proton-carbon $^{2,3}J$ coupling were extracted trough a computer-aided analysis of the heteronuclear coupled and decoupled multiplets acquired in two separate experiments, according to the method proposed by Kover *et al.* [21]. All spectra were acquired at 278° K and the samples were prepared by dissolving compounds 1 and 2 in 0.5 mL of CD_3OD (Armar, 100% D).

3.2. Collection, Extraction and Isolation

Specimens of *Aplidium* sp. were collected at Pozzuoli (Naples, Italy), frozen immediately and kept frozen until extraction. A reference specimen is deposited at the Dipartimento di Chimica delle Sostanze Naturali, University of Naples "Federico II". Fresh thawed animals (8.5 g dry weight after extraction) were homogenized and extracted twice with methanol and then twice with chloroform (4 × 200 mL). The combined extracts were concentrated *in vacuo* and the resulting aqueous residue was extracted with EtOAc. Separation of the EtOAc soluble material (480 mg) was achieved by gradient silica gel MPLC (hexane→EtOAc →MeOH). Fractions eluted with EtOAc/MeOH 9:1 (v/v) were combined and the solvent was evaporated yielding a residue (80 mg) which was subjected to a first chromatography by HPLC on a C18 column (Luna 5 μm, 250 × 3.00 mm) eluting with $MeOH/H_2O$ 85:15 (v/v). Final purification was achieved by a further HPLC separation on a chiral column (Chirex 5001 5 μm, 100 × 4.60 mm) in the same elution conditions, which afforded aplisulfamine A (9.0 mg, 0.10% of dry weight) and aplisulfamine B (3.0 mg, 0.03% of dry weight) in the pure state.

Aplisulfamine A (1). [α]D = +15.6 (methanol, c = 0.001); HRESI-MS (positive ion mode): m/z (%) = 300.2351 $[M + H]^+$, 322.2171 $[M + Na]^+$; ^1H and ^{13}C NMR data (CD_3OD) are reported in Table 1.

Aplisulfamine B (1). $[\alpha]_D$ = −9.7 (methanol, c = 0.001); HRESI-MS (positive ion mode): m/z (%) = 300.2349 $[M + H]^+$, 322.2168 $[M + Na]^+$; ^1H and ^{13}C NMR data (CD_3OD) are reported in Table 1.

3.3. Computational Details

DFT calculations were performed on a Pentium-4 processor at 3.0 GHz using the Gaussian03 package (Multiprocessor). Systematic Conformational Search for the models A and B around S-C2 bond was carried out at the B3LYP level using the 6-31G(d) basis set (range: +48 to −48; step: 30°; number of conformers = 12). All the conformers obtained were subsequently optimized at the B3LYP level using the 6-31G(d,p) basis set.

GIAO ^{13}C calculations were performed using the mPW1PW91 functional and 6-31G(d,p) basis set, using as input the geometry previously optimized at the mPW1PW91/6-31G(d) level. For these calculations, the IEF-PCM solvent continum model, as implemented in Gaussian (methanol solvent), was used. TDDFT calculations were run using the functional B3LYP and the basis sets TZVP including at least 30 excited states in all cases, and using IEF-PCM for MeOH. ECD spectra were generated.

4. CONCLUSIONS

The interesting combination of spectroscopic and computational methods used to assign the absolute stereochemistry of aplisulfamines and, particularly, the original approach we used to assign the relative configuration of an acyclic system composed by an asymmetric carbon linked to a chiral sulfoxide, contribute to the enhancement of theoretical protocols recently applied to solve stereochemical aspects in structure elucidation.

The isolation of both epimers at sulfur brings into question whether they are both of natural origin or, instead, the natural product is only one of them which underwent racemization at the sulfur site during the extraction or partition steps. The latter hypothesis cannot be excluded; actually, the isolation of both aplisulfamines A and B was indeed very fortunate. Having both epimers at the chiral sulfoxide available, we could indeed make a strong case for the stereochemistry assignment at sulfur by application of Mislow's rule as well as for the conformational analysis of S-C2 segment which succeeded in assigning C2 absolute stereochemistry. In addition, the ECD spectra of the natural aplisulfamines, along with the theoretical curves of Models A and B obtained from DFT calculations, are further examples which could implement the case study of Cotton effects of substituted sulfoxides. Our studies evidenced that also for aplisulfamines, containing both a heteroatomic substituent and a chiral secondary carbon directly linked at the sulfoxide group, a simple correlation exists between the sign of their Cotton effects and the sulfur atom configuration.

ACKNOWLEDGMENTS

This research was funded by the EU's 7th Framework Programme FP7/2007-2013 under grant agreement n° 229893 (NatPharma).

REFERENCES

1. Harrigan, G.G.; Luesch, H.; Yoshida, W.Y.; Moore, R.E.; Nagle, D.G.; Paul, V.J. Symplostatin 2: a dolastatin 13 analogue from the marine cyanobacterium Symploca hydnoides. J. Nat. Prod. 1999, 62, 655–658.

2. Hamada, T.; Matsunaga, S.; Yano, G.; Fusetani, N. Polytheonamides A and B, highly cytotoxic, linear polypeptides with unprecedented structural features, from the marine sponge, Theonella swinhoei. J. Am. Chem. Soc. 2005, 127, 110–118.

3. Galbraith, M.N.; Horn, D.H.S.; Sasse; Jenneth, M. Podolactones C and D, terpene sulfoxides from Podocarpus neriifolius. J. Chem. Soc. 1971, 21, 1362–1363.

4. Fenwick, G.R.; Hanley, A.B. The genus Allium--Part 1. Crit. Rev. Food Sci. Nutr. 1985, 22, 199–271.

5. Kuriyama, M.; Takagi, M.; Murata, K. A new amino acid, chondrine, isolated from a red alga. Nip. Suis. G. 1960, 26, 627.

6. Lake, R.J.; Brennan, M.M.; Blunt, J.W.; Munro, M.H.G.; Pannell, L.K. Eudistomin K sulfoxide. An antiviral sulfoxide from the New Zealand ascidian Ritterella sigillinoides. Tetrahedron Lett. 1988, 29, 2255–2256.

7. Murata, O.; Shigemori, H.; Ishibashi, M.; Sugama, K.; Hayashi, K.; Kobayashi, J. Eudistomidins E and F, new β-carboline alkaloids from the Okinawan marine tunicate Eudistoma glaucus. Tetrahedron Lett. 1991, 32, 3539–3542.

8. Makarieva, T.N.; Stonik, V.A.; Dmitrenok, A.S.; Grebnev, B.B.; Isakov, V.V.; Rebachyk, N.M.; Rashkes, Y.W. Varacin and three new marine antimicrobial polysulfides from the far-eastern ascidian Polycitor sp. J. Nat. Prod. 1995, 58, 254–258.

9. Dorman, D.E.; Jautelat, M.D.; Roberts, J. Carbon-13 nuclear magnetic resonance spectroscopy. Quantitative correlations of the carbon chemical shifts of acyclic alkenes. J. Org. Chem. 1971, 36, 2757–2766.

10. Ivanciuc, O.; Rabine, J.P.; Cabrol-Bass, D.; Panaye, A.; Doucet, P.J. 13C NMR Chemical Shift Prediction of the sp3Carbon Atoms in the α Position Relative to the Double Bond in Acyclic Alkenes. J. Chem. Inf. Comput. Sci. 1997, 37, 587–598.

11. Charan, R.D.; Garson, M.J.; Brereton, I.M.; Willis, A.C.; Hooper, J.N.A. Haliclonacyclamines A and B, cytotoxic alkaloids from the tropical marine sponge Haliclona sp. Tetrahedron 1996, 52, 9111–9120.

12. Mislow, K.; Green, M.M.; Laur, P.; Melillo, J.T.; Simmons, T.; Ternay, A.L., Jr. Absolute configuration and optical rotatory power of sulfoxides and sulfinate esters. J. Am. Chem. Soc. 1965, 87, 1958–1976.

13. Axelrod, M.; Bickart, P.; Goldstein, M.L.; Green, M.M.; Kjaer, A.; Mislow, K. Absolute configuration and optical rotatory dispersion of methyl alkyl sulfoxides. Tetrahedron Lett. 1968, 29, 3249–3252.

14. Ottenheijm, H.C.J.; Liskamp, R.M.J.; Helquist, P.; Lather, J.W.; Shekhani, M.S. Absolute configuration of sparsomycin. A chiroptical study of sulfoxides. J. Am. Chem. Soc. 1981, 103, 1720–1723.

15. Matsumori, N.; Kaneno, D.; Murata, M.; Nakamura, H.; Tachibana, K. Stereochemical Determination of acyclic structures based on carbon-proton spin-coupling constants. A method of configuration analysis for natural products.J. Org. Chem. 1999, 64, 866–876. [PubMed]

16. Bassarello, C.; Bifulco, G.; Evidente, A.; Riccio, R.; Gomez-Paloma, L. Stereochemical studies on ascaulitoxin: a J-based NMR configurational analysis of a nitrogen substituted system. Tetrahedron Lett. 2001, 42, 8611–8613.

17. Kobayashi, J.; Tsuda, M. Amphidinolides, bioactive macrolides from symbiotic marine dinoflagellates. Nat. Prod. Rep.2004, 21, 77–93.

18. Ciminiello, P.; Dell'Aversano, C.; Fattorusso, E.; Forino, M.; Magno, S.; Di Rosa, M.; Ianaro, A.; Poletti, R. Structure and stereochemistry of a new cytotoxic Polychlorinated sulfolipid from adriatic shellfish. J. Am. Chem. Soc. 2002, 124, 13114–13120.

19. Bifulco, G.; Dambruoso, P.; Gomez-Paloma, L.; Riccio, R. Determination of relative configuration in organic compounds by NMR spectroscopy and computational methods. Chem. Rev. 2007, 107, 3744–3779.

20. Aiello, A.; Fattorusso, E.; Luciano, P.; Menna, M.; Vitalone, R. Polyaxibetaine, an amino acid derivative from the marine sponge Axinella polypoides. J. Nat. Prod. 2010, 73, 620–622.

21. Kover, K.E.; Hruby, V.J.; Uhrin, D. Sensitivity- and gradient-enhanced heteronuclear coupled/decoupled HSQC-TOCSY experiments for measuring long-range heteronuclear coupling constants. J. Magn. Res. 1997, 129, 125–129.

Index